POLITICS AN[illegible]
145[illegible]

D. M. Loades was [illegible] School and Emma[illegible] to 1963 he was [illegible] University of St An[illegible] Lecturer (1970) an[illegible] University of Durham. He [illegible] at University College of North Wales [illegible] previous publications include *The Oxford [illegible]* (1970), *The Reign of Mary Tudor* (1979) and (ed.) *The End of Strife* (1984).

FONTANA HISTORY OF ENGLAND

Edited by G. R. Elton
Regius Professor of Modern History at the
University of Cambridge

The aim of the series is to reinterpret familiar and unfamiliar aspects of English history. There will be a pair of volumes on each chronological period (except the first) which will throw new light on the age in question by discussing it in relation to contrasting themes.

ALREADY PUBLISHED

Malcolm Todd, *Roman Britain 55 BC–AD 400*
M. T. Clanchy, *England and Its Rulers 1066–1272*
H. E. Hallam, *Rural England 1066–1348*
Claire Cross, *Church and People 1450–1660*
D. M. Loades, *Politics and the Nation 1450–1660*
Anthony Tuck, *Crown and Nobility 1272–1461*
Peter Heath, *Church and Realm 1272–1461*
J. R. Jones, *Britain and the World 1649–1815*
Maxine Berg, *The Age of Manufactures 1700–1820*
Michael Bentley, *Politics Without Democracy 1815–1914*

FORTHCOMING TITLES

Nicholas Brooks, *Warfare, Government and Society 400–1066*

D. M. Loades

POLITICS AND THE NATION 1450–1660

Obedience, Resistance and Public Order

fp
Fontana Press

First published in 1974 by Fontana Paperbacks,
Second impression, March 1977
Second edition, with corrections, October 1979
Reprinted September 1982
Third edition, with new chapter 8 and revisions,
in Fontana Press, May 1986
Reprinted September 1988

Fontana Press is an imprint of
Fontana Paperbacks, part of
the Collins Publishing Group,
8 Grafton Street, London W1X 3LA

Printed and bound in Great Britain by
William Collins Sons & Co. Ltd, Glasgow

For Ann

CONTENTS

PREFACE

For the opportunity to present this study, and for much constructive help and criticism, I am indebted to the General Editor, Professor G. R. Elton. I am also grateful to the University of Durham for giving me a period of sabbatical leave in which to write, and to my wife for her painstaking help in proof reading and correction. Throughout this study the word 'aristocracy' and the phrase 'ruling class' are used to designate all those members of society who were at the time described as 'gentleman', 'armiger', 'esquire' or 'knight' in addition to those bearing titles of nobility; in other words the 'nobiles minor' as well as the 'nobiles major'. The phrase 'political nation' is used with a rather wider meaning, to embrace those merchants, yeomen and other householders who held office or were in other ways men of account in their communities, in addition to the aristocracy. For the convenience of readers, the spelling and punctuation of all English quotations, and of the titles of English printed books have been modernised, and all dates have been given under the new style.

D. M. LOADES

University College, Durham
February 1973

PREFACE TO THE THIRD EDITION

In the twelve years since this book was written, many scholars have contributed to our understanding of different aspects of the period. Some of their arguments and evidence have modified my own views; others have confirmed or strengthened what I wrote in 1973. I have also continued with my own researches, particularly on the reign of Mary, and my interpretation and emphasis has to some extent changed. For all these reasons I felt that the publisher's decision to proceed to a third edition offered an opportunity for many necessary revisions. Chapter eight has been completely rewritten, and an appendix of amendments to other chapters added. The bibliography has also been expanded and brought up to date. Apart from my fellow scholars, whose works I have read, I hope with profit, my main debt of gratitude on this occasion is to my students, both in Durham and in Bangor, for their critical and constructive responses over the years.

D.M.L.

University College of North Wales
Bangor
March 1985

INTRODUCTION

This book is basically a political narrative; the story of the rise and fall of a system of government which may loosely be called the Tudor monarchy. For many years before the fifteenth century the English Crown had controlled a sophisticated administrative machinery, but the political life of the country was principally a question of personal relationships between the kings and the most powerful of their subjects. These relationships operated within broadly defined limits of law and convention, described in the terminology of the time as 'good lordship'. 'Good lordship' was more than a question of feudal contract, and much more than a vague obligation to rule for the general good of the commonwealth. It meant a willingness to acknowledge the special position of those great men who had originally been the monarch's companions in arms; to arbitrate in their quarrels, to listen to their opinions, to employ (and reward) their services. In return, these great men raised their powers to aid the king in war, enforced his laws in time of peace, and even acknowledged an obligation to obey those laws themselves.

This situation owed little to political theory. It was a fact of life which individual monarchs ignored at their peril. If they ignored it more or less deliberately, in pursuit of their own ideals, like Richard II, they might even be deposed by the concerted action of those whose interests and susceptibilities they had offended. If they ignored it out of sheer ineptitude, however, then every attempt would be made to awaken them to a sense of responsibility. This is what was happening in the twenty years after Henry VI attained his majority in 1437. By consistent partiality in the distribution of his favours, by his failure to respond to threats and warnings, and above all by his failure to prevent the law from falling into the hands of predators, Henry demonstrated his inability to grasp the meaning of 'good lordship'. Such dereliction of duty made the traditional processes of government unworkable, and created that chaos of factional quarrels which was the English political life of the 1450s. In these circumstances the existence of a rival claim to the throne, however tenuous, became of paramount importance, and the crisis was largely resolved when Edward, Earl of March, made good his pretensions in 1461.

Edward became a successful king, entirely within the traditional terms of reference, and largely by avoiding his predecessor's elementary errors. He was a 'good lord' and an energetic personal ruler who made his will known and felt. After his death, however, a disputed succession partly undid his achievement, and left the crown in the possession of an insubstantial adventurer named Henry Tudor. Henry was scarcely more fertile in original ideas than Edward had been, but being naturally cautious and suspicious by temperament, he concentrated all his considerable resources of intelligence and determination on building up the security of his dynasty. By sheer application, Henry probably came to know more about his subjects, high and low, than any king who had ever occupied the English throne – and knowledge was power. His careful, and largely successful, treatment of the aristocracy lacked the willing heartiness of Edward, and became more obviously a matter of political calculation. His achievement, too, was precarious, but unlike Edward's it held and became the basis upon which his son and granddaughter were to build.

Without any dramatic developments of policy, Henry VII through his own application and Henry VIII through the application of his minister Cardinal Wolsey, built up the strength of the law and the habit of obedience. After 1497 dynastic and factional strife died away, and the nature of 'good lordship' became subtly changed. Without much affecting the political position of the magnates, the administrative control of the central government over their normal activities was gradually increased. This was done, not by excluding them from positions of responsibility, but rather by multiplying the number and precision of the tasks entrusted to them. By this means they became more dependant upon royal patronage, and more closely associated with the operation of the royal authority. As royal service became a more necessary and attractive element in a nobleman's power and prestige, his capacity for independent or hostile action became proportionately reduced.

By the 1530s the power of the monarchy had been sufficiently consolidated to withstand the strains imposed by the king's 'great matter' and the radical changes which derived from it.

This was a decade full of danger and disaffection, culminating in the great northern rebellion known as the Pilgrimage of Grace. Yet not only did the royal government survive; it emerged from the crisis strengthened by the fact of success, and armed with the beginnings of a new political ideology. The great propaganda campaign mounted by Thomas Cromwell and his servants to overcome opposition to the break with Rome had contained more than a repetitive insistence upon the duty of obedience. It had perforce to envisage a new degree of national autonomy, and a monarchy with extended powers and extended responsibilities. The 'commonwealth of England' began to take on a new meaning, and Cromwell worked with prodigious zeal and energy to translate that meaning into legislation and administrative procedures. His success was partial, and in some respects shortlived, but the major changes of the 1530s were never permanently reversed.

Consequently, upon the pre-existing relationship between the king and the aristocracy was superimposed a new relationship springing from the royal supremacy. The duty of obedience took on additional meaning, and at the same time became accessible to conscientious objections. Awareness of this danger made Henry and Cromwell careful to ensure the maximum participation of the lay aristocracy in both the enactment and the administration of the supremacy. The participation was also substantially increased in a different way when the same men were allowed to purchase large quantities of secularised ecclesiastical property. Thus while the need to enforce new laws and new policies greatly increased the pressure of the central government upon the country at large, that pressure operated through and not against the traditional ruling class – reconciling them to it and building upon the foundations already laid down.

These developments were still only partly digested when further change was initiated in the precarious circumstances of a royal minority. Henry's complex and disruptive matrimonial affairs had left Edward as his undisputed heir, but many years under age and with an uncertain succession beyond his own lifetime. The old king had also left a political situation in which the forces of change and conservation faced each other in unresolved dispute, but with the former in the ascendency. As a result, within two years of Henry's death further attempts were being made to work out the implications of what had been done in the 1530s. Under the guidance of Edward Seymour, Duke of Somerset, the church was subjected to a programme of protestant reform, and a serious attempt was made to protect the rural poor from the effects of inflation and a competitive land market. Both these policies aroused fierce controversy, and the latter alienated the government from the land-owning aristocracy in a manner which Somerset's fragile authority could not afford.

As a result he was overthrown in October 1549, and replaced by an aristocratic group under the leadership of John Dudley, Earl of Warwick. Dudley continued, and accelerated, his predecessor's religious policy, but moved decisively against those elements of social disorder which had been stirred up by Somerset's notions of responsibility. In so doing he repaired the damaged community of interest between the monarchy and the ruling class, and restored faith in the king's 'good lordship'. Nevertheless, when Edward became seriously ill in the summer of 1553, Dudley failed to exploit this renewed confidence in his own interest. In spite of the king's active connivance, he was unable to prevent the succession of Henry's elder daughter, the intensely conservative Mary. After only the briefest hesitation, Mary's claim was endorsed by the 'political nation' in a spontaneous movement which made a profound impression upon contemporary observers.

This movement was a demonstration of confidence in the dynasty but not, as many thought, a mandate to reverse all those policies which had developed since 1530. Mary was expected to follow in her father's footsteps, but she had no intention of doing so, and thus created a fresh political crisis. Without having become committed to Edward's protestantism, the 'political nation' had nevertheless broadly endorsed the national and Erastian position which the monarchy had taken up since 1533. The queen's Habsburg orientation, therefore, and her support for renewed clerical pretensions, cut the monarchy off from the sympathies of the aristocracy as effectively as the social programme of 1549. But this time the ruler was an adult, and there was no Duke of Somerset to take the blame. In effect, Mary's reliance upon her husband, Philip of Spain, upon her husband's subjects, and upon the ultramontane clergy, caused her to be regarded as 'no good lady' by the majority of her own aristocracy. This situation provoked one dangerous rebellion, and a number of more or less serious conspiracies in the brief space of five years, but the Queen survived them. She was able to do so partly because her marriage failed to produce an heir and she failed to exclude her half-sister from the succession; and partly because the aristocracy began to experiment with Parliament as an alternative to rebellion for making their collective wishes known.

The failure of Mary's policies thus had much more than a purely negative importance. Not only did it indicate the extent to which the earlier, Henrician policies had been accepted, but also signified a new willingness to receive a protestant establishment as a necessary support to national autonomy. A few months after coming to the throne, Elizabeth had read these signs accurately enough to embrace the essentially protestant vision of England's destiny which was offered to her by a small but vociferous group of gentry and divines. Having taken this crucial step, however, the queen was then compelled to spend the remainder of her long reign in a successful struggle to retain control over the dynamic politics which this vision had created.

Many seeds sown in the 1530s and 1550s germinated during Elizabeth's forty-four years on the throne. The alliance between protestantism and the royal supremacy produced a new sense of national pride and purpose, but provoked a natural rejoinder in the Bull of Excommunication of 1570 with its consequent tragic dilemmas of conscience and allegiance. The aristocracy's use of Parliament as a means of keeping the queen aware of her obligations, both as a 'good lady' and a 'Godly Prince', led to a considerable development of that institution, fraught with significance for the future. As a 'Godly Prince', Elizabeth was unable to avoid a long and debilitating war with the champion of the Counter Reformation. As a 'good lady' she stretched her inadequate resources, and allowed her patronage to be ominously distorted, in the interests of an expanding and aggressive aristocracy.

During her reign the Tudor monarchy reached, and passed, its zenith. That 'increase of governance' which was characteristic of the Tudor achievement had been accomplished by adapting the traditional concept of 'good lordship', and the Crown's control over the resulting partnership was less secure than it appeared. As the theory of the royal authority became more sophisticated in the late sixteenth century, the practice was again showing signs of wear and tear. Also, in spite of Elizabeth's successful efforts to hold it together, the union between protestant doctrine with its scriptural authoritarianism and the royal supremacy with its Erastian logic was never a wholly harmonious one.

Time, and circumstances, favoured Elizabeth. She lived long enough to pass a united and effectively protestant realm to an undisputed successor of mature age. By 1603 many of the problems which had vexed her father and grandfather had been resolved. The dangerous private resources of the 'overmighty subject'; the inhibiting restrictions of franchises and liberties; even the casual violence of an undisciplined aristocracy; all these were things of the past. But the problems which remained were becoming more rather than less intractable. A ruling class which, having accepted the obligation of staffing the royal administration, could not be persuaded of the necessity to pay for it as well, and royal resources yearly shrinking in relation to the resources of the nobility and gentry. And above all, a Parliament which was rapidly becoming the national forum through which the aristocracy expressed awareness of its strength, and bid for a commensurate voice in the determination of public policy.

The position which James inherited was not one of imminent or inevitable danger, but it was one calling for clear sighted and realistic statesmanship. Intellectual dogmatism of the kind to which the king was prone was thus a serious mistake. Most of the legal and theoretical definitions to which English politics were amenable had been left behind by the course of events, and nothing was to be gained by resorting to them. At the same time James, like Mary, embarked upon an unpopular foreign policy, and showed no awareness of that potent blend of national and religious chauvinism which Elizabeth had 'ridden' with such peril and profit.

For a variety of reasons, therefore, co-operation between the monarchy and the aristocracy began to break down, and in the resulting atmosphere of mutual suspicion, ancient grievances began to appear again in a new guise. The monopoly of royal patronage enjoyed by the Duke of Buckingham undermined confidence in the king's 'good lordship'; the fear of clerical pretensions was revived by the emergence of a 'High Church' party; and the common lawyers refurbished their defences against royal absolutism, as they had done periodically since the fourteenth century. By the time that James died in 1625, the political situation was appreciably worse than it had been in 1603, but certainly not beyond the reach of wise and constructive reforms. Although the positive drive and creative energy had gone out of the Tudor monarchy, most of its mechanism was working with reasonable efficiency, and in spite of having mounted numerous attacks on royal policy the 'country' opposition was both conservative and unsure of its aims.

In less than twenty years, however, tension and difficulty were turned into revolution by the complete failure of the monarch to come to terms with political reality. Just as Henry VI had made the medieval constitution unworkable by his failure to comprehend the responsibilities of 'good lordship', so Charles I made the Tudor constitution unworkable by refusing to recognise the intangible limitations which it imposed upon him. Increasingly isolated from the political and religious aspirations of the 'political nation', Charles came to rely more and more upon a legalistic interpretation of his prerogative, and upon the deep resources of loyalty and obedience which over a century of good government had created.

During the 1630s he endeavoured to use his royal office in a manner for which it had not been designed, and in so doing finally lost the co-operation of the governing and tax-paying classes, with the result that the constitution ground to a halt. Even so, the crisis could have been resolved along the lines laid down by the Long Parliament in 1640-41, had not religious passions been inflamed by revolt in Ireland, and confidence in the king's 'good lordship' been finally destroyed by his attitude of inept dissimulation. For lack of a constructive political alternative, and perhaps because Charles expected to gain a decisive advantage by driving his opponents into rebellion, the country drifted into civil war. But while the king's war aims were clear, those of his antagonists remained negative and uncertain, so that in spite of their greater resources, most of them had no desire to press for a military decision. During 1645 this confusion was eventually resolved in a manner which none of the original protagonists had wanted, by a revolution within the 'parliamentary' party, which took the initiative out of the hands of the existing leaders and placed it at the disposal of Oliver Cromwell and the professional soldiers.

Thus political bankruptcy and deadlock resulted in a genuine revolution which called in a new force from outside the charmed circle of the 'political nation' altogether. At that point the story of the 'Tudor monarchy' comes to an end. What happened thereafter, although of vital importance for the future, is little more than a postscript for the purposes of this book. Much was salvaged from the wreckage, because the revolution was short-lived, and also because it was less profound and self-confident than is sometimes suggested. But the Tudor monarchy was not re-created in 1660. That political system which had evolved after the breakdown of the 1450s, been given new life and direction in the 1530s, and reached its apogee in the England of Elizabeth, was destroyed in the civil war. When the crisis was over, the 'political nation' had to evolve a fresh constitutional balance, and continuity with the pre-war situation was more apparent than real.

In spite of the wide ranging implications of its theme, a work of this kind is not, and cannot be, a general history. I have concentrated upon the relationship between the Crown and the 'political nation', and other factors are taken into account mainly as they affected that relationship. Thus neither foreign policy nor economic developments are considered as subjects in their own right, and religion only insofar as it affected the question of political obligation. The lives and work of ordinary people become relevant mainly in times of crisis, when they riot, or rebel, or impinge in some direct way upon the workings of government. I have made only passing references to 'the sort who do not rule' in other circumstances, usually in connection with the routine work of criminal justice – a subject which is itself handled unevenly because of its varying political importance.

Similarly, this is a study in English history. The affairs of Ireland and of Scotland (even after the union of the Crowns), are treated only in relation to events in England. If such selection seems arbitary and unsatisfactory, I can only submit that selection itself was necessitated by considerations of space and purpose, and that I followed a course which seemed to me to be justified by the nature of the subject. The approach is basically chronological because the situation itself was dynamic and not static. The ageing of monarchs, royal minorities, and the growth of political habits all remind us that the passage of time itself was a factor of considerable importance. Finally, it is a long book. But then a great deal happened in these two hundred turbulent and interesting years – years which saw the gradual transformation of 'good lordship' into patronage of a more recognisably modern kind, and developed the medieval concept of 'consent' in a manner which was to be of great importance for the whole subsequent history of this country.

Part One

THE ECLIPSE OF THE MEDIEVAL MONARCHY

1450-1521

These years saw the breakdown and restoration of medieval government. Coming after a fifteen year minority, the personal rule of Henry VI was a disaster. Not only did Henry make no real attempt to ensure that his laws were justly administered, but he neglected the political necessity to deal equitably with his magnates and councillors. As a result confidence in the public authority of the king was destroyed, and men of all ranks made haste to protect themselves by private arrangements of maintenance and retainder. Feudal and 'bastard feudal' relationships were always close to the surface of medieval political life, and in periods of royal weakness like the 1450s could swiftly turn the country into a battleground of factional interests. In a society accustomed even at the best of times to the need for self-defence, civil order was very much easier to demolish than to rebuild, and the damage wrought during this turbulent decade was not fully repaired until the end of the century.

By 1460 it had become clear that no permanent solution to the crisis could be reached as long as Henry occupied the throne. Since, however, kings were deemed to rule by the will of God and not of their subjects, it was necessary to revive the obsolete hereditary claim of the Mortimers in order to get rid of him. This inevitably introduced a dynastic element into the conflict, which lingered on long after the substantial issues were resolved. Edward IV gained the Crown in 1461, and displayed all the energy and sense of purpose which his predecessor had lacked but for a decade his position was precarious and the restoration of 'governance' was slow and uneven. However, for twelve years after 1471 Edward was unchallenged, and during those years he restored much of the basic financial and political strength of the monarchy. In doing so he relied heavily upon the loyalty of a few powerful families, a conservative policy which brought relatively quick results, but which failed to stand up to the strains imposed by his premature death in 1483. A bitter quarrel between his wife's kin, the Woodvilles, and his brother Richard of Gloucester then resulted in the latter seizing the Crown from the young Edward V – an action which briefly reawakened the factional quarrels of the previous generation. Richard's usurpation created a golden opportunity for the shadowy heir of Henry VI, Henry Tudor, who was able to take advantage of the civil dissension to launch a successful invasion from France.

Once he had made good his claim, Henry's objectives were the same as those of Edward IV – to restore confidence in the royal government and to build up the security of his dynasty. His methods, however, were significantly different. Henry did not place large trust in small numbers, but distributed favours and responsibilities widely and sparingly throughout the ruling class. This was to prove a change of the first importance, reducing the political power of individual magnates and keeping the overall direction of policy much more firmly in the king's own hands. Henry also had an advantage in that strife which had preceded his accession had been relatively brief, and the wounds were therefore swifter to heal. By 1500 the new dynasty was firmly established, and working more effectively than any English government for over one hundred years. In the last years of the reign security hung on a single young life, but the Crown was no longer over-shadowed by a handful of great families. Sustained administrative pressure over twenty years had reduced the political importance of retainder, just as the restoration of good government had reduced its justification. In 1509 Henry VIII could look forward to almost unprecedented freedom of action, and chose to gratify his aristocracy with a foreign war. Whatever the financial unwisdom of such a policy, it earned him the goodwill of men whose co-operation he needed, and contributed to that high level of security which enabled him to destroy so great a magnate as the Duke of Buckingham by the simple process of the law.

CHAPTER I

THE LACK OF GOVERNANCE

'The law serveth of nought else in these days but for to do wrong.' (Complaint of the men of Kent, June 1450)

JUSTICE AND THE SOCIAL ORDER

Anger and discontent are commonly the measure of disappointed expectations, and the men of Kent went to the root of their grievances in protesting that the king's courts no longer provided the justice to which his subjects felt entitled. This was a malfunction which had afflicted English government before, but by 1450 it had reached the proportions of a major crisis. As such it was primarily a crisis of confidence, and had little to do with the foibles or inadequacies of the legal machinery itself. These were of long standing, and too familiar to be remarked upon. Actions in the Court of Common Pleas dragged on expensively and interminably, while in the King's Bench and at the Assizes innumerable indictments for felony came to nothing because of the cumbersome and inadequate machinery for securing the appearance of defendants. Distraint was totally ineffective against a man with no property, and even if the offender was wealthy, custom had reduced the practice of distraining to a derisory level. Sir John Wingfield, a substantial defaulter, was distrained 47 times to produce a total penalty of £6. 2s. 4d. Even the ultimate sanction of outlawry held few terrors, and that could only be brought about by proclamation at five successive county courts. A similar paralysis can also be seen at a lower level. Between 1381 and 1396 the sessions of the peace in Lincolnshire received 485 indictments for felony; of these 404 never came to trial, and of the 81 defendants who did appear, 76 were either acquitted or pardoned.

The men of 1450 certainly had no grounds for exalted expectations of the effectiveness of English law. If the basis of their complaint had been inefficiency, and the paucity of the protection afforded to the individual subject, they would have been saying no more than the Parliament had said repeatedly throughout the fourteenth century. In fact their grievance was far more radical; the fount of justice itself was dry.

> ... nothing is sped almost but false matters by colour of the law for bribery, dread, or favour, and so no remedy is obtainable in the court of conscience in any way.

A measure of injustice was an inescapable fact of life. However, in a society which had been only slowly and partially converted from self-help to litigation, many men looked upon the law as a weapon of aggression or revenge and would use it as such if they were given the chance. The task of controlling and mitigating such uncivilised behaviour lay with the king, and if he failed then the realm became overrun with injustice, like a clearing abandoned to the jungle. This was in effect what had happened since 1421. It was a sign of the times when, in about 1425, William Paston complained that he had never received the £120 damages awarded to him in a suit against one Walter Asloc, because of the maintenance which the latter had received from Sir Thomas Erpingham. By 1440 such complaints were daily matters. In that year Paston wrote to an aggrieved friend, dissuading him from an appeal to law,

> ... for if thou do, thou shalt have the worse, be thy case never so true, for he [his opponent] is said with my Lord of Northfolk, and he is of his council, and also thou canst no man of law in Norfolk or Suffolk to be with thee against him ...

Paston knew what he was talking about, and it is clear from a number of sources that at this time the machinery of the law was amenable to almost unlimited manipulation by powerful and interested parties. In the hands of a malicious enemy the normally ineffectual legal instrument of distraint could become a deadly weapon and might even be used without any proper process at all, as a pretext for simple plunder.

The key to many of these abuses lay in the official powers of the sheriff. Although much reduced from the vice-regal status of the early middle ages, these officers were still crucial for the operation of the law in the counties, in that they impanelled juries of every kind and administered the writs sent down from Chancery. Consequently it became impossible to prosecute without the sheriff's goodwill, and this might be up for sale, or totally unobtainable. In 1454, when he was contemplating legal action,

Sir John Fastolf included among his financial calculations the payment of a reward to the sheriff to induce him to impanel a jury which would indict his opponent. In these circumstances it is not surprising to find great complaint being made about 'the great kinship alliance and following of sheriffs, as well of them that hath been afore this time as of them that now are in the said shires', or to discover that incumbents were remaining in office for ten or even twelve years, in defiance of many statutes.

The opportunities open to the unscrupulous were considerable. Apart from the control of juries and inquisitions, they could conveniently fail to find an offender, or his goods; they could bail prisoners at discretion, virtually charge what fees they liked, and even let their offices to farm. At the same time, they could harass their own or their friends' enemies most effectually; all services which might command a high price. A powerful and wealthy man might be prepared to expend a large sum to gain control of the office. In October 1450, when his interests were seriously threatened by the Duke of York, it was reported of John Heydon 'that rather than he should fail of a sheriff this year coming for his intent, he would spend £1,000'.[1] Of course, not only the sheriffs were open to these temptations; coroners, stewards, and even the officers of the Chancery might be equally amenable. It was alleged against one Robert Ledeham that, before embarking upon a series of misdemeanours, he had taken the precaution of obtaining a writ of *supersedeas*[2] for himself and a number of his men 'that no warrant of justice of peace might be served against them'.

Contrary to what is sometimes implied, the 1440s were a decade of busy litigation, precisely because legal processes were so amenable to exploitation. Far from being a means of settling disputes, or providing redress, the law had become primarily an alternative method of pursuing private quarrels. In this atmosphere clientage inevitably flourished, because the small man had no more chance of defending himself at law than he had by force. When John Paston was expelled from the manor of Gresham by Lord Moleyns, and attempted to seek a remedy at law,

1 James Gresham to John Paston; *Paston Letters*, I, 157.

2 A writ withdrawing a case from the local to the central courts, where it could be indefinitely protracted. To obtain such a writ in advance (a totally improper proceeding) had the effect of forestalling any legal proceedings in the locality.

he was warned that there was no hope of getting even Moleyns' servants convicted, because the latter had used his influence at court to procure a royal letter to the sheriff of Norfolk, commanding him to 'show favour' to Moleyns. Significantly, Paston, who was a substantial man himself, was advised to seek the protection of the Duke of York. By such means a vicious circle was established.

The malleability of the law necessitated private protection, which in turn perverted the law still further. When Paston and his friends managed to get a commission of oyer and terminer sent down to Norfolk in 1451 for the purpose of undoing their enemies Sir Thomas Tuddenham and John Heydon, Tuddenham had the sessions moved to Walsingham, where his influence was strong, and by appearing with four hundred followers effectively deterred any potential plaintiffs. These special commissions to 'hear and determine' cases in a locality might have general jurisdiction, to cover all offences in a specified area, or specific, which would confine them to single issues. The reputation of such commissions was better than that of the ordinary courts, and they were much sought after by litigants. When John Paston was striving to gain redress against Lord Moleyns, he petitioned Lord Chancellor Kemp for such a commission. He also instructed his agent, John Gresham, to press for a special rather than a general commission, 'for in a general oyer and terminer a *supersedeas* may dash all, and so shall not in a special. And also if the justices come at my request, they shall sit as long as I will . . .'.[8] Clientage in itself was not new, and was not necessarily harmful. Lords who kept great households had always been sources of patronage and profit to their dependants and had ruled their 'countries', albeit in the king's name. The evil feature of the system as it developed after 1420 was the lack of any real restraint from above. Just as feudalism proper had a centrifugal effect which could shatter a weak monarchy territorially, so 'bastard feudalism' intensified the solvent effects of inadequate government.

The system which goes by that pejorative name was in fact a subtle and complex set of relationships, and itself much less stable than is sometimes supposed. At one end of the spectrum lay the formal indenture of retainder, whereby the client normally acknowledged himself

[8] *Paston Letters*, I, 146.

> witholden and retained with and towards the said lord for term of his life, promiting and binding him by the faith of his body and by these present indentures to be true faithful and diligent unto the said lord and with him for to be and his quarrel to take against all persons of what estate, degree or condition soever they be, his ligeance only except.

This type of contract, which derived from the military indentures of the fourteenth century, might be varied in a number of ways. The patron might make a specific undertaking to be 'a good and tender lord' to the client; to pay him a fixed fee, or the profits of a certain estate. The client might reserve other obligations, apart from his allegiance to the king, such as a previous obligation to another lord. An indenture might also specify what kind of service was to be rendered.

Exclusive, or almost exclusive, contracts of this kind were a luxury confined to the greatest magnates, the value of whose 'good lordship' was above suspicion. Others usually had to be content with less formal arrangements. The client might live in his lord's household, or receive an annuity, and wear his livery without the restraint of any written agreement. A man so placed would normally describe himself as the 'servant' of the lord in question, although he might have a household and even a clientage of his own. His relationship with his patron might be one of great personal loyalty, or it might be of the frankest mutual convenience. Formal contracts of retainder were not lightly broken, but arrangements of this sort, which must have constituted the great bulk of 'bastard feudalism' at all levels, were subject to frequent evasion or repudiation. Consequently a lord whom fortune had handled roughly, or ineptitude undermined, might find his clientage melting away with disastrous results.

Beyond this category of servant also lay another, and more tenuous form of association, that of the 'well-willer'. These last were men not attached by any tangible token such as a livery or a fee, but who had some hope (which might be purely temporary) of exchanging benefits to their advantage. In this case the relationship might not be one of patronage at all. Letters addressed to successive heads of the Paston family concerning their various enterprises contain many references to 'them that be to youward', meaning friends and kinsmen as well as dependants of various kinds. On the whole it is a mistake to regard clientage as tending toward stability in the mid-fifteenth century; the majority of its relationships were highly volatile,[4] and provided no kind of effective substitute for royal government.

It is also a mistake to regard 'bastard feudalism' as a purely aristocratic matter; a means whereby great lords pursued their private quarrels while the bulk of the country got on with its normal, peaceful business. We have already seen that no litigation could be contemplated without a measure of 'good lordship', and since no man of any substance either clerical or lay could tell when he might become involved in litigation, the establishment of contacts of this kind was a precaution which could not be ignored. The Celys, wealthy merchant staplers, wore the livery of Sir John Weston and addressed him as 'my lord' – not because they had any intention of following his banner but because they might need his protection and were no doubt prepared to contribute to his coffers in return. Although it may be true that the spectacular violence of these years has attracted too much attention, nevertheless there was a great deal of intimidation at all levels of society, and for this reason the ramifications of clientage also extended throughout the community, although the remedy which this provided was no more than an aggravation of the disease.

The magnates were as much the victims as the beneficiaries of this situation. It is not likely that many ruined themselves by excessive retaining, but since patronage might be fiercely competitive, it was also proportionately expensive; a compulsory game for high stakes. Retainers might answer their lord's summons to war or escort duties, but they would expect to be paid. When Humphrey, Duke of Buckingham, summoned over seventy of his Staffordshire yeomen to London in the summer of 1450 it cost him £17. 7s.; five years later those who fought for him at St Albans were paid a flat rate of 6s. 8d. a head. On occasion it might even be necessary to hire casually by the day, as the Earl of Wiltshire and Lord Bonvile did at Taunton in 1454. The ramifications of a big 'interest' also brought problems of their own, in that clients could easily become dissatisfied if their lords' attentions were too often preoccupied elsewhere, and throw the grain

[4] See, for example, Edmund Paston's comment on the situation in Norfolk in 1447. 'So I feel by him he would forsake his master and get him a new if he wist he should rule; and so I ween much of the country is so disposed.' *Paston Letters*, I, 66.

of their local influence into some other scale. Destructive local feuds gravely aggravated the problem of lawlessness, but the quarrels of Lovel and Hungerford, Bonvile and Courtenay, or Paston and Moleyns were, like the system of clientage itself or the cumbrousness of the common law, no more than contributory factors in the crisis. The root of the trouble lay at the centre, in the person of the king.

THE POLITICAL VACUUM

In Henry VI England was afflicted with the worst possible kind of medieval monarch, a man too capable to be ignored, but not capable enough to pursue any consistent or independent policy. Until 1437 this had been largely concealed by his minority; and although a long minority in itself inevitably weakened the Crown, the real collapse came only after Henry assumed personal control. Signs of this collapse were soon to be seen. As early as 1438 his councillors warned the king about the danger of granting indiscriminate pardons, and the warning seems to have been totally ignored. His generosity was soon a matter of common knowledge. Lands, offices, wardships, pensions, pardons and remissions of debt flowed in a constant stream of royal patronage; on occasion the same office or estate was granted twice, to different petitioners. This could happen even with so senior a position as the Chancellorship of Ireland. In 1449 Sir John Talbot petitioned that he had received this office by Letters Patent, only to arrive and discover the Great Seal in the hands of Thomas FitzGerald, who also displayed Letters Patent.[5] The Council remonstrated and sought in vain to check this prodigal outpouring of the king's livelihood. At first they seemed likely to succeed; a Great Council[6] in November 1437 reappointed the councillors of the minority, and resurrected an ordinance of 1406 which stipulated among other things that all warrants except grants of pardon should only pass with the assent of the standing Council. If this had been effective much of the subsequent trouble might have been avoided, but it seems clear that

[5] *Rotuli Parliamentorum*, V, 167.

[6] The Great Council was, roughly speaking, the House of Lords meeting without the Commons, all peers being summoned by writ. The standing Council was the formal body of royal advisers, chosen by the king, who had taken the Council oath. The 'inner council' was an informal body of those in whom the king placed particular trust. The Great Council fell into disuse under Henry VII.

the king resented such restraint, and that the councillors themselves were divided.

After 1441 there were no more publicly nominated Councils, and attendance at meetings became wider and less predictable. At about this time there was a larger attendance of nobles than at any time since the first years of the century. This probably indicates the end of the ascendancy of the 'old guard' civil servants like Kemp and Cromwell, and a weakening of the collective resolve to defend the public interest against Henry's recklessness. After about 1443 attendance at meetings began to dwindle again, and the reason for this is clear. The Earl of Suffolk was achieving a complete dominance over the king, and the business transacted by the formal Council was withering into insignificance. Suffolk, along with his henchmen William Ayscough, Bishop of Salisbury, and Adam Moleyns, Bishop of Chichester, together with the Chancellor, John Stafford, had constituted themselves into a 'cabal' which met at court, and increasingly monopolised important decisions, including, of course, the passing of royal warrants.

This shift of balance was not accomplished suddenly. As late as 1446 such magnates as the Earls of Salisbury, Huntingdon and Northumberland were attending formal meetings. However, the drift of events is made clear enough by the fact that when Suffolk was out of the country in 1444 the Council attempted to regain control over the issue of warrants but its decisions were simply shelved on his return. By 1447 Suffolk's ascendancy was the dominant fact of English politics. In that year the aged Cardinal Beaufort died, and Humphrey, Duke of Gloucester, was destroyed in circumstances which caused Suffolk to be generally accused of his murder.[7] A special summons had to be despatched, recalling a number of reluctant councillors to their formal duty. The power of Suffolk, like that of Wolsey and George Villiers in the suceeding centuries, depended wholly upon his influence over the king. He had no substantial backing among his fellow peers and had incurred the bitter enmity of the Dukes of Norfolk and York, and of Lord Cromwell, the ex-treasurer. Exclusion from power meant exclusion from the fruits of power; and the dim-

[7] Humphrey of Gloucester, the king's uncle, had been arrested on a charge of treason at the Bury St Edmunds Parliament in February 1447, and had died in custody a few days later. Suffolk had undoubtedly been responsible for framing the charges against him, but there is no evidence to support an accusation of murder.

inished circle of favoured courtiers had exclusive access to Henry's irresponsible largesse. Suffolk himself accumulated a large number of profitable offices and wardships, together with such lucrative grants as the right to export two thousand sacks of wool duty free – a concession which was worth almost £3,500. His supporters were treated with similar generosity. Archbishop Stafford was given £500 in December 1448 for 'diligent services'; while Bishop Lumley of Carlisle, the new treasurer, received £600 in 1446, and a further £1,000 in 1449 of the king's 'mere grace' and presumably in response to petitions, although both these men received official salaries.

Such munificence was out of place in the parlous state of the Crown's finances. About 1440 the average gross income was around £70,000 a year, of which ordinary expenditure accounted for approximately £60,000. At this time the French war was costing at least £20,000 a year, and the Exchequer was well over £150,000 in debt. Between 1440 and 1450 income declined by almost 25 per cent partly for economic and partly for political reasons,[8] while there was no corresponding reduction in expenditure. By 1449 the debt was £372,000, and the government was besieged by creditors, who were mostly Englishmen of all classes from humble tradesmen to the highest members of the nobility. Their chances of satisfaction depended not at all upon the size or duration of the debt, but only upon their ability to gain the intercession of some member of the court circle. A group of London brewers paid a total of £132 to William Lumley, the treasurer's brother, for his aid in securing a payment of £612. The normal method of discharging debts was by assignment on some regular source of income, such as the customs, but the receipt of such an assignment was not necessarily the end of the story. The revenue might well be heavily committed already, and many years might pass before the tallies of assignment could be met. It is significant that one of the worst sufferers in this respect was the Duke of York. When he returned from Normandy in 1446 the Crown owed him £38,666 for his services as lieutenant there. In spite of the fact that he renounced £12,666 of this in return for a prompt settlement, most of his assignments were still unmet in 1450, by which time he was owed another

[8] There were serious interruptions in the wool trade, which reduced income from the Staple, and the increasing discontent of the Commons reduced the size and frequency of subsidies.

£10,000 for his services in Ireland. His own credit was pledged to the hilt, and he desperately needed access to the royal patronage. By contrast Adam Moleyns, who had also incurred heavy expenses abroad but was a secure member of the inner court, secured his own payment in cash and unencumbered assignments within a matter of months.

What was true of finance was also true of justice. It was one of the major achievements of the medieval English monarchy that it had obtained a virtual monopoly of justice; the whole system of the common law was controlled from the centre by means of royal writs. This was one of the reasons for its clumsiness. Also, weakness or corruption at Westminster could rapidly place its procedures in the hands of private interests. Henry was temperamentally incapable of refusing a petition, which meant that access to the king became the determining factor in important litigation. In short, it became futile to go to law if your opponent had an ear at court and you did not. We have already seen a good example of this in the case of Lord Moleyns. John Paston might exclaim contemptuously that a royal letter of the kind which Moleyns produced 'might be had for a noble', but the fact remains that he was unable to take effective countermeasures. Under these circumstances it is not surprising that Suffolk and his friends built up a very large clientage, the ramifications of which distorted the administration of justice up and down the country. Under his protection William Tailboys[9] and his servants conducted a virtual reign of terror in Lincolnshire and in London. They were later accused of committing four murders, eight assaults and innumerable robberies and trespasses; and of breaking up the Assizes at Boston in September 1446 with an armed mob, so that the court was unable to continue its business. As long as his patron was secure in power, there was no chance of bringing him to trial. Typically, he received a royal pardon in November 1448 for failing to appear in answer to some of these charges. Eventually, in November 1449 he crowned his career of crime by storming into the Council chamber at Westminster at the head of 'a great company' with the intention of murdering Lord Cromwell; an offence which the House of Commons, in impeaching him, described as 'the most odious riot that hath

[9] William Tailboys of Kyme. A series of indictments against him and his servants appear, significantly, in the Plea Rolls of the Hilary and Easter terms 1450 (Public Record Office, Placita Coram Rege, KB 27/755-6).

been seen in your [Henry's] time or your progenitors.'

Naturally, Suffolk's hand was felt most heavily in those areas where his estates principally lay, and the chief of these was East Anglia. For several years the sheriff of Norfolk was virtually his nominee, and his agents Sir Thomas Tuddenham, John Heydon and John Ulveston bore themselves with a high hand in the county. Sir John Fastolf complained bitterly of their unrestrained extortions, and the Paston letters make it clear that their weapons were at least as much judicial as physical. In 1448 Margaret Paston wrote to her husband that claim was being laid to his manor of Oxnead by one who boasted of Suffolk's 'good lordship', and that the steward of one of his estates had been outlawed at the 'suit of Sir Thomas Tuddenham'. Resistance was a hazardous matter; in another letter of the same year, Margaret wrote

> Danyell is out of the king's good grace, and he shall down and all his men, and all that be his well-willers; there shall no man be so hardy to do nor say against my Lord of Suffolk, nor none that belong to him, and that have done and said against him, they shall sore repent them.

It is not surprising that a generous fund of hatred accumulated, or that such feelings should have been shared by the Duke of Norfolk, whose own patronage was able to accomplish comparatively little in the shire whose name he bore. Similar if less pronounced situations existed elsewhere. It was almost certainly Suffolk's protection which frustrated attempts to bring Sir Robert Harcourt to justice for the murder of Richard Stafford at Coventry in 1448. This case adds another dimension to the picture because, balked of a legal remedy, Stafford's kinsmen took the law into their own hands and besieged their enemy in his Oxfordshire refuge.

At length, in 1450, the anger and frustration of Suffolk's enemies and victims boiled over. Perhaps he did not fully know the extent to which his agents used his protection for their own purposes; but the problem of injustice, like the problem of extortion and financial mismanagement, was a political one, and only capable of a political solution. It was probably events in France rather than in England which brought this situation to a head. The military position there had deteriorated steadily since the breakdown of the Burgundian alliance in 1435, and by 1442 the English had been glad enough to purchase a truce by accepting the dowerless Margaret of Anjou as bride for their young king. This truce had been renewed for two years on 15 March 1448, at the price of surrendering the remaining fortresses in Maine and Anjou. However, before that time elapsed, in March 1449, the Duke of Somerset as governor of Normandy countenanced the seizure and pillage of the town of Fougères, just over the Breton border, by a freebooting English force.

Such provocation was foolhardy since at that very time the English Parliament was being pressed into grudging and inadequate efforts to repair the feeble defences of the Duchy. The French resumed the war in full strength, and by November Normandy was entirely overrun; Rouen fell on November 6, the same day that Parliament reassembled in London. It may be that the feebleness of the English war effort was due mainly to the fact that the aristocracy had lost interest in campaigning when it ceased to be a source of profitable ransoms, but towards the end of 1449 they were looking for a scapegoat to salve their injured pride, and the Duke of Suffolk lay in the full path of their indignation.

THE CRISIS OF 1450

The new year opened ominously. On 9 January Adam Moleyns, Bishop of Chichester and keeper of the Privy Seal, was set upon and murdered at Portsmouth by a mob of infuriated seamen who accused him of withholding their wages. In the anguish of the moment, Moleyns seems to have made some damaging accusations against his patron, and this, in conjunction with the justifiable fuss which Lord Cromwell was making over Tailboys' outrage, prompted Suffolk to make an attempt to exculpate himself when Parliament reassembled on 22 January. This was a mistake and served only to provoke his enemies into levelling formal accusations against him. On 7 February the Commons presented a petition of indictment bearing eight charges, all concerned with alleged treasonable practices in relations with the French. Some of these were wildly improbable: for example that which accused him of having conspired a French invasion in 1447 for the purpose of deposing Henry VI in favour of his own son, John. Presumably the Commons were determined that the charge should be treason and felt some inhibitions about construing treason from the domestic maladministration of a man who so plainly had the king's confidence. The king's ministers were responsible only to himself, and no perversion of justice, however gross, which was carried out in the king's name could be criminal. No king, however, could be deemed to will his own destruction, and actions falling within the scope of the traditional law of treason must be presumed to have been carried out without his knowledge or consent. In the circumstances there is no doubt that Suffolk would have been found guilty if these accusations had been brought to the Lords, however slender their basis might have been, because the great majority were determined upon his destruction.

In the event, Henry respited the charges for a month, and on 9 March the Commons produced another list of 'misprisions which be not criminal', which went to the heart of the matter:

> Item, the said Duke conceiving himself to be with you priviest and best trusted, by full many years hath presumed upon himself to name to your highness, and caused to be made, divers persons to be sheriffs . . . some for lucre and some to be appliable to his intent and commandment . . .

By such means his own affairs, and those of his clients, had been furthered, while the just expectations of others had been violated and ignored. Nor was this all:

> Manslayers, rioters and common openly noised misdoers, seeing his great rule and might in every part of this your realm, have drawn to him, and for great good to him given, have been maintained and supported in suppressing of justice, and to open letting of execution of your laws, to the full heavy discomfort of the true subjects of this your realm.

Suffolk denied all the charges, of both kinds and placed himself on the king's mercy. Henry, at least partly convinced that his favourite's régime had been harmful, refused to countenance the indictment of treason, but banished him for five years without reference to either the Lords or the Council. This decision satisfied no one. It was not 'of record', and many suspected that it was a mere device to get Suffolk out of harm's way until the furore had subsided and he could be recalled to resume his sway.

There had been savage riots against him in London in January, and a large demonstration later in the same month at Eastry in Kent, which indicated that he might share the fate of Adam Moleyns. The leaders of the latter disturbance had explicitly threatened death, not only to Suffolk but also to the Bishop of Salisbury, Lord Say, and others of his associates. In both these cases also there had been explicit and vocal criticism of the king himself. However correct and reticent the Parliament might have been about the ultimate responsibility for contemporary misgovernment, some of Henry's humbler subjects were voicing their disgust most forcefully – and at some risk, as the number of indictments shows. One typical critic in Sussex declared that he was 'a natural fool . . . and no person able to rule the land',[10] while another and more explicit case was that of William Dalton of Ipswich, who was accused of saying 'that he would that our sovereign lord . . . were as cold at his heart root as the stone under his foot, so we had another king that could better rule this land'.

If there was any intention that Suffolk's banishment should preserve him from the violence of his enemies, that intention was frustrated. He took ship for Calais on 30 April, but the same day his vessel was intercepted by the *Nicholas of the Tower*. The Duke was taken aboard and two days later executed after a form of arraignment. Apparently the master of the *Nicholas* acted on his own initiative, and the fallen minister owed his death entirely to the hatred of the commons. This was evidently the opinion of the court, for while London rejoiced over the death of 'Jack Napes', some wild and misguided threats were uttered there to turn Kent into a wilderness as a reprisal for the murder. Although Suffolk had been the principal object of hatred, his death alone did not suffice to restore confidence in the royal government, and there seemed to be no guarantee that his 'false progeny and affinity' would not carry on where he had left off. Henry made no move to repudiate them, and they inevitably clung to the court as their only means of preservation. Clearly many of the commons felt that if they did not get rid of the whole tribe, their last condition would be worse than their first. It needed only a leader to turn this seething discontent into a large scale rebellion, and such a leader appeared in Kent in May 1450. He called himself John Mortimer and John Amend-all, but his real name was Cade and his origins are obscure. The order for his arrest later stated that he was an Irishman who had lived for some time in the household of Sir Thomas Dagre in Sussex, and

[10] P.R.O., KB 27/760 Rex 3. Such words could be construed as treason, because no overt act was required in the 'imagination' of the King's death. See J. G. Bellamy, *The Law of Treason in England in the later Middle Ages*, 121-2.

subsequently fled to France to avoid a charge of murder. He impressed the royal envoys with whom he negotiated as an educated and intelligent man, but Cade was a common name in the Ashford area of Kent, and it seems that no certainty about him is possible.

Cade was no peasant demagogue. Although he subsequently made serious blunders and paid the penalty, at first he impressed and won the support of many of the Kentish gentry. In the last week of May he was able to take advantage of the traditional Whitsun gatherings to muster large bodies of men from the Weald and north Kent, who came together at Blackheath. Their numbers are hard to guess, but over two thousand were subsequently pardoned for participation, so it is reasonable to suppose that substantially more were at one time or another in the camp.[11] Discipline was good, a fact which probably owed as much to the large number of gentry in the force as it did to the power of Cade's personality. These aristocrats, almost a hundred all told, were headed by Sir John Cheney,[12] and included members of such prominent Kentish families as the Fyneux, the Culpeppers and the Twysdens. The majority of the rank and file were subsequently described as yeomen or labourers, but a significantly large minority were artisans and tradesmen from the towns and villages along the London road. Interruptions to trade and consequent unemployment may help to explain the composition of the rebel host, but economic and social grievances did not feature at all among their stated objectives, except in so far as these were held to result from specific forms of misgovernment.

The rebels' 'Complaint', issued on 4 June, was a comprehensive and in many ways a masterly document, blending as it did an indictment of corruption in the day by day administration of the county with a shrewd diagnosis of the political ills of the country at large, and with a studiously moderate demand for retrenchment and reform. Inevitably the blame was laid upon 'certain persons [who] daily and nightly are about his [the king's] person, and daily inform him that good is evil and evil good'.

Item, [the 'Complaint' goes on,] they say that our sovereign

11 Contemporary estimates averaged about 20,000, but such estimates were nearly always exaggerated.

12 An uncle by marriage of Margaret Beaufort and Esquire of the Body to Henry V. Member of Parliament for Kent in 1449. Sheriff in 1455 and 1464.

> lord is above his laws to his pleasure, and he may make it and break it as him list without any distinction. The contrary is true and else he should not have sworn to keep it . . .
> Item, they say that the king should live upon his commons, and that their bodies and goods are the king's; the contrary is true, for then needed he never Parliament to sit to ask goods of his commons . . .
> Item, it is to be remedied that the false traitors will suffer no man to come to the king's presence for no cause without bribes where none ought to be had . . .
> Item, they say that whom the king will shall be traitor, and whom he will shall be none, and appeareth hitherto . . .

As an appeal against arbitrary government, and an assertion of the rule of law, this could hardly have been bettered in the seventeenth century. Specific complaints were made about the abuse of purveyance,[13] the oppressive conduct of the sheriff and his officers, and the depredations of the ever increasing army of royal household servants. The remedies proposed, however, remind us that we are far from the days of the Long Parliament. The demand was for a resumption of all grants of royal land; the banishment of those who so shamelessly abused the king's generosity; and reliance upon the counsel of the 'true lords', especially the Dukes of York, Exeter, Buckingham and Norfolk.

The actions of the rebels were not as logical or as purposeful as their words. Beyond the presentation of these articles, Cade seems to have had no clear plan, and there are signs of divergent counsels among his followers. Consequently, when the Council temporised and ordered the Kentishmen to disperse, they fell back towards Sevenoaks, uncertain what to do next. This problem was temporarily solved by the incautious advance of a small detachment of the king's forces, the destruction of which restored the rebels' morale and brought the royal army close to mutiny. Many of the latter deserted, saying that they would not fight against men whose only purpose was to reform the commonwealth, and to avoid disaster the remainder were dismissed.

In an attempt to placate the rebels, whose advance could not now be resisted, Lord Say and William Cromer, the unpopular

[13] The requisitioning of supplies and horses for the royal household, at low rates. This was an ancient feudal right, much open to abuse, and the subject of frequent complaints.

sheriff of Kent, were lodged in the Tower, and the king withdrew to Kenilworth, leaving London to its own devices. On 2 July a majority of the aldermen and Common Council decided to admit the rebels, and two days later they succeeded in persuading Lord Scales, the governor of the Tower, to surrender Say and Cromer, who were promptly beheaded and their heads set up on London Bridge. This was the high water mark of Cade's success, and if anyone had been in a position to survey the situation across the south of England on that date he might well have assumed that the authority of the government was on the point of total dissolution. On 29 June Bishop Ayscough of Salisbury, another prominent supporter of Suffolk, was lynched by a furious mob while celebrating mass at Edington in Wiltshire. His murderers are alleged to have robbed his baggage of cash and treasure to the value of almost £4,000, which, if true, suggests that their animosity was well founded. On the same day a large scale riot in Salisbury itself sacked the bishop's palace and destroyed his archives. During July there were also riots and risings at other places in Wiltshire, and in Hampshire, Gloucester and Essex, mostly directed against known adherents of the Suffolk faction.

Meanwhile, fortune had deserted Cade. Either he had become intoxicated by success and abandoned his earlier strictness, or else he had simply lost control of his men. Once in London they fell to plunder, and the reaction against them was swift and complete. On 5 July the citizens enlisted the help of the Tower garrison and expelled them after a sharp struggle. The Council exploited this situation sensibly by issuing a general pardon on 8 July, and the majority of the rebels dispersed to their homes. Cade himself, with a small band of followers, remained in arms, perhaps in an attempt to secure their plunder, or possibly because he knew that his pardon, issued in the name of Mortimer, was not valid. On 12 July a price was set on his head, and the following day he was mortally wounded while resisting arrest; the booty which he had accumulated was seized to the king's use, and his head joined his victims' on London Bridge.

The death of Cade did not mean the end of popular disorder, even in Kent. In September another 'Captain' appeared, one John Smith who gathered several hundred followers at Faversham; but Smith seems to have been no more than a rioter and was speedily apprehended. Similar disturbances took place in the same month in Sussex, Wiltshire and Essex, but being without real leadership or purpose they were suppressed without great difficulty. These later risings, although they had political overtones, are not readily distinguishable from the casual and local agrarian violence which was more or less endemic in medieval society. Such violence, even if directed against hated members of the court, was not likely to attract much sympathy from the aristocracy, and members of all factions united to put it down. The same was true where Lollardy was involved. There are strong suggestions that Lollard preachers played an important part in stirring up feeling against Bishop Ayscough, and one of Smith's followers called William Parminter was accused of acting 'against the laws of the church and the laws and customs of the realm, like a heretic and a Lollard'.

A movement like Cade's rebellion, on the other hand, clearly caught the aristocracy in two minds. We have seen that a number of gentry joined it, and they had every expectation that the House of Commons would receive their 'Complaint' favourably. The king's advisers thought the same and hastily dissolved Parliament before the document could reach it. Since the leaders had no idea of how to proceed beyond the stage of a mass petition, this move baffled them; and what had begun as a powerful political demonstration ended up as a dangerous disorder. The magnates played virtually no part. In spite of his adopting the suggestive name of Mortimer, there is no contemporary evidence to connect Cade with the Duke of York, and the circumstantial evidence is all against it. York himself was still in Ireland on 26 August, and the other leading opponents of the court remained aloof.

Up to this point the initiative in attacking abuses in the government had come almost entirely from the commons: through mob violence, through the vigorous petitions of the lower House, and through the moderate (if unlawfully presented) demands of the men of Kent. Neither of the latter two were in any sense revolutionary, and by the summer of 1450 it must have been clear to all those magnates who were out of favour at the court, and to the Duke of York in particular, that they had been presented with a golden opportunity. The Duke of Suffolk was dead, and a judiciously expressed sympathy for the cause of reform seemed to guarantee both a wide measure of support and the paralysis of effective opposition.

THE HEIR PRESUMPTIVE

Richard of York, as the grandson of Edmund of Langley, fourth son of Edward III, was the heir presumptive to the throne as well as being the greatest subject in terms of possessions and estates. In spite of this, or perhaps because of it, he had been excluded from the court, as we have seen, by the hostility of the Duke of Suffolk. In 1446 a violent quarrel with Moleyns resulted in York's command in Normandy being transferred to Edmund Beaufort, and York himself being despatched to the distant Lieutenancy of Ireland. Instead of appreciating that the disaster which had overtaken Beaufort's command in 1449 might easily have been his own, York continued to harbour against his supplanter a resentment at least as bitter as that which he nursed against Suffolk. Therefore, when the news reached him in August 1450 that Beaufort, now Duke of Somerset, had returned to England and was resident at court, he envisaged the mantle of one enemy descending upon the other to his lasting disadvantage. At the beginning of September he landed at Anglesey and marched towards London.

In fact Somerset did not at once inherit the position which Suffolk had vacated; or, if he did, he used his power with discretion. A judicial commission was set up early in August under the presidency of the chancellor, Cardinal Kemp, to investigate the specific local grievances which had lain behind the Kentish rising. This commission, which included the Duke of Buckingham and the Archbishop of Canterbury, sat in a number of places in the county between mid-August and mid-December, and received a large number of indictments against those who had taken advantage of the previous régime. Many of these accusations give colour and substance to the previous complaints: Stephen Slegge, an undersheriff, had arranged to have a man falsely indicted and then charged him ten marks to arrange his acquittal; Robert East, the keeper of Maidstone gaol, had arrested a woman and forced her husband to bid for her release. Some of the charges went back almost ten years. They were commonplace abuses of power for the most part, but rendered intolerable by the impossibility of redress. The commission, which carried out a number of exemplary punishments, owed nothing to the Duke of York, and it seemed possible that a revival in the power of the Council might go some way towards restoring confidence in the king's justice. That this did not happen was partly the responsibility of York himself.

Half-hearted attempts were made to intercept him on his way from Wales, and he arrived in London just before Michaelmas at the head of about 4,000 men, and full of righteous indignation about the way in which loyal subjects were being treated. The king denied that he had any hostile intention towards York, and promised that a widely based council with full powers would be set up to remedy the defects of the legal system. Meanwhile, as we have seen, in many parts of the country those who felt themselves injured or aggrieved were seeking the Duke's 'good lordship' for purposes of redress – or revenge. As a result the erst while clients of Suffolk made haste to secure the protection of the man who was now closest to the king, Edmund, Duke of Somerset. It soon became apparent that York had received nothing but empty promises, and if there had ever been any chance that Somerset would be an effective friend to 'good justice', that chance had been destroyed by the nature of the legacy which he could hardly refuse.

Having failed in a direct approach to the king, Richard naturally sought the alliance of Parliament to gratify the expectations which were now being rested on him, and which he could not afford to disappoint. The third session of the 1449-50 Parliament, held at Leicester in May, had been an eventful one. The notorious Tailboys had been brought to justice and fined £3,000 for his attack on Cromwell. By an obstinate refusal of subsidies an Act of Resumption was forced upon the reluctant king, and a specific appropriation of revenue made for the household. Even when the subsidies were granted, they were not unconditional but ear marked for the payment of the army, and they were to be administered by four receivers appointed by the Parliament. Lack of confidence in the king's government could not have been spelled out more clearly, but the fundamental problem remained untouched: as long as the king had the unrestricted right to choose his own advisers no amount of reforming legislation could be effective. This was also the Duke of York's problem, although for somewhat different reasons. When Parliament was reconvened in the autumn of 1450 he shared with the House of Commons a pressing desire to reshape the executive.

For a time York was the darling of the Commons and of the City of London. His fellow peers were less enthusiastic; most of them could see little gain in replacing the Duke of Suffolk with the Duke of York. Their real need was for a Council which could arbitrate their quarrels impartially and effectively, and there was no reason to suppose that York would serve them better in that respect than Somerset. The man they were most likely to trust was Cardinal Kemp, and he remained firmly within the court circle for reasons of political principle, being by far the ablest defender of the royal prerogative. Those peers who did adhere to York at this time did so for opportunist reasons, and their conduct lent little credibility to his cause. Norfolk was mainly concerned to recover his authority in East Anglia from the Suffolk faction, which, as we have seen, had largely transferred its clientage to Somerset. There was little to choose between the conduct of Tuddenham and Heydon on the one side, and of such Norfolk dependants as Sir William Ashton and Charles Nowell on the other. Similarly the Earl of Devon was motivated mainly by hatred of Lord Bonvile and the Earl of Wiltshire, who had the ear of the court. Whether York himself had any genuine interest in executive reform is doubtful. The conduct of his agents and dependants in those times and places in which he had an ascendency does not suggest firm moral purpose. However, when the Parliament assembled in November 1450 there were vigorous demonstrations in his favour, while Somerset narrowly escaped the fate of Ayscough and Moleyns. York's behaviour throughout was scrupulously correct. He suppressed disorders in the capital and intervened to rescue his opponents from the mob. He encouraged the passage of an Act of Attainder against Cade and took an active part in the judicial proceedings against the later Kentish rebels. At the same time the Commons took up again the causes which they had been forced to drop in May. A further appropriation of revenue for military purposes was made, and a further Act of Resumption passed.

Nevertheless the resistance of the court was stiffening. A proposal to attaint the deceased Duke of Suffolk was defeated. More significantly a petition for the banishment of 'evil influences' – including the Duke of Somerset and Lord Dudley – from the king's presence was refused on the explicit grounds that it was the king's prerogative to choose his own advisers, and his responsibility alone to see that justice was done. By the time that the Parliament was dissolved in May 1451 it was clear that the

Duke of York was making no progress at all in his bid to entrench himself in power. Moreover it had been publicly suggested in the lower House that Henry should recognise York as his heir, thus re-awakening rumours which had been circulating among the disaffected during the previous summer and increasing the king's suspicion of his powerful subject's intentions.

The prolonged crisis of 1450-51 provides the key to the events of the succeeding years. In spite of the efforts of Cardinal Kemp, which resulted in the proper enforcement of the Resumption Act of 1451, and a further attempt to insist that royal warrants should be approved by the standing Council, there was no general recovery of confidence in the administration. Re-affirmation of the royal prerogative left the complaints of the Kentishmen largely unanswered, and Parliament had failed to assert any control over the king's advisers. What had been achieved, in the purge of the unscrupulous Suffolk and his adherents, had been accomplished by lawless violence, in default of constitutional or judicial redress. The commons saw no reason to suppose that the same situation would not arise again, while many lords must have felt, like the Duke of York, that it was hopeless to look to the king for either favour or impartiality. As a direct result of this, a further, if somewhat different crisis developed rapidly in the autumn of 1451.

The Earl of Devon, seeing no possibility of a favourable outcome in his quarrel with Wiltshire, mustered about five thousand retainers and adherents at Taunton and embarked upon a private campaign against his enemy under the pretext of defending the commonweal. A plundering raid upon Wiltshire's estates near Bath failed to capture him, and at the end of September Devon returned to lay siege to Wiltshire's ally, Lord Bonvile, who had occupied Taunton castle. To suppress this dangerous private war the government called upon the Duke of Buckingham and the Earls of Salisbury and Shrewsbury, but before they could muster enough strength to intervene, the Duke of York himself had appeared and persuaded the opponents to negotiate. Although he had no authority to do so, his success enabled him to pose as a defender of the peace, and to save an important ally from possible destruction. It is difficult to know how far Devon had been provoked into this action; certainly his opponents were not blameless, but characteristically the only legal action taken was the indictment of the Earl for treason and rebellion in January

1452. The charge was substantially accurate, but the absence of any comparable proceedings against his opponents can only have confirmed him in his belief that desperate remedies were necessary and thrown him into the much more ambitious schemes being prepared by his ally and patron.

Some time during the autumn of 1451, York seems to have come to the conclusion that the only possible guarantee of his future security lay in the destruction of the Duke of Somerset and his own acceptance, enforced if necessary, into the inner councils of the king. Towards the end of the year, his agents were busy making plans for risings and demonstrations in his favour in places as far apart as Hereford, Grantham and Cambridge. For this purpose they used both the network of his clientage and the still lively sentiments of the previous year. These activities did not escape the notice of the court, and an angry and suspicious exchange of letters ensued, in which York protested his continued allegiance to the king but was understandably reluctant to appear before him in person.

Finally, in February 1452 the Duke declared himself in a letter to the citizens of Shrewsbury, in which he blamed Somerset for the loss of Normandy, and complained that his own good advice to the king

> concerning the wellbeing and safeguard, both of his most royal person, and of the tranquillity and conservation of all this his realm . . . were laid apart, and to be of no effect, through the envy, malice and untruth of the Duke of Somerset.

To remedy this,

> seeing that the said Duke ever prevails and rules about the king's person, and that by this means the land is likely to be destroyed, [I] am fully determined to proceed in all haste against him, with the help of my kinsmen and friends; in such a way that it shall prove to promote ease, peace, tranquillity and the safeguard of this land.

By the middle of February York had mustered a substantial force on his estates near Ludlow, while in the south west the Earl of Devon and Lord Cobham were preparing to join him with a similar following. As he advanced across the midlands, the prepared risings broke out, giving the appearance of a widespread and spontaneous support.

The truth was somewhat different, and Somerset proved to be

a tough antagonist, partly because his government was in reality rather more effective than that of Suffolk, and partly because York had compromised himself by his frank appeal to arms. The great majority of the magnates rallied to the court, and the civic authorities of a number of towns which had received letters from York promptly forwarded them to the Council. Most disastrous of all, Kent did not stir. York bypassed London in his advance, making straight for Dartford in the apparent expectation of massive support from the men who had rallied to Cade. Nothing happened, and at the beginning of March the royal army closed in behind him, cutting off his retreat to the west. When it came to the point, York did not much want to fight. His hope had been to dictate terms from a position of overwhelming strength, but he had failed to achieve such a position. Fortunately for him the majority of the Council were equally reluctant to come to blows. No doubt Somerset was anxious to destroy his rival, but the bulk of the royal army had been contributed by Buckingham, Salisbury and Warwick, and their more conciliatory advice prevailed.

In the negotiations which followed, York based his justification entirely upon an indictment of Somerset, and seems to have received some sort of an undertaking that his charges would be investigated by the Council. However, as soon as he had dispersed his army he found himself under arrest, while Somerset retained his position at the court unchallenged. In the event no further action was taken against York, and he was soon released, but his political position appeared to have been destroyed. Commissions of oyer and terminer were sent out to all those areas which had supported the rising, and large numbers of indictments resulted. Lord Cobham and the Earl of Devon were imprisoned, and it was to be almost two years before they were discharged.[14] At the same time the Council made strenuous efforts to stabilise the situation and exploit the disillusionment with York's reforming pretensions which had resulted from his overt treason.

In April the Duke of Norfolk issued a careful proclamation in East Anglia, inviting all men to bring forward their complaints without fear or favour, promising them his own protection,

[14] Cobham was imprisoned at Berkhampsted Castle for two years, without being brought to trial; Devon was eventually tried, and acquitted, by his peers in 1454. R. L. Storey, *The End of the House of Lancaster*, 101.

under the king. Later in the summer Henry was also taken on an impressive progress, to Exeter, Bristol and the Welsh marches, where Somerset presided over the indictments and trials of a large number of York's adherents. In the event few of these were actually punished, for over two thousand four hundred individuals purchased the king's pardon. The main purpose of the proceedings was to restore confidence, and this was to some extent accomplished. The measure of the court's success can be seen in the altered tone of the Parliament of March 1453. There can be no doubt that the Commons in all these mid-century Parliaments provide a reasonably accurate picture of the political opinions of the burgesses and minor aristocracy, and their place in the constitution, although extremely limited, was recognised and accepted. We have seen that Cade's followers quoted the Commons' right to vote supply in refutation of the claim that the property of subjects belonged to the king. Similarly the constant stream of petitions, with their horrific tales of injustice and oppression, is a striking testimony to faith in the intercessory function of the House.

To have 'packed' such an assembly was beyond the power of any magnate, however great. The Duke of Suffolk at the height of his power could do no more than place a small number of servants and dependants, and the House as a whole showed him scant respect. Similarly the Duke of York in the autumn of 1450, when he was 'greatly to the liking' of the Commons, was unable to secure the return of all his nominees. Individual peers could usually 'manage' elections in areas where their interests were strong, but could seldom dominate them. After all, some of the men who sat as knights of the shire were as wealthy and as powerful as peers. They might be the 'well willers' of their social superiors, but they were certainly not their minions. It is therefore highly significant that the Commons of 1453 were well disposed towards the government. The country had narrowly escaped civil war, and they were inclined to co-operate rather than obstruct. Subsidies were granted to raise a force of archers 'for the defence of the kingdom' – a necessary precaution in view of the fact that the crews of French ships were disporting themselves with impunity on the Suffolk beaches. The government was also bestirring itself in this direction by equipping a fleet; an English army was again on foot in France, and the last Act of Resumption was bearing some fruit.

The fortunes of York were in total eclipse. His Lieutenancy of Ireland was transferred to the Earl of Wiltshire; his follower Sir William Oldhall was attainted by Parliament, and those who had followed him in the previous summer were deprived of all Crown grants of lands or offices. He had lost both the goodwill of the gentry and such support as he had ever had among his fellow peers. However, it was one thing to defeat the Duke of York and another to remedy those defects and abuses in the administration which had made him powerful once, and might always serve his need again. Some progress had been made, but the Duke of Somerset was not a man whose integrity carried much conviction, and it was in him rather than in Kemp or in the Council as a whole that the king reposed his confidence.

CHAPTER 2

THE COLLAPSE OF OBEDIENCE

If princes consider well their estate, they shall find that their seignories contain more trouble and thought than pleasaunce or delight. (*The Book of Good Manners*).

FEALTY AND OBLIGATION

Fifteenth century ideas on the nature of political obligation were extremely conservative. The liberties and prerogatives of the Crown, as Henry IV had reassured his Parliament, were not for the gratification of the king, but to enable him to keep the good laws, statutes and usages of his progenitors, 'and to do right to all men in mercy and in truth according to his oath'. The king's liberty of will enabled him to preserve intact the liberties and franchises of others; and his grace enabled him to accept innovations where necessary and adapt them to the spirit of existing law and custom. The royal prerogative, and indeed the whole application of human or 'positive' law, operated within the context of the law of nature, which set ultimate bounds to the authority of the king, his Courts and his Parliaments. The king could no more abrogate franchises, or alter the law to suit his pleasure, than he could abolish the jurisdiction of the Church. English constitutional theory was an amalgam of Roman and Germanic concepts, although Roman law had advanced much more slowly in England than in most other parts of Europe. The royal office was thought of both in terms of *maiestas*, and in terms of mutual loyalty and obligation.

By the fifteenth century the formal defiance, or *diffidatio*, had long since disappeared, but it had left behind it a trail of precedents in which monarchs with too great an itch to be *lege solutus* had been disciplined or deposed. In contrasting the *dominium politicum et regale* of England with the *dominium regale* of France, Sir John Fortescue was praising the strength of this Germanic survival.[1] Naturally, this was reflected in the law

[1] Sir John Fortescue (1390? – 1479). A distinguished lawyer who was a close observer of the political events of this period. Appointed Chief

of treason, which combined elements of *laesa maiestatis* with breach of trust and betrayal of the realm. In the twelfth century private war and even rebellion had not been considered treasonable.[2] Since the great statute of 1352 there had been no doubt that levying war against the king was treason, but as late as 1381 attitudes to popular insurrection had been more ambiguous. Many of the participants in the disturbances of that year were indicted only of felony, even those who had been responsible for the death of Archbishop Simon. Similarly, it might be extremely difficult to determine when a private affray, resulting in death and injury, ceased to be felony and became treason. According to the law of arms, war was levied only when the party concerned displayed a banner or device, but this was not accepted as a universal test. Cade's followers were indicted of treason, although they had displayed no banner and had denied that their action was in any way directed against the king.

In fact the English law of treason had become somewhat more 'Roman' in the first half of the fifteenth century, and as we have seen, fears that this process was accelerating formed the basis of one of the rebels' complaints in 1450. Their claim, that it was treason to advise the king to abuse his lawful powers, would not have stood in any court, but it was a natural corollary to the universally accepted principle that the royal authority was limited. Ultimately the factor which preserved the balance so much admired by Fortescue was not the law but the collective will of the aristocracy. The English judiciary enjoyed a measure of independence, for there was no equivalent of the French *cas*

Justice of King's Bench in 1442, he adhered to Queen Margaret in 1461 and went into exile with her. Returning in 1471, he was captured after Tewkesbury, but became reconciled to Edward and served on his Council until forced to retire by old age in 1473. During his exile he wrote several legal treatises of which the best known are *De natura legis naturae* (1463?), *De laudibus legum Angliae* (1470), and *The Governance of England* (after 1470). Fortescue's main argument was that the prerogative of the English monarchy was limited by law (both positive and natural) and by consent. This consent was for some purposes vested in the Parliament, and for others in the whole aristocracy of the realm.

[2] It was not until the Welsh and Scottish wars of Edward I that rebellion came to be regarded as treason. For a summary of the law of treason before this period, see F. Pollock and F. W. Maitland, *The History of English Law before the Reign of Edward I*, II, 500-8.

royaux,[8] but still no writ ran against the king and the only way to check a monarch with theocratic ambitions was by force. For this a pretext might be found in the nature of the coronation oath, but the aristocracy had themselves sworn oaths of fealty to the king which the great majority did not lightly renounce.

Both in theory and in practice the magnates enjoyed a special relationship with the king which was feudal and Germanic in its origin and owed nothing to the civil law. They had been his comrades in arms, and his natural companions and advisers. As we have seen, both popular opinion and their own interests dictated that they should enjoy ready access to the court. That many of them, including the highest, were excluded by Henry and those who enjoyed his confidence was considered to be an abuse in itself. At this point a constitutional custom which might almost be called a principle coincided with the contemporary issue of patronage. Just as the king was a 'natural lord' to his peers, so he was expected to be a 'good lord' to them, in that he would listen to their complaints, adjudicate their quarrels, and distribute honours and rewards. All these things Henry failed to do with any consistency or reliability, and as a result the concept of treason became blurred. Thus, while many of those who supported York in his abortive *coup d'état* in 1452 were indicted of treason for 'compassing and imagining the king's destruction', no such charge was levelled against the Duke himself, and his quarrel with Somerset was sent to a select body of councillors for arbitration. In the days which were coming, it was to become increasingly difficult for a peer to know where his true duty lay, or how to reconcile that duty with his legitimate interests. No accepted doctrine of resistance lay ready to hand, nor were any effective constitutional sanctions available. Had the aristocracy been less divided by their own feuds the political issue might have clarified more rapidly; in the event Henry VI, unlike Richard II or Edward II, did not have to face a virtually united baronial opposition.

This circumstance owed nothing to his own political dexterity, but was rather a measure of the extent to which his government had collapsed. Naturally, this can be seen most clearly in the

[8] Cases of lèse-majesty, which were tried by special process in the king's courts, rather than by normal judicial procedures. Bellamy, *op. cit.*, 12-13.

remote northern marches, where the royal authority, as such, had never been much respected. Here the king's representatives were the Wardens, but their power depended more upon the traditional loyalties accorded to their families than upon the salaries and privileges of their offices, although both were considerable. No Warden could have maintained himself without the backing of at least some of the great border families. Consequently the Percies, Nevilles, Cliffords and Dacres – and particularly the first two – looked upon the Wardenries as their own preserve, and coveted them for the additional power and prestige which they could bring to a man whose resources were already great.[4]

In this area the system of government long established in lowland England functioned only fitfully at best. Tynedale, Redesdale, Hexhamshire and the Bishopric of Durham were franchises where the king's writ did not run. In Westmorland the shrievalty was hereditary in the Clifford family, and in Cumberland the sheriff was excluded from the Percy honour of Cockermouth. References to Cumberland and Westmorland virtually disappear from the records of the central government after 1440, and the Assizes at Carlisle and Appleby became more and more perfunctory. The same would probably have happened to Northumberland had it not been for the substantial city of Newcastle upon Tyne which retained regular commercial contacts with the capital. In this wild region, further disturbed by the constant incursions of the Scots, and occasional open war, the principal social virtues were personal loyalty and courage in battle. Border ballads such as *Chevy Chase*, recounting the exploits of the Fenwicks and the Armstrongs, depict a society devoid of normally accepted concepts of right and wrong, where faithfulness to clan or lord was the sole measure of conduct. With such material to draw upon, it is not surprising that aristocratic feuds flourished, or that they were prosecuted with

[4] The Warden of the West March received £1500 a year in times of truce, and £6000 a year in time of war; the Warden of the East March approximately double. The Wardens raised their own troops, and it was up to them to decide how many they needed. Henry Percy, the second Earl of Northumberland, was Warden of the East March from 1417 to 1434, and the third Earl from 1440 to 1461. Ralph Neville, first Earl of Westmorland, was Warden of the West March from 1403 to 1414, his eldest son from 1414 to 1420, and another son, Richard, Earl of Salisbury, from 1420 to 1435 and 1443 to 1460. R. L. Storey, *The End of the House of Lancaster*, 108-9.

uninhibited ferocity.

The harm which could be caused in this area by an irresponsible troublemaker was very great, and such a one was Thomas Percy, second son of the Earl of Northumberland, who was created Lord Egremont in 1449 in the unjustified expectation of good service in the borders. Early in 1453 Egremont took it upon himself to augment the Percy interest by a series of largely unprovoked attacks upon the servants and 'well-willers' of Richard Neville, Earl of Salisbury.[5] Summoned before the Council to answer for these disorders on 7 June, Egremont paid no attention, and a further letter later in the month was equally unavailing. At the end of June Sir John Neville took up the gage, and the disorders spread to the estates of the rival families in Yorkshire. During July and August a series of Council letters and royal commissions were issued in an attempt to discipline the contending parties. On 12 July a commission of oyer and terminer for Yorkshire included the heads of both the contending families, the Earls of Salisbury and Northumberland, presumably in the hope that negotiations would ensue. On 27 July a fresh commission was appointed, this time of councillors learned in the law under the leadership of Sir William Lucy. At the same time, earlier hope having been disappointed, further letters were sent to the two Earls commanding them to discipline their unruly offspring and make them amenable to the new commission. Outrages on both sides continued unabated throughout the late summer and autumn, in spite of the mediating efforts of the Archbishop of York, the Earl of Westmorland, the Mayor of York and others.

There could have been no more convincing demonstration of the utter helplessness of the central government. There was no suggestion that any of these crimes amounted to treason, and the perpetrators were not even excluded from the commissions of the peace! Nothing but ineffectual threats and exhortations came from London, while the two sides mustered substantial armies near Topcliffe in the North Riding. In the event a pitched battle was averted because some kind of disengagement seems

[5] Richard Neville was the first son of Ralph, first Earl of Westmorland, by his second marriage to Joan Beaufort, daughter of the Duke of Lancaster. He was consequently the younger half brother of the second Earl, and relations between the two halves of the Neville family were frequently strained. Richard, Earl of Warwick, was his eldest son.

to have been agreed upon in late October, but that, too, owed nothing to government intervention. No renunciation of allegiance was involved in this confrontation. Indeed, both parties acted as if it were no concern of the king, and the theory as well as the fact of the king's peace had disappeared from view. Nevertheless, in view of the outcome it is significant that in the midst of this quarrel Richard Neville, Earl of Warwick, had also virtually come to blows with the Duke of Somerset. As a result, by the autumn of 1453 the Neville interest stood favourably disposed towards the Duke of York, while the Percies by an automatic reflex inclined to the court.

A FLUCTUATING POLITICAL BALANCE

This alignment could hardly have come at a more crucial moment, because in August the whole future of the government was thrown in doubt when the king suffered a complete mental collapse. For a month or so the inner circle of the Council tried to carry on as though nothing had happened, which partly explains their supine attitude to events in the north, but their whole position depended upon the king, and as soon as his derangement became known their authority was inevitably called in question. A Great Council was consequently summoned early in October to take order for the government and to deal with the dangerous problem of magnate feuds. The importance even of so negligible a personality as Henry VI can be judged by the consequences of his disappearance. Not only did the Duke of Somerset fail to exclude his great rival from the Council, but by the end of the year he was confined to the Tower to answer the long-standing charges about his conduct in France. By that time York had gathered round him a powerful band of allies, among whom the Earls of Salisbury and Warwick were conspicuous, and occupied a prominent place upon the new standing Council which had been set up for the duration of the king's illness. Probably his popularity with his fellow peers was helped by the fact that he was no longer heir to the throne.

Considerably against the odds, on 13 October Queen Margaret had given birth to a son, and should the king's condition prove permanent or fatal a long minority was in prospect. So sudden a reversal of political fortune was accompanied by its own perils, as the preparations being made in London in January 1454 make clear. Mutual distrust seemed likely to turn the Parliament, summoned for February, into an armed conflict. The courtiers, such as Wiltshire, Egremont and Bonvile, feeling themselves to be threatened, boasted of the size of the armed retinues which were to accompany them, while Somerset was reported to be operating from prison an extensive network of spies and encouraging his dependants to harass York and his allies in every way. The latter naturally took their own precautions, while the uncommitted, such as Buckingham and Cardinal Kemp, were forced to do the same for their own protection. According to one report, the judicious Chancellor

> has charged and commanded all his servants to be ready with bows and arrows, swords and bucklers, and all other weapons of war, such as they can use, to wait on the safeguard of his person.

In the event, the balance of power, and the voluntary absence of some of the wilder spirits such as Egremont, prevented any serious outbreak of physical violence, but the danger of civil war was obvious for all to see.

In the circumstances it is not surprising that the Commons were touchy and querulous, or that the Council was somewhat at a loss as to the proper method of conducting business. The death of Kemp in March, and the necessity to appoint a new Chancellor, brought matters to a head. In spite of the most persistent and pathetic attempts to communicate with him, no spark of rationality could be found in the king. On 25 March a deputation of lords waited upon Henry, but neither they nor Margaret were able to obtain any sign of recognition,[6] and the lords therefore had to take the relevant decisions upon their own responsibility. The Earl of Salisbury became Chancellor, and the Duke of York was appointed Protector. The latter position was modelled upon that which the Duke of Gloucester had occupied during Henry's minority, and as such was not a vice-regal office but rather the presidency of the Council. In taking these decisions, the lords set aside the claims of the queen, which had been presented in a most sweeping form, and by so doing turned the strong-minded Margaret into a determined enemy of the Duke of York and all who adhered to him.

The new government was in fact much more widely based than its predecessor, and as a result was soon in a position to

[6] To justify themselves, they left a detailed record of their visit upon the Parliament Roll. *Rot. Parl.*, V, 241.

demonstrate its greater effectiveness. In May 1454 the incorrigible Egremont was again in arms, this time in alliance with Henry Holand, Duke of Exeter, the hare-brained nature of whose activities in this year casts some doubt upon his sanity.[7] Ostensibly Holand was the principal, since his claims to the Protectorship and to the Duchy of Lancaster were the acknowledged cause of the movement. However, since the action all took place in Yorkshire, where Egremont's influence was strong and Exeter's very weak, it seems probable that the Duke was merely a suggestible ass. Unlike the armed gatherings of the previous year, the assembly of these malcontents at Spofforth was treated as treason, and the Duke of York moved against them with a substantial force at the beginning of June. Exeter lost his nerve in the face of impending battle, and fled to sanctuary at Westminster, whence he was taken in July and imprisoned in Pontefract Castle. Egremont was taken by his old enemies the Nevilles later in the year, and confined in Newgate. Judicial proceedings against the lesser rebels commenced at York in mid-June, before a broadly based commission which included the Earls of Warwick and Shrewsbury, Baron Greystoke and Lord Clifford. Most of those indicted were subsequently pardoned, and others were pursued in vain, but at least a small measure of sharp justice was administered.

Perhaps the most significant feature of this whole inconsequential episode is the demonstration which it provides of the ease with which a sizeable disturbance could be raised for no good reason at all. No tangible private quarrel was in view. Egremont made no attempt to direct the assembled force against the Nevilles, and very few of those who obeyed the summons can have had much faith in Exeter's pretensions. It was primarily an assembly of retainers, tenants and servants, apt to the hands of their lords and patrons, and not disposed to question their authority, or consider the nature of the quarrel in which they had been enlisted. No theoretical justification for this attitude could be, or was, advanced; it was a practical demonstration of the way in which clientage had expanded to fill the gap left by the feebleness of the central administration. In the same year,

[7] Exeter's claim to the Duchy of Lancaster was based upon the fact that his paternal grandmother was a daughter of John of Gaunt, a basis so flimsy as to be ridiculous. He was subsequently regarded with grave suspicion by both sides, and died in prison in 1475.

when the Council sent letters into Derbyshire, summoning Sir Nicholas Longford and Walter Blount to answer for a violent affray, Longford's servants seized the wretched messenger and endeavoured to force him to eat the writ. When this failed, they tore the document in pieces, and smashed the Privy Seal with every demonstration of contempt. In the same county in the following year another savage little quarrel was arbitrated by the Duke of Buckingham in the spirit of the ancient Germanic blood feud. The Gresleys and the Vernons agreed to a scale of compensation for injuries inflicted: £13s. 6s. 8d. for a murder, 40s. for a broken leg, and so on. Actions were also initiated at common law, but clearly this was a ritual from which neither side expected to obtain real satisfaction; an element in the quarrel rather than a means of settlement. Where a number of these aristocratic quarrels existed in the same area, complicated patterns of interaction developed. In Derbyshire, the Vernons joined the Longfords, and the Gresleys joined the Blounts, and since the Duke of Buckingham was the Longfords' patron, the Gresleys sought the protection of the Earl of Warwick. Aided in this way by the ramifications of clientage, such disputes could turn a whole countryside into a multitude of suspicious and ready-handed factions, apt to the purposes of ambitious political schemers.

Even the most routine litigation was thus likely to be affected by events at the distant court, with which the participants themselves were in no way concerned. Consider the dilemma of one Steward, servant to Thomas Daniell, impanelled upon a Norfolk jury to judge an issue between John Paston and a certain Francis. Steward wrote to Edmund Paston in great uncertainty, asking what he should do, as Francis was maintained by Sir Thomas Tuddenham. 'He would fain be challenged,' Edmund reported, and went on, 'I counselled him to swear the truth of the issue that he be sworn to, and then he never needed to dread him of no attaint.'[8] This was easy advice to give, but Steward's whole livelihood was at stake in view of Tuddenham's connection with the Duke of Suffolk. It is not surprising that he was anxious to be discharged, nor is it likely that his verdict was unaffected by his circumstances.

At Christmas 1454 the king began to show signs of recovery, and by March the whole political situation at court had been

[8] *Paston Letters*, I, 65 (1447).

reversed. Archbishop Thomas Bourchier replaced Salisbury as Chancellor, Shrewsbury became Treasurer upon the dismissal of Worcester, and the Duke of Somerset, released from confinement and restored to the Captaincy of Calais, resumed his position by the king's side. Northumberland, Clifford and Egremont hastened to London to take advantage of the situation, while York and the Nevilles withdrew to their estates in haste and disarray. This situation was reflected in every shire, as the clients of the newly dominant faction reasserted their control. To reinforce his position, Somerset called a Great Council to meet at Leicester on 21 May, secure in the belief that his rivals would not dare to appear. To this Council the shires were asked to send nominated representatives, presumably in the hope that a body so selectively reinforced would carry something like the weight of a Parliament. It is significant that a formal Parliament was not called; clearly the court felt uncertain of its ability to exercise sufficient influence on the elections.

In the event, York and his allies did come, with great speed and three thousand armed men at their backs. They intercepted the royal party at St. Albans, professing their allegiance to the king, but demanding the removal of their enemies from the Council. At Dartford, three years before, York had been at a disadvantage and unwilling to fight. This time his party was stronger and his inhibitions less, thanks, no doubt, to the presence of the Earl of Warwick at his side. When their demands were refused, York's men attacked without hesitation. The result was not so much a pitched battle as a murderous and successful assault upon Somerset and Northumberland, who, along with Lord Clifford and about fifty of their men, perished in the fighting. The victors treated Henry with scrupulous respect:

> and when all these things were done, the Duke of York entered the abbey and knelt before the king . . . protesting that he had not opposed him but had been against the traitors to his crown. And before York left the king pardoned him and received him into grace . . .

Nevertheless, the Duke's precipitate action was to have disastrous consequences. In the first place it introduced an element of blood feud, in which the Percies, Cliffords and Beauforts sought revenge. In the second place it cleared the way for Queen Margaret to assume the leadership of the 'court party, a development which inevitably identified the Crown with a faction, and led directly to York's death and Henry's deposition. In the short term, however, it seemed rather as though the conditions of York's Protectorship had been re-created. The 'Yorkist' lords, as they may now be called, were not numerous enough to dominate the government on their own, but they had the chief disposal of the Crown's patronage, and were thus in a strong position to attract allies. Consequently Buckingham, the Bourchiers, and the Earls of Worcester and Pembroke soon returned to the Council. At a Parliament which met on the 9 July Henry's acceptance of this situation was proclaimed, and all the lords renewed their oaths of allegiance to the king. The blame for the earlier dissensions was conveniently laid upon the deceased Somerset. The parliamentary Commons were gratified with further measures for the resumption of royal grants, and a new scheme of appropriations for the household.

At the same time, the fragility of this apparent equilibrium was ruthlessly exposed by one of the worst outbreaks of criminal violence in the entire period. The culprit was the Earl of Devon who in October 1455 began a systematic reign of terror in the region around Exeter. His sons and retainers plundered their enemies, frustrated the sessions of the peace, and murdered Nicholas Radford an elderly and respected lawyer. When Parliament re-assembled in mid-November, the wildest rumours of Devon's activities were circulating, and the Commons petitioned anxiously for the appointment of another Protector, to deal with what seemed to be a grave emergency. This expedient was justified on the grounds that the king was indisposed. He was certainly not attending Parliament, but the nature of his illness is unclear; there is no evidence to suggest renewed insanity. York was inevitably appointed to the proposed office, and in December he eventually moved towards the West, with a flurry of proclamations denouncing the Earl and his 'riotous and ungodly demeanings'. When Devon realised that serious action against him was impending, he hastened to submit and was imprisoned in the Tower. His stay there lasted little more than a month. By February the political pendulum was again swinging against York, and the Earl was set at liberty. In spite of the blood-curdling indictments which his enemies managed to present before a commission of oyer and terminer in August 1456, no further action was taken against him, and his sons Thomas and Henry were pardoned for all offences.

During the spring and summer of 1456, the political balance hovered uneasily. The king attended Parliament once more on 25 February, and York's Protectorship came to an end, but there is no sign that the king distrusted him, and in July he went north, apparently as the royal lieutenant to co-ordinate defences against the Scots. However, by this time the queen was his implacable enemy. Not only did his power seem to her a derogation of the royal prerogative, but the greater his share in the patronage of the crown, the less was her own. Not only did he constitute a threat to her position, but, perhaps even more important, to the inheritance of her son. There is no sign as yet that Margaret suspected him of designs upon the Crown itself, but she did suspect him of aiming to establish his family as hereditary Mayors of the Palace.[9] Consequently she was prepared to use any weapon to destroy his credit with the king and the majority of his fellow peers.

In the summer of 1456 such a weapon was placed in her hands by the activities of York's supporter Sir William Herbert in Wales. The Duke had a legitimate claim to the castles of Carmarthen and Aberystwyth, which had been occupied by Jasper Tudor, Earl of Pembroke, but instead of suing or petitioning for redress, he allowed Herbert to retake the castles by force. A Great Council at Coventry in late September was persuaded to act against Herbert, and he was imprisoned in the Tower. For the time being York's friends and the 'neutral' lords prevented any serious action against the Duke, but Margaret was able to use this fact to persuade Henry to purge the great officers of state who had been appointed or confirmed since the battle of St Albans. Archbishop Bourchier was replaced as Chancelor by Bishop Waynfleet of Winchester; Viscount Bourchier as Treasurer by the Earl of Shrewsbury; and the Dean of St Paul's as Keeper of the Privy Seal by Lawrence Booth, the queen's own chancellor. This was a thoroughly partisan administration, and throughout 1457 the queen was engaged in building up the strength of her party. The new Duke of Somerset and the new Earl of Northumberland joined the court, and a number of Crown appointments in the north built up the Percy interest against the Nevilles. Robert Neville, Bishop of Durham, died in July 1457, and was replaced by Lawrence Booth. This ended the Earl of

[9] The position of Charles Martel and his son Pepin, who ruled France in the name of the last Merovingian kings in the eighth century.

Salisbury's influence in the Palatinate, since Booth, who was unable to act without strong local support, relied upon the senior branch of the Neville family, particularly John, Lord Neville, the Earl of Westmorland's younger brother.

CIVIL WAR

The impending political crisis would probably have developed more quickly had it not been for the threat of a French invasion, and the fact that a number of the country's indispensable military commanders were Yorkists – most notably the Earl of Warwick. The glimmer of co-operation which this danger ignited encouraged the optimistic Henry to attempt a major reconciliation in January 1458. By this time the explosive situation in England and the breakdown of civil order were known all over Europe. The king of France and the Duke of Burgundy both fished hopefully in the troubled waters, while James II of Scotland seems to have made up his mind already that the Duke of York was the rightful king. In the city of London there were brawls between the citizens and the students of the Inns of Court, and xenophobic riots which caused the Venetians, Genoese and Florentines to remove their agents to Winchester. The Venetian Senate was so incensed that it prohibited the galleys from visiting London, under heavy penalties. In these unpropitious circumstances, the lords gathered at the capital for a Great Council. Their armed retinues numbered many hundreds, and the city displayed its Yorkist sympathies by admitting the Duke and his allies and excluding their enemies, thus giving the former a considerable strategic advantage. In the event there was no open conflict, and a form of reconciliation was agreed upon whereby the Yorkists gave financial compensation to the heirs of those killed at St Albans – but the fundamental quarrel between the Queen and the Duke was neither mentioned nor alleviated. By the summer of 1458 both sides stood poised for war, while the middle ground was virtually eroded. Only Archbishop Bourchier and the Duke of Buckingham retained to some extent the confidence of both sides.

The country drifted into civil war towards the end of 1458 because mutual suspicion was complete, and there seemed to be no other way of resolving the deadlock. At this stage the initiative lay with the queen, because her objective was clear and positive. She was determined to crush all opposition in the king's name, while her enemies were still professing allegiance to Henry and seeking to defend themselves. Apart from a small set-back at Blore Heath in September, by the end of 1459 Margaret seemed to be in complete command of the situation. The main Yorkist force, which had gathered at Ludlow, had dispersed without risking battle, the Duke going to Ireland and the Nevilles to Calais. To consummate this triumph, a Parliament was summoned to Coventry at the end of November. In these circumstances no one ventured to gainsay the wishes of the court, and the Commons were virtually a nominated assembly. The Yorkist lords were attainted as traitors, their titles extinguished and their properties confiscated. Such ruthlessness was a grave mistake, partly because it seemed to vindicate the claims which the Yorkists had constantly made about the greed and malice of their enemies, and partly because such wholesale expropriations threatened the sanctity of the aristocratic inheritance. Even in an age accustomed to judicial robbery, the Coventry Parliament represented an unprecedented threat to the accepted order and the interests of the ruling class.

The queen's triumph was short lived. At the end of June 1460 Warwick and Salisbury landed from Calais with a substantial force and, by-passing London, marched into the midlands. On 4 July Francesco Coppini, the Bishop of Terni, wrote to the king explaining that the lords had requested his mediation:

> I found them disposed to be devoted and obedient to your Majesty [he went on] and desirous to augment the commonweal of the kingdom, but they wished to come to your majesty and to be restored to favour and their former position, whence they declared themselves ousted and deposed by the envy of their rivals.

Although he was the Papal Legate, Coppini was not in fact an impartial witness of these events because he hoped that a Yorkist dominated England would favour the Burgundian alliance for which he was working. Consequently the Legate's professions of faith in the lords' goodwill towards the king must be suspect, as must his claims that they enjoyed the spontaneous support of the great majority of the commons. However it is clear that, even at this late date, there was no intention to depose the king. Like York's movements in 1452 and 1455, the purpose of this invasion was confined to recovery of control over the feeble Henry. At Northampton on 10 July the Yorkists won a complete victory. Buckingham, Shrewsbury and Egremont died in the fighting, while the king was captured and solemnly taken back to London. A Parliament, called by the Earls in his name, met on 7 October, with the clear intention of undoing the work of the Coventry assembly of the previous year.

How long this blood-thirsty game of 'beggar-your-neighbour' might have gone on is unknowable, but at this juncture the Duke of York returned from Ireland and transformed the situation by laying claim to the throne himself on grounds of indefeasible hereditary right. Even his own supporters were staggered and offended, invoking their oaths of allegiance, and the 'great and notable Acts of Parliament' by which the succession had been determined. In his Irish retreat, York had clearly seen that the logic of his position demanded such a move. Either he must accept defeat, or destroy a situation which he had repeatedly failed to control. In London, the lords were temporarily nonplussed, and tried unsuccessfully to shift the responsibility of decision on to the lawyers. Why they eventually decided to endorse York's claim is not clear.[10] He had a good case in so far as he was the heir general to Edward III by his descent through Philippa, daughter of Lionel, Duke of Clarence; but Henry was the equally undoubted heir male. By common law, real property descended to the heir general, and titles to the heir male, but it was not clear that either of these rules applied to the Crown. Equally York had no better a claim than his uncle Edmund Mortimer, who had refused to countenance a conspiracy on his behalf against Henry V. The lords' eventual decision had neither logic nor sound political sense to commend it. While professing themselves satisfied with the soundness of the Duke's claim, they declined to violate their oaths of allegiance to Henry. Apparently unmoved by the urgent necessity to put an end to the violent political fluctuations of the previous ten years, they proposed a compromise whereby York should be recognised as heir to the throne, while Henry should continue to reign for the rest of his life, or until he chose to abdicate.

[10] The initial reaction was unfavourable, but York, basing his argument wholly upon hereditary right, seems to have undermined the 'constitutional' position based upon parliamentary recognition. His case was also strengthened by the fact that Henry IV had been forced to base his hereditary title on spurious descent from Henry III, rather than upon his genuine relationship to Edward III. E. F. Jacob, *The Fifteenth Century*, 520-2.

This extraordinary suggestion was solemnly embodied in an agreement at the end of October, whereby the Duke was recognised as Prince of Wales and Protector of the realm, while the attainders of the Coventry Parliament were inevitably annulled, the whole parliament being declared null and void by the Statute 39 HVI c. l. Unless it was York's intention to force the king into an early abdication, it is difficult to see why he should have regarded this 'settlement' as giving him the security which he had so long craved. There was not the smallest chance that Margaret, whose staunchest supporters had not been present at the Parliament, would accept the disinheritance of her son. Far from providing for the peace of the realm, such an equivocal recognition of the Duke's claim was an invitation to renewed strife. In the event it lasted hardly longer than it had taken to negotiate, for on the last day of the year the queen's forces trapped an over-confident Protector at Wakefield. York and Salisbury both perished, the former in the fighting, and the latter upon the block.

Towards the end of January Margaret, with French and Scottish backing,[11] marched south against the Earl of Warwick, outmanœuvred him at St Albans and recovered possesion of the king. The Yorkists were now in a desperate plight. If they defeated the resolute queen, they could not hope to neutralise her as long as Henry occupied the throne. If she defeated them, they would follow the Earl of Salisbury to execution, for the struggle had become more ruthless with every month which passed. Faced with this prospect they took the only course open to them. Abandoning the hesitations of the previous October, they proclaimed their allegiance to Edward, Earl of March, the eldest son of the Duke of York, as King Edward IV. In later years Yorkist propaganda was to represent the events of these weeks as being the result of a spontaneous revulsion of feeling against the misgovernment of Henry VI. As one chronicler put it 'in his last days there fell great discord through his false counsel that was covetous, [and] he was put down from the crown by all the commons . . .'. There was a measure of truth in this, in so far as the citizens of London refused to open their gates to Mar-

[11] James II, who had favoured York, had died in August 1460, and his son James III was only eight years old. Margaret obtained the aid of the pro-French faction led by James Kennedy, Bishop of St Andrews. The surrender of Berwick was the price.

garet after her victory at St Albans, for fear of plunder by her northern levies, but welcomed Warwick and Edward a few days later.

Principally, however, the new king owed his victory to the magnates. Only a handful were with him in London when his title was proclaimed, but within a fortnight a score of others, including the Bourchiers and the Duke of Norfolk had accepted him. Their reasons for doing so were no doubt various. Some hoped to control him, as they had sought to control Henry, since he was only nineteen and inexperienced in government. Some, now that the spell of Henry's sacrosanctity was broken, saw great advantages in the prospect of a king who would carry out his regal functions in person, and restore confidence in the king's justice. It is unlikely that any were much moved by the arguments of Yorkist legitimacy.

With the support which these lords brought to him, and a small body of Burgundians, Edward left London to bring his adversaries to a decisive battle. Coming up with the queen at Towton near Tadcaster in Yorkshire, on 29 March, he won a hard fought but total victory. Many of the principal Lancastrian lords fell in the battle, while others were taken and beheaded. Henry and Margaret, together with Prince Edward, their young son, and the Dukes of Somerset and Exeter, escaped into Northumberland.

THE NEW KING

This battle did not end the war, but it placed Edward in possession of the reality of power. For three more years Margaret tried, with inadequate French and Scottish help, to regain control of the north from the remote stronghold of Bamburgh. Late in 1463 there were revolts, stirred up by Lancastrian agents, in Lancashire and Cheshire, and the Duke of Somerset renounced his pardon by joining the rebellion. It was not until May 1464 that the last of Margaret's armies was defeated at Hexham, and Bamburgh was taken by assault at the end of the same month. By this time Margaret was in France, seeking the renewed support of Louis XI, and Henry escaped, only to be captured in hiding the following year and lodged in the Tower. North Wales alone continued to hold pockets of Lancastrian resistance, and there the struggle dragged on on a small scale until the end of the decade.

Meanwhile, although handicapped to some extent by the necessity for these military operations, the new king was able to set about consolidating his position in lowland England. The need for strong and impartial government was desperate. While John Paston had attended the parliament of October 1460, his wife wrote to him,

> Ye have many good prayers of the poor people that God should speed you at this Parliament, for they live in hope that ye should help to set a way that they might live in better peace.

The Pastons, naturally sympathetic to York, were gravely alarmed by Margaret's successes early in 1461 and greeted Edward's victory with relief, but there was no swift or noticeable improvement in the peace of the county. In June a neighbour, Thomas Dennis, the coroner of Norfolk, was kidnapped and murdered,[12] and Margaret Paston wrote to her husband in July that Dennis's widow was in a pitiable state of fright. Margaret was also afraid for her own safety, since the Duke of Norfolk had seized Paston's great house at Caistor and placed all his property and dependants in jeopardy. 'The world is right wild,' reported one of Paston's agents at the same time.

Part of the trouble seems to have stemmed from the new king's anxiety not to pursue obvious feuds. When he pardoned John Heydon, there were bitter complaints that 'the king receiveth such of this country as have been his great enemies and oppressors of the commons, and such as have assisted his highness be not rewarded'. Edward certainly showed no great partiality for John Paston, especially when he suspected him of ignoring letters under the Privy Seal, and did not risk offending the Duke of Norfolk on his behalf, when he petitioned against the wrongful seizure of Caistor.[13] Perhaps, in spite of their protestations, the Pastons did not really want royal justice so much as Yorkist patronage and protection. At any rate, Edward took great pains to find an impartial sheriff for the county,[14] and sent a stern message to the justices of the peace that he intended to see his laws obeyed.

In general, there is no doubt that Edward made strenuous

[12] This crime was actually committed by a gang led by the parson of Snoring, but some contemporary opinion was inclined to blame the Duke of Norfolk. *Paston Letters*, II, 24.

[13] *Paston Letters*, II, 53.

[14] Sir Thomas Montgomery, who was released from duties in the household for that purpose.

efforts to improve the administration of the law, particularly by extensive use of commissions of oyer and terminer, and by his own energetic progresses. His subjects were encouraged to present petitions to him direct, and he took an active personal interest, particularly in cases involving members of the aristocracy. At the same time, bearing in mind the limited resources at the disposal of any medieval king, it would have been unreasonable to expect a sudden transformation in a situation which had been deteriorating steadily for almost forty years. Such evidence as there is of popular discontent with the royal government in these years suggests the disappointment of partial or extravagant expectations rather than of reasonable hopes. The commons of Norfolk, cheated of their vengeance against Heydon and his associates, were threatening revolt in January 1462. Later in the same year a rising in Dorset claimed explicitly: 'We commons have brought King Edward to his prosperity . . . and if he will not be ruled after us . . . as able we were to make him king, as able we be to depose him.' The Yorkist magnates could have claimed no more, but this was an attempt to exploit a weakness in the king's position, not a legitimate criticism of his government. Other evidence suggests that, although there was no immediate diminution of lawlessness, there was a new sense of urgency in prosecution, and a willingness to inflict drastic penalties. When a rising broke out in Gloucestershire in February 1464, the leaders were before a commission of oyer and terminer within six days, and nine of them were sentenced to a traitor's death. Most important of all, the king was always willing to intervene if he was convinced that a private interest was perverting justice, as he did in 'the matter of William Huet', where a duly convicted defendant had escaped punishment through the maintenance of the Earl of Warwick. In acting thus he was performing his royal duty as it was traditionally understood, but it did not always make him loved.

When his first Parliament assembled in November 1461, Edward and his ministers set out to strengthen his position with a series of significant measures. First of all they registered a long and eloquent defence of the king's title, in which they attributed the injustice and oppression of Henry's reign to the wrath of God, incited by the vile act of usurpation perpetrated upon Richard II by Henry's grandfather. This totally unhistorical piece of propaganda formed the basis of a myth which was to survive until the present century. Its immediate purpose was to rescue the Crown from the ruck of factional strife, and perhaps to warn evil-doers that they could not expect the same indulgence from a legitimate ruler.

Secondly, the hearing of indictments was withdrawn from the jurisdiction of the sheriff's tourn, on the grounds that these officers were abusing their position by filling up the juries with their own servants, and arresting and fining defendants at their pleasure. In future all indictments presented at the tourn were to be handed over to the justices of the peace to be heard at quarter sessions. We have already seen that many complaints had been made in recent years about corrupt and partial sheriffs. Presumably it was felt that there was safety in numbers, and that the commission of the peace might be less amenable to pressure – or at least represent a variety of interests.

Thirdly, a series of 'articles' was drawn up to limit the practice of retaining, along the lines of earlier legislation passed between 1399 and 1429. The lords agreed not to maintain any 'convicted felon or notorious evil doer', to aid in the arrest of such men 'not sparing or letting for any man's sake to whom they may belong', and to give no livery or maintenance to any except their household servants. The king promised his protection to all that should obey the law so defined, acknowledging that danger lay not in the practice, but in its abuse. These articles were in the main line of traditional royal policy; it remained to be seen whether they could be implemented, but their formal recognition was a start.

Finally 113 men, including 13 peers, were attainted for their adherence to the defeated party. The logic of Yorkist propaganda demanded such action, but the vast majority of those so condemned were eventually reconciled and restored. Edward's anxiety to escape from any dependence upon a faction made him all the readier to forget the past in return for present and future allegiance. Sometimes, as in the case of the Duke of Somerset, this generosity was misplaced, but on the whole it was a serviceable policy. The danger of invoking legitimist principles was that it encouraged a reply in kind, and there came into existence a hard core of Lancastrian irreconcilables, such as Jasper Tudor and the Earl of Oxford, permanently available to any foreign power which wished to make trouble in England.

In spite of all that Edward could do, the change of dynasty

inevitably weakened instinctive respect for the Crown. There would not be the same long drawn out reluctance to remove him as there had been to remove Henry, should he prove unable to retain control. As in the early years of Henry IV's reign, the 1460s saw a series of risings and conspiracies, the causes of which lay no deeper than the desire to exploit an already unstable situation. Although some of those involved may have been genuinely devoted to the cause of the imprisoned Henry, for most he was no more than a pretext. It is one of the paradoxes of the period that, while every letter and chronicle deplores the situation and reflects a longing for peace and stability, no trouble-maker great or small had any difficulty in raising an armed and turbulent following. These were not necessarily retainers, much less discharged soldiers from the French wars. Most of them were those same common people who were supposed to crave peace, but who knew only one way to protect their interests or make their voices heard. The chronicler Warkworth,[15] in seeking to account for Edward's temporary eclipse in 1470, wrote that the commons had hated Henry for the weakness of his rule, and persuaded themselves that

> if they might have another king he should get all again and amend all manner of things that was amiss and bring the realm of England in great prosperity and rest. Never the latter, when King Edward IIII reigned the people looked after all the forsaid prosperity and peace but it came not; but one battle after another and much trouble, and great loss of goods among the common people.

Edward had sought and won, an inheritance of great danger and difficulty, in which the risks of success were almost as great as those of failure. The Earl of Warwick expected an unchallenged supremacy in the royal counsels and viewed the young king's energy and sense of responsibility with mounting distrust.

As long as Lancastrian resistance continued, Warwick was not only fully employed, but also a virtually independent military commander in the north. Early in 1464, however, he was sent on a diplomatic mission to France, to negotiate an agreement for the mutual exclusion of political refugees. Louis XI, who was apprehensive of a possible alliance between England, Burgundy and Brittany, was anxious for a full peace, to be sealed by a

[15] J. Warkworth, *Chronicle*, ed. J. O. Halliwell, Camden Society 1839, 46-51.

marriage between Edward and his sister-in-law Bona of Savoy. Warwick was personally much in favour of this arrangement, and Edward allowed him to bring his negotiations close to success. Then, in September, the king revealed that he was already married and that the protracted French negotiations had been mainly for the purpose of extracting better terms from the Burgundians. Edward's bride, whom he had married on I May, was Elizabeth Woodville, daughter of Lord Rivers and widow of Sir John Grey. The king's announcement caused 'great displeasure to many great lords, and especially to the larger part of all his Council'. Within a few days reports had reached France of an open breach between Warwick and Edward, and Louis was expecting the former to make an attempt upon the crown. The reasons for this hostile reaction were various. Elizabeth was of relatively humble descent on her father's side;[16] her antecedents were Lancastrian; and she had a numerous family, including two sons by her first marriage. Also, of course, she blocked the way to an advantageous diplomatic marriage. Rumour had exaggerated Warwick's reaction. He was certainly offended, for his advice had been ignored and he had been made to look foolish, but there was as yet no open estrangement.

WARWICK'S CONSPIRACY

By the summer of 1467, however, relations had deteriorated sharply, partly on account of the advancement of the queen's family, and partly because of Edward's foreign policy. As England and Burgundy grew closer to a definitive alliance, Louis began to lay plans to exploit his good relations with Warwick in the hope of persuading him to restore Henry VI. This intention was being talked of in diplomatic circles and had quite possibly come to Edward's ears, but the only sign which he gave of suspecting the Nevilles' intentions was to dismiss Archbishop George Neville from the Chancellorship in June 1467. Meanwhile Warwick was cultivating the friendship of the king's brother,

[16] Her mother was Jacquetta of Luxembourg, daughter of Pierre, Count of St Pol. Jacquetta's uncle, John, had been one of Henry V's most important allies in France, and her first marriage (in 1433) had been to John, Duke of Bedford. Bedford had died after two years, and she had then married the son of her chamberlain, Sir Richard Woodville. J. R. Lander, 'Marriage and politics in the fifteenth century; the Nevilles and the Wydevilles', *Bulletin of the Institute of Historical Research*, 36, 119-53.

George, Duke of Clarence, and his intention at this stage seems to have been rather to elevate the latter to the throne than to risk involvement with the formidable Margaret of Anjou. If Edward saw any signs of impending trouble, he ignored them, and the conspirators were able to take him completely by surprise in July 1469.

Their action was a pure *coup d'état*, unaccompanied by any substantial movement among either the magnates or the commons. At first no mention was made of any intention to remove Edward. All the familiar clichés of the previous decade reappeared. The king was to remove evil councillors (the Woodvilles), refrain from taxing his subjects (a large sum had been raised in 1468 for an expedition which had not materialised), and to take the advice of his true lords (Warwick and Clarence). Edward, quite unprepared, was captured in Buckinghamshire before any resistance could be organised, and his captors proceeded to implement their first demand by beheading Rivers, Sir John Woodville, the Earl of Pembroke and Richard Herbert. It then became apparent that Warwick did not know what to do next. The fragile civil order began to dissolve as riots and disturbances broke out from Norfolk to Northumberland. Some of these were explicitly Lancastrian, but most seem to have been simply private quarrels. The Parliament which the Earl had intended to call at York was abandoned, partly because of the disorders and partly because there seemed to be no prospect of persuading it to endorse Clarence's claim, which was based upon the unsupported assertion that Edward was illegitimate. By October Warwick was forced to release his prisoner, and Edward returned to London where the great majority of the magnates rallied to him. The king seems to have tried to regard the whole episode as a bad joke and displayed no vindictiveness. By the end of the year Warwick and Clarence were also in London, apparently reconciled.

However, if Edward thought that his over-mighty subjects had learned a salutary lesson from their failure, he was mistaken. Instead, they seem to have concluded that success could only come through a seemingly spontaneous and widespread insurrection – very much the attitude which Richard of York had taken in 1452. For this purpose certain of Warwick's adherents, such as Lord Scrope and Sir John Conyers, began to stimulate popular agitations in the north by spreading rumours of new taxation and judicial oppression. These tactics were particularly successful in Lincolnshire, where Lord Welles had taken advantage of the king's captivity to launch a private attack upon the loyal Sir Thomas Burgh. Fearing reprisals, he and his son, Sir Robert Welles, were amenable to Warwick's scheme. As Sir Robert later confessed:

> The cause of our great rising at this time was grounded upon this noise raised amongst the people, that the king was coming down with great power into Lincolnshire, where the king's judges should sit, and hang and draw great numbers of the commons . . . a servant of my said lord of Clarence told us the same. Also my lord of Clarence's servant Walter that came with us to Lincoln stirred and moved often times our host . . . that at such time as the matter came near the point of battle they should call upon my lord of Clarence to be king.

The intention seems to have been to induce the king to walk into a trap by going north against the Lincolnshire men, while Warwick and Clarence, still professing their loyalty, should move a force to cut him off from London. In the event, Edward moved too fast, attacking and dispersing Welles' force before any help could reach them. From papers captured after the battle, as well as from the presence of a number of Clarence's liveries on the field, it became apparent what was afoot. Reaching York towards the end of March, the king proclaimed his brother and Warwick rebels and traitors, while they, failing to raise any adequate force to confront him, fled, intending to return to Calais. However the king's orders had anticipated them, and they were refused admission to the town. At the beginning of May they landed in Normandy.

Had it not been for the international situation this would have been the end of Warwick's pretensions. As it was, Louis seized the opportunity to implement his plan of 1464 and negotiated a reconciliation between the Earl and Queen Margaret. As a result, early in September Warwick was able to land at Exeter with an Anglo-French force of about two thousand. As a professed adherent of Henry VI he was in a much stronger position than he had been in the previous year. He was accompanied by such staunch Lancastrians as the Earls of Pembroke and Oxford, and was speedily joined by the Earl of Shrewsbury and Lord Stanley. Edward, who had once again neglected adequate precautions, was in Yorkshire with a small force. The only sizeable army on foot which he could call upon for support was that recently raised by Lord Montague for the defence of the north. Montague was Warwick's brother, but had hitherto been loyal to Edward. Now he deserted him upon a personal grudge,[17] and the king was caught between two hostile forces. Warned of Montague's treachery in the nick of time, he fled, first to Lynn and then overseas to Burgundy. Warwick's bloodless victory had taken less than a month to accomplish.

Edward's flight makes it almost impossible to judge the real strength of Lancastrian sentiment, or what motives, apart from sheer self-preservation, may have inspired the lords and commons to accept Henry's readeption so calmly. If Edward had taken any reasonable precautions, it would never have happened. We have seen that Warkworth was of the opinion that the common people had come to the conclusion that there was nothing to choose between them; but we have also seen that this was probably unjust. There is no reason to suppose that Henry's reconstituted government, with Warwick as Protector, would have worked any better than before. Friction between Warwick and Margaret was inevitable as soon as the latter should appear on the scene. Also, the French alliance was unpopular, and Warwick was unable to persuade Parliament of the wisdom of a war against Burgundy, which Louis was demanding in return for his earlier help. Margaret delayed in France, apparently unable to believe that Edward was really beaten, and her lack of confidence communicated itself to England. As a result, when Edward landed at Ravenspur on 14 March with a small Anglo-Burgundian force, he was faced by divided councils and virtual paralysis. As one chronicler noted, the 'great part of noble men and commons in those parts were toward the Earl of Northumberland, and would not stir with any lord or noble man other than with the said Earl, or at least by his commandment', and the Earl of Northumberland did nothing. The powerful Lancastrian peers, incredibly, refused Warwick's summons on the grounds that they were waiting for Margaret. Only Montague, Oxford and Exeter were with the Earl, and their behaviour was so hesitant as to be

[17] Montague had been created Earl of Northumberland in 1464. In 1470, when Edward wished to restore the Percy line, he had persuaded Montague to accept a marquisate in return for the surrendered Earldom. Montague apparently felt he had been cheated.

suspicious. Perhaps most important of all Clarence, disappointed with his position in the new régime, betrayed his erstwhile colleagues and rejoined his brother. Thus on 11 April Edward was able to re-enter London unchallenged and three days later annihilated Warwick's inadequate forces at Barnet. The Earl was killed in the rout.

Thanks to their own hesitations and foolishness, the king was able to defeat his enemies in detail. Margaret arrived in England at last on the day of Warwick's death. Belatedly, many of the old Lancastrians rallied to her, but they lacked both speed and resolution. Before she could join forces with the Welsh followers of Jasper Tudor, Edward caught and utterly defeated her army at Tewkesbury on 4 May. Prince Edward, the Earl of Devon and many other leaders were killed, while Margaret herself was taken prisoner. A few days later the last Lancastrian force – of Kentishmen under Thomas Neville the Bastard of Fauconberg – surrendered to Richard of Gloucester. Louis XI, disgruntled by Warwick's failure to bring England into the war against Burgundy, came to terms with Duke Charles, and made no further attempt to aid his erstwhile protéges. On 21 May Henry VI died in the Tower 'of pure displeasure and melancholy' according to a contemporary, but more probably by Edward's orders.

CHAPTER 3

THE RESTORATION OF AUTHORITY

Wherefore me thinketh, that if the king might have his livelihood for the sustenance of his estate in great lordships, manors, fee farms and such other demesnes, his people not charged, he should keep to him wholly their hearts, exceed in lordships all the lords of his realm, and there should none of them grow to be like unto him, which thing is most to be feared in all the world. (Sir John Fortescue, *The Governance of England*)

RETURN TO TRADITIONAL GOVERNMENT

In spite of its dramatic character, the brief readeption of Henry VI left remarkably few traces behind it. The Parliament of November 1470 was not even recorded upon the Rolls. The principal consequences were the deaths of Henry himself, of Prince Edward his son, and of the Earl of Warwick. The first two took the heart out of the Lancastrian cause for the next fourteen years, leaving the claim in the ineffectual hands of the fifteen year old Henry Tudor.[1] The third freed the king from the challenge of his most powerful and dangerous subject. In the summer of 1471 Edward was able to pick up the threads of his policies more or less where he had been forced to drop them ten months previously. The victories of Barnet and Tewkesbury had not in themselves solved any of the fundamental problems afflicting English government, but they had placed the king in such a strong political position that his earlier attempts at retrenchment and reform could be brought significantly nearer to success.

Edward was a man without originality or imagination. The fact that he had twice been surprised by rather obvious con-

[1] The posthumous son of Edmund Tudor, Earl of Richmond, and grandson of Owen Tudor and Katherine, widow of Henry V. His mother, Margaret Beaufort, was the daughter of John Beaufort II, Duke of Somerset, and a great-granddaughter of John of Gaunt by Catherine Swynford. The Beauforts had been legitimated, but excluded from the succession by statute. This could possibly be challenged on legitimist principles, and therein lay Henry's claim to the throne.

spiracies is indicative of his straightforward and unreflective attitude. His views on the nature of government were expressed on his behalf (and in his presence) by the Chancellor, Robert Stillington, in the Parliament of 1468:

> Justice [is the] ground well and root of all prosperity, peace and public rule of every realm, whereupon all the laws of the world be grounded and set, which resteth in three; that is to say the Law of God, Law of Nature, and Positive Law ... What is Justice? Justice is every person to do his office that he is put in according to his degree or estate.

Stillington went on to point out the evil legacy of injustice and disorder which Edward had received from his predecessor, but there was no suggestion that new methods or ideas were called for. The king intended that the three estates – the Lords Spiritual, the Lords Temporal and the Commons – should serve him in their traditional capacities. Far from showing hostility to the magnates as a class, or seeking to undermine their authority, Edward relied upon them as much as any of his predecessors had done. There was no alternative. Even if he had wished to do so, the king could not have afforded a professional bureaucracy of the kind which Louis XI was building up in France. Nor, in view of the grip which clientage had established in the previous half century, could he have expected to appeal successfully to the gentry as a class, or used them as a curb on their social superiors. Instead, we find him relying heavily upon the Bourchiers in Essex, the Stanleys in Lancashire and Cheshire, and the Duke of Norfolk in East Anglia. Perhaps the best example of his policy in this respect is Edward's use of William Hastings. Hastings was a man whose personal loyalty was always above suspicion,[2] and when the king wished to provide for the security of the midlands at the beginning of his reign, he raised Hastings to the peerage and endowed him with the estates of the attainted families of Butler and Beaumont. Most years thereafter saw anything from one to four midland sheriffs wearing Hastings' livery. His extensive and well documented network of retaining was a source of strength to the king as well as to himself, and was undertaken with Edward's full knowledge and approval. At the very end of the

[2] He managed Edward IV's escape in 1470 and organised his return in the following year. It was also he who persuaded Clarence to abandon the Lancastrian cause. Hastings' retainers, and others who were 'towards' him to the number of nearly three thousand, were among the first to join Edward when he landed at Ravenspur in 1471. W. H. Dunham, *Lord Hastings' Indentured Retainers*, 23.

reign John Russell, Bishop of Lincoln, wrote 'the politic rule of every region well ordained standeth in the nobles', and Edward never showed any sign of doubting the truth of his maxim.

The titular peers were not a numerous group[3] and mortality was heavy, quite apart from the troubles. About fifty nobles were executed or died in battle during the second half of the century, but 25 per cent of noble families died out in the male line every twenty-five years under normal conditions, and that rate was not much increased between 1450 and 1500. Nor, apart from junior branches of the royal family, were many ancient lines extinguished. Propaganda deliberately exaggerated the carnage, as did the ignorance of some contemporary writers, like the Croyland monk who bewailed the 'deaths of nearly all the nobles of the realm'. In fact the ranks of the peerage were being constantly replenished from among wealthy commons, which makes it artificial to distinguish the peers too sharply as a social or political group. Edward created thirteen new titles between 1461 and 1471, nine of them in the first year of his reign, a recognised procedure for strengthening his position. Henry had created no fewer than fifteen in the three years 1447-50, but Edward, unlike Henry, was his own political manager and distributed his favours with a judicious hand, striving to avoid the monopolisation of power by a faction which had lain at the root of the troubles of the 1450s. By elevating the Woodvilles through marriage and ennoblement, he strove to balance the otherwise overweening power of the Nevilles. Lord Rivers became Earl Rivers, and seven of the queen's kinswomen married into the families of Buckingham, Exeter, Norfolk, Arundel, Essex, Grey of Ruthin and Herbert. Warwick's brother, William, became Earl of Kent in 1461, and John Neville, Lord Montague (temporarily) Earl of Northumberland in 1464. Also, by generosity to defeated enemies, he sought to avoid the creation of irreconcileable hatreds. As we have seen, only a handful of those attainted in 1461 were not restored by the end of the reign.

On the whole, the king respected and shared the magnates' view of their own position and responsibility. Only men of

[3] There were 51 lay peers in 1436, the same number in 1447, and 54 in 1489. For purposes of comparison, the taxation returns of 1436 also listed 183 'greater knights' and 750 'lesser knights'. J. R. Lander, *Conflict and Stability in fifteenth century England*, 173. The fullest account of the late medieval peerage is in K. B. McFarlane, *The Nobility of Later Medieval England* (Oxford, 1973).

wealth and substance could serve the king effectively, because they alone commanded respect and obedience among the commons. Men of insufficient substance would only be held in contempt, or 'for their great necessity do great extortion and oppression upon the people'. It was for this reason that in 1440 a statute had forbidden the appointment of justices of the peace worth less than £20 per annum, and in 1478 another deprived George Neville of the Dukedom of Bedford on the grounds of his poverty. There was no suggestion that office under the Crown could make good any deficiencies in the 'natural authority' of the holder.

THE WORKINGS OF JUSTICE

It was this concept of office, which Edward had neither the will nor the means to abandon, which made the abuse of justice such a recalcitrant problem. The Pastons were probably typical in looking upon the king as a sort of superior patron whose commissions were, or ought to be, weapons in their family armoury. In 1465 they were protesting as vigorously as ever about the partiality of the sheriff of Norfolk, and worrying lest the Duke of Suffolk should procure a commission of oyer and terminer to use against them. But at the same time Margaret wrote to her husband,

> I would right fain that John Jenny were put out of the Commission of the Peace, and my brother Will Lumner were set in his stead . . . for I know verily he oweth you right good will . . . If there be any labour that Dr Alyn be justice of the peace, I pray you for God's sake let it be letted if you may.

Such an attitude was part of the very fabric of society. Just as the law was a means of harassing or ruining an enemy, so an office was a source of profit or influence rather than a means of doing the king's will. In 1475 the House of Commons brought to Edward's attention an extreme example of the consequences of similar views in Hereford and Shropshire. In response to previous complaints of 'great murders and robberies', a special commission including a number of leading councillors had been sent to the area, and had found that juries were being intimidated and indictments suppressed. As soon as the commission departed matters were worse than before, because those who had ventured to speak up under the commissioners' protection were now exposed to their enemies' revenge,

> whereof no manner remedy nor punishment afore duly was

> had, nor of likeliehood should be had, without your high presence there, or great might and power sent by your highness into those parts.[4]

Only constant vigilance and application by the king himself, it seemed, could provide a remedy for this deep seated malaise. In 1462 we find Edward hearing cases in person in the court of King's Bench, and throughout his reign he moved tirelessly around the country, hearing petitions, adjudicating quarrels, and overseeing the administration of his nobles. Gradually, after 1470, this policy seems to have been successful in securing a greater measure of co-operation from the ruling class, and hence restoring confidence. This is an achievement which it is almost impossible to quantify. We cannot talk in terms of improved conviction rates, fewer pardons, or even fewer cases of riot and mayhem coming before the courts. The formal records of the judiciary and administration were extremely slow to reflect the real effectiveness of government, in so far as they did so at all. There were, however, fewer and less sensational petitions to Parliament for redress, no repetition of the large scale terrorism of Courtenay or Egremont, and no reappearance of the mass discontent of Cade's rebellion.

Once Edward had made it clear that he was strong enough to defeat attacks upon his position, and that he meant to be obeyed, the traditional resources of government were sufficient. Nothing succeeded like success. In the latter part of his reign Edward was conspicuously well served by his magnate clients, by his brother, Richard of Gloucester, and by their retainers. He also had a numerous clientage of his own below the magnate level. These men, knights and squires of the body, grooms of the chamber and other similar *curiales* acted as sheriffs, coroners and justices of the peace. As the king's own men, they were especially amenable to his control, and, more important, immune from manipulation by other interests. Appointments connected with the administration of the royal estates also provided opportunities to expand the king's power. As the Croyland chronicler wrote,

> he [Edward] had taken care to distribute the most trustworthy of his servants throughout all parts of the kingdom, as keepers of castles, manors forests and parks [so] no attempt whatever

[4] The only legal remedy which the petitioners could think of was that acquittals of notorious felons by intimidated juries should be declared void, which was done. *Rot. Parl.*, VI, 159.

> could be made in any part of the kingdom by any person . . . but what he was immediately charged with the same thing to his face.

These same men also served, along with trusted magnates, on the commissions of oyer and terminer which Edward particularly favoured, as flexible and powerful judicial instruments.[5] Similarly the Council which the king established to run the estates of the Principality of Wales was used to keep a watchful eye on that turbulent region, and to provide some much needed stiffening to the upholders of law and order.

However, it was upon the royal Council proper that Edward chiefly depended. The absence of records for most of the period makes it impossible to discuss the composition of that body with any certainty. Professor Lander has assembled from external evidence the names of 124 men who were styled 'councillor' at one time or another during Edward's reign. In the period 1461-1470 these comprised 20 nobles, 25 ecclesiastics, 11 officials and 4 others. In the period 1471-1483 there were 21 nobles, 35 ecclesiastics, 23 officials and 9 others. Many of these 'councillors' can have attended only infrequently, and the composition of the normal working council must remain elusive,[6] but it is clear that the great officers of state were the most assiduous in attendance, and that the king, having taken what advice he chose, made the decisions himself. It was before this body, sitting quite often in the Star Chamber, that most of the magnates' quarrels were adjudicated, and the unruly disciplined. Here, on 24 October 1472, Lord Grey was summoned to answer a complaint by the mayor and burgesses of Nottingham that he had unlawfully maintained rioters against the king's peace. The case was not a straightforward one, and Grey was no more than admonished against unlawful retaining, but it could no longer be supposed that offences of this kind would go unnoticed.

Apart from such cases before the Council, which we have no means of counting, little use seems to have been made of 'extraordinary justice'. The use which John Tiptoft, Earl of Worcester, was specifically authorised to make of his office of Constable,

[5] Edward issued 77 such commissions in the course of his reign, as against 41 issued by Henry VII. Lander, *Conflict and Stability*, 102-3.

[6] J. R. Lander, 'Council, Administration and Councillors 1461-1485', *Bulletin of the Institute of Historical Research*, 32, 138-80.

was not as exceptional as was once supposed[7] The executions which he carried out after the battles of Hedgerley Moor and Hexham were clearly within the traditional scope of the law of arms, since the victims had been taken in open war against the king. The more controversial trials of the Earl of Oxford and Aubrey de Vere in 1462, which the chronicler Warkworth described as being carried out 'by the law of Padua' (i.e. Roman law), were probably conducted by the Constable because the charges included one of conspiring to murder the king while marching under his banner. In any case, it was within the king's accepted prerogative to convict a subject of treason by mere 'declaration' of his own personal knowledge of his guilt. After Tiptoft's death on the scaffold for high treason during Henry's readeption, the Court of Chivalry was used again in the summer of 1471 for the trial of much humbler insurgents in Essex, but with what result is not known. The strange office of 'king's promoter of all causes . . . concerning crimes of lèse-majesty' to which Robert Rydon was appointed in 1482, seems to have existed for some years, but in what way it functioned (if at all) is obscure. The only major exception to Edward's reliance upon the normal procedures of the common law was the extensive use which he made of Chancery to adjudicate and settle property disputes. There was nothing original in this, but naturally the Chancery decisions commanded more respect as the overall power of the Crown revived.

THE ROYAL PURSE

If the evidence of their complaints is to be trusted, the commons of England felt only one grievance as acutely as the lack of justice and that was financial oppression. In 1450 the men of Kent had protested against the extortions of royal officials; in 1470 the men of Lincolnshire feared punitive fines; in 1468 and 1475 foreign observers expected serious disorders to follow parliamentary votes of direct taxation. Edward received an average of about £11,000 a year from Parliament, when allowances are made for inefficiency in collecting what was voted. This was not a great sum, but when it came to the point the king was extremely unwilling to fight the foreign wars which were the

[7] For a discussion of Tiptoft's use of the office of Constable and Marshal see Bellamy, *op. cit.*, 160-2.

traditional and necessary pretexts for such grants. At the beginning of his reign he had undertaken to 'live of his own', and some of his subjects regarded the conversion of extraordinary revenue to ordinary purposes as a serious abuse.[8] At the same time, the king had every excuse for parsimony. In 1460 the Crown had been in debt for over £300,000, and in spite of a moderately successful resumption of alienated lands in 1451, its net income was hardly sufficient to service this enormous liability. Edward was forced to borrow heavily, but, unlike Henry's, most of his loans came from foreign bankers or from the city of London. He thus avoided incurring political as well as financial debts, and made strenuous efforts to meet repayment dates, with some success.

However, the two pillars of traditional royal finance were the customs revenues and the Crown lands, and it was only by substantially increasing his income from these sources that the king could hope to become solvent. There was no attempt to increase customs rates until the following century, but the administration, which had declined woefully in the last decade of the previous reign, was rigorously tightened up. Between 1473 and 1481 royal surveyors with wide powers were introduced into eleven principal ports. This was not a new idea, but it had lapsed almost thirty years before, and Edward's surveyors were paid unprecedented salaries ranging up to £50 a year.[9] At the same time a series of damaging prosecutions for smuggling induced the Merchant Adventurers to introduce their own disciplinary machinery for members who attempted to evade their obligations. By the end of the reign the annual revenue from the customs was approaching £40,000, partly as a result of increasing trade, but more largely as a result of improved methods of enforcement.

The royal estates were potentially, as Sir John Fortescue realised, a greater source both of wealth and of political strength, but they did not reach that level during Edward's lifetime. It was here that Henry's prodigality had struck hardest; hence the Commons' constant pleas for resumption during the 1450s, and Fortescue's arguments for an inalienable royal demesne. Edward passed a total of four Acts of Resumption, in 1461, 1465, 1467

[8] Heavy and improper taxation was one of the grievances alleged by Warwick and Clarence in their proclamation of 12 July 1469. J. Warkworth, *Chronicle*, 45-51.

[9] The income which was generally considered adequate to support gentry status at this time was about £20 per annum. £60 per annum was the average for a 'lesser knight'.

and 1473. Each of these was riddled with specific exemptions, but such concessions were not granted indiscriminately. Every one was examined and authorised by the king personally, so that he not only recovered extensive lands but was able to carry out a thorough overhaul of his patronage. The resumption of direct control over the royal patronage was probably of greater political importance than any increase in revenue. Almost equally important were his inquisitions into the feudal rights of the Crown. By concealing military tenures the aristocracy had defrauded Henry VI's government of aids, of wardships, and even of escheats. This was well known, and general enquiries were constantly being authorised, but since these had elicited no protests, it is probable that they had had no effect. Edward examined the Chancery records himself, in conjunction with a few trusted officials, and 'exacted heavy fines from those whom he found to have intruded and taken possession of their estates without prosecuting their rights in the form required by law'. Loud complaints from the offending parties testify to the reality of these penalties. It was by such means, and by confiscations resulting from attainders, rather than by any significant increases of rents that the revenues from the Crown estates were increased. Net income from this source increased from less than £10,000 per annum in 1461 to about £28,000 by the end of the reign.

Estate management was an art which developed rapidly during the fifteenth century, partly as a result of economic pressures generated by the reduction in the working population after the Black Death, and partly because of the need to have ready cash for the mobilisation of retainers and others at short notice. Well organised estates, like those of Sir John Fastolf, had by 1450 regional receivers and auditors to collect and disburse money coming in from stewards or other officers, and to keep a constant check upon the honesty and efficiency of their operations. The royal estates, by contrast, were inadequately controlled by the cumbersome machinery of the Exchequer. The Exchequer was principally a debt collecting organisation, and while it was extremely tenacious in recording and pursuing sums owed to the Crown, it had no means of providing working balances, and no local officials.

In spite of the fact that the self-contained Duchy of Lancaster lands, which were most efficiently administered, had been in the hands of the Crown since 1399, no attempt had been made to extend Duchy methods to the remainder of the Crown lands. This step was taken by Edward, beginning with those lands resumed in 1461. Gradually, the whole estate was reorganised, except for those parts which were let out on long leases, so that all rents and dues were paid to local receivers, and by them to Receivers General, whose jurisdiction might cover up to ten counties. These men, who were trusted royal servants, then accounted not to the Exchequer but to the king's Chamber, the financial department of the household. For example John Milewater, the Receiver General in the Welsh Marches, accounted for just over £1,520 in the two years 1461-3. Of this he disbursed about £700 in fees and upon royal warrants. The balance of £820 was despatched 'to the coffers of the lord king' in three instalments.

The great advantage of using the Chamber to handle these revenues was that the facts of both income and expenditure were immediately available for the king's inspection. Edward III had used it for the same purpose, but after 1399 it had sunk into obscurity. The bureaucratic machinery of the Exchequer was not abolished – too many vested interests were at stake for that to have been possible – but it became mainly a repository for audited accounts. By 1480 only quite insignificant revenues were following the 'ancient course', but the Upper Exchequer continued to track down and prosecute those whom more informal procedures may have overlooked.

Of the remaining financial resources available to the Crown one, the French subsidy gained at Pecquingy, must be overlooked as an occasional windfall.[10] Another, the profit which the king derived from trading on his own account, was probably small and in any case hard to calculate. More significant both politically and financially, although equally difficult to assess, were 'benevolences' and the profits of justice. The former were virtually private taxes which the king demanded personally of his wealthier subjects, usually when he visited them on a progress. These were most used in the early years of the reign when, as Professor J. R. Lander has put it, Edward was 'living from hand to mouth'. How much resentment they caused is difficult to say, but neither Edward nor his successors were able to exploit them

[10] By this treaty Edward obtained an indemnity of 75,000 crowns, a ransome of 50,000 for Margaret of Anjou, and an annual subsidy of 50,000 which was paid for about six years.

as a means of dispensing with parliamentary grants.

The profits of justice were the fines and other amercements imposed by the courts. These were extremely irregular in their incidence, but might be substantial after troubles had been successfully quelled. For instance, after Fauconbridge had surrendered in May 1471,

> immediately . . . was the Lord Denham and Sir John Fogg and divers others made commissioners, that sat upon all Kent, Sussex and Essex that were at the Blackheath, and upon many others that were not there; for some men paid 200 marks, some £100, and some more and some less, so that it cost the poorest man 7 shillings which was not worth so much, but was fain to sell such clothing as they had, and borrowed the remnant, and laboured for it afterward; and so the king had out of Kent much goods and little love.

Henry VII was not the first to realise the disciplinary value of punitive fines. However little they may have loved him, there was no more trouble in Kent while Edward lived.

Finally, perhaps a mention should be made of the recoinage of 1464, by which one contemporary thought that the king 'had great getting', and which the Venetian agent in Bruges reported as causing much resentment and discontent in England. This was designed to alleviate the shortage of money by attracting more bullion to the mint. To do this it was decided to strike more coins from the pound weight of silver, giving the appearance of a greater return, in slightly lighter coin. As a result the values of all the standard coins had to be adjusted. No serious economic hardship resulted from this, and the complaints seem to have been mainly superficial; 'many men grotched passing sore for they could not reckon that gold so quickly as they did the old gold . . .' (a grievance with a very modern ring). If the commercial classes felt any resentment, it did not much affect their political attitude. As Warkworth reported, it was because Edward 'found great comfort in his commons' that he 'ratified and confirmed all the franchises given to cities and towns, and granted to many . . . more new franchises than was granted before, right largely . . .'

The second part of Edward's reign saw no domestic upheaval greater in scale than a local riot, although in 1473 the irreconcilable Earl of Oxford seized St Michael's Mount and held it for five months before he could be dislodged. In 1475 there was a brief war with France, and the Duke of Burgundy, disgruntled at the outcome, sought to stir up trouble in England, without success. The extent to which English politics had recovered their stability can be judged in some measure by the fate of the Duke of Clarence. Clarence had fallen out with his brother, Richard of Gloucester, and in spite of his foolishness was a great magnate – at least as powerful as the Duke of Exeter had been in 1454. However in 1477 he crowned a series of dangerous escapades by procuring the judicial murder of a certain Ankarette Twynho, on a charge of having poisoned his wife. This he did in the worst tradition of the overmighty subject, by intimidating the jury. Shortly after, he was personally indicted of treason by the king, and attainted by Parliament.[11] By this time it did not need a military campaign, even to bring so great an offender to book.

RICHARD AS PROTECTOR

When Edward died in 1483 he had achieved a great deal. He was the first English king to die solvent since Henry II in the twelfth century. Of his justice, the Croyland Chronicler wrote,

> the lord king was compelled to perambulate the country together with his judges, sparing no one: even his own servants received no less than a hanging if they were detected in theft or murder. Such vigorous justice, universally carried out, put a stop to common acts of robbery for a long time to come.

And in the following century Sir Thomas More could observe that he had left the realm 'in quiet and prosperous estate, for the displeasure of those that bore him grudge for Henry's sake the sixth . . . was well assuaged . . . And many of them in the mean season grown into his favour, of which he was never strange.' At the same time this peace and prosperity were a highly personal accomplishment, and in one vital respect he failed. Although he had married at the age of twenty-two his first three children were all girls, and dying at the age of forty-one he did not live long enough for his eldest son to have reached his majority.

A royal minority would in any case have tested the political peace which Edward had established, but in 1483 the situation was aggravated by two unfortunate circumstances. The new

[11] The murder of Ankarette was not mentioned in the Act of Attainder, which referred only to conspiracy to alienate the loyalty and affection of the king's subjects, *Rot. Parl.*, VI, 193.

king's uncle, Richard of Gloucester, and his mother's relatives, the Woodvilles, bitterly mistrusted each other; and Edward had left two conflicting sets of instructions for the regency government. One, contained in the will which he had drawn up before leaving for France in 1475, had named the queen as Regent. The other, not explicitly set down in writing but well authenticated by his councillors, placed control in the hands of his brother Richard as Protector, following the precedent set by Henry V in 1422. There is no doubt that the latter represented Edward's real intention just before his death, and the queen's claim was not pressed, but sufficient ambiguity remained to cause debate and disagreement within the Council. Those who favoured Richard, pressed for a full Protectorate, with custody of the king's person and extending until he came of age. Others wished to compromise by making the office little more than the nominal presidency of the Council, while those most favourable to the Woodvilles claimed that it should terminate with the new king's coronation. This last suggestion, if carried out, would have had the effect of leaving Elizabeth in something very like the position which had been envisaged in 1475.

When the king died on 9 April most of the strategic advantages lay with the Woodvilles. Prince Edward was with Earl Rivers at Ludlow; Elizabeth herself was in London; the Marquis of Dorset, the queen's son by her first marriage, was Constable of the Tower, and her brother Sir Edward Woodville commanded the fleet. The significance of these appointments was greatly increased by the fact that Edward had mustered a great armament shortly before his death, with the intention of renewing the French war. Arms, men and money were all available in the capital. By contrast Richard was at Middleham, in Yorkshire, far from the centre of power and with no great force ready to hand. On the other hand he had the sympathy and active support of two of the greatest magnates of the earlier régime, the Duke of Buckingham and Lord Hastings, the late king's Chamberlain.

There is no reason to suppose that at this stage Richard had any designs upon the Crown itself. He had served his brother with conspicuous loyalty, not only in the crises of his career but also in the more mundane work of civil administration. During the 1470s he had ruled the north with a firm and judicious hand, so that he was both popular with the commons and respected by the magnates. That interpretation of his life which sees it as a progressive series of bloody crimes, designed to eliminate all who stood between himself and the succession, is the creation of Tudor propaganda. It has no foundation either in fact or in contemporary opinion. Richard was, however, a much more imaginative and apprehensive man than his brother, inclined to exaggerate dangers which could not be accurately assessed. He seems to have been convinced (on what evidence it is impossible to guess) that the Woodvilles meant not only to exclude him from the chief power, but to bring about his ruin and possibly his death. When he heard, towards the end of April, that his enemies were pressing for a very early coronation and intended to represent that as ending his protectorate, he decided to strike at once. In this his plans were materially aided by Hastings, who succeeded in persuading the queen to limit to 2,000 men the escort which was to accompany Earl Rivers and the young king to London. To have brought more, he argued, would have been unnecessary and provocative. As a result Richard and Buckingham were able to intercept the royal party at Stony Stratford on April 30. Rivers, who seems to have been taken completely off his guard, was arrested along with several other members of the household, and the royal escort was dismissed.

It was now the turn of the Woodvilles to be convinced that their lives were threatened. In spite of their strategic advantages, there was no question of an appeal to arms. However sinister his actions might appear to them, Richard was lawful Protector and in possession of the king's person. There was no certainty that they could have persuaded anyone other than their own dependents to fight against him. The queen and Dorset fled to the sanctuary at Westminster, while Sir Edward Woodville, out-manœuvred for the loyalty of the fleet, escaped to Brittany. The Duke of Gloucester reached London on 4 May, and his authority was immediately confirmed in its fullest form by the Council. Within a few days he had re-modelled the administration to his own liking, and conferred upon his ally Buckingham immense power and jurisdiction in the west country and the Welsh marches. By the end of May there were already some who suspected that Richard's ambitions extended to the throne. It is not likely that this was so, because the Council, with his full knowledge and approval, had arranged Edward's coronation for 22 June and prepared plans for a Parliament which was to meet on

25 June. This Parliament was to be asked to confirm his appointment for the duration of the minority.

As with the decision to act against Rivers, it seems to have been fear and suspicion which precipitated the Protector into the actions which led to his usurpation. Certain of the Council, who had hitherto been well disposed towards Richard, began to turn against him, either because they suspected his intentions or simply because they found his extreme animosity towards the Woodvilles unreasonable. One of these was Lord Hastings, who had secretly opened negotiations with the queen through his mistress, Jane Shore. At a council committee on 12 June Richard suddenly confronted Hastings with his knowledge of these negotiations and charged him with treason. There was no attempt at proper judicial process. Even the law of arms was not invoked. Hastings was simply executed out of hand on the Protector's orders.

Already armed forces had been summoned from the north 'to aid and assist (the Protector) against the queen, her blood adherents and affinity, which have intended and daily doth intend to murder and destroy us and our cousin the Duke of Buckingham'. So that when the lords and commons arrived in London for the coronation and the Parliament which was to follow it, they found Richard and his ally commanding the situation with irresistible strength. They also found it being confidently asserted that the young king and his brother were illegitimate because their father had been contracted to Lady Elizabeth Butler, and had consequently invalidated his subsequent marriage. Richard's *coup* showed every sign of hasty contrivance, and of the ruthlessness of chronic insecurity. The story of Edward V's illegitimacy was a hoary scandal which Clarence had once tried to spread. Richard had known of it for years, and never previously shown any signs of believing it. However there was no arguing with his physical force, and no voice was raised in protest when the quasi-Parliament petitioned the Protector to accept the crown on 25 June. The following day he assented to the petition, and was crowned with great splendour on 6 July.

RICHARD'S UNEASY REIGN

The apparent ease of this triumph was deceptive. The execution of Hastings had deeply outraged contemporary opinion, which was not deceived by the subsequent proclamation of his alleged offences. No man felt secure. 'With us is much trouble,' a London correspondent wrote to Sir William Stonor the following week, 'and every man doubts other.' He added significantly that Hastings' retainers had shifted for themselves and taken service with the Duke of Buckingham. This was not all. Edward and his young brother disappeared from public view about the time of their uncle's coronation, and it was widely believed that they either had been, or were about to be, killed.[12] Towards the end of August, and by means which are not really clear, popular discontent with this situation in the south and east of England began to transform itself into a movement to rescue the princes before it should be too late. At first there seem to have been no leaders of note, and the king contented himself with appointing commissions of oyer and terminer to deal with the offenders.

By early October, however, far from being suppressed, the malcontents were gaining strength and beginning to look towards the exiled Earl of Richmond. This change seems to have been partly the result of fresh reports of Edward's death, and partly of the surreptitious influence of the Duke of Buckingham. Why the Duke chose this moment to defect from Richard, who had so recently and so largely extended his authority, is obscure. Dissatisfaction with his position seems improbable, and so does any genuine revulsion of feeling. He may have been consulting astrologers, but perhaps the most likely explanation is that he fancied himself as a kingmaker, and reverted to his Lancastrian antecedents. In the event his action proved ill-judged. He was proclaimed a rebel on 15 October, and the insurrections which broke out immediately afterwards in East Anglia, Kent and Surrey were too scattered to be effective. Apart from Buckingham himself there were no leaders of the first rank, the most significant being Sir John Fogg and Sir Richard Guildford. The Duke of Norfolk with a substantial force managed to place himself between the East Anglian rebels and those from south of the Thames, and defeat them in detail. Buckingham, delayed in his march from the west by floods, and depressed by the small response to his appeals, found his forces melting away. Before the

[12] The Italian chronicler Dominico Mancini, who left England early in July, reported that there was much lamentation in London 'after [Edward's] removal from men's sight', and that there were already rumours that he was dead. Mancini, *The Usurpation of Richard the Third*, ed. C. Armstrong, 113.

end of the month he had sought refuge in flight, but even this was unsuccessful. He was caught, tried by the law of arms, and executed on 2 November.

Richard's speed and resolution had enabled him to defeat what might have been a most dangerous rebellion with apparent ease; but he was never to enjoy real security. His usurpation had undone much of the patient work of reconciliation which Edward had accomplished and had driven the Woodvilles and their adherents into the arms of Henry of Richmond. Nor did the collapse of Buckingham's rising mean the end of sympathy for Henry in England. It was entirely Richard's own fault that this obscure exile had become, by the autumn of 1483, a serious contender for his crown. At the end of November Henry received 10,000 gold crowns from Duke Francis II of Brittany, and on Christmas day he contracted to marry Elizabeth, the eldest daughter of Edward IV. During 1484 English diplomatic pressure succeeded in squeezing Henry out of Brittany into France, but this was an accomplishment of very doubtful value since Charles VIII was equally prepared to help him and in a much better position to do so. The whole of Richard's brief reign was dominated by the expectation of invasion, and the king spent most of his time at Nottingham, to be the readier to meet the challenge should it come in the west or north. Similarly the single Parliament of the reign, which assembled in January 1484, was much concerned with the confirmation of the king's title, the attainder of Buckingham's supporters, and means to quell the grumbling disaffection which never really died away.

In these circumstances it is difficult to assess the effectiveness of Richard's 'ordinary' administration. The evidence suggests that he intended to continue along the lines which his brother had laid down. A statute was enacted laying down property qualifications for jurors, very much in the spirit of the measure of 1461. Another sought to ensure the proper promulgation of fines made in the King's Bench. The spirit of the king's intentions is probably best reflected in two sets of instructions drawn up in 1484. One was directed to Sir Marmaduke Constable, steward of the honour of Tutbury, ordering him to take the oaths of all inhabitants not to be retained by any lord or other, save the king; and neither to give nor receive livery contrary to statute. He was also to investigate complaints of extortion against the bailiffs under his authority.

The other was prepared for the Council of the North. This body had begun its life as Richard's private council, which he had used, like any other magnate, to administer his wide northern estates. Since Edward had entrusted him with extensive jurisdiction in the area, he had naturally used his council for that purpose also, and he now proposed to establish it as a royal Council on an independent footing. It was to sit at York at least four times a year, and was to have jurisdiction over 'all riots, routs, forcible entries and misdemeanours against the laws'. If it should receive information of any such riot, the Council was empowered to act in the king's name, without waiting for any formal procedure of indictment. The Earl of Lincoln was commissioned as President. The creation of this flexible and potentially powerful instrument of royal government reflects not only Richard's interest in the affairs of the north, but also his awareness of the need to supplement the normal machinery of the law in order to bring casual and irresponsible violence under control.

Like Edward, Richard relied heavily upon the knights and esquires of his household for key positions such as keeperships of royal castles and stewardships of important estates, but there was no time for any 'normal' relationship between the king and his magnates to develop. The financial administration seems to have continued under the momentum which it had developed during the previous reign, except that Richard explicitly renounced the practice of 'benevolences', perhaps in the hope of winning a little much needed popularity. However much evidence the king might give of his intention to govern well and to maintain the law, the fact remained that confidence had been badly undermined once more. There were widespread doubts as to whether a king who had acted as Richard had acted towards Hastings could be trusted to uphold a rule of law;[13] and whether a man who had murdered his nephews could escape the judgment of God. Doubts of the latter kind were re-inforced when his young son Edward died in April 1484. By the time that his wife also died in May 1485 his reputation was so tarnished that he felt obliged to make a public denunciation of reports that he had poisoned her. As the year 1484 advanced there were further

[13] He was also answerable for the executions (almost certainly without trial) of Earl Rivers and Sir Richard Grey, which took place at Pontefract on 25 June.

defections to Henry, and a number of ill co-ordinated and abortive attempts to rise in his interest. One of these, at Colchester in Essex at the beginning of November, resulted in the indictment of a number of Essex and Suffolk gentry, including Sir William Brandon. By the end of the year it was known in England that Henry was fitting out an expedition with French support, and Richard redoubled his defensive preparations, certain that he would be attacked in the spring.

In the event it was August before Henry arrived. He had not waited so long to take unnecessary risks at the last minute, and his abortive attempt to take advantage of Buckingham's rising two years earlier had warned him of the danger of facile optimism. For several months his agents went to and fro across the channel, sounding out the attitudes and resources of the English magnates, and it was only when he was satisfied that a realistic amount of support would be forthcoming that he committed himself to the venture. On 7 August he landed in Milford Haven with about two thousand men, having been secretly assured of a favourable reception by the local commanders, Sir John Savage and Rhys ap Thomas. He was able to march unmolested through Wales, while the small contingents of sympathisers such as Sir Walter Herbert joined his ranks. On 15 August he captured Shrewsbury after a nominal resistance, and was joined by a Staffordshire force under Gilbert Talbot. At the same time he was able to make contact with the Stanleys, the most powerful of his potential supporters. Lord Stanley was his step-father,[14] but had hitherto given Richard no cause to suspect his loyalty and had assisted him actively against Buckingham. However, by the time Henry reached Newport in Shropshire it was clear to Richard that Stanley and his brother had to some extent betrayed his trust. They were powerful in Wales, and Henry's unmolested advance could only be attributed to their connivance. Consequently he seized Stanley's son, Lord Strange, as a hostage for his father's good behaviour. This circumstance was not calculated to warm Stanley's heart towards the king, but it effectively prevented him from openly joining forces with his step-son.

If Richard was disappointed with the failure of his outer de-

[14] Margaret Beaufort's third husband. Margaret herself had lost all her lands in the aftermath of Buckingham's revolt, but Richard had entrusted them to Stanley to administer.

fences, Henry did not have cause for unlimited satisfaction either. No magnate of the first importance had joined him, there was no sign of spontaneous risings elsewhere in the country, and relatively few recruits had joined his standard. When he confronted the royal army at Bosworth in Leicestershire on 22 August he had no more than five thousand men, and was outnumbered at least two to one. Although to some extent Henry's own military inexperience was compensated for by the presence of the Earl of Oxford, the king ought to have had an overwhelming advantage in skill as well as in numbers. In the event the outcome was decided partly by treachery and partly by Richard's reckless courage. Before the battle Stanley had evaded both the commands of the king and the overtures of Henry, remaining aloof with the forces which he had brought to the field. The king, justly suspecting his intentions, detailed the Earl of Northumberland to guard the flank of the royal army against any intervention from that quarter. However, at the climax of the battle, when Richard had exposed himself to danger in an effort to bring Henry to personal combat, Stanley ordered his forces into action and Northumberland made no attempt to stop them. As a result the king was cut off and killed, and his army defeated.

OPPOSITION TO HENRY TUDOR'S RULE

Richard's death made the battle of Bosworth decisive. He was a childless widower and his designated heir was John de la Pole, Earl of Lincoln, his nephew, whose hereditary claim to the throne was no stronger than Henry's own. The victor was generally accepted, if not as the instrument of divine vengeance, at least as the recipient of God's favour. The small numbers involved on both sides are revealing. Richard, although enjoying the immense advantage of *de facto* possession, was regarded by many as a usurper and a murderer and could command the active allegiance of only a small proportion of those who would have rallied to his brother under similar circumstances. Henry, on the other hand was an unknown quantity, a foreign-backed adventurer whose principal advantage lay in the disaffection which Richard had so liberally created. It was not an encouraging prospect for the future stability of English government. Far from welcoming Henry as a deliverer from the chaos of civil war, most Englishmen in 1485 must have felt that the security of Edward IV's later years had been thrown back into the melting pot of political faction. However, a decision had been reached, no doubt by the will of God, and it only remained to make the best of it. Consequently when the writs were issued in Henry's name on 15 September for the election of a Parliament, the procedure was universally accepted without demur.

Henry acted as king from the moment of his victory. He could not logically or safely have done otherwise, since he could not afford to let it appear that his title depended in any way upon the will of his subjects. However, beyond emphasising his blood relationship with Henry VI he wisely made little use of legitimist arguments. When the Parliament assembled on 7 November Richard was denounced as a usurper, and those who had adhered to him in his 'rebellion' were attainted, but no doubt was cast upon the title of Edward IV, and that of Edward V was also tacitly accepted. Since Henry was contracted to marry Elizabeth, no aspersions could be cast upon her father or brother. The business of this first Parliament fell mainly into two categories: financial measures and the adjustment of attainders. The king received the traditional 'grant for life' of the customs revenues and made certain assignments for the maintenance of his household, alleging the usual reasons, such as the abuse of purveyance. An extensive Resumption Act was also passed on the pattern of 1461, reaching back to 1455 but specifying numerous exemptions. A great many Yorkist attainders were naturally repealed, Edward's as well as Richard's, and an Act of Indemnity was passed securing the king's own followers against any legal action which might result from the campaign preceding Bosworth. The inevitable attainder of Richard and his most active supporters was modest in scale, numbering no more than thirty individuals, but was accomplished by the rather unnecessary expedient of dating the king's reign from the day before the battle, which aroused some protest. By this means the extensive estates of the duchies of Gloucester and Norfolk came into the king's hands. In addition there were a number of measures enacted apparently on the initiative of the commons. These were mostly of a commercial nature, but included a statute acknowledging that the Crown was vested in Henry and the heirs of his body. Since there was no question of Parliament conferring a title to the throne, the reason for this enactment is obscure. There was no penal legislation of any significance, and no fresh provision for the administration of justice.

Meanwhile the king had taken what steps he could to secure the peace and order of the realm. A general pardon had been proclaimed to all those in the north who had taken arms on Richard's behalf, and his own summons to his supporters there was countermanded.[15] Apart from those specifically mentioned in the Act of Attainder, no legal action was taken against any man for having supported his *de facto* ruler. On 7 October the Great Seal was entrusted to John Alcock, Bishop of Ely, and the Privy Seal to the Bishop of Exeter, both of whom had been loyal servants of Edward IV; while at some earlier date the office of king's secretary had been given to Richard Fox, a fellow exile. From the first Henry thus made it clear that he was prepared to employ and favour prominent Yorkists as well as the restricted circle of his personal adherents. This was elementary wisdom, since it was clearly in his interest to create as few jealousies and antagonisms as possible, and to take what advantage he could of the good government which had appertained in the 1470s. There seems to have been no repetition of the events of 1455, 1461 or 1470, where a change of régime had resulted in a sudden shift of power in the localities and innumerable attempts to settle private scores. This was probably because so many of the magnates had stood aside, and their clients had been consequently uncommitted. Only in such 'household' appointments as the keeperships of royal castles was there a complete change in 1485, and that came about because, as we have seen, Richard had been careful to fill these posts with his personal servants. For the bulk of the country Henry's accession had been a comparatively painless revolution. But partly for that reason, and partly because the Crown had now changed hands by *coup d'état* five times in less than thirty years, his authority sat lightly on the consciences of most of his subjects.

Henry was always acutely aware of this fact, and his awareness gave him that preoccupation with domestic security which is the most noticeable feature of his policies. At first this anxiety mainly concerned the north, and in December 1485 he struck a note which was soon to become familiar by taking securities

[15] In the immediate aftermath of Bosworth, Henry had issued commissions of array to prevent any possible intervention in the Yorkist interest from Scotland. The commissioners were instructed to mobilise only such as would take a specific oath of allegiance to the new king. The commissions were cancelled on 20 October. P. L. Hughes and J. F. Larkin, *Tudor Royal Proclamations*, I, 4.

from Viscount Beauchmont and the Earl of Westmorland for their loyalty and good behaviour. Like Edward in similar circumstance, as soon as his preoccupations in London permitted, Henry set out towards the north on progress, to show himself to the people and make it clear that he intended his laws to be obeyed. The citizens of York, anxious to efface the memory of their well known loyalty to Richard, gave him a welcome of splendid and submissive pageantry, and the king then returned in a great sweep through the west country, receiving similar homage at Hereford, Worcester, Gloucester and Bristol. In the course of this journey, two conspiracies against him were uncovered. While the court was at Lincoln in March the king learned of a plot by Lord Lovel, one of Richard's staunchest adherents, to take him in an ambush. Lovel's force was small and easily dispersed, but the ring-leader escaped. Then towards the end of April another member of Richard's household, Humphrey Stafford, organised a small insurrection at Warwick. This was also suppressed without difficulty. Sessions of oyer and terminer at Warwick and Birmingham promptly convicted a score or so of his followers, most of whom were subsequently pardoned.[16] Stafford himself was taken from the sanctuary at Culham in Oxfordshire and executed. During the king's absence there was also an obscure episode in London, where two dozen tradesmen were later accused of conspiring his death by assembling in arms bearing a variety of signs and banners, such as ploughs, clouted shoes, woolsacks, a ragged staff and a 'rubec rose'.[17] What lay behind such a bizarre gathering, and why it should have been treated as treason, is not clear.

The small standing of these rebels, and the feeble nature of their attempts must have gone some way towards relieving Henry's anxiety. Their greatest weakness was that they had no cause. Edward, Earl of Warwick, a possible claimant to the throne was in the Tower,[18] and Richard's designated heir, the Earl of Lincoln, had apparently ingratiated himself with the new régime and presided over the conviction of a number of Stafford's followers. The king's position was further strengthened in

[16] P.R.O., KB 27/902 Rex 2 d. etc.

[17] P.R.O., KB 27/900 Rex 10.

[18] Son of George, Duke of Clarence. Born February 1475 and imprisoned by both Richard and Henry. Executed 1499. There were some rumours that he had escaped, and a gathering of Stafford's supporters at Birmingham had raised the cry, 'A Warwick, a Warwick'.

September 1486 when Elizabeth, whom he had married in January,[19] discharged her primary duty with exemplary promptness by bearing him a son. Henry was faced with no prolonged and stubborn rear-guard action, such as had afflicted Edward between 1461 and 1465, and it seemed that the dynastic union of York and Lancaster had sufficiently reconciled those members of the ruling class in whom the embers of conflict were still alight.

Nevertheless, it was to be many years before the English monarchy could rebuild the tenacious loyalty which had protected Henry VI through a long minority, mental illness and proven incapacity. Henry VII had certainly not done so in the first year of his reign, and when a serious challenge did appear in 1487 he found the majority of his subjects as cautious and apathetic as Richard's had been under similar circumstances two years before. This challenge seems to have originated in the fertile brain of an Oxford priest named Richard Simonds. Simonds had in his care a boy called Lambert Simnel, a child of ten years of age, 'son to Thomas Simnel late of Oxford, joiner', as he was later described. Young Simnel apparently bore a striking physical resemblance to the boys of the Yorkist royal house, and Simonds decided to try and pass him off as the Earl of Warwick. Presumably he was too young to pose as Richard of York, the younger son of Edward IV who would have been over thirteen had he still been alive, and Simonds may have believed the current rumours that the real Warwick had disappeared. At any rate he took his protegé to Ireland at the end of 1486, where the Lieutenant, the Earl of Kildare, and several other secular and ecclesiastical peers professed themselves convinced of his identity, and proclaimed him King Edward VI. Meanwhile a web of conspiracy had been spun in his interest in England which involved the dowager Elizabeth and the Marquis of Dorset as well as a number of lesser gentry. Henry exhibited the real Warwick in London, but did not succeed in discrediting the imposture. In the middle of March the Earl of Lincoln suddenly fled to the Netherlands, whither Simnel had been taken in February, and joined the group of malcontents already gathering round the pretender. Lincoln must certainly have known that Simnel was a fraud, and may have been intending to use him for

[19] The delay in bringing about this marriage was not occasioned by any political considerations on Henry's part, but because they were near enough kin to require a papal dispensation. This arrived on 16 January 1486, and the marriage took place two days later.

his own purposes, but whatever his motives he was a useful recruit to the cause.

More useful still was the animosity which Margaret, Dowager Duchess of Burgundy (Edward IV's sister), bore toward Henry VII. Not only did she recognise 'Edward VI', but she sent him and his entourage back to Ireland at the beginning of May with two thousand seasoned German mercenaries. On 24 May he was crowned in Dublin cathedral. By this time Henry was justifiably worried since he could not really judge the extent of the disaffection within England, and the Pretender's forces were already stronger than those with which he himself had won the Crown. Lincoln, commanding the invading army, landed his troops at Furness on 4 June, and encountered no more opposition than Henry had done in Wales. Thereafter he rapidly crossed the Pennines and headed south, while the king, who had been waiting at Kenilworth since mid-April, intercepted him at East Stoke near Newark on 16 June. Lincoln had about 8,000 men, and the king perhaps as many as 12,000, but there had been an ominous reluctance to join the royal standard, and even on the field itself a part of the army held back as though unwilling to be committed. Fortunately for Henry there was no overt treachery, and he did not expose himself to unnecessary personal danger. In spite of the impetus of his attack, Lincoln was decisively defeated and died, along with most of his leading followers, on the field of battle.

Stoke has been fairly described as 'the last battle of the Wars of the Roses'. Thereafter Henry had to face conspiracy and rebellion, but never an army in the field. In spite of the flimsiness of Simnel's imposture the danger had been very great because of the fragility of Henry's own position. Victory had made it less fragile, but only a prolonged period of strong and vigilant government would enable the roots of loyalty and obedience to grow. For the rest of his life Henry devoted himself to the cultivation of those roots.

CHAPTER 4

THE FOUNDATION OF THE TUDOR MONARCHY

God hath ordained him to be our king . . . His wealth and prosperity standeth in the wealth of his true subjects, for though the people be subjects to the king yet are they the people of God, and God hath ordained their Prince to protect them and they to obey their Prince. The Commonwealth of this realm or of the subjects or inhabitants thereof may be resembled to a fair and mighty tree growing in a fair field or pasture . . . But for a truth this tree will never long stand or grow upright in this realm without divers strong roots and fastened sure in the ground. (Edmund Dudley, *The Tree of Commonwealth*)

HENRY TUDOR AS KING

Sir Walter Scott popularised the term 'the Wars of the Roses', but he did not invent the idea of a protracted dynastic conflict springing from the deposition of Richard II by Henry Bolingbroke in 1399. That was created by Yorkist propaganda in 1461, and largely accepted by Henry VII who wished to inflate his own reputation as the ender and reconciler of the feud. It consequently found its way into Tudor chronicles, such as Hall and Holinshed, upon which Shakespeare based his history plays, and thence into the common currency of the English language. As we have seen, it is a misleading idea in many ways. There was no question of a Yorkist claim to the throne until 1460, and the sporadic fighting which spread over more than thirty years from the first battle of St Albans to the battle of Stoke did not bear the character of a coherent sequence of operations. What did occur was a series of quarrels between powerful magnates for the control of a weak Crown; quarrels for which, after 1460, dynastic allegiance provided some sort of a pretext. The restoration of Henry VI in 1470 was no more than an attempt to secure for the Earl of Warwick the kind of control which the Duke of York had sought in vain, and which Warwick himself had failed to obtain over Edward. Henry VII was an adventurer who had only the most tenuous connections with Henry VI, but who was able to grasp the opportunity created when the apparently stable régime of Edward IV was torn apart on his death by the actions of Richard of Gloucester.

These quarrels were not 'party issues' in a modern sense even when dynastic claims were invoked, because only a small proportion of the aristocracy was at any time committed to a Yorkist or Lancastrian theory of the succession. On the other hand the ramifications of clientage and the importance of court favour made it difficult for substantial men to avoid involvement altogether. One who did was Edmund, Lord Grey of Ruthin, who succeeded to his estates in 1440, became Earl of Kent in 1465 and died in 1490. His career of uninterrupted estate management was altogether exceptional. Violent quarrels at the highest social and political level did not merely permit similar methods to be used elsewhere, but actively encouraged and exploited them. It is therefore unrealistic to speak of the thirteen weeks or so of campaigning which led up to the principal battles as though that represented the sum total of the disruption caused by the wars. There has been a sharp reaction among historians in recent years against the traditional tales of carnage and devastation. Our attention has been drawn to the unfortified state of English towns, and to the very slight extent of the plunder and destruction which they suffered; to the building of unfortified houses such as Tattershall and South Wingfield; and to the plentiful evidence of modest commercial prosperity. All this is true, but it should not cause us to ignore the innumerable trespasses and assaults, the petty sieges and savage little affrays which fill the records of King's Bench and the Rolls of Parliament. It was these actions, quite as much as the bigger battles or the activities of noble bandits such as Courtenay and Egremont, which caused contemporaries to regard the 1450s and 1460s as a period of unprecedented disorder. The fact that England did not resemble a country devastated by an invading army does not mean that the effects of the troubles were trivial, or localised in their incidence. The Yorkists exaggerated the extent of Lancastrian misgovernment for their own purposes, just as Henry VII did his best to discredit Richard, but the general horror of rebellion and civil strife which we find throughout the sixteenth century was more than a mere *tour de force* of propaganda. It represented a genuine folk memory of what could happen when

In every shire with jacks and salets clean
Misrule does rise and makes the neighbours war

because the monarchy had failed or been challenged beyond its strength.

Although Henry naturally did not remind his subjects of the fact, the events of the period 1483-87 were really a postscript to the mid-century disturbances. The scale of involvement was smaller and the secondary strife much more limited. After the removal of Hastings and Buckingham in 1483, there were no magnates left with the resources to trouble Henry as Warwick had troubled Edward, or York had troubled Henry VI. This was not because the nobility as a whole was decimated, or consisted of raw parvenus. It was partly an accident of personalities, and partly because many of the old loyalties had broken down since 1471. Richard's actions had weakened some; death, marriage and greater security had changed others; so that there was no clientage system of national scope which could be mobilised by anyone who had the will to oppose him. This fact was of immense importance in the early years of the reign, and its significance was not lost upon either Henry or his son.

In every other respect the ingredients of the political situation were unchanged. Henry's marriage was a gesture of reconciliation, but its main practical value was that it prevented Elizabeth from becoming the tool of a rival. It did not remove the danger of Yorkist conspiracy, which, as we have seen, continued even within her own family. In place of the French interference which Edward and Richard justifiably feared, Henry was confronted by the steady hostility of Margaret of Burgundy and the unstable opportunism of the Emperor Maximilian, heir to the bulk of the Burgundian inheritance. Also the murder of James III of Scotland in 1488 and the accession of the hostile James IV re-opened the perennial problem of the northern borders. Nor was Henry any less dependant than his precedessors upon the co-operation of the nobility in the central government and local administration. His peers were his chosen companions and although, like Edward, he never relaxed his insistence on the fact that he consulted individuals by his own will and choice, their local influence was an essential ingredient in the peace and stability of the realm. When a crisis threatened, such as the invasion of 1487, the king summoned his peers to a Great Council, heeded their advice, and relied upon their retainers to support him in the field.

After the defeat and death of the Earl of Lincoln the cause of 'Edward VI' evaporated, and Henry wisely decided to act as though the danger had never been as real as in fact it was. An Act of Attainder against twenty-five men, varying in status from Sir Thomas Broughton to Rowland Robinson, yeoman, was passed through Parliament later in the year, but there were very few executions. The troublesome Lord Lovel, after Lincoln the most important man involved, disappeared and was never heard of again. Probably he died obscurely of injuries suffered on the field. The priest Simonds was incarcerated for life in an ecclesiastical prison, and Simnel himself was sensibly relegated to the royal kitchens, where a long and obscure life lay before him.[1] The Earl of Kildare made haste to submit, and the king, lacking the resources to make his authority in Ireland more real, accepted his professions of penitence. Only in one respect Henry did go beyond these routine and comparatively perfunctory disciplinary measures. On July 5 he wrote to Pope Innocent VIII requesting ecclesiastical sanctions against the Archbishop of Armagh and the Bishops of Meath and Kildare. In this he was successful, and when Sir Richard Edgecombe was sent to Ireland in the following year to receive the allegiance of the Irish magnates, he bore with him a Bull of excommunication against Henry's ecclesiastical opponents, which the Earl of Kildare and the other Irish lords swore to respect before they received the king's pardon.

The support which he consistently received from Pope Innocent was a considerable asset to the king in the early years of his reign. In March 1486 the Pope had formally recognised his title in a Bull which Henry caused to be printed and circulated throughout the realm – the earliest example in England of the use of the new invention of printing for political propaganda. In the same document the pontiff had called upon all churchmen to denounce conspirators against the king's person or estate, under pain of 'the great curse'. Thus in acting against the Irish bishops, Innocent was honouring an undertaking made in the previous year, and in effect giving a warning to their English colleagues to remain in their allegiance. In view of the part which members

[1] He was promoted from scullion to falconer, and eventually transferred to the service of Sir Thomas Lovell. He died about 1540.

of the episcopate had played in earlier disturbances, (for instance Archbishop George Neville in 1469) this was a gesture of no small value or significance. In addition the Pope's co-operation eased the inveterate problems of ecclesiastical immunities. When he was brought to trial in 1486, Humphrey Stafford pleaded that he had been improperly removed from sanctuary, but in the lengthy legal discussions which accompanied the case. Townshend J. gave it as his opinion that

> no franchise can be made without a grant from the king, because none can grant such franchise – that anyone can have such a place of safety – except the king himself . . . the Pope can do nothing within this realm, for the pardon or dispensation of treasons belongs absolutely to the king.

This opinion prevailed, and provoked no hostile reaction from Rome. Similarly in 1487 an agreement was reached between king and pope which gave the former the right to remove from sanctuary any felon who returned thither after committing a second crime.[2] In view of the use which had been made of major sanctuaries such as Westminster and Beverley by armed gangs, this was an important step. Also in 1489 the Parliament acted to restrict benefit of clergy, an age-old grievance of the lay population, without provoking any major dispute.

FURTHER CHALLENGE TO HENRY'S RULE

Although Stoke was the last battle in which the crown was at stake it was to be another ten years before Henry was completely free from challengers, and that decade also saw other disturbances in which there were no dynastic implications. These popular rebellions, which occurred in 1489 and 1497 were both occasioned by demands for direct taxation, and were linked in spirit with Cade's rebellion of 1450 rather than with the magnate feuds of the intervening years. Neither presented any serious danger to the monarchy, but they served as useful illustrations of the fragility of public order, even where no significant political interest was involved. The Yorkshire rising of 1489 followed upon the decision of the Parliament of that year to grant the king a subsidy of £100,000 in connection with his in-

[2] This agreement was concluded as a result of urgent representations from the king. There had been a serious outbreak of violence from the Westminster sanctuary men when rumours reached London that Henry had been defeated by the Earl of Lincoln. *Calendar of State Papers Venetian*, I, 519.

tended intervention in Britanny.[3] This tax was to be raised, not by the traditional tenths and fifteenths, but by a form of income tax, which had been voted for the discharge of the king's debts in 1487, this caused widespread resentment.

Yorkshire felt particularly aggrieved, partly because there had been a poor harvest in 1488, and partly because the border shires proper had been exempted on account of their obligation for defence against the Scots. When the commissioners for the collection of the tax reached the north in April, 'the people of a sudden grew into a great mutiny', and they referred to the Earl of Northumberland for instructions. The Earl was inclined to be conciliatory, but Henry would not allow him to yield to pressure. When this reply was communicated to the malcontents, they attacked Northumberland and his escort at Cocklodge on 28 April. For some reason which is not clear, the Earl's retainers deserted him, and he was killed. This extraordinary event has given rise to a good deal of speculation. Contemporaries thought that some powerful enemy had suborned his household, and historians have noticed that the king took instant advantage of his death to re-organise the government of the north. However, beyond the fact that one of the insurgent leaders, John a'Chambre, had done good service at Bosworth, there is no evidence for Henry's implication, which is intrinsically improbable. Perhaps the responsibility lay with the so called Sir John Egremont, the subsequent leader of the insurrection, who had been plausibly identified as a bastard of the Percy family.[4] In early May Egremont sought to organise his followers to resist the royal retribution which seemed inevitable, but he had little success. On 10 May the king summoned his loyal subjects by proclamation to put down the rebels, and on 22 May a force under the Earl of Surrey cut them to pieces not far from York. Chambre and a few others were hanged, while Egremont escaped to Flanders. The king, who followed Surrey to the north, pardoned most of the prisoners, but he never got the bulk of his subsidy; only

[3] In spite of unofficial English assistance, the Bretons had been heavily defeated by the French in 1488, and Duke Francis II died shortly after, leaving a daughter, Anne, as his heir. Henry was extremely anxious to prevent the absorption of Brittany by France and in February 1489 concluded the treaty of Radon with the Duchy, whereby he undertook to provide six thousand troops for its defence.

[4] By M. E. James; see 'Murder at Cocklodge', *Durham University Journal*, 1965.

£27,000 was ever collected, and the method was not employed again.

In 1497 the men of Cornwall objected to taxation for rather different reasons. On this occasion the demand was caused by the activities of Perkin Warbeck in Scotland, which seemed to threaten an invasion from that quarter. Two tenths and fifteenths were granted, and a subsidy of the same amount; a total again approaching £100,000. Stirred up apparently by a Bodmin lawyer named Thomas Flamank, the Cornishmen claimed not only that they were too poor to pay, but that the Scots were none of their business. The defence of the Scottish border was already provided for by escuage and border tenure, argued Flamank, and it was not merely oppressive, therefore, but illegal to tax Cornwall for that purpose. The blame was laid on John Morton and Sir Reginald Bray, whose removal from the king's Council was demanded. Apart from Flamank the only leader in the first instance seems to have been a resolute and capable blacksmith named Michael Joseph, but they assembled a following several thousands strong and marched towards London. On the way they were joined by their only recruit of note, Lord Audley, whose motives are obscure but were probably connected with the ruin of his private fortunes. He brought them a slight measure of respectability but no great strength, and the direction seems to have remained in the hands of the original leaders. It is difficult to say exactly what powerful stream of provincialism Flamank had succeeded in tapping. There was more in it than the ostensible grievance of taxation, for Cornwall was, and felt itself to be, a region apart with its own language and the vestiges of its own culture; but nothing of this emerges in the limited records of the movement.

The government was taken completely by surprise, with its armed forces committed in the north and most of the nobility and gentry scattered to their estates for the work of the summer. On the 16 June the rebels reached Blackheath without serious challenge, poorly armed but moderately well disciplined, fifteen thousand strong, having picked up a number of recruits on their march. These latter could have had but little interest in the specific grievances at issue and provide a further demonstration of how easily and lightly large scale violence could be provoked. At first there was panic in London, but the mustering of its own forces and reports of the king's approach on the 17th restored a measure of confidence in the city. By the 18th Henry had twenty-five thousand men before the capital, under the command of Oxford, Essex and Suffolk. The battle was short but sharp and cost the lives of two thousand insurgents. Audley, Flamank and Joseph were all taken, tried and executed, but a general proclamation of pardon was made on 20 June and the remaining rebels were punished through their pockets. Together with Warbeck's followers taken in the same year they paid a total of £14,700 into the royal coffers which was about £1,500 more than the disturbances had cost to suppress.

THE CHALLENGE OF A PRETENDER

There was no trace of Yorkist conspiracy in the Cornish rising, but the circumstances which provoked it form a link with Henry's most enigmatic and persistent rival. Accordng to his own subsequent confession this young man was the son of one John Warbeck, a boatman of Tournai. While visiting Ireland as a merchant's supercargo in the autumn of 1491 he was persuaded to impersonate Richard of York, the younger son of Edward IV. The known promoters of this conspiracy were all humble men, and the circumstances seem trivial to the point of farce,[5] but it rapidly acquired an international significance because of the willingness of neighbouring rulers to seize upon any opportunity to weaken or embarrass the king of England. Charles VIII had been eager to launch such a conspiracy in 1490, and as relations with England moved towards open war, he welcomed Warbeck as a prince. By the summer of 1492 about a hundred English Yorkists had joined the pretender in Paris. However, Henry's expedition in October, and the resulting treaty of Etaples on 3 November put an end to this phase of the operation. Warbeck was expelled from France, only to find a warm and promising welcome in Flanders, where Margaret of Burgundy recognised him as her nephew. Maximilian, angry with Henry for having concluded a separate peace with France, was fully prepared to condone this behaviour, and rebuffed English diplomatic representations. So incensed was Henry that he broke off

[5] The story is that Warbeck was used as a sort of model for displaying the fine garments which his master had for sale, and that the people of Cork leapt to the conclusion that this splendid figure must be a royal prince! In his recent judicious summary of the conspiracy, Professor S. B. Chrimes concludes that Warbeck's appearance in Ireland was 'no accident', but the evidence for earlier conspiratorial intention is mainly conjectural. *Henry VII* (London, 1972), 81.

trade relations with the Low Countries in September 1493, a move fraught with the most serious economic consequences, and a measure of his anxiety over Warbeck's activities.

While Maximilian was parading 'the Duke of York' around Europe, and encouraging his pretensions in every way that did not involve a drain upon his nonexistent resources, the King of England took stock of the security of his realm. In the summer of 1493 the commissions of the peace were purged, and the proportion of councillors increased, while a special commission was appointed to investigate reports of sedition and conspiracy throughout the midlands and the north. The care with which these investigations were carried out, and the extent of the information which came into Henry's hands by various methods, is of the highest significance. While Edward IV had allowed himself to be surprised by conspiracies which were almost common knowledge, and Richard III disastrously lacked reliable information at the time of Henry's invasion, by the early 1490s Henry was conspicuously well served by 'intelligencers' and fully alive to their importance. By 1493 he had discovered Warbeck's true origins, knew the extent of the exiles' resources, and a good deal about their contacts and sympathisers in England. The result was a series of treason trials in February and March 1495 on charges of conspiracy, collecting weapons to levy war against the king, alienating the affections of his subjects, and communicating with the Yorkist exiles. Several of the defendants were highly placed, including Sir Simon Mountford, Sir Humphrey Savage and the Dean of St Paul's. Two were close to the King's person, Sir William Stanley, Chamberlain of the Household, and Lord Fitzwalter, the one time Steward. Stanley, Mountford and two other gentlemen were beheaded, several lesser men were hanged, and the convicted clergy imprisoned. Some of those implicated, such as Savage, succeeded in making good their escape.

The fate of Sir William Stanley deserves some consideration, for he was a very wealthy man and had been one of Henry's closest adherents. He was also the brother of the king's stepfather, now Earl of Derby, and a powerful man in Lancashire, Cheshire and the Welsh Marches. According to his indictment he had sent Sir Robert Clifford across to Flanders in March 1493 to communicate with Warbeck and give him some undertaking of support. He also seems to have uttered indiscreet words to the effect that if the pretender was indeed the son of Edward IV, then he would not fight against him.[6] Stanley undoubtedly had the resources to make a major contribution to any Yorkist invasion, but there is no real proof that he had committed himself. Clifford, in spite of his Yorkist antecedents, appears to have been a paid informer and *agent provocateur*, which casts doubt upon his testimony. Henry reputedly accepted the evidence of his Chamberlain's guilt with great reluctance, but he may well have decided that the slightest sign of disaffection so close to his person must be construed as treason and treated accordingly. Probably Stanley had presumed upon his relationship with the king to make some tentative insurance against a Yorkist restoration, and discovered too late Henry was not to be trifled with.

His execution was an act of judicial severity sharpened by alarm, but it served as an effectual deterrent to other members of the aristocracy who may have been contemplating a similar course. A further powerful commission was appointed early in the summer to investigate and try suspects in twenty-six counties, thus completing what was probably the most massive and effective security operation ever to have been mounted against sedition within the realm. As a final precaution, in the late summer the king set off on a long progress through the west and north east for the obvious purpose of over-awing potential discontent among Stanley's tenants and retainers.

> Dum haec in Anglia geruntur [wrote Polydore Vergil] Petrus Warbek interim in Flandria, quamquam summo afficiebatur dolore, patefactam esse coniurationem, socios ab Henrico supplito affectos, nullam certam spem se habere de aliquo subsidio ex Anglia expectando.

Even Ireland offered little more. By comparison with the spontaneous enthusiasm which Lambert Simnel had evoked, Warbeck was a damp squib, and when Henry sent Sir Edward Poynings across as Lord Deputy in October 1494 he had no difficulty in gaining control of the situation.[7]

[6] W. Archbold, 'The Treason of Sir William Stanley', *English Historical Review*, 14, 529-34.

[7] Kildare was removed from this post in 1492, and temporarily replaced with Walter Fitzsimons, the Archbishop of Dublin. When Poynings was withdrawn in 1496, Kildare was restored. Irish politics were dominated by a feud between the Fitzgeralds, to which Kildare belonged, and the Butlers, headed by the Earl of Ormond. This fact made it possible for the English king to maintain some semblance of rule.

By the summer of 1495 Maximilian was becoming disillusioned with his protegé, and his subjects were restive under the trade embargo. He was therefore prepared to offer the pretender liberal encouragement, and even a little aid, to challenge his fortune in England. Consequently, on 3 July Warbeck appeared off Deal with three ships and a few hundred motley followers. The attempt was a fiasco which fully justified the king's precautions. Where Lincoln had landed with four thousand men or more and met no resistance, Warbeck landed about three hundred who were instantly cut to pieces by the Kentish levies. 'All the villagers said the king would come,' an observer wrote, 'and that this fellow might go to his father and mother who live in France and are well known there.' A number of Englishmen among the invaders were taken prisoner and hanged, while those who were the Emperor's subjects were allowed to ransom themselves, if they could. Warbeck himself, with the remainder of his force, sailed to Ireland where he was joined by the Earl of Desmond, but their combined efforts were insufficient to capture the town of Waterford, and since no further recruits seemed to be forthcoming the pretender withdrew again, this time to Scotland. Here, in the closing months of 1495 he was to receive his final taste of princely honours.

Meanwhile a Parliament had met in October, and tidied up the procedures of the summer. Nine attainders were either declared or confirmed against those who had conspired in Warbeck's interest, while a further fourteen of those who had been killed at Deal or executed thereafter also suffered this form of legal death. On the other hand a number of attainders against Richard's adherents were lifted, and the so-called *De facto* Act removed all grounds for future legal proceedings against any who had been on the wrong side at Bosworth or before.[8] After ten years the king was prepared to regard that issue as dead, and concentrate upon the more important loyalties of the moment. The potential resources of Yorkist conspiracy in England were thus still further reduced, just at the time when the successes of Charles VIII in Italy had inflated Henry's diplomatic value in northern Europe. Charles was understandably anxious that there should be no

[8] The common assertion that this Act was designed to protect Henry's own followers in the event of his deposition is not well founded. Had he lost the Crown, the acts of his Parliaments could have been repealed as easily as they were passed.

repetition of the English invasion of 1492 while his attentions were fully occupied in the south, and had offered Henry any assistance which he might need against the pretender. On the other hand the Holy League, which had been formed to check French ambitions, had an equal need for English sympathy. It had been for this reason that Maximilian had been interested in Warbeck, seeing in his success a means of turning England into a virtual satellite. The pretender's failure in 1495 convinced Maximilian's son, the Archduke Philip, and his ally Ferdinand of Aragon that there was no future in this scheme. In February 1496 Philip was prepared to negotiate the resumption of trade with England, and renounced all further interest in Henry's enemies.[9] By the summer Maximilian, who had committed himself deeply to Warbeck's imposture, was overruled and England was admitted to the League, without, however, accepting any commitment to war with France. Shortly after negotiations were re-opened for a marriage between Ferdinand's daughter Catherine and Henry's son Arthur, and were brought to a successful conclusion in October.

By the end of 1496, therefore, Henry's position among the European rulers was secure, and his dynasty universally recognised. Conversely Warbeck was thrown back upon the sole support of James IV of Scotland, who refused all blandishments from the Holy League to renounce him and thus rob Henry of his pretext for refusing to attack France. He received 'Prince Richard of England' sumptuously, gave him a handsome allowance and married him to Lady Catherine Gordon, daughter of the Earl of Huntly. In return Warbeck undertook to surrender Berwick, and to reimburse his host £50,000 when he had won his kingdom. The expedition which was to accomplish this feat, however, turned out to be little more than a border raid. The Scottish nobles were not enthusiastic, and Warbeck's proclamation met with no response in England. All that had been achieved was to give Henry a pretext for war with which he faced his Parliament in January 1497. As we have seen, this resulted in a rebellion which temporarily paralysed operations in the north, and James drew the hopeful and erroneous conclusion that his protegé's hour had struck. He therefore despatched Warbeck to raise a force in Ireland for a descent upon the south-west, while at the beginning of August he crossed the border in force and laid

[9] This was the so called *Magnus Intercursus* of 24 February.

siege to Norham castle. It was soon apparent that he had misread the omens. Ireland was no longer interested in Warbeck, and it was more as a fugitive than an invader that he reached Cornwall on 7 September, to find the defeated remnants of the rebellion straggling back to their homes. In the circumstances it is remarkable that the pretender had any success at all, but discontents of various kinds were festering among the people of Cornwall, and he succeeded in raising about six thousand ill-armed peasants. The number of even the humblest gentry who joined him could be counted on the fingers of one hand. Failing to gain admission to Exeter on 17 September, and warned of the approach of a royal army, Warbeck gave up and fled to the sanctuary at Beaulieu in Hampshire, while the hue and cry hunted him across the countryside. A few days later he threw himself on the king's mercy, confessing his imposture at length and in considerable detail. As an alien he could not be charged with treason, and Henry kept him in prison, while his humble followers sued for what pardon they could get. Following his usual habit, the king contented himself mainly with financial penalties, and five years later many of the erstwhile rebels were still attempting to extricate themselves from debt. At the end of September the king of Scots, faced by a powerful army under the Earl of Surrey and realising that no help was to be expected from the south, retreated across the border and shortly after concluded a truce for seven years.[10]

The capture of Warbeck was not the end of the White Rose, but it was the end of any serious threat. Such irreconcilable Yorkists as remained could look neither for significant support within England, nor for the backing of any other power in Western Europe. Since no bid for the English crown, successful or unsuccessful, had been made without foreign aid since 1461, the end of this interference was of the first importance. Perkin remained in prison until 1499, when the discovery of an obscure plot brought him to the scaffold along with the Earl of Warwick. It seems that Henry had been alarmed early in that year by the appearance of another bogus Earl of Warwick, one Ralph Wilford. The surviving evidence does not explain why this trivial im-

[10] In December of the same year this truce was extended for the lifetime of the two rulers, and after long negotiations was sealed by the marriage of James to Henry's twelve year old daughter Margaret in 1502.

posture should have frightened the king, but it may have helped to convince him that he would never be free from plots while the young man lived. The Spanish ambassador also urged him to get rid of 'doubtful royal blood' before Ferdinand entrusted his daughter to a Tudor husband. The supposed conspiracy of Thomas Astwood and Robert Claymond which brought about the Earl's execution was almost certainly invented by Claymond, who was subsequently pardoned. From the records of Warwick's trial it is not clear whether he was supposed to be seeking the crown for himself, or whether he was to be a party to the escape and renewed pretensions of Warbeck. In either case his offence was judged to be treason, and Warbeck was also executed. There is little doubt that Warwick was 'framed', and Henry has been widely and justifiably criticised for judicial murder. On the other hand the Milanese envoy could write in the summer of 1499 that there was no commotion in England, 'nor likely to be during the lifetime of the present king'.

With Warwick's death the Yorkist claim devolved upon Edmund de la Pole, Earl of Suffolk, brother to the rebellious Earl of Lincoln. Having been apparently reconciled to Henry, Suffolk took fright in July 1499 and fled to Maximilian's court. Daunted perhaps, by the prospect of renewed agitation in that quarter, Henry succeeded in persuading him to return in the following year, but in 1501 he fled again, and the tattered remnant of the Yorkist exiles gathered round him. Henry struck at such of Suffolk's relations and dependants as remained within reach. Sir William de la Pole (his brother), Sir William Courtenay, Sir John Wyndham and Sir James Tyrell were arrested, along with a dozen or so lesser men. Tyrell, Wyndham and some of the others were executed, and a total of seventeen attainders decreed by parliament in 1504. In so far as there was a conspiracy in Suffolk's interest, it was effectively shattered by these measures, but Henry's suspicious nature had been sharpened by age, and by anxiety following the death of Prince Arthur in 1502, so that he made constant diplomatic efforts to secure the fugitive. At length in 1506 he was successful, and Suffolk disappeared into the Tower until his execution by Henry VIII in 1513. Edmund's eventual death seems to have been no more than a precaution on the eve of Henry's expedition to France, and may have been prompted by the fact that his brother Richard was in the French service. Had the Tudors not faced so many succession problems, the White Rose would have been of no significance after 1499, but in the event their proximity to the throne could still bring death and destruction to the Courtenays and Poles as late as 1540; and Francis I toyed with the idea of raising up a Yorkist claimant until Richard de la Pole, the last of Lincoln's brothers, was killed at Pavia in 1525.

FOUNDATIONS OF TUDOR POWER

The death of Arthur at the age of sixteen was a very serious blow to Henry. Not only did the elaborate and long drawn out negotiations for his marriage appear to have been wasted, but the succession now depended upon the eleven-year old Henry. Should the king die within the next three or four years, the situation of 1483 might very well be repeated. As if to emphasize this danger, in 1503 the king's spies brought him a report of some conversations among officers of the Calais garrison, occasioned by rumours of his own illness, as to what would happen in the event of his death.

> Some of them spake of my lord of Buckingham, saying that he was a noble man and would be a royal ruler. Other there were that spake in like wise of your traitor Edmund de la Pole, but none of them spake of my lord Prince . . .

From 1502 until very shortly before he died, Henry's achievements rested upon a knife edge, and this must always be borne in mind when considering the so-called deterioration of his character in the later years of his life.

In the event, his political skill and constant vigilance were rewarded, as Edward's efforts had not been, by the transmission of a secure throne to an adult son, a circumstance upon which the whole subsequent Tudor achievement was based. In stressing the importance of the succession, however, it must not be forgotten that Henry was a successful ruler in his own lifetime, and if he had not been there would have been neither peace nor security to transmit. This success was based, first and foremost, upon his understanding of the need for speedy and reliable information, and the steps which he took to obtain it. Some spies and agents seem to have been employed upon a regular basis, others were casual informers, tempted by large rewards. Sir Robert Clifford was paid £500 for his intelligence from the household of Margaret of Burgundy, and there is no knowing how many other sums paid out in 'rewards' were for similar services. Detailed personal knowledge was the basis of Henry's government. Knowledge of his financial resources enabled him to exploit them efficiently. Knowledge of his enemies' intentions enabled him to frustrate them; and knowledge of offences against the law provided a basis for redress. This thoroughness enabled him, in spite of his troubled legacy, to use the traditional machinery of the English monarchy with an effectiveness not seen since the best days of Edward III.

Nowhere can this be seen more clearly than in the Council, which was the great nerve centre and clearing house for all kinds of business. Henry had brought the nucleus of a Council with him from Brittany, but within weeks after Bosworth this had been expanded into a well balanced group about forty strong. The composition of the Council, then and throughout the reign, closely followed the pattern of the previous twenty years. About a quarter were peers, a similar number lawyers and household officials, while almost half were ecclesiastics of various ranks. Again the records are incomplete, but it is clear that Henry normally presided in person, and individual meetings might consist of any number from five to forty. Forty were present on 9 June 1486 when a variety of matters including the security of London were discussed; and twenty-nine heard a private suit on 5 February 1489; but at half the sixty-three meetings for which records survive, the average attendance was seven. The flexibility of this body, and the variety of ways in which it was used, have caused endless debates among historians.[11] When the king went on progress, for instance, he would designate a number of councillors to accompany him, while others would remain to handle the routine affairs at Westminster. This did not imply that there were two distinct Councils, nor that the membership of either group was constant. Similarly when a group of councillors met in judicial fashion to hear a suit, they were not forming a 'court' that was in any sense separate from the Council itself.

On the other hand there were groups which can best be described as 'committees' of the council, of which the 'Council

[11] For a summary of these discussions see G. R. Elton, 'Why the history of the early Tudor Council remains unwritten', *Studies in Tudor and Stuart Politics and Government*, 1974, 308–39.

learned in the law' was probably the best defined.[12] As confidence in the king's government increased, so the pressure of private petitions to the council became overwhelming. At one time special days were set aside for hearing such petitions, but this seems to have been inadequate and a series of *ad hoc* committees were set up to deal with different classes of complaint. The operation of these groups cannot properly be distinguished from the work of the council as a whole, but one of them at least became semi-permanent – that which handled poor men's suits and later became the Court of Requests. Different in nature, although similar in appearance, was that group of councillors designated by the so-called 'Star Chamber Act' of 1487 to hear complaints of maintenance, riots and other abuses. In this case the Chancellor and six other specified officials formed a disciplinary tribunal which was in fact separate from the council and derived its authority from statute. It is not clear how effectively this tribunal functioned, or exactly why it was established in such a manner. It had no connection with the later Court of Star Chamber, and seems to have lapsed after a few years. Some of the cases which came before this tribunal were Crown cases, but very little of the extensive judicial work of the council itself was undertaken on the initiative of the Crown, and only a minority of cases dealt with actual breaches of the law.[13] The majority were more in the nature of arbitrations, and the rapid growth of this side of the Council's business indicated that the desperate need of the mid-century period was at last being met.

The names of 227 men described as councillors have been recorded for the whole reign, and their standing within the council must have varied greatly. Some seem to have attended so rarely that they did not even take the council oath. Others were summoned only when their special skills were required. At the opposite extreme a handful of trusted advisers were hardly ever absent from the king's side. These were the men whom foreign observers tended to call his 'secret council' – men such as John Morton, Richard Fox, Reginald Bray and Edmund Dudley.

[12] For considerations of this aspect of the council's work see D. M. Gladish, *The Tudor Privy Council*, and R. Somerville, 'Henry VII's "Council learned in the law"', *E.H.R*, 54, 1939, 427-42.

[13] 194 cases have been published and analysed by C. G. Bayne and W. H. Dunham in *Select Cases in the Council of Henry VII*, Selden Society, 1958.

Their position was extremely influential, but it was also personal because they were not members of a separately constituted 'cabinet', and they had no collective voice except in the Council as a whole. Nor did they resemble the princely favourites of Henry VI's reign, for although one or two powerful magnates such as Jasper Tudor and the Earl of Oxford enjoyed this intimate relationship with the king, Henry like Edward made his own decisions and kept the control of patronage very firmly in his own hands.

We have seen that Henry was bound to rely heavily on the aristocracy, both in his Council and outside it. His preference for so called 'middle class' servants has long since been exposed as a myth. Nevertheless in several important respects he departed from the practice of Edward's reign, and still more from that of Richard. Edward had relied heavily upon a few families and upon individuals such as Hastings. Richard had shown signs of carrying this further in the immense powers which he conferred upon Buckingham, and in the fact that he created the Earl of Northumberland Warden General of all three marches and Captain of Berwick, thus giving him a practically vice-regal status in the north. Henry, by contrast liked to spread his trust and favours more evenly, partly because he wished to conciliate existing factions, and partly because he was aware of the jealousies which would result from the creation of provincial 'satraps', however reliable and loyal. This he did, not by building up a new class of local administrators at the knightly level, for such a class had existed since the thirteenth century, but simply by making more equitable use of the men who were already 'great in their countries'.

At the beginning of his reign the position in the north was potentially dangerous, and Henry felt obliged to release the Earl of Northumberland from captivity after a few weeks because his absence was creating a political vaccuum. The only restriction which Henry felt able to place upon his power was to suppress the Wardenry of the West March and to rule it through Lord Dacre as deputy. In 1488 he took the Captaincy of Berwick out of the Earl's hands, in spite of the fact that the latter was doing him good service, and entrusted it to a courtier, Sir William Tyler. Then in 1489, as we have seen, Northumberland was killed. His son was a minor and the king's ward, a blow from which the power of the Percies never recovered.[14] Henry placed the vacant Wardenries in the hands of his three year old son and appointed the Earl of Surrey as lieutenant. A perfunctory attempt was made to revive Richard's northern Council, but the real power lay with the lieutenant and the officers whom he appointed. In the Welsh marches the king's first thought had been to rely upon his uncle the Duke of Bedford, but in 1493 he re-created the Council which Edward had established for his son in 1471, and young Arthur as Prince of Wales kept his household at Ludlow. After his death in 1502 this Council continued to function effectively for the remainder of the reign, but thereafter fell gradually into disuse and was moribund by 1520.

Over the remainder of the country the problems were less acute, and the king's policy is harder to evaluate. It was obviously based to a considerable extent on patronage, particularly grants of office, but threats and penalties played a much greater part than hitherto. These took three main forms: fines for actual breaches of the law, recognisances for good behaviour, and the careful exploitation of feudal rights. The first applied equally to all classes of society, and might be straight-forward or obtained by the sale of a pardon. The second was a traditional expedient the use of which Henry greatly extended, so that all officers were placed under bonds for the proper discharge of their duties, which might be as high as £40,000 in the case of the Captain of Calais. The third consisted mainly of wardships[15] and escheats which Henry, like Edward, investigated thoroughly and used both for financial profit and political control. Wardship, indeed, was one of the most powerful weapons in the king's armoury for dealing with recalcitrant aristocratic families – the Percies being the outstanding example during this period.

The success of these policies depended entirely upon the king's ability to enforce payment, and this was achieved not by any

[14] The fifth Earl was only eleven years old when his father died, and was never able to regain the offices which his father had held. The Tudors continued to regard the Percies with suspicion until the death of the 6th Earl in 1537.

[15] The heir of a tenant-in-chief who was under age became a ward of the king, which meant that the estate passed temporarily into the hands of the Crown, or of a royal grantee. Control over the marriage of the heir (or heiress) went with the estate, which thus became a valuable prize. Later in the sixteenth century such wardships were frequently sold to the highest bidder.

overwhelming display of strength, but by constant, meticulous and well-informed administrative pressure. Every opportunity was exploited, but there are clear indications that in the case of peers Henry was far more concerned to ensure obedience to his will than to obtain large sums for his coffers. For instance Lord Abergavenny became liable for a fine of £70,000 in 1506 for unlawful retaining, but Henry did not attempt to exact so enormous a sum. Instead he imposed a fine of £5,000, and compelled Abergavenny to enter into two additional recognisances, one for his allegiance and the other not to enter the counties of Kent, Surrey, Sussex or Hampshire without the king's licence. In 1506 Lord Dacre made a bond for £2,000, and in 1507 the Earl of Northumberland one for £5,000 under similar circumstances. Given the innumerable feuds and disputes which divided the aristocracy as a result of the wars and prevented the emergence of anything in the nature of a concerted 'baronial opposition', this was an extremely effective way of imposing discipline. It was also a means of keeping the aristocracy at work in the king's service, thus providing one aspect of the 'governance' which was so sorely needed. Little as they may have loved him for it, Henry nevertheless succeeded by his judicious distribution of 'kicks and ha'pence' in making the nobility more dependant upon, and more involved in, the work of the central government than they had been before.

The financial profits of these policies were also substantial, and probably supplied the major motive for their application to lesser men. In 1493-4 the Crown received £3,000 from forfeited bonds. Eleven years later the equivalent sum was £35,000. Other profits of justice were less spectacular, but none the less considerable: £1,000 a year after 1504 for the escape of prisoners; nearly £4,000 in 1504-5 for the sale of pardons, and so on. There is no space here to enter into the controversy which has raged over Henry's allegedly rapacious and unjust exactions, but he certainly encouraged his agents to use their legal powers to the full. These men had an additional motive for zeal in that they might receive a proportion of their takings in lieu of a salary, and although Henry was too careful a supervisor to be the victim of large scale peculation, nevertheless it is probable that the law was stretched in being used as a fiscal instrument. At the same time the peace and order of the realm benefited. The work of Sir Edward Belknap as Surveyor of the Royal Prerogative in the last year of the reign provides a good example. Belknap and his assistants worked on a commission basis, exacting fines for outlawry. They collected £3,000 in about seven months, and were hated as ruthless extortioners, but in the process they made outlawry the real legal sanction which it was supposed to be and had not been for centuries.

In other respects Henry continued the financial policies of Edward. After an initial period of hesitancy due to ignorance and inexperience, he reverted to the use of the Chamber as his principal treasury, and followed his predecessor's practice of careful personal inspection and auditing of the accounts. From 1493 the Exchequer was excluded from land revenue accounting and the receivers were instructed to account to a Council committee sitting in the Chamber. This committee was shortly to be known as the Court of General Surveyors, and in common with the practice of other departments, took bonds of its officers for the performance of their functions. Partly because of this careful supervision, and partly because of the thorough investigation of concealments and feudal obligations, receipts from the Crown lands went up steadily, until by the end of the reign the net revenues from that source averaged £40,000 per annum.[16] Customs receipts continued at about the same level after a slight decline in the early years, and in spite of his acknowledged interest in trade Henry did little in this respect beyond continuing the careful methods of his predecessor. In spite of the trouble which it caused in the early years of his reign, Henry did not do particularly well out of direct taxation. His Parliaments voted him sums which averaged out at £12,000 a year, but much of this was never collected. On the other hand, because of his cautious foreign policy he contrived to spend even less than he received on military expeditions, and made a handsome profit out of Charles VIII's eagerness to invade Italy. In 1491 Edward's expedient of a benevolence, banned by Richard, was revived and letters of assessment under the Privy Seal were sent to many substantial householders. It was in connection with the collection of this that 'Morton's Fork' was alleged to have been invented, and resistance was stubborn until the assessment was confirmed by Parliament in 1495.[17] Overall, Henry's financial policies were undoubtedly successful, but not as profitable as

[16] B. P. Woolfe, *The Crown Lands, 1461-1536.*
[17] Eventually this benevolence raised nearly £50,000, and the Com-

either contemporaries or some subsequent historians believed. In May 1499 Raimondo de Sonaro, the Milanese envoy, reported that the king of England had amassed an 'infinite treasure . . . which he constantly augments', and at his death he was described as the 'richest lord that is now known in the world'. In fact he was solvent, but not very much more.[18] This was important, but in itself no more than Edward had achieved. The more far reaching significance of Henry's methods lay in the development of administrative techniques and a noticeable increase in what might be called 'density' of government, which increased the power of the Crown and diminished the possibility of large scale disorders.

The assertion that justice was corrupted in the later years of Henry's reign by the greed of the king and his officials must be regarded as 'non-proven'. The probability is that there was no serious abuse, because the king's record as a legislator and justiciar was in every other respect an excellent one. He adhered to the existing tradition of judicial independence, retaining Richard's judges and replacing them only on death. He also accepted the opinion of Hussey, C. J., that the judges should not be consulted by the king in respect of cases which the Crown was intending to bring before them – a decision which James I would have done well to remember. At the same time the king initiated a much larger quantity of legislation than Edward had done to improve the effectiveness of the common law. A statute of 1485 significantly increased the authority of the courts by allowing actions to be brought against tenants to uses,[19] who

mons in Parliament thought it more equitable than normal taxation. Storey, *op. cit.*, 109.

[18] Estimates of what Henry left vary from 'about two years' revenue' (c. £230,000) to £9,100, although the latter must be regarded as a minimum since it takes no account of plate or jewels. The traditional figure of £1,800,000 was invented by Bacon, and probably exceeds the gross income for the entire reign.

[19] A tenant to uses was one who held land on trust for another under a feudal tenure. Since the law had hitherto not recognised this arrangement it had been impossible to sue such a tenant who refused to surrender the agreed proportion of his profits to the 'user'. Such a tenant might be a corporation, or a group that was constantly renewed, thus avoiding feudal incidents.

had hitherto been almost immune from legal responsibility, while another Act of 1491 on the same principle decreed that feudal incidents should be due on the death of the user, thus limiting the possibilities of evasion. Although the Crown stood to gain by both these statutes, other feudal lords gained as well, and the effect was to strengthen the position of large estates. A series of acts was also passed to strengthen the law against perjury and against riotous assembly, while the abduction of heiresses became a felony in 1487. There were also two statutes designed to make the courts more useful to ordinary litigants. One in 1487 ordained speedier execution upon writs of error, and the award of costs, while the other in 1496 admitted poor men to sue *in forma pauperis*, which meant that no fees were charged for writs and the Chancellor assigned counsel and attornies without payment. Nevertheless there were still many kinds of grievance for which the common law could provide no remedy, and the boom in Chancery litigation continued, as well as the flood of cases which we have already noticed coming before the Council.

In the supervision of local government Henry followed earlier precedents in using the justices of the peace to curb the sheriffs. An act of 1496 decreed that an action for trespass should lie against a sheriff who exceeded or abused his powers, and that such actions should be tried by the justices in their sessions. Apart from this he did not much increase the work of the justices, and made no significant changes in the composition of the commissions. Individuals were removed for crime or unsatisfactory conduct, but the balance of magnates, ecclesiastics, lawyers and gentry remained about the same. So also did the size, which remained constant at about seventeen or eighteen per commission throughout the second half of the century. At the same time, there was some tightening of control, reflected in more frequent revisions and in the extraordinary act of 1489 which compelled justices to make proclamation of their own shortcomings at every quarter sessions, and to invite the people to complain direct to the king in Council if they were not satisfied that they were getting good justice. There is no means of knowing how far this was complied with, but the king's determination to improve the standard of law enforcement cannot be doubted. As a sign of changing times a handbook for justices, the *Boke of Justyces of Peas*, which may have had some official backing, was published in 1506.

Such evidence as can be meaningfully interpreted indicates that these justices, lectured and cajoled, but also much more effectively backed up by the Council, were seriously tackling problems of disorder by the end of the reign, even over such explosive issues as maintenance and retaining. This was a subject to which Henry gave considerable attention, encouraging prosecutions under the existing law against men below baronial rank, but at first making no serious attempt to check the practice among his peers. Not only were numerous retainers an essential adjunct to the dignity of a nobleman, but such retinues still formed the readiest source of soldiers in the event of war. An act of 1487 forbade any other man, of whatsoever rank, to retain the king's tenants or officials, and decreed loss of office for any of the latter who accepted such maintenance. Then in 1502 a curious proclamation forbade all men in the counties of Kent and Sussex to accept any livery other than the king's. Why Henry should have made this selective prohibition is not clear, and it does not seem to have been very effective. Finally in 1504 came the well known Statute of Liveries, which had the appearance of a blanket prohibition but also provided for a system of licences. This had the considerable advantage of giving the king a discretionary control over the extent of retaining by his peers. The majority almost certainly continued the practice as before, but they did so by the king's indulgence. Any individual whose loyalty might become suspect could be brought sharply to heel by prosecution under the Act, as was done with Lord Abergavenny in 1506. This realistic measure, which represented a significant development of the monarch's traditional attitude, remained the basis of royal policy for the next half century.

When Henry died in 1509 he bequeathed to his son, not the enormous treasure of legend, but a working Council and administration capable of governing the realm in his name. The spectacular sacrifice of the unpopular Empson and Dudley in 1510 has served to conceal the extent to which England continued to be governed by the old king's servants down to the emergence of Wolsey in 1512-13. Henry VIII had no taste for the dull business of administration and was only too willing to allow Warham and Fox to get on with it. However, the old councillors grumbled and remonstrated, and began to oppose his plans to seek glory and profit in a new French war; so Henry listened all the more readily to his suave and competent Almoner. Wolsey was every bit as willing as the older men to shoulder the burdens of routine administration, and he knew better than to lecture his young monarch on the nature of his royal responsibilities. Thanks to his father's watchfulness there was no rival claimant, and no stir of sedition. The crown had not changed hands in such auspicious circumstances since the death of Henry IV in 1413. The young king's youth and glamour caught the public imagination, and he was loved where his father had been feared and respected. Nevertheless, behind the scenes the care and watchfulness of the earlier régime seems to have continued. No doubt in due course it would have run down had Henry's attitude not changed, but before that could happen Wolsey had assumed the main responsibilities of government, and he was as vigilant in the king's interest as Henry VII had been in his own. By the end of 1514 Wolsey was in effective control of the administration, and most of the confidential reports which would once have gone to the king were going to him. In addition his own numerous servants provided him with a great variety of information, which, after his personal influence over the king, was the secret of his power.

These are years in which the main interest of English history shifts away from sedition and law enforcement towards foreign war and diplomacy, and with these matters we cannot be much concerned, except in so far as financial demands caused resentment. In the decade following Henry VIII's accession there was only one disturbance of sufficient importance to warrant mention and that was the so called 'Evil May Day' of 1517. Towards the end of April the London apprentices were stirred up, apparently by a radical preacher, to attack the French, Flemish and Italian residents in the city. Disturbances of this kind had a long history. As we have seen, there had been a fierce outbreak against the Italians in 1456; the Hanse merchants had been attacked during the previous reign, and lesser riots were frequent. On this occasion about two thousand apprentices, reinforced by a few professional criminals, went on a rampage. The Italians were armed and ready and beat them off, but many other houses were plundered. There seems to have been no loss of life. More remarkable than the disturbances was the speed of the government's reaction. The garrison of the Tower was alerted, and within twenty-four hours Wolsey, Norfolk and other lords had brought a substantial force to aid the mayor in restoring order. According to some contemporary observers the damage would have been much worse without this prompt suppression, but nevertheless the official policy was extremely severe. Over four hundred of the rioters were arrested and about forty hanged. By 5 May there were over five thousand troops in the city and gibbets at every gate. Such fierce punishment aroused widespread resentment because it seemed out of proportion to the offence. Eventually on 19 May the remaining prisoners were pardoned by the king in a public ceremony, but the episode left a much deeper impression than its innumerable predecessors.

Foreign wars traditionally kept the aristocracy in a co-operative frame of mind unless they were totally disastrous, and Henry's wars enjoyed a fair measure of success. The young king has been frequently criticised for squandering his resources during these years, but in this respect his expenditure was probably a sound investment. There are distinct signs that after many years' quiescence, the nobility were becoming restive in the later years of Henry VII's reign, as royal pressure increased rather than relaxed. Consequently the new king's actions in calling a Great Council and cancelling many outstanding obligations, may have saved him from serious trouble. At the same time the rapid plunge into war and the contemporaneous rise of Wolsey prevented any attempt by the nobility to take advantage of their young king's inexperience to gain control of the administration. Neither Henry nor Wolsey ever reverted to the suspicious policy of recognisances, but the latter at least remained very much on the alert for any sign of sedition or dangerous pretentiousness in that quarter.

As the years passed and the king's marriage failed to produce a male heir, Wolsey's watchfulness increased, and early in 1521 he persuaded the king to act against the Duke of Buckingham. In terms of his resources, Edward Stafford had all the makings of an overmighty subject: great estates, fortified castles, armouries, many servants. He was also a distant kinsman of the king, being descended from Thomas of Woodstock through his daughter Anne, and had been mentioned as a possible claimant in 1503. In personality he was proud, rash and intemperate – despising Wolsey and inclined to despise the king for trusting him. In spite of all this he apparently enjoyed Henry's favour, and had played a leading part in the negotiations with the Emperor at Gravelines in 1520. However, for some time Buckingham had been inclined to listen to voices which told him what a good king he would make, and his ungovernable temper made him enemies. Thanks to the grievances of 'divers servants that the Duke had put from him' Wolsey began to hear rumours of these foolish conversations, and sent him a private warning to desist. Then towards the end of 1520 an anonymous informant wrote to Wolsey, not only in terms which show how far the danger had progressed, but also how faithfully he was following in the footsteps of Henry VII:

> The king that dead is, whom God pardon, would handle such a case circumspectly and with convenient diligence, for inveighing, and yet not disclose it to the party or otherwise by a great space after, and always grope further, having ever good await and espial to the party . . .

By the beginning of 1521 Wolsey had his hands on several members of the Duke's household who were prepared to testify against him: Charles Knyvet, his surveyor, Robert Gilbert, his chaplain, and a certain Margaret Gedding, who may have been his mistress. When this information was placed before the king, he was seriously alarmed and made elaborate preparations to apprehend the offender. The precautions were unnecessary, for Buckingham responded to a summons to court in mid-April without any sign of suspicion. To his great astonishment he was arrested on his arrival in London and lodged in the Tower. However rashly he may have talked, or allowed others to talk, it seems almost certain that he had no treasonable intentions, but his contempt for Wolsey was a serious mistake. The evidence produced at his trial on 10 May was circumstantial and inconclusive, but Henry had clearly made up his mind that he was guilty, and the peers duly convicted him. His wealth and his proximity to the throne made the slightest indiscretion dangerous, and with the dynasty in such a fragile position a challenge of this kind was easier prevented than cured. There is no reason to suppose that he was 'framed', or a victim of the Cardinal's malice, and his trial was perfectly well conducted by the standards of the time. At his execution on 17 May he grudgingly confessed that he had offended 'through negligence and lack of grace', which was probably a fair assessment of the situation.

The manner of Buckingham's fall is a striking illustration of the extent to which the royal authority had recovered from the debilitating effects of factional and dynastic strife. By 1521 the wars of York and Lancaster were significant mainly as a weapon in the royal armoury of propaganda. The Earl of Warwick and Richard of Gloucester had become bogeymen, whose historical purpose was to illustrate the nemesis of treason and usurpation. They represented those forces of darkness and chaos from which England had been rescued by Divine Providence in the shape of Henry Tudor, and which still lay in wait (or such was the obvious implication) to take advantage of any lapse of loyalty or obedience to the king.

to the royal [illegible] the [illegible]

[illegible] and [illegible] the [illegible]

[illegible]

[illegible] the King [illegible]

[illegible] the [illegible]

[illegible] the church [illegible] and [illegible]

[illegible] considered [illegible]

[illegible] the [illegible] also [illegible]

[illegible] Cromwell [illegible] a vast [illegible] in the [illegible] commons, and [illegible] decade [illegible] did not [illegible]

[illegible] time [illegible] of [illegible] the [illegible]

[illegible] placed [illegible] in the [illegible] the royal [illegible] used in the [illegible]

Part Two

THE ESTABLISHMENT AND TESTING OF THE TUDOR MONARCHY

1521-1570

These were the years of high drama and striking achievement. The private resources of great men no longer in themselves constituted a serious threat to the royal power. The politics of personal ambition now centred upon the court, and the predominant importance of the king's favour was becoming a reality as far away as the marches of Scotland. Against this background of successful government in the medieval tradition, the events of the 1530s raised new and perilous issues. Utilising to the full the resources which previous success, dynastic anxiety and lay anti-clericalism had placed at his disposal, Henry challenged the church over the 'great matter' of his first marriage. His radical solution worked. By securing both practical and theoretical control over the church in England, the king transcended what had hitherto been considered as an inviolable limitation upon his authority. In the shadow of this triumph the remaining secular franchises were also swept away, leaving the country and its people uniformly exposed to royal jurisdiction in a manner which had never hitherto been attempted. This substantial achievement was secured in the first instance by the indefatigable labours of one of the greatest administrative geniuses of the century, Thomas Cromwell. Cromwell persuaded the 'political nation' to accept a vast potential expansion in the power of the central government, and the two troubled decades which followed his death did not affect that fundamental fact.

At the same time, the political conquest of the church inevitably plunged the Crown into those religious conflicts which had been stirred up by continental humanists and reformers. In spite of Cromwell's reforming tendencies, Henry had no desire to make his church autonomous in doctrine as well as jurisdiction. His death, however, placed power temporarily in the hands of men with a different vision, who saw the royal supremacy as a weapon to be used in the service of evangelical faith. Such views were not popular, but the experiment was too brief to cause serious damage to the royal authority, and the men who held them were quickly replaced by the chances of hereditary succession. Queen Mary was equally a woman of vision, but in place of an England autonomous and evangelical, she raised the banner of a catholic England, finding security in the international embraces of the ancient church and the Habsburg empire. This combination the 'political nation' rejected with a unanimity which exposed the limitations of the Henrician achievement, and revealed clearly that the augmented royal power still rested upon the traditional basis of co-operation and consent.

Given time, Mary's intractable idealism could have undone not merely her father's work but her grandfather's as well, and left the monarchy and aristocracy in irreconcilable conflict. In the event she was not given time, and her half-sister Elizabeth, who succeeded her in 1558, was a very different woman. Elizabeth was a realist to her fingertips, and a politician of great skill. She was also wholly committed to her father's policies, and to that extent in sympathy with those who had opposed her sister. However, two conflicting religious ideologies in the short space of eleven years after Henry's death had destroyed the viability of his conservative settlement. Elizabeth was therefore forced to embrace a fully protestant church, and in so doing to sacrifice a measure of political initiative to the zealous evangelicals. For the first decade of her reign she strove, with considerable success, to minimise the disruptive consequences of her choice, and to reconcile advanced reformers and conservative Erastians in the interests of national unity. In this she was aided rather than impeded by the rebellion of 1569, and by the unequivocal reassertion of political catholicism in the papal Bull of 1570. Thereafter national security, and a sense of national purpose, were associated with the protestant faith, and that faith had been placed firmly at the disposal of the monarchy by the settlement of 1559.

CHAPTER 5

THE ADMINISTRATION OF CARDINAL WOLSEY

Let every man therefore wait on the office wherein Christ hath put him, and therein serve his brethren. If he be of low degree, let him patiently therein abide, till God promote him, and exalt him higher. Let kings and head officers seek Christ in their offices, and minister peace and quietness unto the brethren; punish sin, and that with mercy . . . (William Tyndale, *The parable of the Wicked Mammon*)

VIOLENCE AND SOCIAL CHANGE

Henry VII had not cured the propensity of his subjects to take the law into their own hands. Foreigners still commented upon their quarrelsome violence, and upon the large numbers of thieves and other criminals who defied the severest laws. Throughout the sixteenth century English men and women continued to be uninhibited in their exhibitions of emotion, which found outlet in copious tears, extravagant language, and an irritability well-nigh incredible to the modern observer. This last was partly at least due to the constant pain and discomfort of undiagnosed and untreatable illness. Professor Stone has observed that the poor of this period suffered from persistent malnutrition, and the rich from chronic dyspepsia through over-indulgence in an ill-balanced diet. Since all men between the ages of sixteen and sixty were required by law to keep weapons in their houses for the king's service, neither of these conditions was conducive to the public peace. Aristocratic violence had certainly been diminished both in scale and ferocity but the gentry continued to set an anti-social example to their inferiors. Nor were magistrates and royal servants immune from such temptations. In 1502 Sir Robert Harcourt, a justice of the peace and officer of the Crown, was accused of instigating an attack on Eynsham Abbey and using his influence at quarter sessions to prevent redress. In 1524 Sir Ralph Egerton, Treasurer of the household to Princess Mary, used his armed servants to beat off the lawful claimant to an estate in Cheshire. Many other similar examples could be cited. In 1501 Sir Ralph Ellercar was tried by a special commission of oyer and terminer for a 'great riot' in Northumberland.[1] The following year Margaret Bassett, niece and heir of William Blackett of Staffordshire, was abducted by his enemies the Vernons with over one hundred armed servants, and the resulting pursuit ended in a dangerous brawl.[2] It is significant, however, that all these cases are quoted from the records of the Council or the courts, and not from the unheeded complaints of the victims.

The eventual conquest of this endemic violence was the result of well over a century of persistent effort; a century which saw no radical innovations in either legislation or judiciary, but a steady development of social and political attitudes. In this process every aspect of the administration played a part, gradually producing a climate of opinion in which the aristocracy were accustomed to look to the central government alone for office, authority or redress. In 1520 it was still realistic for a substantial knight such as Sir Thomas Tempest to seek his career and preferment in the household of the Earl of Northumberland, or Sir William Eure in that of Lord Darcy. By the 1580s such careers were to be found only in the service of the Crown. Even by 1540 the political power of the Duke of Norfolk lay not in his hosts of tenants or retainers, but much more in his influence at court and the number of his servants and 'well willers' who were strategically deployed in the central administration. This was accompanied by a steady transformation in the nature of 'good lordship'. As the element of physical protection diminished, the need for swift mobilisation also disappeared, with the result that the old style retainer committed to obey his lord's summons in arms was replaced by the political client whose support and advice increased his patron's weight in the Council or the House of Lords. Thus both the formality and the scale of patronage were diminished, for power no longer lay in 'manred' – the ability to command personal service – but in wealth and in political dexterity. The households of almost two hundred servants, such as attended the Duke of Buckingham in the early

[1] Reported in the Appendix to the *4th Report of the Deputy Keeper of the Public Records*. P.R.O., Baga de Secretis, KB 8/3, bundle I.

[2] For an account of this episode, and a discussion of its significance, see E. W. Ives, 'Ralph Egerton of Ridley', *Bulletin of the John Rylands Library*, 52 (2), 1970.

years of Henry VIII's reign or the Earl of Northumberland in the 1520s, had disappeared by the end of the century. 'Tall fellows' were no longer in demand, even for prestige purposes, and conservative writers were grumbling that great lords, instead of having 'the best blood in the land at their commandment' now preferred to have 'the sweat of their brows in [their] coffers'.[8] As we shall see, this represented a social change of the greatest importance, and one in which the disciplinary pressures of the central government played a considerable part. It was a great step forward in both the unification and the pacification of the realm that the king should be seen as, to quote the words of Professor Stone, 'a better lord than the Earl of Derby'.

The early years of Henry VIII's reign inevitably saw some relaxation of his father's iron grip. As we have seen this was politically necessary and represented a change of tactics rather than of strategy. However legal many of the expedients of the old king's later years may have been, they had been bitterly resented, and when Henry promised in his first proclamation that 'his grace shall provide for the reformation of the great extremity and rigour wherewith his said subjects have been grievously vexed and troubled in time past', he was making a gesture of conciliation. The new king had much to gain and little to lose by magnanimity, since the mere fact of his accession had removed the chief incentive for repressive policies. Similarly, when he issued commissions of oyer and terminer, as was customary at the beginning of a new reign, he included in their terms of reference not only every conceivable kind of treason, felony or misdemeanour, but also an investigation

> de omnibus et singulis transgressis contemptibus et offenc' contra formam Statuti de magna carta de libertatibus anglie edit' aliarum statutorum quorumcunque edit' aut contra legem et consuetudinem regni nostri Anglie quoquo modo facet'.

Large numbers of indictments seem to have been presented before these commissioners, although the only records which survive are of those which were eventually transferred to the court of King's Bench. Most of these are for ordinary crimes, but a few present abuses in government. For instance, Sir Amyas Paulet

[8] Gervase Markham, writing about 1624, was mourning a way of life which had already passed. The crucial period for this change of values seem to have been between 1580 and 1620. L. Stone, *The Crisis of the Aristocracy*, 210-17.

was accused with two others of procuring false verdicts and inquisitions for the king in the Isle of Wight; and the customs officers of Hull for making unlawful charges. The impression created is one of extensive petty oppression, but little that could be represented as the serious misuse of power. Richard Empson and Edmund Dudley, who were also indicted at this time, may well have been the greatest offenders, but they were also clearly scapegoats whose unhappy function it was to provide the principal demonstration of the good intentions and royal virtues of King Henry VIII.[4]

Henry expressed the gravest concern for the welfare of his father's soul in the light of these disclosures, but he never showed any sign of wishing to dismantle the main structure of his policy. There were wild rumours that the Duke of Buckingham was to become protector of the realm, and that the Earl of Northumberland would recover full control of the north, but in fact the elder statesmen of the previous reign remained in power, and these magnate pretensions (if they ever really existed) were effectively checked. Such measures as were taken had the full approval of these councillors, as well as of the king himself. Certain aspects of the work of the Council Learned came under attack from the common lawyers and were discontinued. Measures were also passed in the first Parliament of the reign to check abuses in the work of inquisitions, and to stop the practice of proceeding in cases below the level of felony on mere information, without presentment by a jury, a procedure which had been approved by statute in 1495. There were several other reforms of this nature, and they were not unimportant, but it would be a mistake to exaggerate the 'reaction' of 1509-12, which was more a revulsion of feeling than a significant change of political direction. It is true that Henry VIII did not provide the same purposeful control of policy that his father had done, but that was on account of his youth and temperament, not because he was convinced that that policy was wrong. When he found in Wolsey a servant of his own to carry the main burden of administration, he chose a man as committed to the merits of prerogative government as Henry VII had been.

[4] Their attainders were very speedily reversed; that of Dudley in 1511, and that of Empson in 1512. Henry VII was alleged to have been contemplating action against them in the last months of his life.

WOLSEY IN EFFECTIVE CONTROL

Wolsey's rise was rapid. He had been a royal chaplain since 1505, and became Henry's almoner on his accession. His personal ascendancy began almost at once. 'Who was now in high favour, but Master Almoner . . . who ruled all under the king but Master Almoner?' wrote George Cavendish, Wolsey's gentleman usher and biographer. The secret of this success was not witchcraft as some suspected, but an instant readiness to gratify his master's whims, combined with an insatiable appetite for hard work. His value as an administrator at the highest level was proved by his management of the logistics of the French campaign of 1513, and from then on he had no rival in the king's confidence. Warham and Fox, far from regarding him as a rival and an upstart, almost certainly welcomed his appearance on the scene. Both were anxious to retire from active politics and regarded him as a man who could be trusted to continue most of the policies which they had helped to implement. It is probable that Fox had promoted Wolsey's career in the first two years of the reign, lest Henry should fall too far under the influence of magnate councillors such as the Earl of Surrey. After collecting a number of lesser preferments, Wolsey became Bishop of Lincoln in March 1514, Archbishop of York in September of the same year, and Lord Chancellor on the resignation of Warham in December 1515. Meanwhile, on the king's urgent representation he had been created a Cardinal in September 1515, and eventually after persistent pressure, he became Legate *a Latere* in July 1518.

No English prelate had ever held such an accumulation of secular and ecclesiastical offices as this grazier's son from Ipswich. It is not surprising that he was unpopular, for his pride matched his success, and his personality was as flamboyant as the king's. For fifteen years he carried the main burden of government, and Henry seemed to be completely overshadowed by his great minister. But appearances were deceptive. Although he might neglect business completely for weeks on end, the king was always capable of intervening with decisive results and would overrule the Cardinal without hesitation if he felt inclined. In matters which interested him, such as relations with France, or naval armaments, he could show a capacity for rapid assessment and decisive action which frequently took foreign envoys by surprise. At the same time his capacity for sustained application was slight, and it was Wolsey who shouldered the responsibility for justice and finance, for the working of the Council and the good order of the Church. Perhaps only the Cardinal himself realised that his seemingly unshakable power depended entirely upon the king's will and confidence.

It was natural that Wolsey should keep a close watch upon the lay magnates. Not only was this necessary in the interest of good government, but they were bitterly resentful of his power and anxious to seize any opportunity to discredit him. So strict was this vigilance that some later claimed to have been afraid even to grumble audibly about his doings, but there can be no doubt that Henry approved of his minister's watchfulness. Indeed at some time in 1520 he actually wrote to Wolsey (a thing he very seldom troubled to do) urging him to 'keep good watch' on the Dukes of Buckingham and Suffolk, and the Earls of Northumberland, Derby and Wiltshire. What lay behind this outburst of suspicion we do not know, but it may well have been some early hint that Buckingham's loyalty was in doubt. As we have seen, the latter ignored all evidence of such surveillance, to his utter undoing.

At the same time warfare, and the lavish and frequent amusements of the court kept Henry on reasonably good terms with the majority of his peers. They served him in France and in Scotland, and were rewarded with grants of land and titles. In 1514 the Dukedom of Norfolk was revived for Thomas Howard, Earl of Surrey, and a fresh creation made of the Dukedom of Suffolk for Charles Brandon, Viscount L'Isle, the king's boon companion and fellow jouster. Between 1510 and 1525 two Marquisates and five Earldoms were also created or restored, without counting the titles conferred in the latter year upon Henry's illegitimate son.[5] Many attainders of the previous reign were reversed, but in this the king did no more than follow the normal practice. So generous was he with grants in the first five years, however, that in 1515 he had to be persuaded to accept

[5] The Marquisate of Dorset for Thomas Grey in 1511; the Marquisate of Exeter for Henry Courtenay, Earl of Devon, in 1525; the Earldom of Cumberland for Henry Clifford in 1525; the Earldom of Devon for Henry Courtenay in 1511 (restoration); the Earldom of Lincoln for Henry Brandon in 1525; the Earldom of Rutland for Thomas Manners in 1525; the Earldom of Worcester for Charles Somerset in 1514. The titles of Henry Fitzroy were Duke of Richmond and Earl of Nottingham. There were several further creations in 1529.

an Act of Resumption (6 Henry VIII c. 25.) which spoke in unflattering terms of the 'improvident' way in which the Crown's resources had been distributed. The court was gay and magnificent, with frequent tournaments and splendid diplomatic missions, so there was less discontent than there might otherwise have been over Wolsey's administrative monopoly, but the fact remains that he adhered very closely to the policy of Henry VII and distributed small responsibilities with a judicious hand.

The short-lived revival of magnate activity in the Council which marked the beginning of the reign was over by 1512, and thereafter the Cardinal increasingly absorbed the whole of that body's political functions. Formally, it continued to function very much as before, except that the king did not preside, but in substance its regular and recorded meetings were almost exclusively concerned with routine administration. Such of the committees as continued, notably the General Surveyors, were also of this nature. Except on those rare occasions when the king intervened to assert himself, all political decisions not of the first importance were taken by Wolsey and put into effect in Henry's name. So far had this process gone by 1525 that the king complained that he was 'devoid of council', and in the following year a scheme of reform was drawn up by Wolsey in the Eltham Ordinances. Here it was laid down that a group of seven or eight councillors of the middle rank should always be attendant upon the king's person, unless he gave them leave to depart. More significantly, this scheme also proposed to divide the Council into two parts: in effect an inner and outer council. The former, about twenty strong, was to be the king's political and executive instrument the members of which would be in regular attendance when the duties of their other offices under the crown permitted. The latter, which included the Chief Justices, would be called upon piecemeal as required. There is no sign that this plan was put into effect as long as the Cardinal remained in power, but during the following decade something very like it was to be implemented.

Wolsey deliberately channelled the energies of the Council into judicial work, partly because he himself found this congenial, and partly because of the unrelenting demand. The activity of Henry VII's Council in this respect seems to have lapsed with his death, and the paucity of the records makes it hard to discover when it was resumed. Certainly by 1520 a great quantity of such business was again being handled, and it was from this period that some later writers traced the origin of the Court of Star Chamber. Sir Thomas Smith, writing in 1565, observed judiciously:

> This court began long before, but took great augmentation and authority at the time that Cardinal Wolsey . . . was Chancellor of England, who of some was thought to have first devised the court, because that he, after some intermission by negligence of time, augmented the authority of it.

In fact the Court of Star Chamber did not originate at any identifiable point in time, since it was not in any sense an offshoot or committee of the Council, but the whole Council sitting in its judicial capacity. As such it was assisting the king in his traditional function of justiciar and derived its authority from the ancient prerogative of the Crown. In 1532 a plaintiff could refer to a decree as having been made 'in [the] most honourable court of Star Chamber', whereas ten years before the same body would have been described as 'the Council sitting in the Star Chamber'. Wolsey made no institutional innovations, but he did encourage so much business as to necessitate a more formal system of record keeping and an expanded secretariat. As in earlier days, the main pressure came from suits 'betwixt party and party', but the disciplinary aspect of Star Chamber work was not negligible. A large proportion of the private suits were of a disciplinary nature, since they related to the riotous assemblies, affrays and the like, for which the conciliar jurisdiction was stiffened by a number of statutes. This was on account of the greater speed and convenience of its procedures, rather than because the common law courts were unable to deal with the offenders. Wolsey was a man without any legal training and was inclined to regard the complex safeguards of the common law as so many gratuitous obstructions in the path of justice and order. As we have seen, there was something to be said for this point of view, but naturally the common lawyers attributed Wolsey's attitude to the fact that he was Chancellor, and in his insatiable pride wished to elevate the jurisdiction of equity above that of the ordinary courts. It is certainly true that the Cardinal encouraged suitors to apply to the equity courts wherever possible and that this led to a great expansion in the work of Chancery as well as of the Council.

Quite apart from Wolsey's ambitions, there was a genuine need for equity upon a large scale. So formalised were the procedures of the common law that no new type of writ could be developed, which meant that no cognisance could be taken of wrongs which were not remediable under the traditional forms.[6] This might mean that no redress could be obtained at all, or that it could be obtained only by resorting to far fetched legal fictions which necessarily jeopardised the success of actions based upon them. Only statute could modify the common law beyond the restricted range of judicial interpretation, and statutes were inflexible and extremely expensive. Also, the common law was such a technical jungle that the skill of the advocate was always a major factor in obtaining a favourable verdict, and such skill commanded a high price.

Pleading *in forma pauperis*, which was supposed to overcome this difficulty for the poor, never seems to have been very popular and may have been discouraged by the lawyers themselves. In the equity courts the pleading was in writing, and in English, and a speedy decision could be reached upon the principles of rough justice. The problem of poor men's causes had always been a difficult one, and a Council committee had existed to deal with them since the reign of Edward IV. By about 1497 this committee had acquired the institutional character of a court, with formal records, and confined its functions to the law terms, although it would always receive petitions at other times. In 1516 this court was appointed to meet in the White Hall of the palace of Westminster, and soon began to be known as the Court of Requests. The decisions of this court were subject to review by the Council as a whole, and there were also councillors specially in attendance upon the king to receive poor men's petitions, but from this time onward the bulk of 'poor men's causes' were heard in the White Hall. The only serious drawback of the equity courts was the limited range of penalties which they could impose. Since they could not touch life or real property they were virtually restricted to fines or imprisonment, and all treasons and felonies lay outside their jurisdiction.

According to Sir Thomas Smith, one of the main causes which inspired Wolsey to reactivate the judicial functions of the council was the need 'to repress the insolency of the noblemen and gentlemen of the north parts of England, who being far from

[6] Hence Maitland's observation that the common law maintained 'where there is no remedy there is no wrong'. *Equity*, 299.

the king and the seat of justice made almost as it were an ordinary war among themselves, and made their force their law'. Social conditions in the northern marches had changed little in the previous century, and although the liberties of Tynedale and Redesdale had been incorporated in Northumberland by statute in 1497, their people were not in fact any easier to govern than they had been before. After the death of the fourth Earl of Northumberland in 1489, Henry VII had ruled mainly through lieutenants and had relied upon the co-operation of Lord Dacre and the semi-courtier Lord Darcy. This had been successful to some extent, with the Percy interest in abeyance, because the Dacres and the Cliffords neutralised each other and the king was able to set about building up a local clientage of his own. This he did by appointing members of gentry families to posts in the royal household. These posts carried with them fees, access to the king's person and patronage, and an obligation upon the holder to use his local authority in the interests of the crown. As we have seen, both Edward and Richard had used this policy to some extent in lowland England, but the established patronage of the great northern families had given them little scope in the marches, and they had relied almost exclusively upon magnate support. Henry VIII continued his father's policy in this respect, and between 1490 and about 1520 there was a significant movement among the younger generation of northern gentry to seek the king's favour. For instance, Sir Edward Radcliffe of Dilston in Northumberland became one of Henry's Esquires of the Body some time before 1516, whereas his father, Thomas Radcliffe of Derwentwater, had been a fee'd man of the fourth Earl of Northumberland. Similarly John Pennington of Cumberland was in the king's household by 1496, although his father, who lived until 1518, had always been a staunch adherent of the Percies. The Curwens, and the Plumptons and Constables in Yorkshire were other families which followed a similar course.

This development was to continue, and in the course of time would transform the political situation in northern England, but in the 1520s the old order had been no more than modified. Indeed in 1515 Henry reverted to an earlier pattern of government by placing the Wardenries of all three marches in the hands of Thomas, third lord Dacre, who held these offices until his death in 1525. Dacre was not so much a trusted servant of the Tudors as a reliable antagonist of the Percy interest, and there are clear signs that in the last years of his life Wolsey regarded him as a danger and an embarrassment. Certainly the influence of the Dacre family among the lawless dalesmen of the West March was so great that Henry Clifford, first Earl of Cumberland, who was appointed to the Wardenry in 1525, had to be dismissed two years later in favour of William, fourth lord Dacre. At the same time it proved impossible to find anyone of sufficient weight to continue in command of the East and Middle Marches without Percy support, and in 1527 the sixth Earl of Northumberland was appointed to these offices from which his father had been so carefully excluded. Wolsey's attempt to revive the Yorkist Council of the North between 1522 and 1525 met with little success.[7] In theory this council was to serve the infant Duke of Richmond, the king's lieutenant, and enjoyed very wide civil and criminal jurisdiction over both Yorkshire and the marches, but in practice it could make no impression upon the entrenched position of the northern lords. After the Cardinal's fall, in 1530, its operations were restricted to Yorkshire until the major reorganisation which was to follow the Pilgrimage of Grace in 1537. Far more fruitful in terms of royal authority was the policy of steadily expanding the royal estates in the north, which Wolsey pursued contemporaneously with the extension of crown patronage. This brought the king into the area as a major power in terms which the established families could recognise, and gave a firm basis upon which to rebuild the administration in the later 1530s.

The lawlessness of the Welsh marches was a slightly less intractable problem, because there was no equivalent of the constant menace of Scottish intervention, nor of the safe retreat which Scotland could provide. Nor were the great marcher families, such as the Herberts and the Stanleys, accustomed to the degree of unfettered dominion which the Percies and the Nevilles had enjoyed. Nevertheless the constant feuds of the Welsh gentry, and the extremely high rates of common crime such as robbery and homicide, made the area a difficult one to control. The Prince's council which had been continued after

[7] R. Reid, *The King's Council in the North*. In 1527 the Council confessed its impotence in attempting to deal with Sir William Lisle, and it was this failure more than anything else which convinced Wolsey of the need to employ the services of the Earl of Northumberland. M. E. James, *A Tudor Magnate and the Tudor State*. Borthwick Papers, No. 30, 12-13.

Arthur's death in 1502 had long since ceased to perform any useful function when Wolsey revived it in 1525 for the nine year old Mary. For about nine years, under the presidency of Bishop Voysey of Exeter, this body strove without much success to bring order to the marches. Neither its powers nor its personnel were really equal to the task, and it was only to be after a major reorganisation in 1534 that it became an effective instrument of the central government.

Wolsey had little taste or aptitude for institutional engineering, just as he had little understanding of the common law. His highly personal methods of government were based upon the management of men rather than upon the creation or modification of machinery. Consequently. during his period of power there was little reforming legislation beyond the continuance of statutes passed in the previous reign. It was typical of him that he should have sought to place conscience above the law, ignoring the diverse and uncertain interpretations which this must have brought about. Probably, had he had more time and energy to spare for domestic affairs, he would have taken steps to increase the influence of Roman law in England.[8] There was ample justification for the mistrust with which the common lawyers regarded him, although they were wrong in attributing his attitude to mere arrogance. 'The king ought for his royal dignity and prerogative to mitigate the rigour of the law where conscience hath the more force,' he claimed after his fall. His concept of government had little room for established procedures and conventions, or for the safeguards which these offered to the subject. 'In what uncertainty shall the king's subjects be when they shall be put from the law of the realm to be ordered by the discretion and conscience of one man?' Christopher St German was to write later, voicing the suspicions of the Cardinal's enemies. His failure to appreciate the strongly constitutional nature of English politics was Wolsey's greatest weakness as an administrator, and the cause of much of the hatred which he incurred.

In his fourteen years as Chancellor, he met only one Parliament, in 1523, and on that occasion he distinguished himself by going down in person to the House of Commons in an attempt to bully the members into granting a subsidy of 4 shillings in the pound. The Speaker, Sir Thomas More, who was in no sense

[8] J. A. Guy, *The Cardinal's Court* (1977).

an opponent of the Crown, was forced to point out that this visitation was contrary to the long established freedom of the House to debate without outside interference. The members, already incensed by Wolsey's contemptuous refusal to listen to a deputation, were made yet more unco-operative by this ineptitude. In the event they would grant only one subsidy of £150,000 in four annual instalments, and imposed such a complicated schedule of assessment that efficient collection was rendered almost impossible. Henry had been living beyond his means for about ten years, pursuing a foreign policy which necessitated constant recourse to extraordinary revenue, and Wolsey had no sense of his financial limitations. Although he continued the earlier policy of Chamber accounting and careful supervision,[9] money to him was only a means to gratify the king's ambitions, and he regarded the long established machinery of direct taxation with ill-concealed impatience. In 1513 Parliament had granted a subsidy of £160,000, but a year later only £50,000 of this had been collected, and a supplementary grant had to be made to raise the remainder. In 1515 this process was repeated, as the total realised was still short of the original figure. At a time when the war was costing upwards of £100,000 a year this degree of support was totally inadequate, but Wolsey paid no heed to the implied warning. There was money enough in England, therefore the king should have it. In 1522-3 he resorted to a series of forced loans on strict individual assessments, and raised over £350,000. By comparison the subsidy extracted from a reluctant Parliament in the following year was both laborious and unrewarding. It seemed a straightforward conclusion that there was more to be gained by direct pressure than by scrupulous constitutionalism, and with the concurrence of the Council Wolsey determined at the beginning of 1525 to make a further massive assault upon the wealth of the king's subjects.

On the 21 March letters missive were sent out for what was optimistically termed an 'amicable grant' of one-sixth of the incomes and moveable goods of laymen, and one-third of the equivalent wealth of the clergy. The reaction was immediate and general, so that by the beginning of May Henry was forced to

[9] Several statutes in the early years of the reign confirmed the immunity of the General Surveyors from Exchequer process, thus securing the essentials of the Chamber system, although it was probably Wolsey's servants rather than himself who carried out the supervision.

write to his commissioners to proceed 'doucely', in spite of the fact that in some areas the people had risen in arms against them.[10] It seems clear that there were widespread spontaneous uprisings among the common people, who protested their poverty and their loyalty to the king. The gentry were more inclined to temporise by offering partial payment, but were reluctant to aid the commissioners in suppressing the commons. There was no identifiable leadership, but the storm centre seems to have been along the Suffolk-Essex border, and particularly the town of Lavenham. On 11 May the Dukes of Norfolk and Suffolk reported that the situation had been brought under control, but that there were still a number of armed gatherings which had not been dispersed, and that many of the favourably inclined were not daring to pay for fear of reprisals after the commissioners had withdrawn. The clergy were equally reluctant, if less violent in their protests. Like the laity, they disliked the arbitrariness of the 'grant' almost as much as its weight, pointing out with justice that if the king 'should now and also in time to come thus, by his Grace's letters missive, privy seals and other ways, hereafter require aid of the spirituality as often times as it shall please his Grace so to do . . . the church and clergy shall at length be put to such impossible charges as they shall not be able to bear'. London was resolute in its refusal to contribute, in spite of Wolsey's hectoring, and a general insurrection seemed a distinct possibility. Should such an eventuality come to pass, Norfolk reported with secret satisfaction, the commons' quarrel would be with Wolsey alone, as they reputed him to be solely responsible. The dislike which the aristocracy felt for the Lord Chancellor did not increase their zeal to suppress the movement.

In the event there was no insurrection, because Henry cut his losses and abandoned the imposition. This he was able to do with a show of fatherly benevolence, casting yet further odium upon his minister by claiming to have been unaware of the severity of the demands being made. Probably the Cardinal was not as solely responsible as he confessed in public, or as he was universally believed to be, but accepted the blame in order to save his master's face. Otherwise it is difficult to understand how he could have retained the king's confidence after such a dangerous débâcle. The opposition to the 'amicable grant' could hardly have been more successful had it been a concerted political de-

[10] *Letters and Papers*, IV, 1318; 8 May.

monstration, but remarkably little is known about it. The whole episode was quietly consigned to oblivion. No legal proceedings were taken, and there were no subsequent complaints of extra-legal punishments. This has served to obscure its importance, which is unfortunate because it provided an excellent demonstration of the vulnerability of Henry's government to a certain kind of pressure. This pressure, which can perhaps be best described as 'quasi-rebellion', had no dynastic overtones, and did not intend to bring the Crown into jeopardy, but was concerned to bring about a change of policy. At the time certain of the king's officers wished to regard the demonstrations as treasonable, but this point of view was not accepted, which may perhaps have encouraged the idea that such political pressure was legitimate and should not incur the odium of rebellion. As we shall see, the delicate distinction between opposition and treason was to be one of the main problems in the suceeding century. We find it in the Pilgrimage of Grace, in 1549, in the rising of the northern Earls, and even in the opening phases of the civil war.

During Wolsey's period in power relatively little treason came before the courts, although on three occasions special proclamations were issued ordering the arrest of troublemakers in specified areas, and the investigation of their crimes.[11] An obscure conspiracy occurred in 1523 in Westminster and in Coventry, which resulted in a certain Francis Philips and three others being tried for seeking to raise war against the king and depose him. Murder and robbery were also involved, and Francis and two of his colleagues suffered traitors' deaths, but their antecedents and their purposes are unknown. More interesting from the legal point of view was the trial in 1519 of John Cowley, a London yeoman, and several others for treasonable words spoken while the defendants were in custody in the Marshalsea. The words alleged included such remarks as 'I ask a vengeance upon the king . . .' and 'The king is dead and is kept secret at Windsor by means of my lord Cardinal . . .'. Cowley and three others were convicted and executed, while two were acquitted.[12] Treasonable words were as well known to the common law in the period immediately before the act of 1534 as they had been in the previous century.

[11] Yorkshire and Northumberland, 16 July 1524; Coventry, 6 November 1525. Hughes and Larkin, *Tudor Royal Proclamations*, I, 143, 144, 150.
[12] P.R.O., King's Bench, Controllment Rolls; KB 9/475 (2).

The relative domestic peace of these years has enabled historians to see more clearly the growth of official concern with two long standing problems which were beginning to change their nature and significance. The first of these was the practice of enclosing common land and open fields for more convenient and profitable farming 'in severalty'. A considerable amount of enclosure had been carried out during the fifteenth century, particularly in those arable regions of the East Midlands where open fields had predominated for centuries. As long as there was no pressure of population this process had caused little resentment, but by the end of the century the voices of discontent were audible. Where enclosure was carried out in the interest of improved arable farming the complaints were usually technical, but where the purpose was to convert the land to sheep pasture, or to some non-productive purpose such as a deer-park, the grievances might be bitter and justified. Sheep farming was remunerative and required little labour, so that landlords were naturally tempted, where the law allowed them, to expel their tenants and put the fields down to grass. In fact the majority of tenants enjoyed full legal security, and the scope for arbitrary action on the part of manorial lords was very limited, but in suitable areas tenants at will and others without legal estate might suffer severely.[13] It was the complaints of these victims which began to reach the ears of the Council in the early years of the sixteenth century, and it was their cause which humanists and social reformers were to embrace so warmly and indiscriminately over the next fifty years.

The government's attitude was consistently hostile to enclosure, partly because of the dangers of uprooting even a small proportion of the population, and partly because of ill-founded fears about the supply of grain. As early as 1489 an Act of Parliament prohibited the pulling down of houses and the conversion of land from arable to pasture, while in 1517 Wolsey caused to be issued the celebrated enclosure commissions to enquire into the extent of the evil. The returns from these commissions

[13] A legal estate might consist in a freehold or a lease, both protected by the common law, or a copyhold, equally protected by the customary law. However, certain kinds of tenure which appeared to enjoy protection, such as demesne copyhold, did not in fact do so. E. Kerridge, *Agrarian Problems in the Sixteenth Century and after.*

indicated that the rate of enclosure was much slower than it had been before 1485, but the evidence of social disruption was sufficient to justify an intensification of the government's anti-enclosure policy. A series of prosecutions in Chancery resulted, and in 1526 outstanding offenders were summoned by proclamation to appear, and to enter into recognisances before the commissioners. In the same year, and again in 1529 all unlawful enclosures were ordered to be destroyed.

THE GROWTH OF RELIGIOUS DISSENT

The second problem was religious, and was concerned partly with dissent and partly with anticlericalism. The Lollard heresy was long established in England, having stemmed indirectly from the teachings of John Wycliffe in the late fourteenth century. By 1450 persecution had destroyed its intellectual and social standing, so that hitherto we have seen it only as a constituent element in plebian riots. Towards the end of the century, however, there are clear signs that it was recovering its vigour, and in 1499 the Venetian Sonaro reported upon the re-appearance of the Lollards as though they were a new phenomenon. 'A new sect of heretics has appeared in England (who) say that baptism is unnecessary for the offspring of Christians, that marriage is superfluous . . . and that the sacrament of the altar is untrue.' He also correctly observed that the ecclesiastical authorities had commenced a new round of persecution. This was particularly concentrated in the Thames valley and in Berkshire, and as Sonaro's description suggests, it caught some very strange fish in its net. There were also Lollard cells in London, and it was no doubt from one of these that the traitor John Cowley derived his opinion 'that no man should receive the sacrament of the altar but at the hour of death'. Cowley also claimed 'that he would lever hear a bagpipe than a mass sungen', which would suggest a touch of the newer reforming ideas were it not for the fact that his words were uttered in 1518.[14] From this background, too, came Richard Hun, whose death in the Bishop of London's prison in December 1514 caused one of the biggest anti-clerical demonstrations of the century. Hun was a cross-grained fellow who became rather unnecessarily embroiled in litigation with his local incumbent, a man named Thomas Dryffeld. Having

[14] P.R.O., KB 9/475 (2).

lost a case in the bishop's court, he then attempted to sue Dryffeld for slander in King's Bench, and while this was still *sub judice* launched another suit, claiming that the Rector and his associates had offended against the statutes of Praemunire. The main Praemunire Act, that of 1393 (16 Richard II, cap. 5) had been the result of a quarrel between the papacy and the English monarchy, and had been rather imprecisely directed against the exercise of ecclesiastical jurisdiction without the king's consent. Hun was not the first private litigant to appeal to this Act against the sentence of a Church court, but in the circumstances the Bishop of London naturally regarded his action as provocative.

At the end of November 1514, Hun was arrested upon a charge of heresy. A search of his house revealed some Lollard books, and there is a certain amount of independent evidence to suggest that the charge may have been well founded. However, he was never able to answer it, and his death caused an immediate accusation of murder to be levelled against the bishop's officers. In all probability they were guilty, and certainly the behaviour of Bishop Fitzjames at this juncture was highly discreditable. Not only did he use his influence with the Council to get the indictment suppressed, but also caused his own court to pronounce the dead man a contumacious heretic, with the result that his family was reduced to penury. Popular opinion in London was outraged by this evidence of malice, and the chronicler Wriothesley summed up the general reaction when he wrote that Hun 'was made a heretic for suing a praemunire'. The case was well calculated to focus lay resentment, because it had always been a major grievance of the laity that when heresy was in question the clergy were judges in their own cause. When the Parliament met in February 1515, the powerful sentiments of anti-clericalism prevailing in the City were soon reflected in the House of Commons. As a result the demand arose for the renewal of the temporary act of 1512 restricting benefit of clergy for all serious offences to those in major orders. This provoked Richard Kidderminster, the Abbot of Winchcombe, to preach an outspoken public sermon, denouncing any such measure as contrary to the liberties of the Church. Parliament appealed to the king, and this angry resumption of the ancient debate over criminous clerks was called before the Council.

Henry, like his father, was a loyal son of the Church, but not inclined to tolerate defiance of his jurisdiction, and his attitude towards both benefit of clergy and rights of sanctuary was generally in accordance with the agreement of 1487.[15] Consequently he was much incensed by the arguments of the ecclesiastical lawyers, which sought not merely to repudiate that position, but to overturn the long established English practice whereby indicted clerics appeared in the king's courts to plead their clergy. By November 1515 the dispute was showing signs of further escalation. Convocation contemplated heresy charges against Henry Standish, the principal royal spokesman, and the common law judges accused Convocation of a breach of praemunire. At this point Wolsey, whose dual role must have been an extremely difficult one, tried to persuade Henry to refer the dispute to Rome, but the king was not to be drawn. Instead he asserted the freedom of the English Crown from any earthly superior and refused to allow Standish or any other prominent anti-clerical to appear before Convocation. In the event a compromise was reached, whereby the charges on both sides were abandoned, and the parliamentary measure was quietly dropped. Nevertheless in 1518 Standish became Bishop of St Asaph, and the Reformation Parliament of 1529 was to pick up the anti-clerical theme almost exactly where that of 1515 had been compelled to lay it down.

However by that time a new element had been added to the situation through the appearance of Lutheran ideas from Germany. At first these were influential mainly within the university of Cambridge, and Wolsey showed a pronounced reluctance to allow persecution. In spite of having burned Luther's works at Paul's Cross in 1521, the Cardinal proved remarkably tolerant of such reformers as Bilney and Latimer, and even engaged some scholars suspected of similar opinions to staff his new college in Oxford. Like many other contemporary prelates who were statesmen rather than theologians or pastors, he probably made the mistake of supposing that the German reformer was nothing more than a sort of intellectual Lollard, and that the English Church had no reason to fear his impact. Wolsey was neither a scholar nor a humanist, but he was a patron of both, and belonged to a generation which contained few zealots. As for ecclesiastical reform, he was quite prepared to admit that it was

[15] On 28 January 1518 John Cowley was taken from the sanctuary of St Martin's in London by Sir Thomas Lovell. He pleaded breach of sanctuary at his trial, but the plea was disallowed. P.R.O., KB 9/475 (2).

an excellent idea, but showed no taste for the personal sacrifices which it must have involved, and had no leisure from his pressing political commitments. The Cardinal's failure to use his unique combination of powers to improve the conditions of the English Church was to prove a disastrous oversight. Not only did his lethargy and bad example stimulate the growth of reforming ideas; they also caused good catholics to turn away in despair from the papal authority which he represented and to seek redress directly from the hands of the king. Wolsey's early tolerance of the reformers did not make them love him and did nothing to mitigate the hatred with which he was regarded by anticlericals of all classes. Also it soon became apparent that he had underestimated the revolutionary potential of the German theology, and conservative ecclesiastics blamed him loudly for his lack of resolution.

In England the new reformers were remarkable mainly for their skilful and resolute use of printed propaganda, a medium hitherto little employed either by the government or its opponents. Learned men like Sir Thomas More doubted whether many of their contemporaries could read,[16] but it seems clear that the ability was more widespread than they realised, and that most communities could at least hear the new works read aloud in inns and private houses. This created an unprecedented problem of discipline and control which speedily outgrew the resources of ecclesiastical administration. In 1524 Bishop Tunstall of London issued an order prohibiting the importation of printed books, or their publication in England, but as a measure of censorship this seems to have been almost totally ineffective. The reading habit was growing fast, and there was an avid market for such controversial literature. Both zeal and profit tempted the smuggler. In 1528 Hans van Ruremond, a stationer operating in London, was apprehended and forced to do penance for importing five hundred copies of William Tyndale's English New Testament, but such successes were rare. At about that same time Bishop Nix of Norwich admitted that he and his episcopal colleagues were quite unable to stem the flood. The only solution was an

[16] Arguing in 1533 against the need for a vernacular translation of the scriptures, More wrote, 'If . . . the peoples souls should needs perish but if they have it translated into their own tongue, then must there the most part perish for all that, except the preacher make further provision besides . . .'. *The Apology of Sir Thomas More* (1533).

appeal to the king, and in January 1530 appeared the first of a long series of proclamations against heretical books.[17] Henry might object to ecclesiastical pretensions, but he had no sympathy with doctrinal dissent, and his own work against Luther, *Assertio Septem Sacramentorum* had earned him the title of 'Defender of the Faith'. His proclamation invoked the early fifteenth century statutes, which had been framed against the Lollards, and ordered all judges and magistrates to put them into effect.

There was more in this reaction than a fatherly concern for his subjects' souls, real as this was in Henry. In the first place the peasants' revolt of 1525 had alarmed monarchs all over Western Europe and alerted them to the explosive possibilities of religious dissent. 'Wicked sects of heretics and Lollards,' the proclamation declared, '. . . soweth sedition among Christian people, and finally do destroy the peace and tranquillity of Christian realms, as late happened in some parts of Germany, where by procurement and sedition of Martin Luther and other heretics were slain an infinite number of Christian people.' A second proclamation in June 1530 also emphasised the king's concern to control religious propaganda, and close co-operation between royal and episcopal officials resulted in a series of prosecutions during 1530. In December of that year a certain Richard Bayfield, a trafficker in the forbidden literature, was burned for heresy. Secondly, Henry was much preoccupied during these years with the jurisdiction of the church, and prepared to welcome any opportunity to strengthen his hand in the interminable negotiations with the papacy for the annulment of his marriage.

HENRY'S 'GREAT MATTER'

A detailed consideration of the so-called 'divorce' would be out of place in this context, but it is important to realise that by 1525 the unfortunate Catherine had become doubly an incumbrance. Not only was she past the child-bearing age and had left the king without a male heir, but she was also a zealous and active worker for the Habsburg alliance which Henry and Wolsey were now anxious to repudiate. The latter planned to cement

[17] Misdated 'before March 1529' in *Tudor Royal Proclamations*, this proclamation was actually the first step in the campaign against heresy, initiated by Sir Thomas More as chancellor. G. R. Elton, *Policy and Police*, 218 n. 5.

his new French alliance by replacing her with a French princess, probably Renée of Anjou, and went to France in the summer of 1527 to complete the negotiations in person. While he was away it became clear that Henry had no intention of marrying Renée, or any other princess, but had set his heart on Anne Boleyn, the daughter of Lord Rochford. When news of this reached Wolsey, he was seriously alarmed. Not only was it an ominous sign that the king had deceived him, but the Boleyns were known to be his enemies, and might well become the spearhead of a determined attempt on the part of the lay aristocracy to overthrow him. Thus if he succeeded in honouring his undertaking to free Henry of Catherine, he would do so to his own peril; while if he failed he could hardly hope to retain what was left of the king's confidence. In the event the complexities of the case and the vulnerability of the papacy to Habsburg pressure gave him no chance to determine the issue. On the 31 July 1529 his legatine court at Blackfriars was adjourned, and shortly after the king's 'great matter' was revoked to Rome. By the end of August foreign ambassadors were instructed not to visit the Chancellor, and important affairs of state were being handled by a triumvirate of Norfolk, Suffolk and Rochford. On 21 September Wolsey was commanded to surrender the Great Seal and retire to Esher. Just over two weeks later, on 9 October he was formally charged with a breach of praemunire.

The injustice of this charge, and the conviction which followed it, was matched only by its effectiveness. In spite of his status as a prince of the Church the Cardinal's position in England was utterly destroyed, and the temporalities of all his benefices were forfeit to the king. If Henry had ever been in any doubt about the extent of his power over the English Church, Wolsey's fall must have removed it. However, hardly had this decisive action been taken when the king relented, and the vultures which had been gathering round the fallen minister were temporarily dispersed. His praemunire was pardoned, and some part of his goods restored. Unfortunately Wolsey could not reconcile himself to exclusion from power, and his intrigues to recover the king's favour provoked his enemies to further action against him. In April 1530 he was commanded to withdraw to his Archbishopric, which he had never visited, and he seems to have nourished some hopes of making himself an influence in the north. A certain indiscretion in his relations with Chapuys, the

Imperial Ambassador, and perhaps a forlorn hope that the Pope would intervene on his behalf brought about his final downfall. His physician, Agostini, was arrested and confessed to carrying letters which were supposed to be soliciting intervention on his behalf. On 4 November he was arrested on his way to York, and commanded to return to London to face charges of treason.

As soon as it became known that further proceedings against him were intended, all sorts of enemies made haste to lay their accusations. 'Every man discloseth the rancour and malice that secretly before they carried in their breasts covered,' as a later writer expressed it.

> The nobility [he went on] . . . although they fawned on him outwardly, yet did they swell against him in envy inwardly. The gentlemen attending in the court for that little was to be had at the Prince their master's hands but by his means . . . bore mortal malice to him. The gentlemen of the country for that he earnestly laboured that the houses of husbandry which they had destroyed might be re-edified . . . desired his destruction.[18]

The charges varied from plotting rebellion to endangering the king's life by exposing him to the infection of smallpox. 'And so every man had one thing or another against him, but all would have it to be no less than treason. They feared lest if at any time he should be restored to the king's favour, he would not leave their malice unrevenged.' However, before any of these accusations could be put to the proof, Wolsey had passed beyond treason or rehabilitation. At Leicester Abbey on 29 November he died, and was buried in the Abbey church.

He was not an easy man to replace, as Henry had realised within a few weeks of his first exclusion from office, missing his well-informed and efficient services. Nevertheless, Henry had paid a price for these services. The Cardinal's omnicompetence had tended to cut the king off from his subjects, and particularly to cut the aristocracy off from the royal patronage, thus diminishing his 'good lordship'. Although he had to some extent screened Henry from unpopularity, this in itself had disadvantages, in that men were readier to resist policies when they believed them to be a minister's rather than the king's. This happened over the 'amicable grant', and it is hard to see how the

[18] 'Chronicle and defence of the English reformation' in *The Papers of George Wyatt*, ed. D. Loades, Camden Society, 4th series, V, 144-5.

policies of the early 1530s could have won acceptance if they had not obviously emanated from the king himself. As long as Wolsey was alive there were constant rumours of his return to favour, and his successors laboured uneasily in his shadow. Once he was dead, the pattern of government seems to have reverted temporarily to that which had existed before his rise, with an inner group of the Council carrying the main burden of business. This group consisted of Norfolk, Suffolk and Rochford, along with the new Chancellor, Sir Thomas More, and the king's secretary, Stephen Gardiner, who became Bishop of Winchester in December 1531. There was one important difference, however, from the pre-1515 period, and that was the part played by the king. Henry was passionately concerned to win his matrimonial freedom, and for about three years after Wolsey's fall acted as his own chief minister, trying one expedient after another to get his own way.

It was this determination, more than anything else, which brought the so-called 'Reformation Parliament' into existence in November 1529. The laity, and particularly the Commons, had lost none of their anti-clerical potential since 1515. If anything their indignation had waxed in the face of Wolsey's manifold abuses and his failure to undertake any practical measure of reform. Consequently they were only too willing to attack ecclesiastical jurisdiction, and to put the Church under pressure. Henry seems to have hoped that this would be sufficient to bring Pope Clement to terms. He would offer to restrain the hostility of Parliament in return for the desired annulment. However, Clement was not in a position to yield to this blackmail, even if he had wished to do so, since the sack of Rome by an Imperial army in 1527 had placed him virtually in the Emperor's hands, and Charles V for several reasons was determined to frustrate Henry's purposes. Catherine was his aunt as well as his staunch political ally, and the Emperor was anxious to prevent the possible understanding between England and France, which Henry was seeking to strengthen his bargaining position. As a result the king soon found himself facing an *impasse*. From statutes against such traditional grievances as excessive probate and mortuary fees, and clerical pluralism, the king and his advisers progressed to selective praemunire proceedings against individual prelates and clergy. At the end of 1530 general charges under the Praemunire Acts were launched against both Convocations, upon the specious ground that they had acquiesced in Wolsey's Legatine authority. Strange as these charges were, the leaders of the English Church were in no position to resist. For generations English bishops had been virtually appointed by the Crown, and the sees used to reward loyal and zealous civil servants. Men such as Warham and Tunstall had looked to the king all their lives, and their habits of obedience did not readily change. In January 1531 the Convocations submitted and agreed to pay fines totalling £118,000.

Meanwhile Henry had been seeking for another way out of his dilemma. In 1530 his agents in Rome had been instructed to search for documentary evidence proving that the English Church was subject to the papacy only in matters of heresy. They were unsuccessful, but dark hints were soon being dropped in diplomatic circles about the Imperial status of England, and the pre-Augustinian origins of its religion. It was soon to be argued openly that Christianity came to England with St Joseph of Arimathea and was officially accepted by 'King Lucius' in the second century. If a favourable verdict in his 'great matter' could not be obtained from the curia, then perhaps some decision could be reached in England which might be made to serve the purpose. However, none of these threatening gestures produced a satisfactory reaction, and Henry did not yet see his way clear to put them into effect. Consequently the House of Commons returned to the charge early in 1532 with a comprehensive 'Supplication against the ordinaries', which contained sweeping condemnations of clerical jurisdiction and practices. Faced with the possibility of major legislation against them, the Convocations chose instead to throw themselves on the king's mercy by accepting a series of royal demands, which in effect surrendered the jurisdictional autonomy of the English church. The surrender took place on 15 May 1532, and the following day Sir Thomas More, who had used all his influence and ability to dissuade the bishops from yielding,[19] surrendered the Great Seal.

[19] Professor Elton has argued that More was fully committed to opposing the king's policy over the Submission, and did his best to create an opposition group in the House of Commons. *Studies in Tudor and Stuart Politics and Government*, I, 155–73. There is also a good deal of evidence to suggest that, in spite of the weakness of their position, resistance was stiffening among the bishops in the weeks before the crucial decision was taken. M. Kelly, 'The submission of the clergy', *Transactions of the Royal Historical Society*, 5th series, 15, 97-119.

CHAPTER 6

THOMAS CROMWELL AND THE CRISIS OF AUTHORITY

I see no cause why any man should be offended that the king is called the Head of the Church of England rather than the Head of the realm of England . . . the Church of England consisteth of the same sorts of people at this day that are comprised in this word realm of whom the king is called the Head. Shall he not, being called the Head of the realm of England, be the Head of the same men when they are named the Church of England (Stephen Gardiner, *De vera obedientia oratio*).

THE BREAK WITH ROME

The controversial work of the 'Reformation Parliament' made it a controversial assembly, both at the time and since. Eustace Chapuys, who was totally committed to the cause of Queen Catherine and whose sources of information were not always reliable, believed that the members had been intimidated or bribed into doing the king's will. Twenty years later, when he was preparing to repeal its statutes, Stephen Gardiner claimed that it had been 'cruelly constrained' to reject the papal authority. In the reign of Elizabeth the violently partisan biographer of John Fisher alleged that '. . . The Common House was so partially chosen, that the king had his will almost in all things that himself listed'.[1] Even the chronicler Edward Hall, who was himself a member, asserted that the House was full of the king's servants. However, all these writers had their own reasons for wishing to impugn the integrity of the decisions reached between 1529 and 1536, and in fact the elections seem to have been conducted on exactly the same lines as those for any other Parliament in the preceding century. In the counties, where a uniform franchise had been established in 1430, the seventy-four knights of the shire were selected in accordance with the struc-

[1] Richard Hall, *The Life of John Fisher*, 68.

ture of the local aristocratic hierarchies. Where a county was dominated by a single great family, both the members would be its nominees. Where the leadership was less clear cut there was normally prior agreement for a suitable division, as in this case between the Greys and the Hastings in Leicestershire. Only in the event of great complexity, or irreconcilable feud, would there be a genuine electoral contest. Thus the king's influence over the county elections was almost entirely second hand and depended upon which of the magnate and gentry families were most firmly attached to the court.

In the boroughs, from which the great majority of the members came, there was much greater variety. In this Parliament 236 members represented 117 boroughs,[2] ranging from the wealthy and independent City of London to the grass grown ruins of Old Sarum. The more important the town the more likely it was to be represented by its own burgesses, and these members would not normally be committed to anything except their own interests. At the other end of the scale many small and poor boroughs were only too glad to surrender one or both their seats to nominees of neighbouring magnates, who would agree to serve without wages. It was here that the direct patronage of the Crown could sometimes be effective, and a royal official of humble standing and promising ability be provided with a place. However, in the majority of cases the Crown benefited only indirectly, through aristocratic families which either were, or could be made to feel, committed to royal policies. At a later date, and even in bye-elections to this parliament, the decisive voice in this process would be that of the leading minister, but in October 1529 there was no leading minister, and no clear cut policy to attract commitment. The 'invasion' of the borough seats by gentry was not a new phenomenon. It had been going on since the early fifteenth century, in spite of periodic attempts to impose residence qualifications, but it does seem to have become rather more pronounced in this Parliament. Younger sons and influential lawyers were the principal beneficiaries of this development, and the presence of the latter in increasing numbers in the lower House was to be a fact of great political significance. Biographical information is available for almost a hundred borough members in this Parliament, and of these about

[2] Two members from each enfranchised borough, except London which sent four.

a half were resident merchants and administrators. The remainder were country gentry, lawyers and courtiers in approximately equal proportions. By the end of the century the proportion of genuine burgesses would be down to about one-sixth. For the most part the county members were men well known both in their counties and at court. The borough members tended to be one thing or the other, except in those rare cases where a prominent gentleman occupied a borough seat for some special reason, as Sir Ralph Ellerker did at Scarborough, or Sir John Seymour at Heytesbury.

There were undoubtedly royal servants in the House of Commons, and clients of men high in the king's confidence, but the pattern of legislation cannot be explained in terms of an induced or enforced subservience. Opinion about the 'Great Matter' was deeply divided, but Parliament was never called upon to express a direct decision over what was, and remained, an ecclesiastical cause. Catherine was generally popular, and Henry's treatment of her was widely criticised at all levels; but the urgent need to settle the succession, and the prevailing temper of anticlericalism, made the majority of members perfectly willing to harry the Church in the king's interest. The 'Supplication of the Commons against the ordinaries' was probably a government measure in its final form, but it accurately reflected lay hatred of canon law and ecclesiastical courts. If anything the Commons were disappointed with the submission of the Convocations, because it contained no guarantee of reforms in this direction, beyond placing the whole matter at the discretion of the king. The true significance of this submission was probably understood by very few on either side, since jurisdictional quarrels between kings and popes were frequent, and the legislative authority of the Parliament had not been invoked as it had been in the statutes of Praemunire. Apart from the acts of 1529 which we have already noticed, the only measure which had taken a statutory form before the crisis came to a head at the beginning of 1533 was that proposing to restrict the payment of Annates. In retrospect this appears significant, but at the time, with its conditional implementation and mendacious preamble, it was no more than another attempt to enforce the pope's co-operation.[3]

[3] 23 Henry VIII c.20. The preamble complained that '. . . it is well perceived by long approved experience that great and inestimable sums of money be daily conveyed out of this realm to the impoverishment of

The submission of the clergy should be seen in the same light.

The decisive moves were not made in Parliament, but at court and in Rome. In August 1532 the irresolute hostility of Warham was ended by his death. A swift and bold solution to the problem now seemed both necessary and possible. By the end of the year legislation was already being planned, and Anne Boleyn was known to be pregnant. In January 1533 Henry nominated to the see of Canterbury a man well known as an advocate of his cause, Thomas Cranmer. Incredibly, in the circumstances, this nomination was accepted by the pope without demur in February, and Cranmer was duly consecrated in the following month. Clement was certainly warned of the danger of this appointment, but chose to ignore the warnings, apparently out of a misguided desire to do the king of England some service which was within his power. Within a few days of his installation, Cranmer wrote to Henry requesting permission to hear and determine the 'great matter', and the king replied in a letter which showed that his ideas had advanced considerably since the previous May. He described the Archbishop as enjoying his spiritual jurisdiction within the realm 'by the sufferance of us and our progenitors', making no mention of the papal confirmation which he knew perfectly well Cranmer had secretly repudiated. It was a delicate matter for a subject to cite his sovereign before a court the authority of which derived, by implication, from the sovereign himself. Such a questionable proceeding needed the largest possible demonstrations of support, and it was for this purpose that the Parliament was called upon to pronounce the Archbishop's court competent.

The Act in Restraint of Appeals, which received the royal assent at the beginning of April, was very much an occasional measure. In spite of its flamboyant preamble, it did not define a consistent jurisdictional position, and did not even clearly exclude the appeal which Catherine herself had lodged four years previously. A draft proposal which would have had the effect of putting the Parliament itself in the position of judge was never

the same, and especially such sums of money as the Pope's Holiness, his predecessors, and the court of Rome by long time have heretofor taken . . .'. This represented a popular myth, in fact the sums concerned were insignificant.

implemented,[4] and the members may well have felt at the time that they had committed themselves to nothing which had not been the common currency of political discussion for the previous two years. The Convocations were less equivocally placed, and their submissions of the previous year now took on a new significance. They were not called upon to discuss the general issue of jurisdictional relations with the papacy, but to give a specific opinion upon the canon law of the marriage. Although this was not officially a judgment of the case, no more than a handful of the assembled clergy had the courage to follow Bishop Fisher's lead and defend the original papal dispensation.[5] On 5 April, after a long debate the southern Convocation declared by a large majority that Henry's union with Catherine had violated a divine law from which no pope could dispense, and a few days later the northern assembly followed suit, although with rather greater reluctance. In doing so they had obeyed the king and disregarded the inhibition which the pope had placed upon such discussions *lite pendente*. Thereafter there seemed to be no reason to fear the concerted opposition of the representative institutions of either the clergy or the laity, and on the 10 May Cranmer opened his court of Dunstable. Catherine consistently refused to recognise his authority, and two weeks later the inevitable judgment was pronounced against her. The king was free to acknowledge that he had already re-married, and it gradually became apparent that in the process of satisfying his conscience, Henry had taken a step of incalculable importance for the future of the English Church.

When the news of Cranmer's action reached Rome, the king was immediately ordered to take back his discarded wife upon pain of excommunication, and it was only at this juncture that it seems to have been understood in the curia that the situation in England had implications far beyond the particular case in dispute. In July the payment of ecclesiastical taxation virtually

[4] Scarisbrick, *Henry VIII*, 311. There were two draft bills before the final version. *Letters and Papers*, VI, 311, (4) (5).

[5] Pope Julius II had granted this dispensation in 1503 for Prince Henry to marry his brother Arthur's widow, on the assumption that the first marriage had been consummated. Henry later claimed, on the basis of Leviticus xvii, 16 and xx, 21, that such a union was contrary to Divine Law, and that the pope had acted *ultra vires*. For a full discussion see Scarisbrick, 163-97.

ceased when the conditional act against Annates was activated by Letters Patent. In September the suspended sentence of excommunication took effect, and shortly afterwards Henry issued his appeal to a General Council, which had been prepared before, for use as a last resort. Henry claimed throughout that since the pope's own authority was an issue, he could not properly judge the case, and this appeal acted to some extent as a lifeline, connecting him with the traditional framework. It is very doubtful whether the king expected, or wanted, such a council to meet. Thereafter continuous negotiation was at an end, and it became necessary to make provision for the government and functioning of the Church, which suddenly found itself cut off from its ancient roots. In the two parliamentary sessions of 1534 a series of acts was passed for this purpose. The submission of the clergy in 1532 was given statutory confirmation, thus formally acknowledging the role of the king in the making of canon law. All papal taxation was diverted to the royal coffers; the Archbishop of Canterbury was authorised to issue all ecclesiastical licences and franchises; and provision was made for the appointment of bishops by the king. Finally the Act of Supremacy set out explicitly the claims which Henry had in fact already made good, declaring the king to be in every sense the earthly Head of the English Church.

Whether by accident or design, the government's tactics in this crisis had spreadeagled the opposition. Anne Boleyn's unpopularity was very great, both among the courtiers whom she affronted, and among the common people who openly abused her as a 'goggle-eyed whore', but there was no such general condemnation of Henry's bold defiance of the pope. Anticlericalism, and a widespread feeling that the papacy had done, and would do, no good in England to a large extent neutralised the discontent caused by the 'divorce' itself. We have already seen that dislike of Wolsey had encouraged a tendency to look to the king as the protector and reformer of the Church. This, together with the fact that few people either understood or felt strongly about the issues involved, confined opposition to the royal supremacy to a small number of intellectuals and religious conservatives.

What the government very rightly feared was the appearance of any respected leader who might disturb this somewhat puzzled acquiescence, and awaken the piety of the nation on the pope's behalf. This did not happen, partly because the pope himself gave no lead, partly because the foreign aid which would have been essential for success was not forthcoming, and partly because of the severity with which potential agitators were treated. The best known of these at the popular level was Elizabeth Barton, the so called 'Nun of Kent'. She was a woman with a long and undistinguished history of prophetic utterance, who in 1527 had taken it upon herself to warn the king of the iniquity of his matrimonial plans. As Henry persisted, a group of Canterbury clergy led by Dr Edward Bocking induced her to give a more political flavour to her prophecies. If Henry married Anne Boleyn, she declared, he would cease to be king in the eyes of God, would be deposed, and would die a villain's death. These were dangerous words, not because there was any specific reference to the supremacy, but because they were designed to transform the animosity against Anne Boleyn into a political weapon for the reversal of royal policy. In July 1533 the nun and her principal adherents were arrested, and their inflammatory propaganda effectively suppressed. All seven hundred copies of *The Nuns Book* were seized and destroyed before they could be distributed. Later in the year the Council denounced her as a fraud and a harlot, and she was hanged along with five of her supporters in April 1534.[6]

Elizabeth Barton's fate was intended to be more than a warning and the Council cast its net wide in the hope of implicating others of Catherine's friends. John Fisher, her most outspoken advocate, was convicted of misprision of treason, and an attempt to implicate Sir Thomas More was frustrated only by the scrupulous correctness of his dealings with the nun. More was no demagogue, but he was respected for his learning and integrity, and was known to be a deeply committed opponent of the king's policies. The praise of humanist and catholic biographers has tended to conceal the fact that he was looked upon both at home and abroad as the one man capable of stirring up his fellow-countrymen to frustrate Henry's purposes. Whether he could in fact have done so is beside the point. The government

[6] These six were condemned by Act of Attainder, not by common law (25 Henry VIII c.12). This Act contained a long propaganda section denouncing their crimes, and a proviso that it should be proclaimed, but the offence for which they suffered did not actually become treason until later in the year. G. R. Elton, 'Treason Law in the Early Reformation', *Historical Journal*, II, 2, 211-36.

can hardly be blamed for denying him the opportunity. In April 1534 he refused to take the oath of the succession and was imprisoned in the Tower. Later in the same year the 'malicious' rejection of the king's title of Supreme Head was made treason by statute, and More was brought to trial under that Act and convicted. Vindictive as Henry's treatment of him may have been, there is no doubt that as the law stood at the time of his trial, he was guilty. If there was any injustice in his condemnation, it was because his own view of the situation was correct and the statute itself was 'directly repugnant to the Law of God'. The issue was one of such fundamental importance that no agreement is ever likely to be reached upon it, since the whole nature of the positive law was in question. More's death aroused widespread indignation, but it was overshadowed, particularly in the eyes of continental observers, by the almost simultaneous execution of John Fisher. Fisher, Bishop of Rochester and a newly created Cardinal, was a prince of the Church, and a man of fiery and dangerous eloquence. Unlike More, he was guilty of treason in its traditional definition as well as under the terms of the recent act, since in 1533 he had secretly appealed to the Emperor to use force in defence of the papal cause.

Considering the magnitude of the revolution which was being wrought, the number of those who suffered death for their opposition was not great – about one hundred in all.[7] At the same time many of those who died were not, as More, Fisher and Elizabeth Barton were, politically significant. The brutal treatment accorded to the Carthusians of Syon and a number of other humble people both clergy and laity was justifiable only on the doubtful assumption that the commons were on the verge of general rebellion. In fact these people probably suffered not because of the danger which they represented, but because Henry would tolerate no wilful defiance once it had come to his attention. Some fled abroad to avoid an intolerable pressure upon their consciences, but they were few in number by comparison

[7] G. R. Elton, *Policy and Police*, 387. 110 people are known to have been executed for various treasons (exclusive of rebellion) between 1532 and 1540, while another 17 probably were. Of these nearly 40 died for riots and conspiracies which did not directly result from opposition to the king's policies, while in 15 cases the nature of the treason is not known. Counting all the doubtful cases, the maximum number of victims for opposing the 'great matter' is 88. Another 12 died in prison.

with the religious refugees of the next generation. Reginald Pole, scholar and royal kinsman,[8] and Richard Pate, who absconded from a diplomatic mission, were the most important. For most Englishmen of all classes the crisis petered out in the kind of grumbling which is so frequently reflected in the court records of the period. There was no rebellion, and although some of the aristocracy, such as the Earl of Shrewsbury, managed to avoid paying court to Anne as Queen, they were not prepared to run the risk of conspiracy, let alone of overt action.

PROPAGANDA AND CONTROL

The failure of the opposition to crystallise in 1533-4 was due in part to the complex nature of the issues, which could not produce the kind of straightforward defiance which had been so effective in 1525, and in part to the thoroughness of the government's methods. This can be seen at all levels, in the management of parliamentary business, in the sharp increase of official propaganda, and in the speed and efficiency with which rumours of sedition were followed up and prosecuted. Such thoroughness would have been impossible under the kind of junta which succeeded Wolsey and must be attributed to the emergence of another chief minister with exceptional gifts – Thomas Cromwell. Cromwell was a common lawyer by training, who had begun his career in the Cardinal's service, but had survived his master's fall without discredit and by 1531 was already rising in the confidence of the king. He entered the Council as a humble official about the end of 1530, and two years later, without having received any appointment of the first rank, was Henry's most influential adviser. It is unlikely that he originated the policy which culminated in the royal supremacy, because Henry was not the kind of man to be led in such a matter. On the other hand he was a master of ways and means, and having perhaps assessed the direction in which the king's mind was moving, set himself to remove all those impediments, legal and psychological which lay in his path.

Being much less conventional than his master, he felt no personal qualms in making a complete break with the papal juris-

[8] Reginald Pole was the third son of Sir Richard Pole and Margaret, Countess of Salisbury, the daughter of George, Duke of Clarence. He was licensed to live and study abroad in 1532, but earned Henry's undying enmity by writing *Pro Ecclesiasticae Unitatis Defensione* in 1536.

diction, but realised that if such a step was to be accomplished peacefully it required the most careful formulation. Hence the emphasis upon the alleged usurpation by the papacy of powers traditionally and properly belonging to the English crown. Both to the lawyer and to the common man precedent was of the greatest importance, and the best way to persuade either to accept a new situation was to represent it as the revival of an old one. This method had the great advantage of presenting a cut and dried argument which was at once flattering to national pride and gratifying to anticlerical prejudice. In addition every measure brought before the Parliament was drafted and re-drafted to minimise controversy, and to draw determined opponents of the policy into the open. It would be idle to pretend that the members were not under pressure, but it was a pressure of management and argument rather than of bribery or coercion. The decision to use statutory instruments to change the jurisdictional status of the English Church, on the other hand, need not be attributed to Cromwell. Statute had long been recognised as the most authoritative form of pronouncement available in positive law, and the king did not need Cromwell to tell him that if such a course was to be taken, it must be taken by that means. The possibility of declaring the autonomy of the English Church by purely ecclesiastical means, that is through Convocation, was not considered because of the need for lay support, and because Henry had no desire to create an English patriarchate.

Before 1530 England had seen very little in the way of organised propaganda. The two most significant achievements of that art had been the successful attribution of the troubles of the 1450s to the usurpation of Henry IV, and the skilful denigration of Richard III. In each of these cases the principal instrument had been the spoken word; orations before Parliament, sermons, and tales and rumours for popular consumption. In the latter case, also, the process was aided by the fact that Richard had already acquired a reputation for 'frightfulness' before his death. The new art of printing was scarcely used at all before 1520, and the first to realise its potential impact were not the servants of the government but the religious reformers. We have already seen how quickly censorship became a problem, but neither Wolsey nor the king himself seems to have drawn any lessons from that development. Henry's tract on the sacraments, printed in 1521, was intended as a contribution to a learned theological debate, and was not for popular consumption. When the divorce issue first began to create tension between England and Rome, it was again the religious reformers who first saw the possibilities of the situation. Any enemy of the pope was potentially a friend of reform, and William Tyndale's *Obedience of a Christian man*, published in Antwerp in 1528, went a long way towards advocating the absolute authority of the temporal ruler over laity and clergy alike.[9] Little as he might approve of their theology, Henry could not afford to suppress the pungent anticlericalism of Tyndale, or of Simon Fish, whose scurrilous *Supplication of the beggars* of 1529 opened up a whole new range of propaganda possibilities. By the time that the king was ready to take decisive steps to secure control over the English Church, a wide variety of arguments, legal, historical and pastoral, were already circulating on his behalf.

Some of these were actually employed in the preambles of the relevant statutes, and it is clear that Cromwell was swift to appreciate their value. Once a course of action had been decided upon, no persuasion was neglected to make it acceptable. The lawyer Christopher St German's *Doctor and Student*, advocating the severe limitation of ecclesiastical autonomy, a dialogue first published in 1530, went through four editions in 1531 including two from the royal printer Thomas Berthelet. In 1532 another work by the same author *Spirituality and Temporality*, also received two printings, while the anonymous *A Glass of the Truth* provided a further strongly worded defence of the king's 'divorce'. Thereafter each year of the decade saw a fresh batch of books and pamphlets defending Henry's proceedings at every level from the philosophical to the frankly popular. Some of these were the work of humanist scholars such as Thomas Starkey and Richard Morison, who accepted Cromwell's patronage when the English humanist movement divided and some of Erasmus's disciples followed Sir Thomas More into opposition.[10] Some were written by leading ecclesiastics like Stephen Gardiner and Cuthbert Tunstall, who were placed under the strongest

[9] Tyndale, like all protestants, reserved ultimate authority to 'the word of God', that is the scriptures, but the difficulties which this was to create for the royal supremacy were not at first apparent.

[10] For a consideration of the split in the English humanist 'movement' and its consequences, see J. K. McConica, *English Humanists and Reformation Politics*.

pressure, not merely to add to the stream of argument but also to provide convincing evidence of their loyalty to the crown. Among these was Gardiner's *De vera obedientia*, which was probably the ablest intellectual defence of the royal supremacy.[11] Also in 1535 appeared the first English translation of the *Defensor Pacis* by the fourteenth century antipapalist Marsilius of Padua. Where the contents of these books were directed to serious reasoning, and not to mere abuse of the clergy, or of Catherine and her friends, they tended to follow two lines, one functional, the other historical. The functional argument started by accepting the institution of a visible Church, and then proceeded by a series of scriptural citations or *a priori* assertions to the conclusion that the purposes of this Church were concerned with the life to come, and it could therefore have no 'lordship' in the present world. This being so the rule of the Church was merely an aspect of the rule of each Christian society, and was therefore vested in the head of that society, to wit the Prince. The historical argument also accepted a visible Church, but claimed that in its primitive purity it had admitted no single Head save Christ, and that the pretensions of the Papacy were a comparatively late corruption, for which Gregory VII was usually blamed. Since, however, God had not intended anarchy in his Church, he must have intended it to be ruled by the civil magistrates – *quod erat demonstrandum*.

There was certainly an element of disingenuousness in some of this propaganda, but much of it was sincere enough, as far as it went. It is intellectually unsatisfactory, not because it was dishonest but because it was groping tentatively to fit a theory to an existing situation. Whatever might be pretended, the royal supremacy was in fact a new development, and many of its implications had still to be worked out. For instance, although it was quite clear that the king was claiming and exercising the ancient *potestas jurisdictionis* of the Church, it was not certain how far he was claiming the *potestas ordinis*, the spiritual func-

11 Gardiner, who had supported the divorce project from the beginning, was deeply disturbed by the resulting attacks upon the Church, and had played a leading part in compiling the 'Answer of the ordinaries' to the commons 'Supplication'. Under pressure he reconsidered his position and saved his career by writing *De vera obedientia*. In this work he tried to maintain a delicate balance between the royal supremacy and traditional doctrinal orthodoxy, which was to prove untenable in the following reign.

tions which included excommunication and the administration of the sacraments.[12] Hitherto the canon law had always been accepted as an aspect of the divine law, but now it was 'the Pope's law', and of no authority except in so far as it was confirmed by the king. How, in these circumstances, was the divine law to be defined – and could it exercise any effective control over the vagaries of the positive law? Also, there were more tangible and immediate problems. Was the supremacy personal to the king, or was it exercised in conjunction with the Parliament, representing the will of the Christian society? Did the Bishops derive their spiritual as well as their temporal authority from the king? And above all, what control did the Supreme Head enjoy over the doctrine and worship of the English Church? Many of these questions took a long time to answer, and the limitations of official Henrician theory were to be ruthlessly exposed in the period after 1547. 'As they be distinct in places, so they have distinct ministers and divers heads in earth', declared the authoritative *King's Book* of 1543, '. . . yet be all these holy Churches but one holy Church catholic.' This was not a view which commended itself to Hooper, or Ridley, or the later Cranmer. Nevertheless, considering that so much of it was produced by authors writing from hand to mouth, this propaganda was both coherent and effective. It provided adequate intellectual covering for those who did not wish to expose themselves to the king's wrath, and respectable arguments to quieten officious consciences. At the more popular level it also succeeded in presenting the king as the defender and protector of his subjects against those clerical frauds and oppressions from which they believed themselves to have been suffering for so long.

Not all Cromwell's propaganda came off the printing press. He also made extensive use of reforming preachers, such as Hugh Latimer, who, if they could steer clear of blatant heresy, made extremely effective advocates for the supremacy. Their passionate sincerity commanded respect, and their eloquence was superior to anything that the conservative churchmen could produce. Although they were soon to have grave reservations about

[12] Henry himself never claimed the power to administer any sacraments, and the *Bishop's Book* of 1537 explicitly renounced any claims to consecrate clergy. However, Cranmer was prepared to make that claim on the king's behalf, under certain conditions, and his view was echoed in *King's Book* of 1543. D. Loades, *The Oxford Martyrs*, 43-7.

Henry's performance as a Godly Prince, the majority of them remained fully committed to the doctrine of non-resistance and insisted that obedience was due to the king as a matter of the highest religious duty. 'Obey him . . . ,' urged Latimer, 'and that for conscience.' The king was God's servant, and answerable to Him alone for his doings. 'The office of a magistrate is grounded upon God's word, and is plainly described of St Paul, writing unto the Romans, where he sheweth that all souls, that is to say all men, ought to obey magistrates for they are ordained of God.' As we shall see, this did not amount to a doctrine of total subservience, and fully fledged protestantism later turned out to be a very two-edged weapon in the hands of the secular authorities, but in the context of the 1530s these preachers, who were not yet acknowleged protestants, made a substantial contribution to what has been called the 'cult of authority'.

At the opposite end of the scale, the suppression of dissent was a matter of equal concern. It became high treason to write or publish any work against the king's title, or against each rearrangement of the succession. At the beginning of 1536 a proclamation ordered the surrender and destruction of all works by John Fisher and other pro-papal writers, and at the same time suppressed those venerable nuisances the pardoners, who were still hawking indulgences around the superstitious and ill-informed. In November 1538 the machinery of censorship was further developed. No English book printed abroad was to be brought into the country on pain of forfeiture of goods and imprisonment, and no new book was to be printed in England until it had been examined and licensed by some of the Council, or others appointed. Eventually, in July 1546, a sort of index was established, prohibiting the works of eleven named authors. These proclamations made clear the delicacy of the king's position. He never abandoned his hostility to the doctrines of Luther, and the works of protestant writers such as Bilney, Barnes and George Joye shared a common condemnation with those of papalists like Fisher and Pole. It is hard to say how effective this censorship was. Protestant works continued to come into the country in fair numbers, and several cases before the Council indicate that production in England also continued, but the records of punishments and prosecutions are very fragmentary. There are virtually no references to the smuggling or production of Romanist propaganda, and it seems likely that this was never a serious problem. Disapproval of the king's proceedings from this side was more commonly verbal, and the records of King's Bench are liberally sprinkled with the indictment and trials of such offenders. The treason Acts of 1534 and 1536 had given additional emphasis to the law in this direction, and the incidence of cases was very much higher than in any previous period. They varied greatly in seriousness, from the old man trudging to Worcester market who blamed the inclement weather upon the king's unnatural goings-on, to the Prior of Lenton near Nottingham, who in 1538 declared of Henry,

> The devil is in him, for he is past grace; he will never amend in this world. I warrant him to have as shameful a death as ever king had in England. A vengeance on him.[18]

The frequency with which such utterances resulted in trial and punishment reflected both the extent of the problem and the vigilance of the authorities. We have, of course, no means of knowing how large a risk these careless talkers ran, but there are plenty of illustrations of the way in which the machinery of apprehension worked. For example in 1535 a certain David Leonard, an Irishman working in Somerset, delivered himself of some unflattering opinions of Anne Boleyn. John Horsey and Robert Hill, two local craftsmen, reported his words to the tithingman of a nearby village, who in turn informed the justices of the peace. The latter ordered Leonard's arrest, informed Cromwell, and requested instructions. Stories of this kind make it clear that the government enjoyed a fair measure of co-operation at all levels. In the great bulk of the delations and letters which investigations of this kind produced, there is a striking assumption on the part of Cromwell and those who served him that ordinary subjects would do their duty in reporting disaffection, and on balance it would seem that this confidence was justified. Cromwell's concern with proceedings of this kind was persistent and meticulous. His influence with the king, which was paramount from 1532 to 1539, made him a good master to serve, and he used the immense ramifications of his patronage to build up an information service far beyond any-

[18] P.R.O., KB 9/542/11. Seven other monks of the same house were involved in this treason, and were tried and convicted with him, although it is not clear how many were actually executed. P.R.O., KB 29/171/31. For a further consideration of this case, see Elton, *Policy and Police*, 350, 359 n. 4.

thing that Wolsey had achieved, and not equalled again until the days of Cecil and Walsingham. Whatever he may have done with the central administrative machinery, Cromwell was no legal innovator. Except for the extensions to the treason law which we have already noticed, his aim was to enforce the law as it stood, by maintaining a constant pressure upon commons and gentry alike to use the channels of communication and prosecution which were open to them. This can be seen in the Chancellor's addresses to the judges and justices of the peace, and in Cromwell's own enormous surviving correspondence. No case was too small for his attention, and his attitude is well illustrated in a letter written by Lord Sandys in 1538:

> I should commit them [the suspects] to ward or else take surety for their forthcoming when they should be called to answer for their offences . . . and then to advertise his lordship [Cromwell] with the depositions, which should be seen and answer made for the order of such persons, being indeed or thought offenders.

Every hint of treason was pursued, and like Wolsey, Cromwell acquired a reputation for listening at every man's keyhole. He was hated by some and feared by many, but his efficiency ensured that criticism of the king's policies was kept under control and did not generate a dangerous political opposition.

The main instruments of this control were the courts of common law. Unlike his predecessor, Cromwell had no affection for the civil law, and was not reluctant to wrestle with recalcitrant juries, or run the risk of acquittal through defective indictments. In a number of recorded cases treason proceedings failed for one or other of these reasons, and it is certainly not true that conviction on that charge was a foregone conclusion.[14] Attempts were made to improve the efficiency of common law processes, but these were more in the interests of ordinary justice than to prevent the escape of putative traitors. Juries might still be corrupted or overawed by local interests, and in such cases remedy could be provided by the court of Star Chamber. For instance, when Sir Matthew Browne persuaded the sheriff of

[14] There are records of over thirty acquittals in cases of treason between 1532 and 1540, either through 'favour of the jury' or through technicalities. For instance one Robert Lenton, accused in 1536 of possessing popish books, got off because his indictment did not repeat the place and county of his domicile when relating his offence. KB 27/1113/Rex 14. Elton, *Policy and Police*, 305, 387.

Surrey to impanel a jury which would acquit a servant of his named Hanley, and followed this up by offering the jurors bribes, he was prosecuted before the Council. Star Chamber continued to be mainly concerned with party issues, and where cases were initiated by the Crown it was usually for this sort of reason, rather than because there was any question of sedition. In 1538 a plan was drawn up to extend the jurisdiction of Star Chamber by giving it the task of receiving charges from the 'inferior courts of inquisition', such as the leets and hundred courts, but this proposal, which would have involved a curious amalgam of equity and common law, never seems to have been put into effect. On the whole the evidence suggests that Cromwell and his agents were punctilious in their observance of legal forms, but ruthless in their determination to bring offenders to trial, no matter whether the charge was treason, murder or felony. In the present state of our knowledge it is very difficult to say how far the general administration of the law improved during this period, but the increase of 'governance' which is so noticeable in the field of political discipline was certainly reflected in the treatment of other disorders, crimes and misdemeanours.

REVOLUTION IN GOVERNMENT

The 1530s were a decade of extensive re-organisation in the machinery of the central administration, and thanks to the work of Professor Elton the name of Thomas Cromwell has become firmly associated with the concept of a 'revolution in government'. In this aspect of his work, Cromwell was not so much an innovator as a systematiser. Bureaucratic methods of the kind which he applied had been used before, but hitherto their use had been interspersed with periods of intensely personal government, such as the reign of Henry VII. After 1540 there was no return swing of the pendulum, so that the continuous evolution of the modern Privy Council and Secretaries of State can be traced from Cromwell's reforms. If, as seems probable, he was responsible for making permanent a type of bureaucratic government which had previously appeared only intermittently, then the term 'revolution' is an appropriate one, and the importance of the achievement can hardly be overstressed. Early in 1534 Cromwell became Principal Secretary, an office of household origin which had already become politically significant in the hands of Stephen Gardiner. This position he turned into the hub of the administration, building up a clerical staff on the lines of a modern department, which acted as a clearing house for every conceivable kind of public business. Knowledge creates power, and the information which was constantly passing through the Principal Secretary's hands gave him an unchallengeable supremacy in the council, as well as his effectiveness in the kind of police work which we have already examined. He was also responsible at a later date for the re-organisation of the financial administration in the wake of the royal supremacy, erecting the Court of First Fruits and Tenths to handle the revenues then coming from the church to the crown, and the Court of Augmentations to control the great landed wealth acquired from the dissolved religious houses. The Courts of Wards and of General Surveyors were also established on a more formal basis to oversee the feudal revenues, and those derived from the existing royal estates. These Courts not only checked peculation and concealment, they also covered the country with a new network of royal officials, Surveyors, Receivers, Auditors and others. The existence of such posts added a new dimension to the Crown's patronage and created as many additional sources of information and agents of control.

The legislative programme of the Parliament from 1533 to 1539 was the heaviest which had ever been seen and remained unsurpassed until the nineteenth century. In managing this programme, and initiating much of it, Cromwell not only displayed great skill as a tactician, but also a considerable amount of political idealism. In his eyes statute was not merely the highest instrument of the positive law, but the pronouncement of a sovereign authority. By 1540 it had become in effect no less, because although political theorists refused for many years to surrender the concept of a divine or natural law superior to that of the state; in practice after the repudiation of the Roman jurisdiction that superior law was simply defined to suit the requirements of current policy.

As we have seen, the government of the Church was reorganised in a series of Acts, and Cromwell became Viceregent in Spirituals, presiding at Convocation and exercising extensive ecclesiastical patronage in the king's interest. At first it had seemed that the royal supremacy would make little difference to the routine business of ecclesiastical administration, but

Cromwell's sympathy with the reformers soon resulted in attacks on clerical pluralism, reductions in the number of feast days, and most important of all, the appearance of an authorised English translation of the bible. It also resulted in a wholesale attack upon the monasteries. Whether this policy originated from Cromwell or from the king himself is not clear, nor is it quite certain when the crucial decisions were taken. When the royal commissioners were sent out early in 1535 to conduct a general visitation and assessment of these houses, it seems to have been the government's intention to prune and reform, rather than to abolish. However, as the visitation progressed the tone of Cromwell's instructions changed, and it became clear that it was the commissioners' duty to find fault.[15] Perhaps the king had decided that in the parlous state of his finances, nothing less than a wholesale appropriation would be acceptable. It may also have been feared that such establishments were centres of popish intrigue, although the vast majority of the religious had taken the oath of supremacy without objection. According to a later story, Cromwell had not originally intended to proceed against the monasteries by statute for fear of the repercussions, but was overruled in the Council. If this is true, the actual procedure adopted may have been a compromise. In 1536 all those houses worth less than £200 a year were dissolved and their property taken into the king's hands, on the specious grounds that the small establishments had decayed and became corrupt, while true religion still flourished in their larger neighbours. In 1539 the remainder fell, ostensibly because the religious vocation had collapsed, but in fact because the great majority of priors and abbots had surrendered their houses in the face of bribery and threats.

A vast landed wealth thus came into the king's possession, equivalent to about 10 per cent of the entire landed wealth of the country. Had this been converted into a permanent endowment for the Crown, the whole subsequent history of the English monarchy might have been different. Instead, the bulk of it was sold between 1540 and 1560, mostly at a fair market price, (about twenty times the clear annual value) and passed into the hands of the aristocracy and country gentry, with incalculable

[15] For a full consideration of this visitation, and the change of policy which it involved, see M. C. Knowles, *The Religious Orders in England*, III.

consequences for their economic and political power. The financial benefit to the Crown was thus great, but evanescent. On the other hand the opportunities for patronage were not neglected, and it has been asserted with some truth that by distributing the profits of this spoliation as he did, Henry created a vested interest in the royal supremacy which doomed all counter-revolutionary attempts to failure.

The absorption of the ecclesiastical jurisdiction by the Crown was undoubtedly the greatest single augmentation which the royal authority had ever received, but within two years it was followed by another, less dramatic but still of great importance. We have already seen that most of the great secular franchises, such as the Earldom of Chester and the Duchy of Lancaster had long since fallen to the Crown by the course of feudal law, and that there were precedents from the late fifteenth century for the termination of lesser franchises by statute. In 1536, taking advantage of the success which had attended the acts against the pope, Cromwell launched a great statute for the resumption of all franchises and liberties 'appertaining to the imperial crown of this realm (which) have been severed and taken from the same by sundry gifts of the king's most noble progenitors.' Another Act swept away the Welsh marcher lordships, and placed the whole of Wales under the normal English shire government of sheriffs and justices of the peace. From the 1st July 1536 'all original writs and judicial writs and all manner of indictments of treason, felony or trespass, and all manner of process to be made upon the same' ran in the king's name alone. Thanks to the royal supremacy, the great liberties of the Church fell with the rest, although the Bishopric of Durham was to retain the empty shell of its palatine status for another three hundred years.

By the end of 1536 the realm of England was jurisdictionally united as never before under the authority of the king, and the complex hierarchy of powers which had checked and limited the medieval monarchy had disappeared. Men at all levels of society were to become increasingly aware of the intrusive presence of the central government, and they frequently did not like it. This dislike was particularly strong in the north, and, as we shall see, contributed largely to one of the most dangerous rebellions of the century, but Cromwell was not deterred and energetically followed up in the localities the centralising policy which he had formulated in parliament. Like Wolsey, he sought to build up groups of gentry in direct dependence upon the Crown to combat the influence of the great border families. This was not, however, a straightforward policy and involved a great deal of manœuvring among conflicting loyalties. For instance in the West March, where the most powerful figure at first was Lord Dacre, the Crown tended to favour the Cliffords and deliberately increased the power of such Percy dependents as Sir Thomas Wharton. In the East March, where the sixth Earl of Northumberland was predominant, the royal patronage was not directly used against him, because the Earl himself fell heavily under the king's influence, and made Henry his heir when he died in 1537. Here the concern was mainly to prevent the Percy interest from slipping into the hands of younger and more energetic members of the family such as Sir Ingram Percy, who bitterly distrusted Cromwell's insidious tactics.

Perhaps the best example of the way in which a new situation was developing in the north is provided by the fall of Lord Dacre in 1534. In the course of a feud with Sir William Musgrave, Dacre became involved in a highly dubious relationship with the Armstrongs of Liddesdale and certain other Scots, whom he incited to attack Musgrave's lands. News of this reached London, and Dacre was charged with high treason. However, for this charge to be good in law, a true bill would have to be found in Cumberland, and a commission was appointed to sit at Carlisle and investigate the charges. Both this commission, and the two juries which presented the formal indictments were well staffed with royal clients. Wharton and Curwen, Lowther and Musgrave, were not merely willing to do the king's will, but with the king's support had become strong enough to challenge the traditional dominance of Dacre or Clifford. In the event, Dacre was acquitted by his peers, but this owed nothing to his local strength. The Earl of Cumberland became Warden of the West March, and it was left to Dacre to recoup his fortunes as best he could by studious loyalty during the forthcoming rebellion. Significantly, when it seemed likely that the Dacre estates would become forfeit to the Crown, hopeful letters began to reach Cromwell out of Cumberland, asking to be 'remembered'. The fall of the great northern abbeys, such as Holm Cultram, produced a similar response, which indicates that the ancient distinction between the marches and lowland England was becoming blurred.

The collapse of the Pilgrimage of Grace[16] enabled this process to be carried a stage further. The northern Council, which since 1530 had been a feeble body with its jurisdiction confined to Yorkshire, was reconstituted and its authority transformed. It became an independent council, established by royal commission, with both equity and common law jurisdiction over the whole of the north. As such it was a bureaucratic machine, controlled from the centre, and competent to handle all kinds of offences. It was not only a northern Star Chamber, but also, being armed with commissions of the peace and of oyer and terminer, could try felonies and treasons, wielding the penalties of death and forfeiture. The members of this Council were for the most part lawyers and administrators, with a proportion of local gentry and headed by a Lord President who was either an ecclesiastic or a nobleman of proven reliability. This institution, with its flexibility and wide powers, was to prove a valuable instrument of government policy, but it did not cure the problems of the north, and at times of crisis such as the rebellion of 1569 was liable to be brushed aside. Nevertheless, in conjunction with the slow transformation being wrought in northern politics by the pressure of Crown patronage, it brought about a marked improvement in the general governability of the region.

As we have seen, the similar council in the marches of Wales had been reconstituted in 1534, but its authority was greatly extended by the statute of 1536, which gave it competence in all the seventeen shires of Wales, Monmouth, Hereford, Shropshire, Worcester, Gloucester and Cheshire. Like its northern counterpart, it was both a local Star Chamber and a court of common law, but in 1543 four Courts of Great Session were set up by statute to exercise common law jurisdiction in Wales, which greatly reduced its function in that direction. After the abolition of the marcher lordships, the lawlessness of Wales lost what little political significance it still possessed and became almost entirely an administrative problem, with which this Council coped in a methodical and unspectacular fashion for over a century.[17] Cromwell obviously believed in the value of local

[16] See pages 185-6.

[17] Alone of the conciliar courts, the Council in the Marches was re-established in 1660, and not finally abolished until 1689. Its history in the seventeenth century was much less controversial than that of Star Chamber or the northern Council.

councils wherever a region seemed to present special difficulties, and in 1538 tried the same methods in the south-west. The problem here may have been the rather artificial fear of magnate disaffection, stimulated by the so-called 'conspiracy' of the Marquis of Exeter, or it may have been the vulnerability of the area to foreign invasion. Certainly the local justices were slack and needed more direct oversight, but this did not necessitate the establishment of a council, and Cromwell simultaneously provided for this by securing the appointment of one of his most valuable and efficient servants, Richard Pollard, as sheriff. For whatever reason the Council in the West may have been established, it must soon have been judged superfluous since within ten years it had disappeared, leaving only a handful of session records behind it.

The career of Richard Pollard serves as a reminder that even the best institutions could do no more than contribute to the effectiveness of government. As in the north, so over the remainder of the country, Cromwell's success depended more upon a network of local patronage and a well informed control over the commissions of the peace than upon his celebrated constitutional engineering. To this extent his power was as personal as that of Wolsey or Henry VII had been, but the changes which he made in the machinery of government nevertheless had the effect of somewhat diminishing the importance of personalities in the future. Nowhere is this more evident than in the Council itself. Unlike Wolsey, Cromwell made no attempt to monopolise the business of advising the king and seems rather to have encouraged increased formality and the regular attendance of a defined body of councillors. These men were for the most part office holders, such as Sir Thomas Audley the Lord Chancellor, the Duke of Norfolk and the Earl of Wiltshire. They formed a small and compact group of working administrators who met wherever and whenever required, which commonly meant every day either at court or at Westminster. As long as his power lasted, Cromwell's was the dominant voice, but when he fell in 1540 the reformed Council continued to function along the lines which he had laid down and kept a formal written record of its business. In the 1540s and thereafter we can see it keeping a close watch on sedition, overseeing the work of commissioners and other royal officials, supervising defence and the garrisons of Berwick or Calais, and intervening with increasing frequency in the affairs of the Church.

From about 1536 onwards it is proper to speak of the Council as an institution, and although its effectiveness continued to depend heavily upon the personality of the monarch and the abilities of the individual councillors, it never lost that character and never ceased to function, even under the most adverse circumstances. At the same time the institutional evolution of Star Chamber was also completed, and it can be seen as a body distinct from the Council proper, or Privy Council as it may now be called, but staffed by the same men under the character of judges. Although the Privy Council never ceased to handle suits and petitions in a quasi-judicial manner, the great bulk of this work had now transferred to Star Chamber, and in this respect Cromwell did little more than recognise the practice of his predecessor.

THE PILGRIMAGE OF GRACE

In many ways, therefore, Thomas Cromwell was a successful minister; perhaps, in view of the difficulty of the tasks which faced him, the most successful to serve any Tudor monarch. Above all he was a master at winning consent to the king's controversial policies, and the magnitude of this achievement can best be judged by looking at the point where his persuasiveness and vigilance most conspicuously failed, the great northern rising known as the Pilgrimage of Grace. There was no single cause of the Pilgrimage, in the sense that taxation was the cause of the rising of 1489 or the demonstrations of 1525. Among the commons the dissolution of the monasteries was generally unpopular, and had given rise to a whole crop of rumours about the confiscation of church goods, while the proposal to introduce registers of births and marriages aroused fears of new taxation. In some places there were particular grievances against grasping landlords, and always in the background the incalculable fear of strangers and outsiders, in the shape of royal commissioners and other government agents, interfering decisively in the traditional social and religious life of the region. This last was also a factor motivating the aristocracy, although in their case the resentment was more likely to be directed against a particular individual who had secured the benefits of royal favour, or against Cromwell himself, who was generally regarded as the king's evil genius. The aristocracy were also greatly exercised about the Statute of Uses, which had been passed in 1536 for the purpose of putting an end to that convenient device and enforcing strict entails upon estates held by knight service. They complained with some justice that the north was seriously under-represented in Parliament,[18] and that their interests had not been considered. Operating upon this assortment of discontents were the efforts of many petty demagogues and preachers, political leaders calculating their own advantage, and the pursuers of private quarrels. Over all, perhaps the most important single factor in the later stages, was the personality of Robert Aske; but it was the situation which turned Aske into a leader, not he who created the situation.

The movement began at Louth in Lincolnshire at the end of September 1536, the immediate cause being the appearance of the royal commissioners for the subsidy voted earlier in the year. During the first week in October there were spontaneous risings of the commons all over the shire, risings in which the clergy played a prominent part, and towards which the attitude of the gentry was ambivalent. Later on these gentlemen were to claim that the fury of the commons had taken them unaware, and that they had lent countenance to the rebels out of fear. The truth seems to have been rather different. In spite of the stigmas hurled against them by royal propaganda, many of these men were familiar with the court and with the real intentions of Cromwell's policies, which for the most part they opposed. They also resented the intrusion of royal favourites, particularly the Duke of Suffolk, into the landed hierarchy of the county.[19] In fact they were more than willing to take advantage of the popular demonstrations as a means of coercing the government into a change of policy. Consequently they encouraged their servants and dependents to join in, and were easily persuaded to draw up the Articles of the movement which were approved by a mass gathering of over 10,000 men at Lincoln on 7 October. Only about eighteen gentlemen were actively involved, but many more must have been sympathetic, because there was virtually

[18] The nine northern counties, Northumberland, Cumberland, Westmorland, Lancashire, Yorkshire, Cheshire, Derby, Nottingham and Lincoln, possessed between them only fifteen enfranchised boroughs; fewer than the single southern county of Wiltshire. Durham was not represented at all.

[19] M. E. James, 'Obedience and dissent in Henrician England: the Lincolnshire rebellion of 1536', *Past and Present*, 48, 1-78.

no attempt to suppress the demonstration, and the sheriff, Edward Dymocke, professed himself completely helpless. The king was understandably suspicious of this helplessness. In his intructions to the Duke of Suffolk, appointed Lieutenant to deal with the rising, he urged him to discover 'if it be likely that so few villeins and labourers could have stirred or raised, in despite of so many gentlemen, their own tenants against themselves or us'. 'Many of the gentlemen,' he considered, 'be not as whole as they pretend.'

At the same time, these men had no desire to be rebels or traitors. Their professions of loyalty to the king were sincere as far as they went. They wanted to get rid of Cromwell and to reverse many of his policies, but when it came to the point they were not prepared to appear in arms against their lawful sovereign in order to achieve these aims. When Henry's unequivocal rejection of their demands reached Lincoln on 10 October, they gave up and sued for pardon. Significantly, in spite of some bitter complaints on the part of assembled commons, the latter accepted this decision and dispersed, which would hardly have been the reaction of an uncontrollable *jacquerie*. Nevertheless the king, or Cromwell, wisely decided to accept the pleas of coercion, and the rising became officially represented as the fury of 'the rude and ignorant people' stirred up by a few erring priests and monks. This interpretation was clearly reflected in the judicial proceedings which followed. Ninety-five tradesmen and labourers were convicted of high treason, and some twenty-five clergy, among whom the canons of Bardney and the monks of Barling featured prominently. Among the gentry only Sir John Hussey and Thomas Moigne, the Recorder of Lincoln, were considered to have committed offences too flagrant to be overlooked. Hussey and Moigne were executed along with the more prominent clergy, and about forty of the rank and file.[20]

In isolation the Lincolnshire disturbances would have been of only secondary significance, but in the event they detonated a very much larger explosion. The men of Horncastle had been the first to march behind the banner of the five wounds of Christ, but the same symbolism had an immediate appeal across

[20] The pardons of about twenty are recorded in the King's Bench Rolls, and Elton records some thirty-five others. *Policy and Police*, 387; P.R.O. KB 29/171/39.

the Humber in the East Riding, where the men of Beverley were mustering as early as 8 October. In this region Robert Aske, a lawyer and a Percy dependant of strong religious idealism, immediately emerged as the leader, although he later denied responsibility for the original assembly. There was no organised opposition, and by 13 October the companies from the East Riding and Marshland were marching to York, where the citizens had already declared for them. There Aske issued a proclamation which struck the notes to be consistently echoed through the remainder of the rising.

> For this pilgrimage we have taken it for the preservation of Christ's Church, of this realm of England, the king our sovereign lord, the nobility and commons of the same, and to the intent to make petition to the king's highness for the reformation of that which is amiss within this his realm.

At the same time he sent to the mayor of York a copy of the pilgrim's articles, which listed five demands: that the dissolved religious houses be restored; the Statute of Uses repealed; the fifteenth recently voted by Parliament remitted; 'low born' councillors around the king (particularly Cromwell and Sir Richard Rich) dismissed; and certain bishops suspected of heresy removed from office. At this stage there was little to distinguish this movement from that in Lincolnshire, which had just collapsed, but within a few days the news arrived of further risings in Northumberland, Durham, Cumberland, and the North and West Ridings. Everywhere these had the appearance of spontaneous outbursts among the commons, and it is true that the grievances over gressoms[21] and border tenures, enclosures and rack renting had combined with religious apprehensions to produce an explosive mixture. Nevertheless it is the aristocracy who provide the keys to an understanding of the situation. Two years previously Chapuys had believed that a number of northern lords including Lord Darcy and the Earl of Derby were seriously disaffected and would be willing to co-operate with an Imperial invasion. Such an invasion was not a practicable proposition, and Chapuys was always too sanguine, but he certainly had some first hand evidence to support his ex-

[21] A 'gressom' or ingressum was a fine paid by a tenant to his lord on entry to his holding. These fines were supposed to be defined by the custom of the manor, but some lords had been taking advantage of the weakness of custom to exact higher fines.

pectations.[22] At the same time, whatever Aske and his colleagues might think about their Pilgrimage, no one who knew Henry could doubt that he would regard involvement in such a movement as treason, and the greater the offender the more unforgiveable the offence.

Consequently the aristocrats who became deeply involved tended to be men of the second rank, like Sir Thomas Percy and Sir Christopher Danby, and the gentlemen everywhere followed the example of their Lincolnshire brethren by going through an elaborate charade of coercion before taking the pilgrim's oath. Of the five northern Earls two, Westmorland and Northumberland, remained somewhat equivocal in their attitude. Both professed their own loyalty but either allowed or could not prevent their kinsmen and dependants from joining the rising. The other three, Cumberland, Derby and Shrewsbury, committed themselves to the court after only the briefest hesitation. These decisions were of the greatest importance, particularly the latter two. The fact that Derby was able to prevent the pilgrims from making any significant headway in Lancashire, and that the conservative Shrewbsury could keep much of south Yorkshire quiet, casts a significant light on events elsewhere. The sweeping success of the rebellion in Northumberland, Durham and North Yorkshire must have been due in no small measure to the leadership, covert or otherwise, of servants of the Percy and Neville interests. In Cumberland the Clifford Earl was an unpopular figure on account of his harsh estate policy, and his service to the Crown was virtually confined to holding Carlisle. The pilgrim musters at Penrith and Kirby Stephen seem to have been led by local clergy, but in this region the operation of the Dacre interest is an imponderable factor. Lord Dacre himself had no stomach for further risks, but his servants and dependants were by long tradition hostile to the Cliffords, and it seems unlikely that their animosity would have slept through the rising. In Westmorland the commons may have been genuinely on their own, since the only brief surviving description of their grievances is confined to gressoms, taxes and religious houses, and they claimed explicitly, 'we accept no gentleman of our council because we be afraid of them.'

By the 20 October Aske had a massive force of some thirty

[22] R. B. Smith, *Land and Politics in the Reign of Henry VIII* (the West Riding of Yorkshire), 169-70.

thousand men near Pontefract, and it seemed that the whole of the north was supporting him. On the 21st Pontefract castle yielded to him, and a considerable number of gentry, including Lord Darcy and Sir Robert Constable joined the rebel council. South of the Don the Duke of Norfolk and the Earl of Shrewsbury had only about eight thousand men under arms, and there were extensive rumours of disaffection in the south. In fact the pilgrims were poised at precisely that point where a decisive military success could have swept them triumphantly forward. But neither Aske nor Darcy was seeking such a victory. Like other rebels before and after, they denied that they were traitors, or that they had any intention of harming the king or his estate. Unlike some, they were also sufficiently sincere to allow their opportunity to slip away. Time was against them, as it is against all commanders who have to keep large forces inactive. Also, their demands had grown a good deal more elaborate since the York articles, and had come to include such matters as the renunciation of the royal supremacy and the rehabilitation of the Princess Mary,[23] which were beyond the reach of possible concession. That Aske should have hoped to gain his way upon issues of this kind without defeating the king in the field showed a degree of naivety incompatible with the political leadership which he was exercising and reveals startlingly how fragile the political resources of the pilgrims really were. Henry instructed Norfolk to temporise and agreed to receive a deputation consisting of Sir Ralph Ellerker and Robert Bowes. To them he vigorously defended his policies and promised a general pardon in return for submission. Meanwhile the truce which had been established in the north at the beginning of November was wearing thin. Rumours that royal forces were mustering, and the appearance of Richard Morison's forthright *Remedy for Sedition* seemed to offer no promise of satisfaction. Nevertheless Aske's pacific policy prevailed, and when Ellerker and Bowes returned on 21 November, they declared themselves satisfied of the king's

[23] There was some fear that Henry's statutory tinkering with the succession might let in the Scots claim. Article 3 ran, 'Item we most humbly beseech our dread sovereign lord that the lady Mary may be made legitimate and the former statute therein annulled, for the danger of the title that might incur to the crown of Scotland, that to be by Parliament.' *Letters and Papers*, XI, 1246.

good faith and mercy. A further pilgrims' council met at Pontefract on 2 December and drew up a definite list of twenty-four articles, which ranged from the royal supremacy and the succession to the petty extortions of escheators. What the king offered was very much less: a general pardon, and a Parliament to meet wherever and whenever the rebels wished. To this Norfolk added on his own initiative an undertaking to allow the abbeys to stand until such a Parliament had met. These terms the pilgrims accepted, partly because they trusted Henry's good faith, but also because it was now clear that they could gain no more without resort to arms. Many of the commons were not satisfied, but by this time their numbers had greatly diminished and no leader emerged who was willing to continue the struggle. On 8 December Lancaster Herald proclaimed the royal pardon, and they dispersed to their homes.

The rebellion was over, and the king had committed himself to very little. On the other hand he had been unable to punish a massive, if temporary defiance of his authority. There must have been many men in the north in December 1536 who wondered whether Henry was really prepared to forgive such a dangerous demonstration. One of these, Sir Francis Bigod, trusted the king's mercy so little that he preferred the doubtful security of a revived insurrection. Bigod was a protestant who had no time for the pope or the old religion, but who strongly objected to the centralising policies of the government, and believed that the king's promises of pardon and redress were alike worthless. In mid-January 1537 he led a small rising in the East Riding, which collapsed within a matter of days and served only to precipitate the vengeance which he had feared. Only in Cumberland, where the impatient commons sought to revive the situation of October by attacking Carlisle, was there any response to Bigod's initiative. Without gentry leaders this riot was easily suppressed, but between them Bigod and the men of Cumberland had given the government sufficient pretext to embark upon a policy of sharp repression. The Duke of Norfolk declared martial law in the West March, and during the spring there was a systematic round-up of leaders of the original Pilgrimage. Over one hundred and thirty executions followed, including Darcy, Aske and Sir Thomas Percy as well as Bigod. There was not a flicker of resistance, and by the summer of 1537 the king's position in the north was stronger than at any time hitherto. As we have seen, the Council of the North was reorganised in that year, and in July the Earl of Northumberland died, leaving the Percy inheritance in the king's hands.

As if to emphasise this augmentation of his strength, Henry appointed Sir William Eure as Warden of the East March and accelerated his policy of relying on loyal gentry families, commenting that 'we will not be bound of a necessity to be served with lords. But we will be served with such men of what degree soever as we shall appoint to the same.' No previous king could have said as much, and it was not an idle boast, but an ironic comment on the recent massive attempt to repel interference with the northern way of life. The failure of the Pilgrimage may have been due as much to its leaders as to the king, but the benefit to the central government was significant and lasting.

CHAPTER 7

HENRY VIII AND HIS LEGACY

Yet this I note concerning rebels and rebellions, although the devil raise them, yet God always useth them to his glory, as a part of his justice. For when kings suffer their under officers to misuse their subjects, and will not hear nor remedy their peoples wrongs when they complain, then suffereth God the rebels to rage, and to execute that part of his justice that the partial prince would not. (*The Mirror of Princes.*)

THE FALL OF CROMWELL

Henry's confidence in Cromwell does not seem to have been shaken at all by the powerful evidence of his unpopularity which the Pilgrimage provided, yet within four years he had fallen, the Statute of Uses had been virtually repealed, and a strong reaction against 'heretic' ideas was in progress. In 1543 the Princess Mary was placed again in the order of succession, behind Jane Seymour's son, Edward (born 1537), but ahead of Anne Boleyn's daughter, Elizabeth (born 1533).[1] It could be said, therefore, that the rebellion indirectly achieved several of its aims; and the cost to the aristocracy had not been high, except in the case of the Percies. Many of those who had covered their participation with a thin cloak of coercion, like Sir Thomas Tempest, or Edward Dymocke in Lincolnshire, were later to do the Crown good service, and receive prominent marks of favour. However, it would be too simple to conclude that the king appreciated the force of the rebels' argument, and discreetly gave ground as soon as he could do so without appearing to yield to threats. This may have been true in the case of the Act of Wills of 1540, which emasculated the Statute of Uses,[2] but the religious reaction and

[1] 35 Henry VIII, c.I. This Act did not specify the succession beyond Elizabeth, but in Henry's Will, stamped on 30 December 1546 it was provided that, in the event of all his children dying without heirs, the crown was to pass to the descendants of his younger sister, Mary (the 'Suffolk' line). Thus the descendants of his elder sister, Margaret (the Scottish line) were excluded, as the pilgrims had demanded.

[2] For full and conflicting accounts of these two Acts and their im-

the fall of Cromwell were almost certainly brought about by the international situation, and the rehabilitation of Mary did not remove the provision to which the pilgrims had most objected, that in the last analysis Henry should be empowered to bequeath the crown by will.

When the threat of the rebellion was over, Henry's reaction was not to seek for points which he could gracefully yield, but to tighten his security arrangements. The reorganised Council of the North was a product of this determination, and so was the Council of the West. So too, in a different way, was the fall of the Courtenays and Poles. These two families represented the last sprigs of the White Rose. Henry Courtenay, Marquis of Exeter, was the son of Catherine, a younger daughter of Edward IV, while Margaret Pole, Countess of Salisbury, was the daughter of George, Duke of Clarence. In happier days, before he began to embark upon dangerous and controversial policies, Henry had shown no suspicion of these families and had accorded them every mark of favour. However, the zealous papalism of Reginald, Margaret's exiled son, and the sympathy of the ladies of both families with Catherine of Aragon, brought them into danger.

When it began to be whispered in the south-west that Courtenay was the true heir to the throne and would 'bring better days', the king and Cromwell decided to act. Sir Geoffrey Pole, Reginald's younger brother, was arrested in the late summer of 1538 and seems to have been terrified into making incriminating statements about all his relations. As evidence of treasonable intent these were flimsy enough – reports of cryptic conversations and country gossip – a mere hint of association with the Emperor – but in the circumstances they were sufficient. On November 4 the Marquis and Lord Montague, Margaret's eldest son, were arrested, and the French Ambassador reported,

> Il y a bien longtemps que ce Roi m'avait dit qu'il voulait exterminer ce maison de Montague, qui est encore de la Rose Blanche, et de la maison de Pole dont est le Cardinal.

The two peers were brought to trial on 2 and 3 December, convicted, and executed on the 9th. On the 4th December, Sir Geof-

plications, see J. M. W. Bean, *The Decline of English Feudalism*, 270-302, and E. W. Ives, 'The genesis of the Statute of Uses', *EHR*, 82, 677-695. On balance, Ives has the better of the argument.

frey Pole, Sir Edward Neville and three lesser men were also convicted, although Sir Geoffrey was later pardoned and left to the tender mercies of his own conscience. In all these cases strict legal propriety was observed, but it is clear that the victims' fate was determined by who they were rather than by what they had done. This was even more clearly the case with the Lady Margaret herself, who would admit nothing, and against whom even her feeble younger son could not be induced to testify. An Act of Attainder was needed to condemn her in the summer of 1539, and it was two years after that before a minor 'White Rose' conspiracy in Yorkshire eventually brought her to the block.

Meanwhile, Henry's position in Europe became more and more perilous. In June 1538 Charles V concluded a ten year truce with his perennial enemy Francis I of France and thus for the first time created a serious possibility of combined action by the two great catholic powers against schismatic England. In December of the same year Pope Paul III took advantage of this favourable turn of events to promulgate the sentence of excommunication passed against Henry three years before, deposing him and absolving his subjects from their allegiance. Not surprisingly, Cardinal Reginald Pole was his most active and zealous agent in seeking to stimulate a crusade against 'the most cruel and abominable tyrant'. In January 1539 Francis and Charles entered into a pact not to negotiate separately with England, and Henry's attempts to win the sympathy of Scotland were frustrated by the return of Cardinal David Beaton. The early months of 1539 were dominated by the fear of invasion, but this strengthened rather than weakened the king's hold upon the country. Musters were held, defence works repaired and rebuilt, and Henry restlessly toured the scenes of activity. There were a few executions for treason, mostly of clergy for preaching against the royal supremacy, but no suggestion of an extensive 'underground movement' preparing to co-operate with the landing which was generally expected. It was one thing to criticise the king's policies, but quite another to aid and abet his foreign enemies.

At the beginning of 1539 Henry was completely without allies, a position which violated the most elementary principles of renaissance diplomacy. He therefore entered into negotiations with the protestant League of Schmalkalden, who regarded his advances with ill-concealed suspicion. Discussions commenced for the formation of an anti-papal consensus, but the Lutherans insisted upon a comprehensive confession of faith, and although some of the king's servants may have been willing to work in this direction, Henry himself would not budge. By the time that a Schmalkaldic delegation reached England in April any small hope of agreement which might have existed had disappeared because Francis I had broken his agreement with the Emperor, and re-opened direct communications with England, which Henry rightly understood to signal the breakdown of the temporary *entente*. By the summer Pope Paul had given up hope of his desired crusade, and Pole was recalled to Rome, his footsteps dogged by English spies and possible assassins.

In this atmosphere, Henry drew back from radical religious commitment, and the Duke of Norfolk introduced in the House of Lords his six theological questions which became the Act of Six Articles. These articles in no way modified the royal supremacy, but they did represent a sharp rebuff for those who had been hopefully seeing in the break with Rome a first step to the establishment of an evangelical Church on the Saxon or Swiss model. The passage of this Act in June 1539, after much heated debate, has been generally interpreted as a defeat for Cromwell, and the first serious crack in the edifice of his power. In fact, it is not quite clear where Cromwell stood, for although he had certainly patronised men of a reforming tendency, there is no proof of his opposition to this measure, either before or afterwards. After the Act became law, it was he who manœuvred the reforming bishops Shaxton and Latimer into resignation, and it was he who, in November 1539, was appointed by proclamation to supervise and control the publication of an authorised translation of the scriptures.[8] This, together with the unabated stream of anti-papal propaganda, indicates the very limited nature of the reaction. The Act of Six Articles was not a surrender to continental pressures so much as an attempt to allay the anxieties of conservative Henricians and strengthen the 'national front' against the pope. The summer of 1539 saw a crescendo of plays, pageants and interludes designed for the same purpose, crudely and boisterously mocking papal pretensions and glorifying the

[8] Hughes and Larkin, *Proclamations*, I, 286. A draft proclamation, of April the same year, had intended to set limits to the availability of English scripture, but it was never issued and Henry never actually yielded to conservative pressure on this point.

king. The Londoners, at least, seem to have enjoyed themselves hugely.

The same parliamentary session passed the controversial Statute of Proclamations, which has also been taken to indicate a weakening of Cromwell's authority. The Act as passed did little more than give a parliamentary stiffening to royal proclamations, in order to make them easier to enforce. Indeed it could be claimed to have extended the competence of Parliament into the field of the traditional prerogative, and thus to have been quite consistent with Cromwell's known predilection for statutory methods. On the other hand, there is some evidence to suggest that the eventual measure enacted was less radical than Cromwell had intended, and this has been interpreted to mean that the minister was rebuffed by the House of Commons and frustrated in his intention, which was no less than to elevate proclamation into a legislative instrument. The evidence of the parliamentary drafts is not conclusive, and this interpretation is mainly based upon the assumption that Cromwell was primarily concerned to extend the prerogative by any available means. Such an assumption would mean that his previous use of Parliament had been wholly opportunist, and this can not be convincingly maintained. The controversy is a vexed one, and involves the whole interpretation of Cromwell's career, but the balance of probability is that it was never his intention to give the king the power to legislate by proclamation, and the final form of the 1539 Act is therefore no indication that his power was tottering.

The minister's fall, when it came in June 1540 was sudden and to some extent mysterious. Certainly he had been largely responsible for the Cleves marriage, which had proved so bitterly disappointing, but Henry's own enthusiasm had been no less, and the king continued to desire a political understanding with the Lutheran princes, in spite of his dissatisfaction with the Lady Anne. In fact there are no signs of a major divergence in policy between the king and his minister, and there was no significant change of direction after the latter's death. The explanation must lie in the personal rivalries and animosities of the court. Cromwell had many enemies, including the religious conservatives, of whom Stephen Gardiner was by far the most able, and the Dukes of Norfolk and Suffolk, whom he had outdistanced in the political race in 1533 and 1534. These enemies succeeded in gaining the king's ear in the early part of 1540, but how they did so, and what arguments they may have used, can only be very imperfectly deduced.

Probably Catherine Howard, Norfolk's niece, was their main instrument, a vivacious and somewhat promiscuous young woman with whom the ageing king rapidly became infatuated after the fiasco of his marriage to Anne of Cleves at the very beginning of 1540. For a short time Catherine exercised the same kind of influence over Henry that Anne Boleyn had wielded at the height of her power, but she did not possess her predecessor's intelligence or judgement and was little more than a vehicle for her uncle. This, together with skilful insinuations of heresy, may have been sufficient to undermine the king's confidence in Cromwell. Like Wolsey, he had laid himself open to accusations of coming between the king and his subjects, and of controlling the royal patronage in his own interest, by the very efficiency with which he had performed his duties. Whether, in the crucial weeks of decision, Henry remembered the fury of the pilgrims and the need to be a 'good lord' to his peers can only be conjectured. Some of the charges which eventually appeared in the Act of Attainder, such as issuing commissions without the king's knowledge, and usurping the royal authority, together with the emphasis placed upon his base birth, certainly echoed the complaints of three years before.[4]

So powerful a man could not be brought down without a struggle, and Cromwell was not the victim of casual malice but of a carefully organised campaign. Early in April Marillac reported that 'the bishops' were coming back into favour, and that the minister was in serious danger. He added, significantly, that if Cromwell survived this crisis it would be on account of his diligence rather than his policy. The French Ambassador seems to have believed throughout that Gardiner and his episcopal supporters were the real protagonists against him, and there is very little evidence of the part played by the lay aristocracy. At the end of April, when he was raised to the peerage as Earl of Essex, it seemed that Cromwell had won, and he was certainly in full control of parliamentary business at that stage, but the violent

[4] Ostensibly these were the main charges, and read very like the old fashioned crime of 'accroaching' the king's power, but no attempt was made to bring a common law action on those grounds.

doctrinal disputes in both houses during May probably undermined his fragile triumph. By the first week in June the half concealed struggle was at a point of balance, the air was full of rumours and nobody knew who was most in danger. On 1 June Bishop Sampson of Chichester, an ally of Gardiner's, was suddenly arrested, and Marillac believed that five other bishops were about to share his fate. Instead, it was Cromwell who went to the Tower, arrested at the council board on 10 June. The same day a 'detection' of his treasons was made public, and copies sent to the king's envoys overseas.

Two days later the fallen minister wrote to Henry from prison a letter which strongly suggests the real basis of the king's indignation against him. In it he protested that he had never been either a traitor or a sacramentary, that is one who denied any kind of Real Presence in the eucharist. Henry had a positive horror of this radical heresy, which went far beyond the doctrines of Luther. As we have seen, the king had been fully engaged in negotiations with the Lutherans, and he had also played an active part in the latest outburst of theological disputation, so it could not be plausibly alleged that these things had been done without his knowledge. If, however, he could be convinced that Cromwell's real intention was to further the cause of the sacramentaries, then the latter's fall would be assured. This, it seems, was what happened and may explain Marillac's conviction that the bishops were the ringleaders, in spite of the obvious involvement of Norfolk and his family. Once out of power, Cromwell was hastened to his doom, not by trial but by Act of Attainder since the charges against him would hardly have stood the test of the common law, and executed on 28 July. Two days later the reformers Barnes, Jerome and Garret went to the fire at Smithfield, condemned by the same procedure for heresies 'the number whereof were too long here to be rehersed'. The victims themselves were uncertain of the charges against them, but the manner of their death and Barnes' hot denial of sacramentary and anabaptist opinions, links their fate with that of the fallen minister, and suggests that they suffered to give colour to the notion of a radical conspiracy.

Whoever may have played upon his prejudices, the responsibility for Cromwell's fall and death lay with the king. Age and sickness had made Henry increasingly irritable and unpredictable, and from this point on his formidable personality was neither guided nor restrained by any servant of the first rank. The political history of England in the last seven years of the reign is the history of the king's own moods: his doubts, his fears, and his aggressive search for renewed youth.[5] Primarily it is a history of wars and negotiations, but from our point of view these were years of administrative consolidation, of religious uncertainty, and of an increasingly imminent royal minority. No attempt was made to reverse the bureaucratic developments of the 1530s, and the disciplinary activities of the Council seem to have been augmented rather than abated. In the north the flourishing career of Lord Wharton, who became Warden of the West March over the head of the Earl of Cumberland in 1544, indicates the strictest continuity of policy. A lengthy proclamation of 8 July 1546 summed up nearly twenty years of press censorship, and nowhere is there any proof that Henry's undoubted personal control led to the repudiation of earlier achievements. This is as true of religion as it is of administration. In spite of Marillac's assertion that 'the old doctrines' were again in favour, the reaction was never more than half-hearted. A proclamation of May 1541 ordered the Great Bible to be placed in every parish church, and repeated attempts by conservative ecclesiastics failed to deprive Cranmer of the king's favour. Once the brief 'sacramentary' panic was over, Henry began once again to show favour to reforming ideas, and this tendency was accelerated after his marriage to Catherine Parr in July 1543. The conservative party never gave up and as late as 1546 scored a success in the case of Anne Askew, but their attempts to implicate the queen were unavailing.

Catherine was a sober, pious woman of humanistic learning and mildly reforming sympathies, whose influence over Henry in the last years of his life was very considerable. It was her unenviable task to rescue the king from the morose ruination of his last attempt at youthful passion after Catherine Howard's infidelities had been expiated upon the scaffold. She reconciled him to his elder children, and thus played some part in the final determination of the succession. Most important of all, by her patronage of reforming humanist scholars such as Roger Ascham and Sir John Cheke she helped to ensure the protestant education

[5] A useful and thorough examination of Henry's later years is *The Mask of Royalty* by L. B. Smith, although some of Professor Smith's conclusions are controversial.

of the young Prince Edward, a process which has left Henry's own doctrinal conservatism during these last years in some doubt. How large a part the queen played in the politics of the court is uncertain, but she was sympathetic to Edward and Thomas Seymour, the brothers of Queen Jane, and the former, who had been created Earl of Hertford in 1537, was the dominant figure at court by 1545.[6] The Duke of Norfolk had been badly shaken by his niece's fall, and was soon further weakened by the indiscreet behaviour of his son, the Earl of Surrey. In March 1543 a number of Londoners were examined by the Council for discussing the Howard family's claim to the throne, a topic which implied the gravest danger for the Earl himself, since it was linked with his name rather than his father's. The peril seemed to pass, but at the end of 1546, when Henry's days were obviously numbered, the Duke and his son were both struck down by charges of countenancing these very claims. Although Norfolk was saved from the scaffold by the king's own death, the power of his family was in total eclipse as the new reign opened.

THE MINORITY GOVERNMENT

The legacy which Henry bequeathed to his nine year old son was no easy one. Certainly, there was no open disaffection. The last conspiracy in the north, a plot to seize Pontefract early in 1541, had been effectively dealt with by the northern Council, and the king's great progress to the north later in the same year seems to have pacified or suppressed discontent there for a number of years to come. On the other hand the French and Scottish wars had so drained the treasury that by 1545 Wriothesley, the Lord Chancellor, and Paget, the Principal Secretary, were corresponding in tones of despair, and the disastrous expedient of debasing the coinage was resorted to.[7] This bedevilled the exchanges, so that Edward's Council was to find credit expensive and difficult

[6] Hertford was a successful soldier who had made his reputation mostly in Scotland. His brother Thomas is supposed to have paid his attentions to Catherine before she married Henry, and married her shortly after the king's death.

[7] Between 1542 and 1547 the wars cost over £2 million, at a time when the royal revenues (including sales of monastic land) were probably running at about £300,000 a year. By 1547 nearly £800,000 worth of monastic land had been sold, about two-thirds of the total acquired. By contrast, the suppression of the Pilgrimage of Grace had cost only about £50,000.

to obtain, and added to the hardships caused by the bad harvests of the middle 1540s. The French war was ended in the summer of 1546, but the Scots had succeeded in repudiating the terms imposed upon them after their defeat at Solway Moss in 1543, and the few Scottish lords who still favoured an English marriage for their young queen were in total disarray when Henry died.[8]

Most serious of all, the religious situation was highly unstable. Officially, the doctrine of the Church had been laid down by the Act of Six Articles and the *King's Book* of 1543, both conservative and orthodox documents. In practice the king had given considerable encouragement to the reforming party in the last months of his life, and at the time of his death they were completely in control. Gardiner, the only conservative prelate who might have stood effectively in their way, had been excluded from the 'regency council' by Henry's explicit decision, and there were no conservative peers of sufficient power to balance Hertford and Lisle,[9] who were of the new persuasion. Religious change was therefore generally expected, and the expectation had an unsettling effect both upon those who desired it and those who dreaded it.

Finally, there was the fact of the minority itself. No doubt attended Edward's title to the throne, but in spite of all his efforts Henry had not been able to hand on his crown to an adult son. His will, duly sanctioned in advance by Act of Parliament, laid down the subsequent order of succession clearly enough, but the fact remained that real dynastic security rested upon one life. The old king was aware of his failure, and did his best in his own imperious way to remedy the defect by providing for a body of executors of his own choosing to act as his son's Council. It was a forlorn hope. Not even a king as awesome as Henry had become could rule from beyond the grave, and the new régime had to do the best it could with its own resources to wield the formidably augmented powers which were

[8] Henry's intention had been to bring about the union of the Crowns on his own terms by persuading the Scots to marry the infant Mary to Prince Edward. His angry and violent reaction to Scottish attempts to escape from their treaty obligations caused this project to be termed 'the rough wooing'. See A. J. Slavin, *Politics and Profit; the early career of Sir Ralph Sadler* (Sadler was Henry's envoy in Scotland).

[9] John Dudley, son of Edmund Dudley. Restored in blood 1510, created Viscount Lisle 1542, Earl of Warwick, February 1547, Duke of Northumberland, October 1551.

the positive side of his legacy.

The shape of this régime was soon sketched out in a few significant actions. From the first it was clear that Henry's plan for a ruling Council of equal members was unworkable, and within a matter of days the leadership which Hertford had already enjoyed in the old king's lifetime was formally acknowledged in his elevation to the position of Lord Protector. Thanks to the co-operation of Paget he had been able to secure custody of Edward's person within hours of his father's death, and his accession to power was not seriously challenged. Also, in the first fortnight in February there was an extensive distribution of honours and appropriate endowments, ostensibly, and probably genuinely, planned by Henry. Amongst others, Hertford became Duke of Somerset, John Dudley, Viscount Lisle, became Earl of Warwick, and Lord Chancellor Wriothesley became Earl of Southampton. This last promotion is the strongest indication that Henry was really responsible, since Wriothesley was a conservative, and very soon after was deprived of his Chancellorship and his seat on the Council.

Most important of all, however, was the decision of the Council at the beginning of February that the jurisdiction of all bishops had lapsed with the death of the late king, and that new instruments should be drawn up in Edward's name, renewing their spiritual authority. This decision, which Professor Jordan has called a 'starkly Erastian interpretation of the Act of Supremacy', clearly reflects the influence of Cranmer, who had already stated in a private opinion to Henry that no form of consecration was necessary for a bishop, and resolved at a blow the doubts and uncertainties which had surrounded the authority of the episcopate since 1534. They were to be regarded simply as royal officials. To an alert conservative like Gardiner this action conveyed a sharp warning of impending change, and he took up the challenge swiftly in the hope of dissuading the Council from embarking upon a course of unforeseeable consequences for the fragile stability of a minority government.

In a long series of letters beginning in February and extending throughout the year, the Bishop of Winchester argued the dangers of religious innovation. First of all he pointed out to the Protector that he had a solemn duty 'to deliver this realm to the king at eighteen years of age as the king his father, whose soul God assoil, left it'. To introduce change, he went on, could only have the effect of weakening the royal supremacy itself, since the pope 'wanteth not wit to beat into other princes' ears that where his authority is abolished, there at every change of governors shall be change of religion'. Naturally, he objected to the terms of the new commissions, which implied that the bishops were mere delegates. He was not a delegate, he claimed, but an ordinary, that is one who had jurisdiction in his own right by virtue of his orders, and had always been so accepted under the old king. Gardiner never explicitly asserted that Edward's youth debarred him from the full exercise of the supremacy, he merely pointed out the unwisdom of making decisions of such vital importance, when the king might decide to reverse them on reaching his years of discretion. In a typical letter of 12 June he wrote

> A king's authority to govern his realm never wanteth, though he were in his cradle. His place is replenished by his Council, as we have now my Lord Protector. And yet it is a difference in the judgement of the people to direct and order things established, and to make in the highest innovations.

Up to this point the bishop had been arguing generally, but the Royal Injunctions of July 1547 gave him a more specific target at which to aim. These Injunctions were in no sense radical, but they did enjoin the readings of Cranmer's *Homilies*, one of which, 'On Justification', clearly taught the Lutheran doctrine of justification by faith alone. This, claimed Gardiner, was contrary to the teaching laid down in *The King's Book*, which had been authorised by statute as the standard of orthodoxy. Therefore the injunctions were a breach of statute law, and 'if any, although he be deputed by the king, do in execution of spiritual jurisdiction extend the same contrary to any Common Law or Act of Parliament, it is a praemunire both to the judge and to the parties, although it be done in the King's Majesties name . . .'. The king's task was to uphold the law, and it would be both a peril to the realm and an encouragement to seditious anabaptists if he should fail to do so. It ill became Cranmer, he concluded bitterly, to set such an evil example of disobedience to authority.

Gardiner's opposition to the Injunctions resulted in his imprisonment, but confinement did not interrupt his flow of protest and expostulation. In October he returned to the charge.

> If your Grace would have this for a precedent [he wrote to Somerset], that whatsoever the king's Council, for the time of a prince's minority shall send to be preached, must needs be

received without allegation, of what strength is the Act of Parliament against the Bishop of Rome?

The protestants called their fond opinions the law of God, he claimed, and sought to ride roughshod over the law of the land; they set up their private opinions against the public authority, and were thus a menace to the security of the state.

However, before the end of the year Edward's first Parliament had swept away the *King's Book* and the Act of Six Articles, thus destroying the legal foundation of Gardiner's argument and forcing the bishop to reassess the basis of his objections. This he certainly did with great reluctance, since a lifetime of royal service had given him a deep instinct of obedience, but during the next two years it gradually became clear that his concept of the royal supremacy was hedged about by more limitations than he had ever found it necessary to admit while King Henry was alive. Fundamentally he believed that the supremacy could only operate within the confines of traditional doctrine, even when there was no single visible authority to define what that doctrine was. To make the essential distinction between matters within the competence of the supremacy, and matters beyond it, he and his fellow conservatives made use of the reformers' concept of *adiaphora*, or 'things indifferent'. Thus matters of ecclesiastical jurisdiction, such as the appointment of bishops, the regulation of fasts, or even the abolition of monasteries and chantries, could be regarded as indifferent to salvation, while the preaching of justification by faith alone, or the denial of transubstantiation could not. Gardiner's legalistic arguments had been genuine enough up to a point, but the real reason for his opposition to protestantism was that he believed it to be false doctrine.

The legislation of 1549, which converted the official doctrine of the English Church to what was, from his point of view, heresy, therefore turned these arguments back upon him. The painfulness of this dilemma to one who was a lawyer and civil servant rather than a theologian was acute. In the summer of 1550 he was even prepared to accept the Prayer Book and the Act of Uniformity for the sake of his allegiance, but refused to subscribe to a set of articles admitting that they were 'good and godly', and that his former opposition had been wrong. For this refusal he was sequestered from his bishopric and eventually deprived, a series of events which finally drove him to renounce the royal supremacy altogether as soon as Mary's accession had made it safe to do so.

Gardiner was the leader of the conservative ecclesiastics, but he was not the only bishop to be deprived for his opposition to the religious policy of Edward's governments. Bonner of London, Day of Chichester, Heath of Worcester and Tunstall of Durham also failed to accommodate their consciences, and all likewise returned eventually to the papal obedience. With their defection the national catholicism of the Henrician church was extinguished and the royal supremacy became an exclusively protestant concept. Of course, those same laws and policies which made it necessary for the conservatives to re-think their principles of obedience, facilitated the righteous submissiveness of their opponents. 'The King's statutes and ordinances,' proclaimed Latimer, '. . . are God's laws, forasmuch as we ought to obey them, as well as God's laws and commandments.' 'The office of a magistrate is grounded upon God's work,' declared the same preacher on another occasion, 'and is plainly described of St Paul, writing unto the Romans.'

The Edwardian Church was every bit as much an instrument of government propaganda as that of Henry had been. Sermons, homilies and exhortations of every kind urged the sacred duty of obedience to the Prince, terming rebellion '. . . the puddle and sink of all sins against God and man'. So obvious was the alliance of convenience between the protestant divines and the secular politicians that the conservatives regarded the reservations of the former with pardonable scepticism. The king was not a pope, explained Latimer, because his subjects were not obliged to take what he did for an article of faith. 'The king and his Council may err; the Parliament Houses, both high and low may err.' This was all very well, but when the conclusion was that the subjects' duty in the event of such error was confined to passive protest, sceptics might be forgiven for seeing such protestations as mere face-saving formulae, designed to protect the 'professors of the Gospel' from the grim implications of total Erastianism. The sincerity and religious conviction which actually inspired them became evident only when political power had been stripped away.

The programme of liturgical and doctrinal change moved slowly at first. Before the first Parliament of the reign opened on 4 November 1547 only the Council decision of February and the Royal Injunctions of July had departed from the Henrician standard, and neither of these would have seemed particularly meaningful to ordinary people. Nor, indeed, did the Acts of this Parliament itself bring about many positive innovations. Except for that decreeing that bishops should be appointed by Letters Patent, they were mostly negative, sweeping away not only the Six Articles but also the statutory restrictions on printing and the anti-Lollard laws of the fifteenth century. The effect of these measures was not so much to create freedom as to encourage uncertainty and strife. At the same time the abolition of the chantries began the very rapid erosion of religious practices which were both widespread and popular. The Parliament of 1545 had passed a measure granting the property of these foundations to the Crown on the grounds of financial necessity, but it had not been implemented, and when it was reactivated two years later the pretext had significantly changed. The chantries were now 'superstitious', being based upon the 'false doctrine' of purgatory, and were swept away as popish survivals. Since this not only involved rich colleges and guilds, but also obits, 'lights' and the other humble pieties of the poor, the effects of this dissolution were felt and resented in every parish in the land.[10] It was not until March 1548 that Cranmer's English Order of Communion introduced the first liturgical change, and began to steer the Church towards a positively protestant position. There was then a pause of almost a year before the first *Book of Common Prayer* was authorised by Parliament, and it was not until June 1549 that the Act of Uniformity which had accompanied it came into force, and the English Church became for the first time officially, if mildly, evangelical.

Up to this point, religious policy had been the result of intimate collaboration between Cranmer and Somerset, but the latter's fall from power in October 1549 substantially changed the climate of the Privy Council. Briefly it seemed as though a catholic reaction would ensue, but for reasons of his own the man who had supplanted the Protector, John Dudley, Earl of Warwick, threw in his lot with the more radical reformers and combined with them to bring pressure to bear upon Cranmer and increase the pace of change. As a result the Prayer Book was extensively revised in 1552 to remove all traces of the Mass, which

[10] 1 Edward VI, c.14. For a detailed study of a regional sample of reactions see C. J. Kitching 'The distribution of Chantry property in the diocese of York' (Unpublished Ph.D thesis, Durham 1970).

was the radicals' principal abomination, and a new Act of Uniformity for the first time imposed penalties upon the laity for attending any other form of worship.[11] At the same time the government sought to lay its hands on all such church plate and other goods as had become 'superfluous' for the greatly simplified services of the new liturgy, thus dramatically fulfilling the predictions which had helped to stimulate the commons of the north to rebellion sixteen years before.

POPULAR REACTION TO THE REFORMED CHURCH

These changes inevitably caused opposition and discontent, which to some extent justified the warnings which Gardiner had originally uttered. But the disciplinary problems which faced the government on this account were neither as severe nor as widespread as might have been expected. Indeed, at the beginning of the reign it was protestant activists rather than conservatives who caused the most trouble. As soon as the news of Henry's death was known there was an outburst of iconoclasm in London, and the churchwardens of St Martin's in Ironmonger's Lane stripped their church of images to paint the inside walls with texts of scripture, 'whereof some were perversely translated'. In May the Council issued a proclamation against rumours of impending change, and by November assaults upon clergy of the old persuasion within the capital had become serious enough to necessitate similar action. An outburst of protestant propaganda, much of it popular and scurrilous, stimulated endless furious discussions about the sacrament of the altar, and the radicals simply ignored the ecclesiastical laws relating to festivals of the church. The same happened with the Lenten fast in the spring of 1548, in spite of the Council's attempts to aid the clergy in enforcing it. In September 1547 the Imperial Ambassador reported that the government was doing its best to restrain popular demand for reform, and that the people of London 'clamour for novelties of all sorts'. In spite of their willingness to relax the stringent laws of the previous régime, neither Cranmer nor Somerset had any intention of being stampeded into reform by pressures from below. Up to a point protestant propaganda was useful to them, and the so-called toleration of this period was probably designed

[11] 5 & 6 Edward VI, c.1. The previous Act had only imposed penalties upon the clergy for using any other form. The penalty for a first offence was six months in prison.

to give it scope, but intensified disciplinary activity towards the end of the year makes it clear that the government intended to control the pace as well as the direction of its policy. Outside London there is much less evidence of aggressive protestant conviction, although some communities in East Anglia and the home counties were running ahead of the government, like the people of St Ives in Huntingdonshire who purged their church of 'abuses' in the summer of 1547. There were also a few magnates of advanced views, who turned their households into hotbeds of radicalism. The most famous of these was the dowager Duchess of Suffolk, whose residence at Grimsthorpe in Lincolnshire became the model of a 'godly commonwealth'.

Such parish records as survive show a wide variety of responses to the successive stages of reform, but there can be no doubt that the prevailing climate of opinion was conservative among clergy, people and aristocracy alike. At the same time the royal supremacy had become deeply rooted in the political consciousness of all classes, and the reluctance which Gardiner felt to disobey the commands of his lawful sovereign was truly representative. It was treason to resist or deny the king's ecclesiastical authority, and treason not only involved appalling risks but was regarded with a genuine abhorrence reinforced by twenty years' effective propaganda. Very few had either the education or the intellectual capacity to reason with themselves in the sophisticated manner of the Bishop of Winchester, and fewer still could have drawn his delicate distinctions between the proper and improper exercise of the supremacy. Consequently the discontent which was undoubtedly created by the dissolution of the chantries and the removal of images found remarkably few outlets in action.

There were a number of riots in the midlands and south-east during the summer of 1548, which some observers attributed to religious causes, but the actual motivation seems to have been chiefly social and economic. Only in the south-west did there develop a large scale demonstration in which religion clearly played a dominant part. There the men of Cornwall had conceived a savage hatred against their Archdeacon, an unsavoury adventurer named William Body. His appearance in the county in 1547 had provoked a riot, and when he returned in 1548 to carry out the government's instructions for the removal of images, a mob set upon him and murdered him at Helston on 6

April. There was more to this attack than personal animosity, and the temper of the commons was so rebellious that the justices were forced to cancel the quarter sessions and call for the support of their Devon colleagues. However, in the event the rising petered out and ten of the ringleaders were tried and hanged. One of these, a yeoman named John Resseigh, had declared at the height of the tumult that he and his fellows would have their religion as King Henry 'of blessed memory' had left it. They would accept no changes decreed by the Lord Protector, nor by King Edward until he had reached the age of twenty-four.

During the twelve months which followed the anger of the Cornishmen was further stimulated by reports of the impending abolition of the mass, reports which conservative clergy deliberately spread; and probably exaggerated. Consequently, when it became known that the new liturgy was to be introduced on Whitsunday 1549, the signal was given for a larger and much more dangerous outburst. Towards the end of May the commons from the villages around Bodmin gathered in a camp outside the town, and recruited a local gentleman named Humphrey Arundell to act as their leader. Arundell was a man with a troublesome reputation, but he carried some weight in the locality, and seems to have co-operated willingly with the group of priests who had given the movement its original cohesion. Early in June the Cornishmen advanced into Devon, where a simultaneous and independent rising had taken place among the commons at Sampford Courtenay.[12] There the villagers had compelled their priest to continue with the mass and had murdered a local gentleman who attempted to quell the disturbance. Far from seeking gentry leadership, the men of Devon seem to have been inspired by a social animus altogether lacking among their Cornish neighbours, and the justices of the peace could do nothing to check or disperse the great gathering which had assembled at Crediton by 20 June. When the news of these developments reached London, Somerset's first reaction was to treat them as the result of ignorance and misunderstanding, rather than a deliberate desire to defy his authority. He sent Sir Peter

[12] The ultimate intention of the rebels is not very clear. It seems that the advance into Devon was mainly for the purpose of linking up with the movement there, and not a first step in a greater advance. See F. Rose Troup, *The Western Rebellion of 1549*, Julian Cornwall, *The Revolt of the Peasantry, 1549*, and A. L. Rowse, *Tudor Cornwall*.

Carew, a Devon man recently living in Lincolnshire, to rally the local gentry and persuade the misguided commons to disperse. Carew failed partly because he bungled his approach and partly because he found some of the gentry too ready to make sweeping concessions. His men also set fire to some barns on the outskirts of Crediton, and this had the effect of ruining his credentials as a negotiator.

In spite of Carew's report emphasising the danger of the situation, the Protector persisted for the time being in his lenient attitude. His resources were already strained by extensive enclosure riots, and the necessity to provide against the danger of war with France. So although he sent Lord Russell, the Lord Privy Seal, down to the west on 24 June with instructions to provide for the 'good order and quiet' of the region, he was unable to give him a sufficient force to operate against the rebels. This apparent lack of resolution undermined the confidence of the gentry in neighbouring Wiltshire and Somerset, so that Russell was unable to recruit any effective assistance. Further east, in Hampshire and Sussex, the people waited 'in a quavering quiet' for some decisive move. Had the rebels followed the example of their predecessors in 1497 and moved resolutely towards London, there might have been a general conflagration in the south of England. It seems certain that they were stimulated by a much wider range of grievances than appeared in the 'articles', which were the work of the clerical leaders. Many of the rank and file were especially hostile to the gentry, regarding them as the principal beneficiaries of the new religious order. One contemporary (admittedly hostile) described the latter element as follows: 'a number of vagabonds would have no justice, a band of thieves would have no state of any gentleman and yet to put all in one bag, a sort of traitors would have neither king nor good subjects.' In the event, they decided instead to consolidate their hold on the south-west, and at the beginning of July turned back to besiege Exeter. This move was their undoing, because although a substantial majority of the citizens shared their conservative views, the city fathers refused to countenance treason and stoutly resisted their attacks. While the insurgents' energies were concentrated on the siege, Russell continued his efforts to raise an adequate army. It was slow work, and by 18 July he still had less than two thousand men, while Somerset was forced to divert reinforcements to deal with other risings in Oxfordshire and Norfolk. It was not until the end of July that Russell felt strong enough to advance, and by that time even the Protector seems to have abandoned his leniency, since he wrote on the 27th that if any more should 'speak traiterous words against the king and in favour of the traiterous rebels, ye shall hang two or three of them . . . And that will be the only and best stay of all those talks.'

Once the government had an army in the field, the result was not long in doubt. A series of sharp engagements culminated in a decisive victory at Clyst St Mary on 4 August, and two days later the siege of Exeter was raised. By this time Russell had a force of about eight thousand, including a contingent of Italian mercenaries, and was able to press on into the far west, where the structure of local government had been in ruins for over two months. Additional urgency was given to this campaign by the outbreak of war with France on 8 August, and the fear that French assistance might keep the rebellion alive. A final and desperate battle was fought at Sampford Courtenay on 16 August, which may have cost the rebels as many as four thousand casualties, and left a large number of prisoners in Russell's hands. One or two clergy, caught *flagrante delicto*, were hanged on the spot in their 'popish vestments', but for the most part the execution done in battle was deemed to be sufficient, and there were no extensive judicial proceedings. Arundell and three others, two of them minor gentry, were taken to London for trial, and later suffered traitors' deaths. Had it not been for the simultaneous, if differently motivated, disturbances elsewhere, and Somerset's reluctance to understand the real anger of the rebels, this insurrection would never have assumed dangerous proportions. It lacked the covert aristocratic support which had made the Pilgrimage formidable, and its leaders showed little skill in either strategy or propaganda.

The 'articles' which they sent to the Council at the end of June were unintelligently contrived and clumsily phrased. For the most part they simply demanded the retention of the traditional liturgy with its full apparatus of gesture and imagery, and the return of those laws which would bring persecution upon all who disagreed with them. The authors showed no real sign of understanding catholic theology, let alone the intentions of the reformers. They demanded the withdrawal of the English bible, 'for we be informed that otherwise the clergy shall not of long confound the heretics', and they rejected the English liturgy on the curious grounds that some of them, being Cornish, knew no English. There was no mention of the pope, but the recall of Pole was requested, and the re-erection of some, at least, of the abbeys. Finally, as a strange afterthought, they demanded that no gentleman should be allowed more than one servant for every one hundred marks of his revenue.[13] Although ostensibly a petition each article began 'Item, we will have . . .', and all conventional protestations of loyalty to the king were starkly omitted.

In some respects these articles were as offensive to the aristocracy and to educated conservatives as they were to reformers and should not be taken as representative of the quality of conservative opposition in general. They also presented the government with excellent propaganda opportunities, which were eagerly seized by Cranmer and by Nicholas Udall, both of whom lengthily denounced the rebels' presumption and ignorance and drew the conventional conclusions, that popery led to rebellion and rebellion to anarchy. There was no further serious attempt to resist the progress of protestantism by force. Perhaps the element of *jacquerie* in the south-western rising, together with the more explicitly social disturbances elsewhere, convinced the conservative aristocracy that they must uphold the authority of the Council; no matter what its religious policy. Thus the radical measures of 1550-53 provoked no revolt in spite of their unpopularity. Caught between violent social protest and a protestant supremacy, the aristocracy decided that the preservation of order was more vital to its interests than doubtful issues of theology, and threw its weight behind the oppressive legislation which followed the overthrow of the Protector in the last months of 1549.

THE ENCLOSURE CRISIS

In many ways Somerset had been an enlightened and effective ruler, but the long summer crisis of 1549 had exposed his weaknesses. We have already seen that enclosures were an ancient grievance, and that the traditional policy of Tudor governments had been to protect tenants wherever possible. This legacy the Protector laudably accepted, but with insufficient understanding

[13] Article 13. This was naturally seized upon by government propagandists as revealing the true anarchic purposes of the rebellion.

of either the limitations of his own position, or the aggravation which the problem had recently undergone. Prices, particularly of foodstuffs, had risen sharply; by 100 per cent since the beginning of the century and by over 30 per cent since 1530.[14] Coming on top of over one hundred years of stable or declining prices, this inflation was regarded as a mystery and an outrage. Lacking any understanding of economic problems, contemporaries immediately sought to blame human agents, and the landlords were popular targets. Moralists and pamphleteers denounced them as 'unnatural lords . . . step lords', and ran two problems conveniently together by blaming both vagrancy and inflation on the insatiable greed with which they screwed up their rents and evicted tenants to make the utmost profit from their lands. Certainly there were good and bad lords, but this view of the situation was nearer to a myth than an oversimplification. Nevertheless, it combined explosively with the peasant egalitarianism which was never far below the surface of rural society. Consequently, although there was no noticeable increase in the rate of enclosure after 1540, there was a rapid build up of indignation, and hedge-breaking riots increased in frequency and violence.

Economic distress had been intensified by bad harvests, as we have seen, and confidence in the currency reduced by the debasements of 1542 and 1546. In addition, there can be little doubt that a steady increase in population, beginning in the later years of the fifteenth century, had created a land hunger in which comparatively trivial changes in the pattern of land use might cause quite disproportionate distress and anger. The evidence suggests that the lords were as much the victims of inflation as their tenants, in many cases more so since long leases on fixed rents were common in the early part of the century, and even entry fines were often inflexible. This meant that they had every incentive to use whatever means were available to increase their revenues, and wherever the land was suitable for sheep farming, it was likely to be more profitable than arable. It also meant that those tenants who were not protected by law, such as demesne copyholders and tenants-at-will, or those whose leases conveniently fell in, might be made to pay for the privileged posi-

[14] All 'price rise' statistics are controversial approximations. For a good summary of modern scholarship on this important subject see R. B. Outhwaite, *Inflation in Tudor and Early Stuart England.*

tion of their fellows. Naturally landlords pleaded their own poverty in justification of their actions, and they had at least as much cause to do so as their detractors had to complain.

During the 1540s this situation was aggravated by the propaganda of the so-called 'commonwealth men'. These men, of whom John Hales, Sir John Cheke and Robert Crowley are the best known, were humanist scholars and idealists, who looked for the establishment of Christian justice within the state, as their medieval predecessors had looked for it in Christendom at large. They were not in any sense social revolutionaries, believing firmly in the subordination of the commons to the aristocracy and of the whole realm to the king. 'The maintenance of these heads [the gentry],' Thomas Starkey had written 'is the maintenance of all civil order and politic rule here in our nation.' For this very reason, however, it was of the utmost importance that the gentry should have a sense of social responsibility towards the inferior whom God had called them to rule.

> Consider [says Crowley addressing the landlords], that you are but ministers and servants under the Lord our God, and that you shall render a straight account of your administration . . . That you are lords and governors cometh not by nature but by the ordinance and appointment of God.

This sense of responsibility, they all agreed, was grievously lacking among the aristocracy of their own day. 'Thy princes are wicked and companions of thieves,' thundered Latimer, whose protestant zeal embraced the same notions of order and duty. 'Beat down and destroy with all your power and ability that greedy and devouring spirit of covetousness which now so universally reigns,' wrote Nicholas Ridley as Bishop of London to the preachers of his diocese.[15] The Lord Protector, himself an idealistic man and a sincere protestant, was convinced that the remedy lay in his own hands.

He took up the campaign against enclosures where Wolsey had laid it down, seeing in this single issue the quintessence of the problem. In June 1548 a lengthy proclamation announced that existing statutes against enclosures were to be strictly en-

[15] The protestant leaders were already conscious that they were being exploited by secular minded gentlemen, and strove unavailingly to maintain the moral authority of the Church. Dudley was to give the *coup de grâce* to this attempt when he refused to countenance an effective reform of the canon law in 1552.

forced, and at the same time a royal commission on the lines of Wolsey's enquiry of 1517 was sent into the midlands to investigate the extent of the encroachments. In acting thus, Somerset was heeding the 'commonwealth' lobby led by John Hales rather than his colleagues in the Council, who seem to have been unanimously opposed to such a course. Early in 1549 a number of draft bills against enclosures were submitted to the Commons by this lobby, but they were so blatant in their social animus that they had no chance of acceptance, and even Somerset knew better than to lend them countenance. He did, however, secure the passage of a subsidy Act which provided for a tax on sheep specifically designed to make enclosure for pasture less profitable.[16] Growing evidence of opposition among the gentry, as well as within the Council only made him more determined. 'Maugre the Devil, private profit, self love, money and such like the Devil's instruments, it shall go forward and set . . . a stay in the body of the commonwealth,' he declared. Moral conviction of this kind makes for insensitive politics, and Somerset was ignoring the all-important fact that his own power, and the whole structure of the administration for which he was responsible, depended upon the co-operation of those very men whom he was so willing to castigate.[17] That co-operation had already been strained to breaking point by the burdens resulting from the Protector's obsessive pursuit of the war against Scotland, burdens which made his high-handed censoriousness over their own financial operations particularly galling. Even if such an attitude had been wholly justified, which it was not, the resulting policy would have been unworkable. In the event it proved to be destructive of the social order he was so anxious to preserve.

The commons had already been encouraged by 'common-

[16] 2 & 3 Edward VI, c.36. The passage of this Act through a hostile House was no mean achievement, for as a contemporary wrote '. . . it pricketh them most which be chosen to be burgesses'. Somerset certainly had no means to pack or intimidate Parliament. Jordan, *The Young King*, 178.

[17] The autocratic streak in Somerset was strong. In *The King's Council in the Reign of Edward VI*, D. E. Hoak has argued convincingly that he virtually succeeded in ruling without the Council from December 1547 to October 1549. The fullest account of Somerset's policies is given by M. L. Bush, *The Government Policy of Protector Somerset*.

wealth' writers and protestant preachers to see the source of their distress where they wanted to see it, in the greed of their social superiors. In the summer of 1548 they were further encouraged by the Protector's actions to see him as their ally, and to expect immediate redress. Such expectations were bound to be disappointed, because only a prolonged period of intense pressure could have overcome the resistance of the gentry, and this Somerset lacked the resources even to mount, let alone sustain. As a result, anger and frustration boiled over in a series of large riots, not directed against the king but against the men who were, as often as not, his local representatives. Somerset refused to see the warning, and early in the summer of 1549 the whole situation exploded in a manner which seemed to contemporaries to herald the total breakdown of the social and political order.

The greatest single rising began on 20 June as an enclosure riot at Attleborough, in Norfolk. Within a few days the leadership of a local yeoman named Robert Kett had transformed the aimless fury of a small mob into a purposeful demonstration against the county gentry. By 12 July he had an orderly camp on Mousehold Heath, outside Norwich, and an estimated sixteen thousand men under his command. Such a force was quite beyond the resources of the local justices to disperse, but there was little violence until 23 July, when the rebels took the city of Norwich against the attempted resistance of the civic authorities. They then despatched to the Council in London a set of twenty-nine articles detailing their complaints. These present a very marked contrast to those from the south-west. All but about three or four of them request specific legal and economic reforms, mostly of a moderate and reasonable kind; for instance, number 13 runs, 'We pray your Grace to take all liberty of leet into your own hands, whereby all men may quietly enjoy their commons with all profits.'[18] Insofar as they show any religious attitude, it is sympathetic to the reformers, and the whole document is scrupulously respectful of the king's authority. This development placed Somerset in the gravest difficulty. He had great sympathy with the rebel cause, and he also had a series of other risings on his hands which seemed to be more dangerous and subversive. At the same time he could neither ignore such a large-scale movement nor yield to implied threats. Repeatedly by

[18] The Court Leet was theoretically a royal court, but was normally under local control, which presumably was thought to lead to inequitable distribution of common rights.

proclamation and by direct message he tried to persuade the rebels to disperse, promising a general pardon and at least a measure of redress. No success attended these efforts as the rebels, with justice, suspected artifice, and on 30 July a force was despatched against them under the Marquis of Northampton. The result was a fiasco. Northampton had no glimmer of military capacity and fled at the first sign of determined resistance, whereupon his army, bereft of leadership, promptly followed him. Had the rebellion concealed a political purpose this would have been the moment of danger, but Kett had no idea how to exploit his victory, and his army remained on Mousehold Heath awaiting the next government initiative.

This came in the last week of August, when the Earl of Warwick arrived outside Norwich with twelve thousand men. Either the Protector himself had decided on severe repression, or his hand had been forced, for Warwick was the leader of that group upon the Council which distrusted his social policies and within a few weeks was to remove him from power. Once again the rebels professed their loyalty to the king, and a final attempt at negotiation was made, but they were no more ready to trust their aristocratic enemies than before, and the effort was futile. Using martial law, Warwick hanged any rebels he could find within the city and began systematic operations against the camp. Faced with daily demoralising losses, on 26 August Kett decided to risk battle. The next day his force was overwhelmed by the royal cavalry, and 'Dusindale' was filled with slaughtered bodies, as a local rhyme had prophesied.[19] About three thousand of the rebels perished in the battle, and another fifty or so, including Kett and his brother, were tried and executed for treason. We do not know how many died by martial law, but an eye witness account, written down long afterwards, suggests that the number may have been as high as two hundred and fifty.[20] By the end of August the government was more or less in command of the situation, since Lord Grey of Wilton had earlier sup-

[19] The battlefield of 'Dusindale' has never been accurately identified. The story of the Delphic prophecy comes from Holinshed, and may be an embellishment.

[20] Alexander Neville, who in 1549 had been a young man in Norwich, published in 1575 *De furoribus Norfolcensium Ketto Duce*, in which he mentions three hundred as having been executed. Only about fifty are recorded as having died for treason, so if his overall figure was approximately correct, the balance may have suffered summary punishment.

pressed a similar but less well organised rising in Oxfordshire and Berkshire, but the Protector's policy was in ruins and the aristocracy were very seriously alarmed.

Naturally their alarm was shared by the scholars and divines whose words had been so dramatically misconstrued. Neither the 'commonwealth men' nor the protestant divines had ever countenanced rebellion, in spite of their fierce criticism of the gentry. They had been concerned to awaken a sense of duty in their governors and to plead the case of the poor, not to suggest that the latter should take the law into their own hands. The humanist Sir John Cheke wrote *The true subject to the rebel* and *The hurt of sedition* as government propaganda, and a new edition of Cranmer's *Homilies* was forthright on the subject of obedience. 'I never saw so little discipline as is nowadays,' lamented Latimer; 'men will be masters . . . and no disciples.' Such unruliness, he went on, was sinful in the eyes of God and would bring more punishment than earthly rulers could inflict. To Gardiner, the explanation was simple. Protestantism was the religion of disobedience, undermining all authority: 'liberty of life hath borne such swing that good life beareth no rule . . . O devilish liberty, I would to God Germany had kept thee still.' Like Luther at the time of the peasants' revolt, the English protestants in 1549 had to produce convincing evidence of their willingness to uphold authority if they were not to see their evangelical programme hopelessly discredited.

They were therefore in no position to rally to Somerset's support when Warwick's well contrived *coup* placed him in the Tower in October. Especially since the Protector, in a final misguided gesture had actually called upon the commons in the king's name to protect him from the evil intentions of his peers. Nor were they able to offer any effective resistance to the flagrant secularisation of the Church, which, as the next few years were to show, was the price which Warwick and his allies demanded for their support of evangelical reform. It is not surprising, therefore, that by 1553 protestantism was widely regarded as the tool of unscrulpulous political adventurers, or that many protestant leaders were prepared to welcome persecution as a means of restoring their integrity.

Somerset's fall was the signal for a series of repressive measures designed to make any repetition of the disorders of the summer impossible. A new Treasons Act resurrected several of the laws of Henry VIII, repealed in the hopeful days of 1547. Several thousand German and Italian mercenaries were recruited, although Warwick progressively abandoned any attempt at a constructive foreign policy as his financial position became more and more desperate.[21] The Protector's lax attitude to the press was abandoned in favour of renewed censorship, controlled by a committee of the Council, and fierce penalties were prescribed for unlawful assemblies and attacks upon enclosures. These measures were largely effective, because no one in a powerful or influential position was prepared to oppose them. Many of the old peerage families, who might have challenged the power of the Seymours and Dudleys, such as the Staffords, Courtenays, Percies and Howards, had been broken in the previous reign. The survivors, although hostile to parvenus and sympathetic to the old religion, were as anxious as Dudley himself to keep the commons in subjection. This was common ground to all peers and gentlemen, no matter what their attitude to Edward's councillors, and consequently the disciplinary machinery of the law continued to function with surprising efficiency in spite of the weakness of the government in other respects. The Council records are full of the detection of sedition and the punishment of the guilty parties, some cases seeming of the most trivial kind. However the government and its agents knew well enough that once a riot had been allowed to develop it could rapidly outrun the normal resources of local order, and much damage could be done before outside help was available. Therefore the greatest vigilance was justified, and also the deliberate encouragement of military preparedness among the gentry, particularly those known to be 'sound' in religion – which was a good acid test of commitment to the régime.

Just before Somerset was overthrown a group of Kentish gentlemen led by Sir Thomas Wyatt the younger produced a scheme 'to strengthen the king's part with a power of the

[21] Dudley was forced to make very extensive grants of royal land and annuities to maintain the questionable loyalty of his associates. The war with France was quickly ended, the fleet laid up, and the garrisons withdrawn from Scotland. There was certainly no failure of the revenue administration, but much of the Crown income was improperly dispersed. The situation was aggravated by continued rapid inflation, and by the collapse of the Antwerp Cloth trade in 1550. Jordan, *The Threshold of Power*, 116-80.

choice of his most able and trusty subjects, which might be upon a very short warning in a readiness, well armed and ordered against all sudden attempts either at home or abroad'. They were specifically motivated by the recent rebellions and by the fact that the gentry had proved so incapable of swift and effective action. Their proposal amounted to the setting up of a select militia, consisting of gentlemen appointed by the Crown, and something very like the armed retainers of the previous century. The scheme was never officially accepted, but Wyatt and his fellows set up a sort of 'vigilante' system in Kent, and other gentry may have done the same elsewhere. Dudley certainly encouraged his own particular friends and supporters to keep 'private bands' by dispensing them from the Act of Retainers.[22] In 1550 the Council also decided to create a small force under its own control, and it may have been this that Edward was referring to in December 1551 when he wrote to Barnaby Fitzpatrick, mentioning 'the musters of the new erected gendarmery'. There is no evidence of its ever having been used. The occasional expedient of appointing military lieutenants for counties or groups of counties was put upon a regular footing during this period, and by the beginning of 1553 it must have seemed that Dudley was in command of sufficient military resources to secure himself against any kind of domestic opposition. As long as he governed in the king's name, and while the most likely enemy was the rebellious commons, this was no doubt true. But in the spring of 1553 Edward, still only in his sixteenth year, became seriously ill, and the heir to the throne by his father's will was the Princess Mary, thirty-seven years of age and Dudley's bitter antagonist on every issue whether political or religious.

[22] For example, on 29 March 1552, Lord Wentworth received a licence to retain eighty gentlemen and yeomen in his livery, over and above his household servants – and a pardon for all offences against the Statute of Retainers committed since the previous 25 April. *Calendar of the Patent Rolls, Ed. VI*, IV, 347.

CHAPTER 8

RELIGIOUS REACTION AND THE SPANISH MARRIAGE

> If the Crown were the Queen's, in such sort that she might do with it what she would, both now and after her death, there might appear some rightful pretence in giving it over to a stranger Prince, but seeing it belongeth to the heirs of England after her death, ye commit deadly sin and damnation in unjustly giving and taking away the right of others . . . (John Bradford, *The copy of a letter*, 1556)

QUEEN JANE

John Dudley, created Duke of Northumberland in October 1551, exhibited many of the characteristics of the overmighty subjects of the previous century. Unlike Somerset, he never took the title of Protector, and therefore never assumed a formal responsibility for the direction of policy. From his chosen position as President of the Council, he consistently thrust the young king forward, encouraging him to play an increasing role in public business. How long Edward, who showed clear signs of becoming as strong-minded and as wilful as his father, would have tolerated this kind of manipulation is uncertain, but as long as he lived the Duke's personal influence over him remained paramount. The consequent ability to control royal patronage was the real foundation of Northumberland's power, as it had been of De la Pole's or Beaufort's, and a constant flow of pensions, offices, grants and preferential sales maintained the appearance of a firmly committed following among the gentry and aristocracy. In reality, however, Dudley was hardly more popular than De la Pole had been at the height of his power. Among the commons he was generally, and justly, held responsible for the judicial murder of the fallen Protector,[1] whose largely undeserved

[1] Somerset had been released from arrest in February 1550, and restored to the Council in April. However, Dudley rapidly came to distrust the revival of his influence, and he was rearrested in September 1551. In November he was tried

reputation for benevolence gave him a Banquo-like revenge against his supplanter. Northumberland's social policy was seen, by contrast with Somerset's, as harsh and repressive. In fact it was realistic, and probably achieved rather more. Although the Enclosure Commissions and the tax on sheep were abandoned, prosecutions for depopulation were stepped up, and fresh legislation in 1552 was designed to protect husbandry, curb usury, and provide additional encouragement for poor relief. In face of a deteriorating economic situation, caused partly by the temporary collapse of the English cloth market in Antwerp, partly by poor harvests, and partly by the ravages of the 'sweating sickness', Northumberland was compelled to give a high priority to the maintenance of order. In spite of tensions and minor disorders, there was no repetition of the upheavals of 1548–9, but success in such a thankless task contributed nothing to his popularity. Religious conservatives hated him for his advanced protestantism, and for the ruthlessness with which he had double-crossed them after the fall of Somerset.[2] Many protestant leaders at the same time bitterly distrusted his exploitation of their doctrine, and denounced him as a 'carnal gospeller'. The aristocratic support which he derived from his 'law and order' policy, and from his return to genuine conciliar government after Somerset's autocratic experiments, was genuine enough but largely opportunist. He was not of the royal blood, as Richard of Gloucester had been, nor could he call upon the loyalty engendered by an established family position and great estates. His great estates were of recent acquisition, and his clientage depended upon his political power, rather than the other way round. As we have seen, the power of 'manred' had in any case declined sharply during the previous thirty years, and the threat which Northumberland represented to the authority of the Crown was significantly different from that of his overmighty predecessors.

on a trumped-up charge of seeking to murder Dudley and other councillors – and executed in January 1552. After his own fall Dudley confessed that the evidence against Somerset had been fabricated.

[2] Somerset had been defeated by an alliance of interests, and it was widely believed that his fall would be followed by religious reaction, and even by the appointment of Mary as Regent. However, in the autumn of 1549 Dudley had succeeded in packing the Council with his own adherents, and the conservatives, led by Wriothesley, had been defeated.

The Duke himself had no illusions about the basis of his power, and Edward's deteriorating health during the winter of 1552–3 was a source of great anxiety to him. There seemed to be every likelihood that he would share his father's fate once the protective cover of the young king's life was withdrawn. Late in 1552 rumours began to circulate that he had designs upon the succession. The perpetrators were punished, and seem to have been motivated by nothing more precise than general animosity, but they reflected a popular awareness of his predicament. No doubt contingency plans were in his mind, but it would be a mistake to suppose that the eventual crisis of July 1553 was the result of a long-matured conspiracy, or that it was brought about primarily by the Duke's overweening ambition. Not only was self-preservation uppermost in his mind, but the king also had his own reasons for wishing to exclude his elder half-sister. Edward's protestantism was not simply the product of Northumberland's influence, although it corresponded very happily with his interests, and the young king's anxiety to preserve the reformed church was genuine and acute. At some stage before his illness became serious, Edward drew up his own 'Instrument' for the succession, setting aside the claims of both his half-sisters, as well as that of the Stuart line. In the event of his own death without heirs, the Crown was to pass to the male heir of the Suffolk line; that is to say, to any son who might be born to Frances Grey, Duchess of Suffolk, the elder daughter of Henry VIII's younger sister, Mary. Or, failing that, to the eldest son born to any of Frances's three daughters, Jane, Catherine and Mary. This was hardly an emergency measure. Frances was not pregnant, and had not conceived for several years, whilst none of her daughters was married, and only Jane was of marriageable age. Northumberland's influence on this Instrument, if any, is obscure. It had little legal weight since Edward, as a minor, could not even make a valid will, let alone dispose of the Crown *mero moto suo*, without the consent of parliament. When the latter body assembled on 1 March 1553, the succession was not mentioned. Presumably the king's condition was not considered to be serious enough to justify the risk of unveiling such a dubious document, while Edward remained wedded to his own ideas, and by no means reconciled to the prospect of an early demise. Northumberland certainly knew of his sovereign's intentions, and the marriage which took place on 21 May between his only unmarried son, Guildford, and Lady Jane Grey has to be seen in that light.

It is not certain that anything more sinister was intended than a general strengthening of his position, because tuberculosis is a disease in which there are many remissions, and as late as the end of May hopes were still entertained of the king's recovery. However, in the first week of June his condition deteriorated alarmingly, and his physicians informed the Duke that his death was not only inevitable, but imminent. It was probably not until he received this news that Northumberland finally decided upon his course of action, because the arrangements which he then began to make show every sign of desperate contrivance. There was now no time for the Instrument to be ratified by parliament, even if the members had been willing, and it therefore had to be claimed that the will of the king was sufficient authority – a claim the absolutist pretensions of which far exceeded the limits of normal Divine Right. The judges, and indeed other councillors, reacted with acute embarrassment, but Northumberland was fully supported by the dying king. Mary must not succeed or the whole work of the reformation would be endangered. Between them they overbore all objections, and the Instrument was ratified. But by this time, of course, the document itself was inadequate. There would be no male heir of the Suffolk line before Edward's death, and the Instrument lost its last shred of plausibility. It is not known who carried out the necessary alterations, although they must have been made with Edward's knowledge and consent. The surviving draft, with its erasures and insertions, is an eloquent reminder of the situation. Two important amendments were made; one deleting the provision that Frances should act as Regent if no male heirs had been born to any of her daughters before the king's death, and the second inserting 'the Lady Jane and her heirs male' in place of the original 'heirs male of the Lady Jane'. In the circumstances this made Jane the direct heir, in spite of the fact that her mother, through whom she derived her claim, was still alive. Since she was Northumberland's daughter-in-law, and her sons would be

Dudleys, the Duke was naturally held responsible for this arrangement, which was taken as proof of overweening dynastic ambition. His fellow councillors showed acute symptoms of alarm, and Cranmer at least did his best to dissuade the king from such a dangerous experiment.[3] However, no one could suggest an acceptable alternative. Northumberland cajoled and threatened, and Edward directly invoked their allegiance, until they gave way and signed an undertaking to uphold the amended Instrument. Some comforted themselves with the thought that it could not be treason to obey the king, but most knew better.

When Edward died on 6 July their best chance of security appeared to lie in abiding by their decision, however reluctantly reached, and Northumberland had no intention of allowing them to escape that obligation. His survival now depended totally upon his ability to hold them to their allegiance. They proclaimed Queen Jane, and mustered their resources to uphold her, concealing the news of the king's death for as long as possible to strengthen their position. However, the new regime had neither legitimacy nor popularity to commend it, and the widespread hatred which Northumberland had already incurred was a fatal handicap. Even the protestant Londoners were sulky, and the only Edwardian prelate to make any public pronouncement in Jane's favour was Nicholas Ridley. Preaching at Paul's Cross on 9 July he declared that both Mary and Elizabeth were incapable of succeeding because they had been bastardised by Acts of Parliament which had never been repealed.[4] He also added that the unmarried condition of both princesses made them hazards to the security of the realm, and that Mary was a known adherent of the banished mass. His audience heard him out in stony silence. The unenthusiastic attitude of the

[3] According to his own explanation of his conduct, offered at his trial in November 1553, when he was found guilty of high treason, and later in a letter to the queen. Cranmer, *Works*, II, 442.

[4] Mary had been effectively bastardised by the first Succession Act of Henry VIII (25 Henry VIII c.22) and both daughters by the second (28 Henry VIII c.7). These Acts had not been repealed, but both Mary and Elizabeth had been included in the succession as laid down in 35 Henry VIII c.1. Henry's first Act was finally repealed by 1 Mary st. 2 c.1, 'An Act declaring the Queen's Majesty to have been born in most just and lawful wedlock.'

protestants was of great importance. Although only a small proportion of the total population, they were vociferous, and the natural defenders of the Edwardian settlement which Jane's succession was ostensibly designed to protect. In some places they did support her, and research has only recently uncovered the tracks which they were so quickly forced to hide; but in general loyalty to the Tudor dynasty weighed far more heavily than religion. The attitude of most can be summed up in the self-righteous opinion later attributed to Sir Nicholas Throgmorton:

And though I liked not the religion
Which all her life Queen Mary had professed,
Yet in my mind that wicked motion,
Right heirs for to displace I did detest.

Also, the extent of Mary's conservatism was not generally appreciated, even by her enemies who might have exploited it. Loyalty to the mass, and to traditional pieties, was a commendation to most Englishmen, and Mary had lived unprotestingly under the royal supremacy for seventeen years, since her father had forced it upon her.

The princess had no intention of surrendering her inheritance tamely. She may not have had much confidence in her own abilities, but a belief in her royal destiny was a part of her confidence in God. Secretly warned of her brother's death and of Northumberland's intention to apprehend her, she slipped away from Hunsdon on 7 July and made her way to Kenninghall in Suffolk. From there she proclaimed her title to the Crown, and summoned her loyal subjects to defend her against John Dudley 'calling himself Duke of Northumberland', and the traitors adhering to him. At the same time the Council in London sent out letters to all sheriffs, justices and deputy lieutenants warning them against her 'ungodly pretences' and ordering them to uphold Queen Jane. Foreign observers thought Mary's defiance was absurd. The Imperial envoys, who were friendly to her, reported gloomily that Northumberland controlled all the resources of the kingdom – the treasury, the fleet, and the armouries of the Tower. There was nothing that one woman could do against him, no matter how just her cause. Had the royal finances been in better shape, and had the Duke not been so generally disliked and distrusted, even by those who were ostensibly his allies, this judgement might have been correct. But within a few days tidings began to arrive in the capital of daily defections to her cause, and of great companies of gentry and commons flocking to her standard.

By 13 July the situation of Jane's adherents was becoming desperate. The Earl of Bath, the Earl of Sussex, the Earl of Derby, and innumerable gentry, particularly from East Anglia, had declared for Mary and begun to move to her assistance. Her camp, by this time at Framlingham, was large, well ordered and well supplied. The stoutly protestant Sir Peter Carew proclaimed her in Devon, and Sir Thomas Wyatt in Kent. Had Northumberland still commanded the forces of German and Italian mercenaries who had played such an important part in 1549, he would have had a firm base upon which to build his campaign; but poverty had forced him to pay them off nearly a year before. Nevertheless, the nettle had to be grasped, and on Jane's insistence he had to grasp it himself, since she would not allow her father to leave the capital.

THE CONSERVATIVE ESTABLISHMENT

On 14 July he set out from London with about two thousand men, leaving behind a Council in which he placed no trust. By the 16th he had reached Cambridge, his small force still further reduced by desertion, and his lack of old-fashioned manred ruthlessly exposed by the crisis. On the same day the Earls of Arundel and Pembroke were encouraging their colleagues to escape from his sinking vessel before it should be too late. On the 19th they proclaimed Queen Mary, and denounced their erstwhile leader as a 'conscienceless tyrant'. In Cambridge Northumberland, now deserted by all his men, could only wait until the emissaries of the new sovereign arrived on 24 July to arrest him. There was little hope in flight, and in any case he was a fatalist. The celebrations in London matched those of some mighty victory.

> The Earl of Pembroke threw away his cap full of angelots. I saw myself money was thrown out at windows for joy. The bonfires were without number, and what with shouting, and crying of the people, and ringing of bells, there could no man hear what another said

wrote one eyewitness. There was cause for rejoicing because, although in one sense Mary's bid was the only successful rebellion against a Tudor government, in another (and far more important) sense the dynasty had survived its most dangerous crisis. Had Edward VI succeeded in setting aside his father's will, and the statute which authorised it, the supremacy of statute, so painstakingly built up during the Reformation Parliament, would have been in jeopardy, and with it the whole pragmatic partnership between the Crown and the political nation. It was awareness of this, at least as much as legitimism in the narrower sense, which rallied such overwhelming support to Henry VIII's elder daughter. The Imperial ambassadors were delighted, impressed, and more than a little puzzled by a phenomenon which was so alien to their experience. 'Ce royaulme est populaire' wrote Simon Renard to the Emperor, not meaning democratic in the modern sense, but possessing a large and articulate political class which could not easily be persuaded or intimidated. To a contemporary European, accustomed to the routines of magnate politics, this was an unstable and unpredictable situation, and one which Renard was to view apprehensively during the months which followed.

Meanwhile enthusiastic catholics were telling the new queen that God had favoured her with an especial miracle, and she was well disposed to believe them. Religion was so fundamental a part of Mary's personality that she could only interpret her remarkable triumph as a divine mandate to rescue her fellow countrymen from their twenty-year nightmare of schism and heresy. 'She has no thought but to restore the mass and religion', one contemporary wrote, adding that such a policy was bound to cause strife. Unfortunately Mary conspicuously lacked the worldly wisdom to discriminate between an endorsement of her known position – as lawful heir and a religious conservative – and a mandate for her private priorities – a Habsburg marriage and the return of papal jurisdiction. The problems which arose from this initial misunderstanding were complex, and were to last throughout the short reign.

The first people to be affected, naturally, were the protestants. The English reformers had always taught non-resistance, but to a sincere evangelical by 1553 the calm acceptance of a return to the mass – let alone the papal authority – was unthinkable. Some sought an answer in flight and exile, putting their personal integrity before the plight of the national church; an attitude which the new regime was assiduous to encourage. Others stayed, welcoming an opportunity to testify to their faith by suffering persecution. 'Where the word of God is truly preached, there is persecution, as well of the hearers as of the teachers,' Latimer had written many years before, '. . . [and] where you see persecution, there is the gospel, there is the truth.' But such thoughts were not an adequate consolation to all, and some later abandoned their traditional principles, advocating resistance or rebellion. To the government the obstinacy of this hard core was baffling. They had accepted Mary as their lawful queen, and continued to profess their belief in the royal supremacy, and yet they rejected the catholic church to which she commanded them to adhere. As the advocate Story said to Cranmer at his trial: 'the same laws, being put away by a parliament, are now received again by a parliament, and have as full authority now as they had then.' Yet, in spite of their principles of obedience, Cranmer and his followers refused to obey. What explanation could there be but wilful stubbornness and self-conceit? That their opponents might have a genuine dilemma of conscience the authorities would never for one moment admit. The association between heresy and sedition was automatic, and the queen could never understand that many Englishmen who were perfectly willing to accept her as their lawful queen, nevertheless rejected the faith which was so intimate a part of her personality. The lesson which she chose to draw from the circumstances of her accession was rather that the so-called protestants were nothing but a handful of conspirators around the Duke of Northumberland, without any significant following among the people.

In fact Mary was far less in tune with her subjects than she supposed, and not only in respect of religion, where she was undoubtedly misled by the popularity of the traditional forms. For many years she had been deeply devoted to the memory of her mother, and had never forgiven her father's servants for the humiliations which they had both suffered at his hands. In difficulty and distress she had always turned to her cousin the Emperor, and was as emotionally committed to the Habsburg interest as she was to the catholic faith. As a strategic option that alliance had much to commend it, and represented the normal orientation of Tudor foreign policy, but as a permanent commitment it signified a sacrifice of national independence to which the political nation was deeply averse. This attitude Mary totally failed to understand, attributing it to mere xenophobia. Because of her own background, and the history of the previous twenty years, she was also compelled to employ in high office men whom she did not fully trust. Consequently, before her reign was a month old her principal confidant was Charles's ambassador, Simon Renard, a man whose self-interested influence over the queen seriously disrupted her relations with her own Council. At a lower level this lack of 'Englishness' was soon perceived and commented upon by those very people who had welcomed her to the throne. 'She is a Spaniard at heart,' they muttered, '. . . she loves another realm better than this.' As the reign developed they began to fear involvement in the Emperor's wars, and even annexation to the Habsburg empire. For her part, Mary was never prepared to admit that her subjects were entitled to any opinion upon such matters of high policy, and she did not scruple to tell them so on occasion. Technically she was quite correct, and her reaction was thoroughly Tudor, but because she was not willing to trim the sails of her policies to the winds of political support, her reign developed into a frustrating battle to impose her own priorities.

These problems did not become apparent all at once. At first it seemed as though the new queen's religious policy would be a quiet and tolerant one. On 18 August she issued a proclamation which, while declaring her own position, renounced any immediate intention of coercing the consciences of others. The agitations stirred up by a few radicals in London ruffled the calm surface, but, beyond expelling the refugee protestant congregations, the government for the moment did nothing. This was partly because the queen and her Lord Chancellor, Stephen Gardiner, both believed that protestantism, once defeated, would simply wither away; and partly because of the anxious representations made by Simon Renard. Renard was genuinely fearful that Mary's determination to 'right matters at a single blow' would stir up a rebellion which might sweep her from her throne as swiftly as she had gained it. Events were to prove that the ambassador's fears were wildly exaggerated, but he was new to the job, and playing for a very high stake. Mary's accession had unexpectedly placed in the Emperor's hands, at a very low ebb in his European fortunes, an opportunity which he could not afford to neglect. In informing him of her success, the Queen of England had expressed her filial gratitude and duty. Seizing the moment Charles, or more likely Granvelle acting in his name,[5] instructed the ambassador to sound out the possibility of a marriage alliance. Prince Philip, his only legitimate son, was a widower, and although eleven years Mary's junior expressed himself amenable to the call of duty. The political advantage from the Habsburg point of view would be great. Although it meant offending the Portuguese royal family with whom Philip had been negotiating, it offered at least a firm alliance for the immediate future to complete the encirclement of France, and at most a permanent dynastic union. Mary was easily convinced. She had implicit faith in the Emperor's judgement, and it was obvious that, at thirty-seven, no time could be lost if there was to be any chance of an heir. It was also essential that her potential consort should be a man of political experience, with sufficient prestige and resources to stand above the factions of the English court. By October the secret negotiations were complete, and Mary had sworn upon the sacrament that she would marry the Prince of Spain.

In spite of the valid arguments which supported it, both this decision itself and the manner of reaching it, were mistaken. Stephen Gardiner, and the majority of her councillors, were opposed to the negotiation, and endeavoured to dissuade her. Of her senior advisers, only Lord Paget was fully supportive. The reasons for this opposition varied, but the one most commonly voiced was that Philip, as the heir to more than half of his father's vast domains, would soon have all too little time for England, whose interests would inevitably become submerged by the demands of other territories. The House of

[5]Charles was in very poor health throughout the late summer of 1553, and although these negotiations probably represent his desire and intention, Granvelle was the effective instigator.

Commons, alarmed by rumours of what was impending, sent a deputation to wait upon the queen, with a petition that she should marry within the realm. The French ambassador, Antoine de Noailles, threatened war and began immediate intrigues with any malcontents he could find. Before Christmas anti-Spanish ballads and broadsheets were circulating in the streets of London, and angry members of parliament were digesting the brusque dismissal of their petition. Mary had no intention of being deflected from her purpose. Although she had not taken the initiative, Philip had become her choice; a great prince of her mother's people, and an impeccable catholic. Her honour and her emotions were both fully engaged, and objections which turned out to be prophetic in their accuracy went unheeded. As this situation became apparent outside the court, the seeds of conspiracy were sown. The original leader of this plot seems to have been William Thomas, a protestant and one-time clerk to Edward's Privy Council. Most of those involved, such as Sir James Croft and Sir Edward Warner, had been closely involved with the previous regime, but none had been prominent among Mary's opponents in the summer; indeed Sir Thomas Wyatt and Sir Peter Carew had swiftly declared for her, and Sir Nicholas Throgmorton was probably the man whose warning had enabled her to escape from Hunsdon in time to avoid arrest. With the exception of Thomas, whose leadership was shortlived, and Carew, none of them was, or had been, notable for protestant zeal. The government later ascribed religious motives to them, and they certainly had connections with more obvious reformers, but the recognised protestant leadership disowned them, and their purposes appear to have been almost entirely political. If the queen would not listen to reasonable protest, then she must be made to realise the strength of her subjects' resentment.

How far the conspirators were prepared to go is not clear. A proposal to assassinate Mary was rejected at once, and in their public pronouncements the leaders were careful to insist that their movement was a demonstration and not a rebellion; 'we intend nothing against the Queen, but better counsel and councillors . . .' However, unlike the leaders of the Pilgrimage of Grace, or of the rebellions of 1549, these men had available a plausible alternative candidate for the throne; not the sad and discredited Jane Grey, but the Princess Elizabeth. Her name was never openly invoked, and her complicity was never proved, but there is considerable evidence to suggest that, had the rising succeeded, the queen would have been deposed in favour of her half-sister. It was, at least, a very premature intention. Most of the aristocracy, little as they liked the prospect of Philip as king, were a long way from being convinced that less drastic methods could not prevail. Those who had been implicated with Northumberland were still breathless from their narrow escape, and Mary was, after all, their lawful sovereign. Consequently the number involved was not great and the plot, although grandiose in conception, lacked substance. It was also flawed by the participation of Edward Courtenay. This young man was the son of the Marquis of Exeter, who had been executed in 1538, and had been in prison since his father's death. He was now twenty-six, and the intoxication of unaccustomed liberty had made him frivolous, petulant and unstable. He had been restored to his father's lesser title of Earl of Devon in September 1553, but this had been an act of filial penitence by the queen, rather than in recognition of his qualities. His age and descent made him the only plausible candidate for the queen's hand among the English nobility, and for that reason he was made much of by those who hoped to dissuade Mary from a foreign marriage – notably Stephen Gardiner. Unfortunately he was a poor instrument, and there was never any serious chance that she would have married him, but the news that she had definitely decided on Philip was a great blow to his self-esteem, and threw him into the arms of the conspirators.

For a few weeks he was full of obscure plans to raise the south-west, and his new friends devised a different course to the Crown matrimonial by proposing to marry him to Elizabeth, but he was a dangerous man to trust with a secret. Late in January 1554 his patron Gardiner, having heard some disquieting rumours, sent for him and persuaded him to reveal all that he knew. The conspirators, whose plans had not been intended to mature until Easter, were forced to choose between flight and immediate action.[6] They attempted the

[6]Courtenay's breakdown was in fact the last of a series of incidents which precipitated this crisis, because Renard had also discovered some part of the conspirators' plans. At the same time the Earl's indiscretions had begun before

latter, but their incomplete scheme misfired. Sir James Croft, who was supposed to raise the Welsh marches, never left London. The Duke of Suffolk, with his brothers, Thomas and John Grey, went down to his estates in Leicestershire and raised a small force from among his tenants and kinsmen.

However, it proved impossible to stir up an anti-Spanish panic, and within a few days his neighbour and enemy the Earl of Huntingdon was in full command of the situation. Suffolk's force dispersed, and the three brothers took to flight, but all were captured and lodged in the Tower. Sir Peter Carew did his best to exploit the exposed position of Devon, by persuading the gentry of the danger of a Spanish landing; but although he succeeded in creating a good deal of alarm, the reaction was not as militant as he had hoped, and after a few days he gave up and fled to France. These failures left the whole burden of the enterprise to be borne by the one leader who did succeed in raising a force, Sir Thomas Wyatt.

Wyatt had the advantage of a closely knit group of friends and associates to support him, and Kent was a county of many small interests, not dominated by a few great families. It was also readily accessible to propaganda from London, and had a more turbulent history than any other English county over the previous hundred years. Wyatt began to muster forces at his home, Allington castle, near Maidstone, about 20 January, while his supporters rode around the countryside declaring that 'the Spaniards was coming into the realm with harness and handguns, and would make us Englishmen wondrous . . . vile'. His intention was to persuade the Kentishmen that there already existed a spontaneous nationwide protest against the Spanish marriage, in which they were invited to join. The sheriff, Sir Robert Southwell, was quick to inform the Council that something was afoot, but he could not assess the seriousness of the situation, and was finding his neighbours ominously uncooperative.

The reaction from Westminster was puzzled and hesitant. Gardiner had not been fully frank with his colleagues about Courtenay's disclosures, because he wished to protect that young man from the consequences of his own folly. Nor were any of them certain that the Kentish demonstration was

his interview with Gardiner, and Noailles blamed him principally for the betrayal of the plot.

connected with the wider conspiracy, of which they were already aware. Several highly placed opponents of the marriage, notably the Earls of Arundel and Shrewsbury, were absent from the court. There is no reason to suppose that they sympathised with the rebels, but their retinues were not immediately available and without them there was no military force capable of moving swiftly to disperse the malcontents. Consequently an attempt was made to negotiate, and envoys were sent down to Allington to remind Wyatt that if he objected to the queen's policy, it was his duty as a true subject to sue by petition. Sir Thomas, who was endeavouring to be all things to all men, managed to evade this overture, and on 25 January raised his standard at Maidstone. The same day proclamations were issued at Maidstone, Tonbridge, Malling, and various other places in the county, declaring that the realm was in imminent danger. By the 27th he probably had about two thousand men under arms, not counting detachments at Tonbridge and Sevenoaks. By contrast, Southwell had made almost no progress. Only Lord Abergavenny had made any move to assist him. Sir Thomas Cheney, the Lord Warden of the Cinque Ports, and the most powerful man in East Kent, protested his own loyalty, but declared that his men would not follow him. To complete the sheriff's discomfiture, Wyatt proclaimed him and all who adhered to him traitors to the queen and commonwealth.

By this time the Council had reluctantly decided that a military operation was necessary, but the quarrel between Stephen Gardiner and Lord Paget, which had been disrupting business for two months, made every plan and proposal contentious. Renard and Paget, who had always been the principal protagonists of the marriage, endeavoured to use the situation to discredit Gardiner by accusing him of sabotaging the military preparations, and hinting that he was in league with the rebels. Gardiner, who had long since accepted the inevitability of the marriage, and had played a leading part in negotiating the treaty, exposed himself to this attack by continuing to urge negotiations with the dissidents. As a result the first move was a fiasco. A force of about eight hundred, mainly Londoners, was hastily scraped together under the command of the senile Duke of Norfolk, and sent down to link up with Southwell and Abergavenny. The

Londoners were strongly sympathetic to Wyatt, and deserted to him *en masse* at the first opportunity, in a move which had probably been planned before they left the capital. The Kentish loyalists were completely discouraged, and the queen had no army between herself and a sizeable rebellion. However, hesitancy in the Council was now at an end. Although Renard claimed for himself the credit for persuading the queen to remain at Westminster, the decision was probably her own, and coincided with the majority opinion. Consequently, in spite of his success, time was not on Wyatt's side. He had by now about three thousand men, and the prospect of a favourable reception in London, but no man of any great substance had joined him in arms, and recruitment outside Kent had been disappointing. London was the key, but instead of marching directly on the City, the rebels delayed for four or five days, reducing unimportant places like Cooling Castle. Meanwhile a general proclamation of Wyatt's treason had been issued, and the queen had appeared in person at the Guildhall to appeal to the loyalty of the citizens. By the time Wyatt eventually arrived in Southwark on 3 February, he found that the efforts of his friends had been neutralised, and London Bridge was held against him in some strength. News had also arrived of the collapse of the Duke of Suffolk's foray, and Paget's energy was rallying magnate support to the Crown. Even so, Wyatt displayed no sense of urgency, lingering in Southwark for three days before finally giving up hope of entering the City by that route. On 6 February he made a belated attempt to redeem the situation by rapid march to Kingston bridge, followed by an assault along the north bank of the Thames. By the time he reached London in the early hours of the following morning, the Earl of Pembroke had a force in the field against him, and his own army was much reduced by desertion. The issue was not, however, beyond doubt. Pembroke's men at first made no attempt to attack their depleted enemies, and eyewitness accounts suggest that the Earl's control was extremely fragile. Only when it became clear that the City would not admit the rebels, and that the gates were securely held for the queen, was the spell finally broken. Pembroke attacked with belated resolution; within a few moments Wyatt's force had surrendered, and Sir Thomas himself was on the way to the Tower.

It was not a very satisfying victory from the government's point of view. A relatively small rebellion, without magnate backing, had nevertheless managed for a few days to present a serious threat to the Crown. Its ringleaders could be punished, but dissatisfaction with the Spanish marriage was neither suppressed nor discredited. The participation of the Duke of Suffolk enabled the Council to claim that the object of the rebellion had really been to restore his daughter to the throne, but this was unconvincing, and did not succeed in creating any general association between dislike of Spain and the practices of the Duke of Northumberland. On the contrary, the protestants, who were also blamed by official propaganda, began to gain in credibility from the same association, and those who were soon regarding Sir Thomas Wyatt as a martyr were making the first explicit connection between protestantism and English national feeling. Nor were the Council's own divisions resolved by Wyatt's defeat. Renard, acting on instructions from Granvelle, urged Mary to be severe with the ringleaders, and lenient to the rank and file. Gardiner wished to strike at Elizabeth, but to protect Courtenay, and therefore became the leading exponent of the religious interpretation. Paget was prepared to sacrifice Courtenay, but determined to protect the princess, and advocated a general policy of mercy. The queen herself, after a brief period of anger, was appeased, and listened sympathetically even to the forlorn appeals of Jane Wyatt. In the event about a hundred were executed, a high proportion of them Londoners, but the victims appear to have been chosen without any particular purpose in mind.[7] Elizabeth and Courtenay both escaped with brief periods of imprisonment, while the luckless Jane Grey and her husband suffered. Already attainted, and unprotected by powerful friends, they were easy, if irrelevant prey. By the end of March Noailles, who had failed to move quickly enough to bring aid to Wyatt when it might have mattered, was noting with satisfaction that the projected appearance of the Prince of Spain was still viewed with resentment which might be

[7] This applied to the exactions of fines, as well as to executions. The punishments were nothing like as severe as those which Elizabeth was to exact after the rebellion of 1569, and Renard was greatly dissatisfied with the lack of severity. Loades, *Two Tudor Conspiracies*, 113–27.

stimulated into action when the appropriate time came. Renard, who as a congenital pessimist was of the same opinion, threatened to postpone the visit *sine die* if better discipline could not be maintained.

THE SCHISM ENDED

Tension was high throughout the summer, not least because of the continuing uncertainties over Philip's intentions, but when he actually landed on 20 July, it was something of an anticlimax. He and his followers behaved with unexpected tact and graciousness, and the marriage was concluded without a hitch. There was no military occupation. The alarmists were temporarily discredited, and the King of France was too preoccupied with his campaign in the Netherlands to carry out the threatened interception. Mary's determination appeared to be vindicated, and it now remained to capitalise upon this success. With his son safely installed in England, and likely to get the main credit for a successful negotiation – a credit which they both needed in their constant battle against French influence in the Curia – the Emperor withdrew his objections to a policy of full-scale catholic restoration. Within a few weeks formal steps had been taken towards the ending of the twenty-year-old schism.

This, as we have seen, had always been close to Mary's heart. Within a few weeks of her accession she had received a secret envoy from the pope, and had assured him '. . . that she had always been most obedient and affectionate towards the apostolic see, and that his Holiness had no more loving daughter than herself'. At the same time a series of letters from Cardinal Pole, already appointed Legate for England, urged her passionately to declare her allegiance openly in the interest of her own salvation. Those laws which declared her to be Head of the Church, he urged, were invalidated by the Law of God and needed no repeal. The miracle of her accession had been wrought for this sole purpose, and no mere human considerations should be allowed to stand in her way.

> Shall God grant his help to schismatics and heretics assembled in parliament to reform the affairs of the kingdom [he wrote in fury]? God has given the sceptre and the sword into her majesty's hands for no other reason than

that ribaldry and disobedience to the Holy laws may be punished . . .

Such words reflected the lofty idealism of a man long out of touch with the affairs of his native land, and although it pained her, Mary was compelled to allow more cautious counsels to prevail. Laws passed by parliament must be repealed by parliament, even if this was seen to be a surrender of principle. Also, the restoration of the mass and the restoration of the papal jurisdiction were two quite different things, since the royal supremacy had won a measure of acceptance which had not been accorded to protestant doctrine. Above all, the return of the papacy would raise the whole question of the entitlement to secularised church lands. 'It is my duty to warn your Majesty', Renard had written to Charles, 'that the catholics hold more church lands than do the heretics', and he added that they had no intention of surrendering them, pope or no pope.

The queen had reluctantly agreed that there was no immediate prospect of solving these problems, but she had no intention of allowing her officials to enforce heretical worship. The first session of Mary's first parliament predictably repealed all the Edwardian religious legislation and from 20 December 1553 the English church reverted to the state in which King Henry VIII had left it. As yet, however, there was no persecution. A number of leading protestants had been imprisoned on one pretext or another, and at the beginning of 1554 a sweeping disciplinary campaign was launched, aimed particularly at those clergy who had availed themselves of the opportunity to marry. Hundreds of deprivations followed, including a number of bishops. Ironically Mary, who had abandoned the offensive title of Supreme Head before Christmas, was perfectly willing to use the authority of that office to restore the traditional order, but not to try spiritual offenders. Consequently there were no proceedings for heresy until the papal authority was acknowledged.

In March 1554, at the same time as issuing a set of visitation articles in her own name, the queen also took the quite illegal step of secretly recognising Cardinal Pole's Legatine jurisdiction. Mary clearly believed that good conscience should not be constrained by bad law, and covered her convictions in this instance with only the thinnest of veils. It had been made quite clear in the parliamentary session of November 1553 that neither House was willing to dismantle the royal supremacy, at least until some satisfactory guarantee had been obtained for the secularised church lands, and this neither Pole nor the pope himself was willing to grant at that stage. The second session of April 1554 saw no break in the deadlock. Gardiner seems to have made an attempt to pledge the papacy's consent to such a guarantee, but he was not entitled to do so, and the parliament very properly refused to be drawn.[8] The Chancellor's purpose was partly to take the wind out of Imperial sails, and to safeguard English catholicism against Spanish associations, by negotiating a deal with the Curia before Philip's arrival. For that very reason he was bitterly opposed by the leading English Imperialist, Lord Paget, and another round of their feud, which as we have seen had boiled up over the Wyatt rebellion, was fought out on the floor of the House of Lords. Gardiner's proposals were defeated, and the queen was understandably furious at this public display of conflict between two of her leading councillors. Paget narrowly escaped arrest, and never thereafter recovered Mary's confidence – owing his subsequent rehabilitation and appointment as Lord Privy Seal entirely to Philip. In August 1554 Julius III finally came to the conclusion that he would have to cut the churches' losses in England, thus making serious negotiations possible at exactly the time that Philip, as King of England, was ready to take a hand. Both Philip and his father were now anxious for a quick settlement, and it was only Cardinal Pole, who fully shared Gardiner's misgivings about bringing the pope back in a Spanish baggage train, who stood in the way. However, Pole could not indefinitely defend a position which his master had abandoned. By October he had been convinced that no alternative course was possible, and shortly afterwards the English Council invited him to return to his native land after almost twenty-five years of exile.

These weeks were the climax of Mary's life. By the end of October she was convinced that she was pregnant, and the

[8] Since these proposals never reached the stage of draft bills, they are difficult to reconstruct in detail. Loades, *Oxford Martyrs*, 125–7; *Reign of Mary*, 168–9.

news of this had a strangely calming effect upon the turbulent citizens of London. On 24 November, Pole was welcomed with every sign of devotion and pious enthusiasm, and a few days later parliament, satisfied with the terms of its bargain, petitioned for reconciliation to the Holy See. On 30 November, amid scenes of spectacular emotion, Pole pronounced a solemn absolution, and both he and the queen were convinced that the powers of darkness had been banished for ever. On 2 December Gardiner preached to a packed throng at Paul's Cross on the text *iam nos de somno surgere*, and Habsburg Europe celebrated the triumph of its latest crusader in heretical England. However, below the surface the situation was less satisfactory, and before Christmas serious differences of opinion had arisen about the settlement which was still incomplete until it had been embodied in legislation. The common lawyers, and no doubt most of the lay aristocracy, assumed the papal dispensation to mean that the Henrician statutes were now acknowledged to have created a valid title to the monastic property, which had been vested in the Crown and thus transferred to the purchasers and grantees. Pole, with the queen's support, denied this. The title remained in the church, but the pope was graciously pleased to allow the present holders to continue in occupation. Their title thus depended upon the dispensation itself, which could, of course, be revoked by a subsequent pope.

No open disaffection resulted from this disturbing realisation, but doubt and distrust lingered for the remainder of the reign, and the sharp struggle between Pole and the possessioners over the form of the statute quickly disrupted the superficial harmony of late November. In the short term the greatest gainer from the reconciliation was Gardiner, who was at last placed in a position to implement his policy of sharp religious coercion. Thus, although Pole in no way dissented, the religious persecution which began in earnest in February 1555 was principally the work of the queen and the Chancellor. Mary's mind was expressed in a memorandum which she wrote to the Council early in the same month:

> Touching the punishment of heretics, methinketh it ought to be done without rashness, not leaving in the meanwhile to do justice to such as by learning would seem to deceive

the simple. And the rest to be so used that the people might well perceive them not to be condemned without just occasion, whereby they both understand the truth and beware to do the like . . .

In spite of Gardiner's desire to build up the prestige of the restored ecclesiastical jurisdiction, and the queen's own scruples, it is significant that not only the Council, but the whole machinery of secular administration, played a large part in the implementation of this policy of catholic uniformity. Throughout the following three and a half years we find constant directives and exhortations being issued by the Council to commissioners of the peace for the apprehension of preachers, and the suppression of irregularities. Royal commissions were used, alongside Legatine ones, for enquiries into heretical practices, and for the seizure of protestant books and writings. The effectiveness of the persecution depended, above all, upon the willingness of the lay magistrates to implement it, and in spite of all claims to the contrary, the Marian church was substantially the church by law established, just as its Henrician and Edwardian predecessors had been.

It was partly for this reason that the policy of coercion failed. Although there were zealous persecutors among the gentry, such as Edmund Tyrell in Essex, on the whole the magistrates were apathetic and negligent instruments. As time went on the Council, acting upon the queen's instructions, became increasingly liberal with reprimands and minor punishments, but the effect was slight.[9] Nor was this situation much helped by Cardinal Pole's own priorities, and those which were forced upon him by papal policy. The latter required him, and his bishops, to spend a disproportionate amount of their time and energy taking stock of the chaotic financial state to which the church had been reduced by a combination of neglect and political pressure. The former, by concentrating upon discipline and education, accepted a long timetable of gradual rehabilitation, and did little to stimulate the sense of spiritual mission which was

[9] For instance in letters to the JPs of Norfolk (British Library, Cotton MS Titus B II, 104, May 1554) and Yorkshire (Wombwell MSS, *Historical Manuscripts Commission*, 55, 2 April 1557).

needed to combat protestant activism on its own terms.[10] 'The priests are coming back to take their revenge', claimed the protestant propagandists, and it was a claim which gained plausibility from innumerable disciplinary proceedings and fiscal enquiries. By contrast, the reformers succeeded in bringing about a transformation in their own image. The Duke of Northumberland's apostasy had enabled them to dissociate themselves from his rapacity and unscrupulous opportunism, while at the same time Philip's undoubted role in the resurgence of persecuting catholicism presented them with the opportunity to pose as the spearhead of patriotic resistance to Spanish domination. By the spring of 1555 they also had a faith for which men and women were prepared to die. This dramatic change was partly the government's own fault, because before 1553 protestantism had been viewed by the indifferent as Swiss or German rather than English. By 1555 those same citizens who had pressed to dip their handkerchieves in Sir Thomas Wyatt's blood were crowding round the stakes at Smithfield, shouting encouragement to the victims. Just how spontaneous these demonstrations were is hard to assess. In some cases they were certainly contrived by sympathisers in the crowd, but the majority were at least willing to be influenced, and the demonstrations were usually described by observers as being hostile to the authorities. Nearly three hundred victims over three and a half years was not a sanguinary persecution by European standards, but it was unprecedented in England, and it was unpopular because the English could not be persuaded that heresy was a serious crime. At the same time the heroism of the early victims, particularly Rogers and Hooper, made a deep impression upon many who were not predisposed to favour their cause, and rescued it from accusations of time serving.

To do Gardiner justice, it is clear that he had expected no such reaction, and when it became clear that the heretics would not be quickly cowed or eliminated by violence, he desired to try other methods. Foxe exaggerated when he

[10] Pole's priorities were set out clearly in the draft decrees of his Legatine Synod of 1556–7 (Wilkins, *Concilia*, IV, 126). He tended to distrust preaching (in which he differed from Mary) and to seek for the restoration of good habits and piety. Papal concern with legal and financial proprieties was a major distraction. R. H. Pogson, 'Reginald Pole and the priorities of government in Mary Tudor's church', *Historical Journal*, 1975, 3–21.

claimed that the Chancellor 'gave the matter over as utterly discouraged'; rather, he urged imprisonment, fines and civil disabilities in place of the burnings which were turning into propaganda orgies. However, by the summer of 1555 the queen and the cardinal were fully committed to a course which was not so much a policy as the discharge of a solemn duty. It is debatable whether they might have succeeded in the long run, because both were cut short by death in 1558. Catholic conformity certainly did make progress in the latter part of the reign, but there was no sign of any diminution in protestant activity or determination. Moreover, with the execution of respected leaders such as Cranmer and Ridley, more uninhibited voices were to be heard, notably those of John Ponet and Christopher Goodman, calling upon the godly to arise and smite the 'Jezebel of England'. It is also significant that when the issue was tried in parliament in 1559, there was no catholic party worthy of the name in the House of Commons. The fact is that the protestants were allowed to score a resounding propaganda victory, not, perhaps, as resounding as it was made to appear by the Elizabethans, but nevertheless real and substantial. Both the quality and the quantity of government propaganda was poor, reflecting a lack of intelligent management which was typical of Mary's public relations.[11] Innumerable works of conservative piety reflect a buoyant demand, but hard-hitting and effective defences of government policy, either secular or religious, can be counted on the fingers of one hand. A series of measures, similar to those of Henry's and Edward's governments, prescribed penalties for the production, importation or possession of heretical or seditious works, but their effect seems to have been small.

Gardiner died on 12 November 1555, and his loss was never remedied. He had been the only major English statesman in whom the queen had reposed any confidence, and he was succeeded by an amiable nonentity, Nicholas Heath. This was

[11] There were a few substantial works of anti-protestant polemic, such as Christopherson's *An Exhortation to All Men to Take Heed and Beware of Rebellion* (1554) and Huggarde's *The Displaying of the Protestants* (1556), but no organised government campaign. Loyal ballads and broadsheets were produced, but again not in numbers to suggest purposeful encouragement. *Reign of Mary*, 160–4. J. Loach, 'Pamphlets and politics, 1553–8', *Bulletin of the Institute of Historical Research*, 1975, 31–45.

doubly unfortunate since the optimism of the early part of the year had evaporated, leaving a sour taste behind. In July the queen's vital pregnancy had finally been revealed as a pathological delusion, and Philip had almost immediately departed for the Netherlands. After the reconciliation with Rome, his twelve-month stay in England had achieved remarkably little, except periodic savage brawls between his servants and the citizens of London. He had failed to build up any significant clientage among the English aristocracy, although several had been willing to serve him, and played only a minor and spasmodic role in the government of England.[12] This may have been partly due to the limitations imposed by the marriage treaty, but was more the result of his constant preoccupation with the affairs of other Habsburg lands, and of his hearty distaste for England and the English. In one sense his departure relieved the tension which had been building up during the summer as rumours of the queen's health became more alarming, but it did not solve the problem of his political future. Although Mary would not acknowledge the fact herself, she could not now be expected to bear a healthy child, and by the terms of the marriage treaty, Philip's interest in England would cease with her death. At the same time the stake was a large one, and many politically aware Englishmen suspected that the treaty would be no safeguard should the queen die first. They therefore looked with the gravest distrust upon Mary's known desire to have her husband crowned in England. Legally, such a coronation would make no difference to his position, but the status of a king consort was unprecedented and full of uncertainties, so that the ceremonial possession of a crown was accorded great symbolic significance. *The copy of a letter*, a hastily written piece of anti-Spanish polemic by the Cheshire agitator John Bradford, reflects the confused thinking and powerful emotions which this subject generated.

[12] Philip's most effective interventions in government (as distinct from politics) came over the establishment of the 'select council' just before his departure, and over the appointment of Paget to succeed the Earl of Bedford as Lord Privy Seal. He clearly could have exercised considerable influence had he chosen to do so. He made no attempt to employ Englishmen on his own business elsewhere, presumably because the marriage treaty barred him from appointing Spaniards to offices in England.

> I think that you can never forget the unjust enterprise of the late Duke of Northumberland, and what miserable success it had. Be ye therefore wise and beware by other men's harms; for ye may perceive evidently that God will take vengeance upon wrongful doers.

Bradford's point was that the Crown belonged to 'the heirs of England', in this case, Elizabeth, and he was invoking the same spirit of legitimacy which had served Mary herself so well in 1553.

Partly as a result of this steadily mounting concern, which was not alleviated by Philip's absence, the parliament which assembled in October 1555 was the most difficult of the reign.[13] In the event, only one government measure was actually defeated – that designed to confiscate the property of the religious exiles – but both the fact and the manner of that result were significant. It was defeated upon a division, which was rare even for a private measure, and after an organised demonstration which landed the ringleader, Sir Anthony Kingston, in the Tower. It was the public demonstration of defiance rather than the loss of the bill which was damaging to the government. However, too much should not be made of the incident. The queen got her subsidy, in spite of protests, and the bulk of the legislative activity of the session was normal. In a sense what was not said was more significant than what was, because the issue in everyone's mind – Philip's coronation – was not raised. Mary wrote repeatedly to her husband, asking him to return, lamenting the intransigence of her subjects, and confessing that she dared not press the matter as he wished. But Philip stayed in the Netherlands, occupying himself with what really interested him – the struggle against France – and what was left of his influence in England withered away.

[13] '. . . the present House of Commons, whether by accident or design, a thing not seen for many years in any parliament, is quite full of gentry and nobility (for the most part suspect in matters of religion) and therefore more daring and licentious than former Houses, which consisted of burgesses and plebians, by nature timid and respectful . . .' (18 Nov. 1555) *Calendar of State Papers, Venetian*, VI, 251. In fact the Commons in Mary's parliament were not abnormally obstructive except where, as in this case, they felt their property interests to be threatened. J. Loach, 'Conservatism and consent in parliament, 1547–1559' in Loach and R. Tittler (eds.), *The Mid-Tudor Polity*, 9–28.

The queen was deeply distressed, both by her failure to gratify him and by his persistent refusal to visit her, but her willingness to accept defeat reduced the political temperature, and the government began to get on top of some of its other problems. After an uncertain start, and some ill-advised generosity in the first year of the reign, the problem of inherited debt was confronted. With the aid of the 1555 subsidy, and a Privy Seal loan (much resented, but nevertheless paid), the overall burden began to be reduced, and probably stood at about £130,000 by the early part of 1557.[14] At the same time the Council, by an efficient system of committees and commissions, was coping with the persistent problems of law enforcement and social unrest. The harvests of 1555 and 1556 were bad (the latter one of the worst of the century), but despite that fact, and the continuing discontent caused by the religious persecution and grumbling fears of Spanish intervention, there were no serious disorders. Rumours and alarms were legion, and the Council records give the impression that there were rebels and heretics behind every bush. Whether nervousness made them vigilant or vigilance made them nervous is not clear, but the councillors can certainly not be charged with complacency, and their watchfulness was effective. Foreign observers were frequently at a loss to know what to believe, and on one occasion when a serious conspiracy was reported, it was described as being a symptom of 'the general fear and suspicion which dominate here'.

Only one of these innumerable alarms merits particular mention, and that is the plot associated with the name of Henry Dudley, which was gradually brought to light during the spring of 1556. Dudley himself and most of the others whose complicity can be proved, were insubstantial men, but the plot had wide ramifications among the West Country gentry which were never fully unravelled, and seems to have touched the highest political level. Dudley's intention was to raise a force among the English exiles in France, and to invade with French backing, linking up with simultaneous risings in

[14] Mary had started badly by pardoning the last instalment of the Edwardian subsidy, and then taking out a very large loan to be repaid in Spain, but sound fiscal policies were becoming effective by 1555. *Reign of Mary*, 291–320.

the south and west of England. In the spring of 1556 Henri II did not feel ready for open war, and he extricated himself from the damaging revelations of Dudley's accomplices by disavowing and recalling Noailles, who had been only too obviously implicated. Nor did the English Council wish to respond more forcefully, having problems enough at home without getting involved in expensive adventures abroad. In the autumn, however, the prospects for continuing the much-needed peace began to cloud as Pope Paul IV crowned a year of strenuous anti-Habsburg diplomacy by provoking Philip into attacking him. Henri quickly rallied to the papal side, and Philip began to put pressure on Mary to involve England as well. The queen was willing, but both her subjects and her Council had long dreaded this situation, and emphasised that the marriage treaty had been careful to exclude any such obligation. However, the king was hard-pressed, and his honour as well as his fortunes was at stake, so in March 1557 he returned at length to England, to add his weight to Mary's.

Within the Council only his faithful ally Lord Paget was in favour of war, the majority having already expressed their views frankly in writing:

> It is considered that the common people of this realm being partly many ways grieved, some pinched with famine and want of payment of money due to them, some miscontented for matters of religion, and generally all yet talking of the smarte of the last wars, it might be very dangerous to entangle them now with new wars, especially where necessity of defence shall not require the same . . .

Cogent as these arguments were, councillors did not, in the last analysis, make decisions of peace and war. At this time the issue was resolved by the ridiculous escapade of one Thomas Stafford, a distant kinsman of Cardinal Pole,[15] who descended on the Yorkshire coast with a handful of men and proclaimed himself 'Protector of the Realm'. Whether he was a French catspaw or a dupe of Lord Paget is not clear. He was

[15] Stafford was a son of Cardinal Pole's sister, Ursula, and represented himself in France as the rightful Duke of Buckingham, and heir to the English throne. In the spring of 1557 he was allowed to recruit a small force in France, and he seized Scarborough castle. The fact that he was aided and transported by Jean Ribaut, who is known to have had connections with Paget, makes the real nature of the enterprise uncertain.

quickly defeated and executed, but the incident was sufficient to enable the king and queen to insist on war, and thereby to aggravate all the problems against which the English government was struggling.

The war effort itself was not as contemptible as Spanish observers and diplomats liked to claim, especially considering the devastating effects of the influenza epidemic of 1557–8, which followed the near famine of the previous year. Nor were all Englishmen averse to war. The Earl of Pembroke was able to lead a creditable (and largely volunteer) expeditionary force to the siege of St Quentin. However, it proved impossible to reinforce, despite the king's willingness to pay; and the loss of Calais in January 1558 knocked what stuffing there was out of English zeal. It was probably influenza rather than sheer depression which frustrated the recovery expedition, but the troops were sent home without ever having been fully mustered, and what little was done during the remainder of the war was almost entirely at sea. Philip blamed his English subjects bitterly, and they, with rather more justice, blamed him. Even without major military operations, the cost of the navy, and of the Scottish borders, threatened by Mary of Guise, remorselessly pushed up the debts which Mary's Council had been working so hard to reduce. By the end of the reign they were approaching £300,000, about 80 per cent higher than the burden which the queen had inherited.[16] The church was certainly not immune from the general blight. Cardinal Pole's Legatine powers were withdrawn in April 1557, and he was summoned to Rome to face charges of heresy. The charges were the result of Paul IV's personal malice, and Mary insisted on him remaining at his post, but for the last year and a half of his ministry Pole was a broken man, while English business was neglected in Rome, and lesser men strove by administrative means to maintain the momentum of the catholic restoration at home.

The accumulated misfortunes of the last two years of Mary's reign appear to the modern observer to be more the results of bad luck than misjudgement. It was not Mary's fault that she failed to bear a child, or that the harvest failed, or that the

[16] The navy alone cost £143,000 between January 1557 and November 1558. *Reign of Mary*, 418–20.

influenza was so devastating – or even that the pope hated her husband. However, in contemporary eyes that hardly mattered – indeed natural misfortunes were worse than obvious mistakes, because they could only be attributed to the judgement of God. It was the obvious fact that the queen's God had deserted her which created the peculiar atmosphere of 1558, and may well have shortened her own life. The protestants, of course, had an immediate explanation which they were not slow to produce: persecute God's Elect, and He will revenge Himself in His own way. Nevertheless, not all the blame for this should be laid at the door of a jealous God. The queen's own mistakes and inadequacies played their part. In marrying Philip she had gratified her own wishes at the expense of her kingdom's interest, and although it was a defensible decision the outcome could have been, and was, predicted. In fact the marriage was designed by Charles and Granvelle with scant consideration for England, and for the limited purpose of securing Philip's position in the Netherlands, it worked perfectly well. More damaging than the marriage itself was the attitude of which it was a symptom. In the queen's eyes all the principal changes which had taken place in England since 1529 were evil, and this had several important consequences. The first, and most obvious, was her desire to reverse the main drift of policy; the second was her willingness to believe that the endorsement of her claim in 1553 meant that her subjects shared her views in all important respects (which led in turn to the conviction that all opposition was the work of small minorities); and the third was her unwillingness to repose full trust in anyone who had been associated with the policies she deplored. It was this which led her to confide first in Renard, then in Philip, and finally in Cardinal Pole. As a result her relations with her Council were consistently unsatisfactory. This was not, as Imperial observers tended to believe, mainly a question of numbers. Because of the circumstances of her accession, Mary was forced to assemble a heterogeneous Council,[17] and there

[17] Mary needed a Council as soon as she proclaimed her title – hence the so-called 'Framlingham Council', made up of her earliest adherents. These were mostly men of little political experience, and had to be augmented by more seasoned politicians, as soon as these became available. There were constant tensions between these two groups, but the queen had little choice if her government was to be effective.

were naturally quarrels and divisions among the councillors. Paget made this diversity work to advantage in administration, by allocating different work to specialist groups. At the political level, however, the queen seems to have expected her councillors to give her unanimous advice, and to tell her what to do. When they failed to do so (as any Tudor Privy Council would have failed), she became baffled and angry, and complained that she spent all her time shouting at them to no effect. First Renard and then Feria (Philip's representative in England at the end of the reign) echoed and magnified these complaints.

> 'They change everything they have decided', wrote the latter, 'and it is impossible to make them see what a state they are in . . .'

Such remarks were partly prompted by the refusal of the English Council to take its orders from Brussels, partly by the envoys' desire to magnify their own difficulties and achievements, and partly because they could not openly say that the problem lay in the queen's inexperience and lack of political intelligence.

Mary paid a heavy price for her limitations during her lifetime, just as she paid a devastating price for failure after her death. Perhaps most seriously in the long run, by failing to appreciate the difference between religious conservatism and full catholicism, she drove a wedge between the two, and enabled the protestants to pose as the party of national priorities. Significantly, there was no powerful political interest to defend her policies after her death. As her abler servants, such as Gardiner and Petre, died or retired, they were replaced by men of lesser ability, such as Heath, Bourne and Boxall; and her own favoured servants were generally men of good catholic antecedents and mediocre talent, such as Rochester, Waldegrave and Englefield. Apart from the conservative clergy, the only group among her own subjects for whom she seems to have felt much affection were those whose families had suffered disgrace or disfavour during the previous twenty years. The Howards and the Courtenays were restored to their lands and dignities at the beginning of the reign, and in 1557 the Northumberland title was revived for Sir Thomas Percy. All her major peerage creations were restorations, and at the lower social level rewards went mainly to those who had rallied quickly to her standard in 1553. It was hardly a constructive or forward-looking policy.

At the same time, it would be a mistake to conclude any summary assessment of the reign by emphasising only failures and weaknesses. Not only did Mary preserve the legitimate Tudor succession at the beginning of her reign, she also preserved it at the end. As Renard pointed out, long after he had left England, most of the plots and dangers of the reign had been the work of those who wished to bring Elizabeth to the throne before her time. By defeating these attempts, and eventually (albeit reluctantly) allowing her sister to succeed without dispute, she preserved her country from the dangers of civil war. She also handed Elizabeth an invaluable lesson on the importance of establishing and maintaining good working relations with the aristocracy – a lesson which Elizabeth, if anything, learned too well. At a more mundane level, her financial ministers completed the reform of the Exchequer, planned under Edward VI, and successfully imposed a new book of customs rates – a feat which their successors did not even attempt. The militia was reorganised (in 1558), subsidy assessments updated and improved (1555), and a number of measures passed to improve the administration of the law. Little as Mary may have loved them, she had no option but to employ servants trained in the school of Thomas Cromwell, and they served the commonwealth well. By contrast the preservation of order, a constant preoccupation, was achieved by very conservative means. Licences to retain were issued with even greater freedom than under the Duke of Northumberland, although the recipients tended to be prelates and members of the older aristocracy. In 1555 selected noblemen, such as the Earl of Cumberland, were ordered to muster their servants and tenants for the suppression of 'any sudden stir or tumult'. Such measures provided the basis for the later Elizabethan claim that Mary had ruled through a tyrannical 'popish faction'. Such was certainly not her intention, but she was naturally compelled to rely upon men who were thought to be dependable – and they became both fewer and more distinctively catholic as the reign advanced.

CHAPTER 9

A NEW QUEEN AND A NEW IDENTITY

When it pleased God to send a blessing upon us He gave us His servant Elizabeth to be our Queen, and to be the instrument of His glory in the sight of the world . . .
(John Jewel, *View of a Seditious Bull*)

Looking back on the accession of Elizabeth, Englishmen of later generations were conditioned to regard it as the supreme act of Divine benevolence, but it did not look that way at the time, except to the beleaguered protestant minority. The enthusiasm which greeted her, like that which had greeted Mary, was more the result of relief at a legitimate and peaceful succession than of knowledge of her intentions. Nevertheless, she was quick to perceive that the policies of the previous five years had had many unintended consequences. The conservative national church of Henry VIII had been seriously weakened by the return to Rome, and Rome had been further contaminated in the eyes of most Englishmen by association with Spain. Nor could either side now deny that the settlement of religion was a matter for parliament, since statute had both made and unmade a reformation. At the same time adversity had taught the religious exiles in Germany and Switzerland some new ways of looking at their situation. Temporarily freed from the constraints of an establishment, they had been able to conduct liturgical and intellectual experiments which laid the foundations of English puritanism. They had also begun to dabble with those doctrines of principled resistance which were to be of such great importance in the following century. Thus to Christopher Goodman God could put the sword directly into the hands of the people to punish the idolatry of their rulers,[1]

[1] *How Superior Powers ought to be Obeyed* (1558).

while John Ponet more comprehensively saw the whole authority of the prince as a delegation from the community.[2]

To one of these exile groups also belonged the credit for originating the ideology of England as an Elect Nation, which was to play a fundamental part in the development of the English polity during the next half century. Brooding upon the mysterious ways of the Lord, they came to the conclusion that the Marian persecution was a fiery purgation designed to test the vocation of England to a special place in the divine order. Starting from this assumption, and mixing a little secular nationalism with their eschatology, they were able to prove to their own satisfaction that this was part of an historical evolution beginning with the first establishment of Christianity in Britain. King John's quarrel with the papacy, the Statutes of Praemunire, the condemnation of Wycliffe, and Henry VIII's establishment of the royal supremacy, could all be seen as leading up to this supreme test. Naturally this idiosyncratic view of the history of the Church went hand in hand with a devotion to the Prayer Book and to the English Crown which was not shared by all the expatriots. Some, more completely under the influence of Calvin's Geneva, could see no hope in the policies of princes and looked forward only to converting their homeland into some semblance of 'the most perfect school of Christ'. To those who created the vision of England as a New Jerusalem, however, the monarchy and particularly the enigmatic personality of Elizabeth loomed very large. If their hopes were ever to come to fulfilment, it must be through her, and long before there was any tangible reason to do so, they had convinced themselves that she would lend herself to their purposes. She was to be the new Constantine, or Deborah taking council for the people of the Lord. As soon as the news of Mary's death reached them, they hastened home, while the more cautious and realistic Genevans waited to see what the attitude of the new queen would be.

Her sister's mistakes, and the perils of her own position had meanwhile provided the young princess with a series of valuable political lessons. She was never to forget how dangerous it was to be the heir to a throne, often the unwitting focus of foolish plots, and the name automatically in the mouth of every malcontent. In later years her hesitant treatment of Mary Stuart was to reflect not merely an acknowledgement of her royal

[2] *A Short Treatise of Politic Power* (1556).

status but an understanding of the genuine difficulty of her position. More important, Elizabeth, who was naturally cool headed and detached, had been given an excellent opportunity to observe the realities of political power. Mary's passionate commitment to the Habsburgs and the catholic Church had been frustrated, fundamentally, by the non-cooperation of the aristocracy. 'It boots not how many laws be made,' a commentator had written of Somerset's enclosure legislation, 'for men see few or none put into effect.' The same could be true of any policy.

Power was rooted in the counties, and particularly in the commissions of the peace, and without a substantial measure of backing at this level there could be no hope of effective government. In the late 1540s the gentry had passed through a crisis in their relations with the commons, but their authority in the countryside was less damaged than has sometimes been supposed. They were prepared to welcome the administrative duties which the Crown imposed upon them as tending to strengthen their hold upon their poorer neighbours, and also as forging direct links with the monarchy which made them less dependent upon their social superiors. At the same time, as we have seen, their political awareness at the national level was increasing as they became conscious of the interdependence of politics and administration. Mary, who preferred priests and the ancient peerage, was not a 'gentleman's queen'. Elizabeth understood from the beginning that her relations with this class of her subjects would be of fundamental importance, and that their prejudices and ambitions would have to be taken into account, at least in the general direction of her policies. In 1558 they wanted an end to the threat of Spanish domination and unequivocal security for the lands which they or their predecessors had acquired from the Church.

Mary never wanted her half sister to succeed, and throughout the reign she was in constant danger. Renard did his best to bring her to the block after Wyatt's rising, and Philip's advisers continued to recommend her removal as the best means of securing his own influence in the country. At one point it was intended to marry her to the Duke of Savoy, and any pretext would have been welcome to send her overseas. Gardiner tried on at least two occasions to have her excluded from the succession by statute, and Mary wished to replace her with Margaret Clifford, the daughter of Frances Brandon's sister Eleanor, who had married Henry Clifford, Earl of Cumberland. Margaret's only qualification for the succession was her unimpeachable catholicism. All these attempts failed, and in March 1558 Renard penned a memorandum which recognised the invincibility of her position. By this time he had been out of England for two and a half years, but his observations upon the situation are of considerable interest.

> It must not be forgotten [he wrote] that all the plots and disorders that have troubled England during the past four years have aimed at placing Elizabeth in possession of the government sooner than the course of nature would permit.

There was, he believed, an organised party which had stimulated these conspiracies and assiduously protected the princess's interests. Although he mentioned no names, it is clear that he considered several councillors to be involved and saw the strength of the party in its proximity to the centre of power. How much truth there was in this interpretation it is very difficult to determine. Certainly in the crisis of February and March 1554 Lord Paget was the leader of an influential group who succeeded in frustrating Renard's attempts to bring her to trial, but beyond this there is no conclusive evidence for the kind of organisation which the diplomat suspected. This is not surprising since the utmost discretion would have been necessary in its operation, but the necessity for discretion passed in time and no mention of such services was ever made. Renard was always inclined to over-emphasise the deliberation of his opponents, and in this case probably saw a conspiracy in what was in fact no more than a measure of tacit understanding. In one respect his international preoccupations made him wildly inaccurate. He saw Elizabeth's supporters as allies of the French and believed that French intrigue had contributed to the princess's immunity.

In this connection Philip was wiser than his servant. He realised well enough that the French candidate to succeed Mary was not Elizabeth but Mary Stuart, the grand-daughter of Henry VIII's sister Margaret and currently betrothed to the Dauphin Francis.[8] When it became obvious to him that the English would not tolerate any continuation of his own authority after his wife's death, Philip abandoned his hostility to the princess and

[8] Mary was the daughter of James V, Margaret's son by her first marriage to James IV. She had been queen of Scotland in her own right since her father's early death in 1543.

in the last months of the reign used his full influence on her behalf. Mary Stuart had no backing in England, but the possibility of a French invasion was always present, and Philip rightly judged that English resistance would best be stimulated in defence of Elizabeth's title. Consequently while the queen was coming to the painful and reluctant conclusion that she would have to recognise her sister's right, her husband was already sending his ablest advisers to pay his respects to the rising sun.

THE ELIZABETHAN CHURCH

Thus when Mary died, a great many powerful and conflicting hopes focused on the new ruler. This was natural in the circumstances, and should not be taken to mean that she had committed herself in advance to the policies which were eventually formulated. She was bound to draw back from the Habsburg embrace and end the futile religious persecution, but more than this could not at first have been forecast. She was young, inexperienced in government, and unmarried, all factors which diminished her prospects of success, and although her accession was greeted with relief and popular rejoicing, many experienced administrators must have wondered whether the Tudor monarchy could survive another female ruler. Their fears proved to be groundless, not because Mary's failure had created ideal conditions for Elizabeth's success, but because the latter proved to be a remarkably able young woman with an exceptional capacity for judging both men and situations. 'She seems incomparably more feared than her sister,' wrote the Count de Feria shortly after her accession, 'and has her way absolutely, as her father did.' This was an exaggeration, but a significant one, for Elizabeth 'gloried' in her father and respected his achievements, while Mary's emotions had been engaged by her mother and her mother's people. In 1553 Charles V had sensibly advised Mary to be 'une bonne anglaise', but it was counsel she was incapable of following. Her successor did not make the same mistake.

The problems which faced the new queen in November 1558 were daunting. The country was at war with France, and Henri II 'bestrode the realms like a colossus . . . one foot in Calais, the other in Scotland'. The Crown was £300,000 in debt, and its military forces feeble and demoralised. Although peace negotiations had been under way for some months, England was too weak to carry any weight at the conference table, and whether talking or fighting was bound to be heavily dependent upon Spanish aid. This made any dramatic gestures of national independence impossible and seemed for the time being to guarantee the survival of the existing religious settlement. Indeed every argument of prudence pointed in the same direction, for it was impossible to judge the consequences of overturning the doctrine of the Church for a third time within the space of twelve years. Characteristically, Elizabeth made no statement of her position but continued to enforce the existing laws and prohibited unlicensed preaching by proclamation. Nevertheless, the protestants remained confident of her favour, drawing comfort from the end of the persecution and such studied gestures as her public prayer on the eve of her coronation:

> Thou hast dealt as wonderfully and mercifully with me as Thou didst with thy true and faithful servant Daniel the prophet; whom thou deliveredst out of the den, from the cruelty of the greedy and raging lions; even so was I overwhelmed, and only by Thee delivered.[4]

By the time that Parliament assembled in January 1559 the conservatives were thoroughly apprehensive, seeing in the queen's fondness for scriptural turns of phrase and her willingness to listen to preachers of doubtful orthodoxy confirmations of their longstanding fears. They were almost certainly right, but Elizabeth was more interested in jurisdiction than in religion, and the events of the first session suggest that she would probably have been satisfied with the restoration of the royal supremacy as it had existed at her father's death.

Two circumstances gave her the opportunity to go further. Although Cardinal Pole had died within a few hours of his sovereign, and ten sees were vacant by the time Parliament assembled, the remaining catholic bishops were unyielding in

[4] The whole of Elizabeth's behaviour during her ceremonial entry to London in January 1559 was a long series of propaganda statements and gestures for public consumption. It was a most talented performance, and a full account was almost immediately published under the title *The Passage of our most dread Sovereign Lady, Queen Elizabeth, through the City of London to Westminster, the Day before her Coronation*. (Reprinted in A. F. Pollard, *Tudor Tracts*).

their opposition. Most, like Nicholas Heath, Archbishop of York, willingly acknowledged their allegiance to the queen, but refused on grounds of conscience to have anything to do with the royal supremacy, however conservatively handled. Their hostile speeches and votes were not sufficient to sway the House of Lords, but they made it clear to Elizabeth that she would have to find a wholly new episcopate to run her national church. When Convocation unanimously reaffirmed its adherence to the see of Rome in February, it became equally clear that there would be no conservative churchmen who might prove more amenable. The royal supremacy had become a wholly protestant concept, and the Church 'as King Henry left it' was dead.

The second circumstance was the appearance in the House of Commons of an extremely well organised 'pressure group' of protestant gentry. Several of these, like Sir Anthony Cooke, had been in exile and sympathised strongly with that idealistic view of a protestant England which we have already noticed. They worked in close collaboration with their clerical friends in London, particularly John Jewel and Richard Cox, who had been their leaders in exile. They probably numbered less than thirty in a House which showed an unusually high proportion of continuity with its predecessor, but their message was one of hope and confidence, and this gave them an influence out of all proportion to their numbers. Throughout the first session they pressed hard for a fully protestant establishment similar to that of Edward VI, and by Easter their campaign had succeeded in convincing the queen that she did not have to make concessions to the catholic opposition.

By the end of March the peace negotiations at Cateau-Cambrésis were virtually concluded, and although England had not succeeded in salvaging much from the war, Elizabeth's own position was considerably strengthened. Henri II abandoned his daughter-in-law's pretensions to the English crown and recognised Elizabeth as the lawful queen. Thus although she was technically a bastard in catholic eyes, and incapable of inheriting, no catholic power was prepared to move against her should the pope make any pronouncement to that effect. For the time being there was no danger of his doing so, for Elizabeth had as yet made no move against the Church and the Curia was always poorly informed on English affairs, and she could afford to be less scrupulous about causing offence in that direction. All these factors combined to persuade the queen to abandon the half-measures which she had accepted during the first session and to reconvene Parliament after Easter with the object of completing a full protestant settlement.[5]

To an Act of Supremacy which was substantially unchanged, she now added an Act of Uniformity, restoring the Prayer Book of 1552 with only minor alterations. At first sight this settlement seems to be, as one historian has described it, 'a compromise in which the queen conceded most.' But in fact it was hardly a compromise at all. Doctrinally and liturgically it represented almost the entire programme of the Prayer Book exiles, with the exception of some minor liturgical details which they did not at the time regard as important. Neither the catholics nor the Genevans were accommodated at all; the former for reasons which we have already noticed, and the latter because they had for the most part remained abroad. At the same time, jurisdictionally it was a total victory for the queen, creating a thoroughly Erastian Church which Elizabeth was empowered to govern by royal commission. It was a bargain, certainly, but not a compromise. A bargain which the protestants were prepared to accept because of their self-induced faith in their sovereign as a Godly Prince. Having secured the substance of what she wanted, Elizabeth was never thereafter prepared to budge, in spite of the most persistent clamour for reform, but she succeeded nevertheless in preserving the faith of the majority of her subjects to the end.

Apart from the dwindling number of the bishops,[6] there was little opposition to these measures. Fewer than a dozen lay peers dissented, and there was no organised resistance in the Commons. The contrast between the conscientious attitude of the prelates and upper clergy, and the apathy of the conservative gentry was most marked. There was, to all intents and purposes, no catholic party among the lay aristocracy. Very many, perhaps a majority

[5] Elizabeth seems to have believed, with justice, that Philip's friendship was a political calculation in his own interest and could stand the strain of a religious revolution in England. She also continued assiduously to persuade his envoy, De Quadra, of her own catholic inclinations.

[6] White of Winchester and Watson of Lincoln were sent to the Tower for speaking against the royal supremacy in a disputation which had been staged in Westminster Hall on 31 March.

in all classes, were 'old believers' in religion, but Mary's Church had conspicuously failed to bring about a Counter-Reformation in England, or even to initiate one. The price was paid in the decade from 1558 to 1568, when the new and precarious Anglican settlement was challenged, not by a solid body of the catholic faithful, but by a few individuals. During the summer of 1559 the queen's commissioners toured the country administering the oath of supremacy to all clergy. The number of refusals was under three hundred, which included all but one of the surviving bishops,[7] and a large proportion of prebendaries and others attached to cathedral churches. The vast majority of the parochial clergy conformed. Like their parishioners, most of them probably preferred the mass to the protestant communion, but they were not prepared to make any sacrifices for their preference, and resorted to grumbling and evasion of an unedifying kind. As agents of the new régime they were likely to be useless, but as its adversaries they would also be innocuous, and that was a matter of no small importance. Indeed, even those senior clergy who respectably stood by their catholicism proved ineffective as leaders. A few withdrew into exile and wrote controversial works against the settlement,[8] and the ex-bishops were imprisoned, but most seem to have withdrawn quietly into private life. They were decent and sober priests and scholars, but they had no desire to be disloyal to the queen, and had no fire in their bellies. When the Counter-Reformation did come to England, it was mainly the work of a different generation with different attitudes. Meanwhile the government could afford to be relatively lenient with such amenable dissenters and to adopt a conciliatory policy for the purpose of giving the Anglican Church a chance to take root.

For some months after the summer visitation, the normal government of the Church was suspended and it was not until after the consecration of Matthew Parker to Canterbury on 17 December that regular processes could be resumed. By that time the queen's grip upon ecclesiastical policy was firmly established, and the new bishops found themselves faced with a situation

[7] Kitchin of Llandaff was the only survivor. Elizabeth seems to have hoped originally for the conformity of eight existing bishops. W. P. Haugaard, *Elizabeth and the English Reformation*, 36-8.

[8] Notably Thomas Harding, who took up the cudgels against Jewel's *An Apology of the Church of England* in a controversy which went on for almost a decade.

which was not quite as acceptable as they had at first supposed. Significantly, Parker had not been an exile, and his protestantism was consequently a shade more Erastian than that of his new colleagues. Considering the narrowness of the group from which they were drawn, these men were remarkably able and were to serve the Church well, but their task was not easy. They had accepted the royal supremacy, not as a matter of convenience but of conviction, seeing in the restored protestant establishment the dawning of the climacteric age of England's history, which was to give her a special place in the preparation for the Second Coming. They were therefore shocked and alarmed, not only by the queen's tolerant attitude to the conservatives, but by her own fondness for liturgical ornaments. In November 1559 John Jewel wrote to his friend Peter Martyr that 'doctrine is everywhere most pure; but as to ceremonies and maskings there is a little too much foolery. That little silver cross of ill omened origin still maintains its place in the queen's chapel.' They did not appreciate the political necessity to heal and settle the realm, and their scruples were soon reinforced by the return of other exiles such as Whittingham and Whitehead, who were less committed to 'tarrying for the magistrate', and more inclined to judge the English Church by Genevan standards.

Consequently the first crisis of authority to afflict the settlement came not from the resistance of the catholics, but from the zeal of protestant radicalism. Elizabeth was determined that she, and any of her subjects who so desired, should be at liberty to use any vestments, ornaments or liturgical gestures which had not been prohibited by the terms of the Act of Uniformity. Since that Act had been deliberately vague in a number of particulars,[9] there was in fact scope for a fair amount of conservative expression, and many of the queen's more zealous commissioners had exceeded their powers in the suppression of such practices during 1559. While all the new bishops were opposed to the use of ornaments, they were so in differing degrees. Parker, Barlow, Guest and other moderates regarded images and vestments as inexpedient in a reformed Church and merely tending to super-

[9] 'Provided always and be it enacted that such ornaments of the Church and the ministers thereof shall be retained and be in use as was in the Church of England by authority of Parliament in the second year of King Edward VI . . .' (1 Eliz. I, c.2. para 13). In fact in the second year of King Edward VI (1548) Parliament had made no change in the traditional usages.

stition, while Grindal, Sandys, Jewel and Cox considered them to be absolutely prohibited by the divine law. The crisis itself was provoked by the queen's proposal to order the restoration of crucifixes in the parish churches where they had been destroyed. Jewel and Sandys both thought that if this was insisted upon several bishops, themselves included, would resign. Parker, while disagreeing with the queen's policy, would have been prepared to enforce it as appertaining to the supremacy. In the event a showdown was avoided. Lengthy discussions between October 1559 and March 1560 resulted in a measure of agreement. Elizabeth did not insist upon restoration, Cox was converted to Parker's opinion, and there were no resignations. 'Religion,' Jewel wrote calmly on 5 March, 'is now somewhat more established than it was.' As a result, when further conflict developed over the use of vestments, the bishops were more prepared to present a united front. The situation was also somewhat eased by the attitude of Henry Bullinger, Zwingli's successor at Geneva and the indefatigable friend of the English reformers. When appealed to over the issue of vestments, his opinion was in substantial agreement with that of Parker. Undesirable as such things might be, they could be regarded as *adiaphora*, and need not prevent zealous ministers from giving their services to an otherwise Godly Church which so evidently needed them. Thus when the radicals brought their proposals for further reform before the Convocation of 1563, the bishops opposed them on the queen's instruction, although they were in substantial agreement with what was intended.

The government of the Church in the 1560s was full of subtleties and contradictions of this kind, which baffled the idealism of straightforward protestants. In effect, Elizabeth compromised with her more militant bishops, but was never prepared to be open about it. Thus the 'Interpretations' in which the bishops worked out the detailed application of the Act of Uniformity contained a policy closer to their own views than to those of the queen, but one which they were compelled to enforce upon their own authority. A good example is the formula reached over the vestments issue:

> That there be used only one apparel as the cope in the administration of the Lord's Supper, and the surplice at all other ministrations . . .

This represented the absolute minimum which Elizabeth was prepared to tolerate and had the effect of prohibiting the 'vestment' proper – the chasuble. For this reason the queen gave no official countenance to the 'Interpretations', and Parker complained justifiably of lack of support in dealing with the recalcitrant. Elizabeth was deliberately, if deviously, impeding her more zealous servants in their desire to suppress the remnants of catholicism. At the same time she reacted sharply to puritan nonconformity, which they were naturally inclined to tolerate. Politically, this policy made perfect sense. The conservatives, apart from a handful of militant romanists in exile, represented no immediate threat to her authority, and showed every sign of settling down peacefully if not excessively badgered. On the other hand, some at least of the radicals held views on the nature of the Church which were not really consistent with the royal supremacy at all, and time was not an ally in dealing with them. At the same time such a policy could not be openly avowed by one who was enjoying the considerable benefits of posing as a daughter of Zion. Hence the dissimulations of which the bishops in general, and Parker in particular, were the victims. Unheroic as this was it succeeded remarkably well, largely because of the Archbishop's willingness to shoulder his thankless task. When the militantly protestant Commons of 1563 forced through an Act making a second refusal of the oath of supremacy high treason, the queen countered by ordering the bishops not to administer the oath a second time. Parker transmitted this unwelcome order in his own name rather than

> recite the queen's Majesty's name, which I would not have rehearsed to the discouragement of the honest Protestant, nor known too easy, to the rejoice too much of the adversaries, her adversaries indeed. I had rather bear the burthen myself.

In this way the bishops incurred a good deal of undeserved odium among the militants, but most of the latter retained their faith in the supremacy and continued to press for further reform through the existing constitutional channels.

THE STRUCTURE OF ELIZABETHAN GOVERNMENT

They were encouraged to do this by the fact that religious ideology had penetrated deeply into the realm of secular politics, and the very Erastianism of the settlement, which in some respects they deplored, had turned the House of Commons into an effective forum for pressure and agitation. The first decade of Elizabeth's reign saw a significant shift of initiative in this respect. During the previous thirty years the Parliament had been frequently called upon to endorse or put into effect policies which had been hammered out by the sovereign in Council or Convocation. But by 1563 there had appeared for the first time in the House of Commons a group which had a policy of its own and was prepared to develop techniques of persuasion which made it a real political force. The queen's initial decision to control this group by joining it rather than attempting to defeat it coloured the whole politics of the reign. Elizabeth had no intention of surrendering any aspect of her prerogative, yet found herself working in an uneasy relationship with self-appointed advisers who had clearly defined ideas on all the major issues of the time – the succession and foreign policy no less than ecclesiastical affairs. For many years it remained her preoccupation to employ the energies and abilities of this group, without allowing it to usurp a policy-making role. In the government of the Church, as we have seen, she retained a firm control over the executive, while making concessions in legislation, and a similar pattern was to develop in other fields. At the same time it would be a mistake to regard the puritan party in the Commons as an 'opposition', except in a few specific instances. For all their disagreements the queen, her councillors, and the puritan gentry shared a common basis of policy which not only enabled the régime to work, but gave it a constructive energy which had not been possessed by the governments of either Edward or Mary.

Her sister's failure gave Elizabeth the opportunity to base her régime upon a creative minority, who were able to entrench themselves in power during a decade of relative peace. To the queen herself belonged the credit for seizing the opportunity, and much of the credit for preserving the peace. Above all, she succeeded in managing the human resources which her choice had placed at her disposal, and in restoring stability to English politics after three decades of division and upheaval. Her attitude to government was in many ways impeccably conservative, and this was a considerable source of strength.

> I am but one body naturally considered [she declared shortly after her accession], . . . although by His permission a body

> politic to govern, so I shall desire you all, my lords (chiefly you of the nobility, everyone in his degree and power) to be assistant to me that I with my ruling and you with your service may make a good account to Almighty God and leave some comfort to our posterity on earth.

Whatever misgivings she may actually have felt, in all her public utterances Elizabeth assumed the loyalty and devotion of the whole aristocracy as a matter of course. The commissions of the peace were revised in 1559, in 1562 and in 1564, but there were very few exclusions which can be attributed to suspected disaffection.[10] On the whole this show of confidence was justified, since, as we have seen, there was no attempt to organise a dissident catholic faction. Even those who least sympathised with the queen's religious policies welcomed her robust nationalism and recognised her as King Henry's heir. It was partly for this reason that she was so anxious to prevent the militant protestants from 'rocking the boat' in 1563 and 1566.

When it came to selecting those in whom she was to repose especial confidence, however, her attitude was rather different. Two-thirds of the councillors who had served Mary in her last year were discarded, the only substantial group of survivors being seven peers – the Marquis of Winchester, the Earls of Arundel, Derby, Shrewsbury and Pembroke, and Lords Clinton and Howard. Howard was Elizabeth's great-uncle and a careerist courtier, Winchester Lord Treasurer and a distinguished civil servant, and Clinton Lord Admiral. The others were local magnates of varying antecedents, who had been conspicuous by their absence from court during the latter part of the previous reign. Shrewsbury was also Lord President of the Council of the North, an office in which the new queen retained him. All were men of long experience, conservative in temperament and conformist in religion. Lord Paget, who seems to have owed his rehabilitation largely to Philip after his disgrace of 1554, was among those who lost their seats.

The new councillors whom Elizabeth added were also for the most part men of experience, but in every other respect they

[10] J. H. Gleason, 'Commissions of the Peace, 1554-64' *Huntington Library Quarterly*, 18, 1955. Gleason's maximum figure for six counties is 25, or about 10 per cent of the membership, but there is positive proof for only a handful of these.

were an assorted group. Only two were peers; William Parr, newly restored to the Marquisate of Northampton, and Francis, Earl of Bedford. Sir William Cecil had been Secretary of State under Edward, an office which he now resumed, but the remainder had held only minor posts. Sir Edward Rogers had been imprisoned for involvement with Wyatt, and Sir Francis Knollys had been among the religious exiles in Strassburg. All were known protestant sympathisers and two, Knollys and the Earl of Bedford, were outspoken radicals. The total number in the re-formed Council was under twenty, and although it represented a considerable variety of ideological positions, in one respect it was uniform, and unique. It was an exclusively lay body, containing no divine of any persuasion.[11]

At the court, the other main political focus, the transformation was even more complete than in the Council. Except in the 'civil service' departments of the household the turnover was something like eighty per cent, and the family groups which were to play such an important part in the history of the reign became established very early. There were the queen's own relatives through the ramifications of the Boleyn and Howard families; the Bacon/Cecil/Cooke connection; and the Dudleys – Ambrose, Master of the Ordnance, and Robert, Master of the Horse. It was here, too, that the less discreet supporters of Elizabeth's shadowy years found their rewards. Sir William St Low became Captain of the Guard, Sir Thomas Cawarden Master of the Revels, and Sir Ralph Hopton Marshal of the Household. The court, like the Council, was dominated by intellectual and highly educated laymen, whose taste and patronage was soon to make as profound an impression upon the artistic and educational history of England as their abilities were upon its political development.

Beyond the inner circles of the régime, the pattern of change varied. The civil service showed considerable stability, except in one or two key offices such as the Mastership of the Wards, from which Mary's loyal familiar Sir Francis Englefield was dismissed in favour of Sir Thomas Parry. Within a few years

[11] Nicholas Wotton was technically in orders, and held ecclesiastical preferments, but he had never functioned as a priest and was in any case a specialist diplomat who took little part in the normal work of the Council.

Englefield was to be an exile and Spanish pensioner, while Parry died in 1560, to be succeeded by Sir William Cecil, who developed the post into one of the most influential agencies of his domestic policy. Among the attornies, clerks and local officers of the courts there were few displacements which can be attributed to the change of government.

Among the military and quasi-military servants of the Crown, on the other hand, the story was very different. Sir Edward Warner returned to the Lieutenancy of the Tower which he had lost under Mary; Sir James Croft became Captain of Berwick, and Lord Cobham Lord Warden of the Cinque Ports. All these men had been in trouble for rebellion or conspiracy against the late queen, and amongst the lesser military commanders the anti-Marian cast was even more pronounced. The names of the field officers who served in Scotland, France and Ireland in the early years of the reign read like a roll call of the surviving followers of Wyatt and Dudley. It was thus that Elizabeth employed the restless younger sons who had been so ripe for mischief. In these small wars they found rewards, glory, and as often as not an early grave. At little cost or risk to herself, she justified their expectation that she would be 'a liberal dame, and nothing so unthankful as her sister'.

By 1560 a clear pattern had emerged in the central government, where the queen had contrived to create a working partnership between the old fashioned xenophobic and anti-clerical magnates of the kind who had served her father so well, and the new protestant nationalists. In the formation of policy her confidence was given mainly to the latter, who were also strongly represented in the House of Commons, but she remained acutely aware that the former wielded great power in the localities, and spoke for a weighty body of aristocratic and popular opinion. The success of her régime would depend upon her ability to hold these different, but not necessarily incompatible groups together, and in doing this a realistic policy of social discipline would be a great help. Elizabeth had none of the dangerous idealism of the Duke of Somerset, and the new generation of protestant leaders did not share the social preoccupations of Hales and Latimer. There was still agrarian distress, and inflation continued, but the pressure of agitation had eased considerably since the late 1540s, probably because no further encouragement had been given from above. 1556 and 1557 had been years of bad harvests and steep price increases, which had added to the anxieties of Mary's Council, but outbreaks of violence had been few and by the end of the decade the situation had returned to normal. The queen's attitude towards her humble subjects was firmly paternalistic, and in this she was generally supported by magnates and gentry of all shades of opinion. Many of the details of the great Statute of Artificers of 1563 were highly controversial and long debated, but the principles inspiring that measure were not seriously disputed,[12] and it was certainly not a partisan issue as between 'new' and 'old' believers.

This is not the place in which to weigh the merits of Elizabeth's economic policies, but the labour of applying them was of considerable significance in the development of local government. In 1565 Sir Thomas Smith listed the duties which by that time fell to the justices of the peace:

> the repressing of robbers thieves and vagabonds, of privy complots and conspiracies, of riots and violences, and all other misdemeanours in the commonwealth . . . also at other times by commandment of the prince upon suspicion of war, to take order for the safety of the shire, sometimes to take musters of harness and able men, and sometime to take order for the excessive wages of labourers and servants, for excess of apparel, for unlawful games, for conventicles and evil order in ale houses and taverns, for punishment of idle and vagabond persons, and generally . . . for the good of government of the shire.

A formidable catalogue, and one which demonstrates yet again the dependence of the government on such men. There was, however, another side to the story. The frequency with which he encountered the local gentry as the representatives of the Crown, with the full weight of the law behind them, engendered in the ordinary man habits of obedience which could not in the nature of things be too discriminating. In other words it was not always clear when a gentleman was acting as a justice, and when as a landowner. During the previous reign there had been a case where a justice had attempted to treat a private disagreement

[12] For a careful examination of this Statute and its evolution, see S. T. Bindoff, 'The making of the Statute of Artificers' in *Elizabethan Government and Society: essays presented to Sir John Neale.*

with his tenants as sedition against the queen and had taken the case to the Privy Council before the truth was discovered. Burdensome as the minute regulation of economic affairs might be, it strengthened the authority of the gentry as a class and as individuals, and for that reason they accepted it. Nor is it likely that the government was altogether unmindful of this effect. Elizabeth and her advisers were entirely conventional in their desire to preserve and strengthen the social hierarchy, and the disciplinary element both in the Statute of Artificers and in the numerous proclamations which followed it was considerable. As a recent scholar has written: 'wages and apprenticeship legislation was as much designed to keep men in their jobs as to keep jobs open for them, and agrarian legislation was as concerned to keep labourers on the land as to keep the land available for them.'[13] The average justice of the peace, who did not expect to receive lucrative offices or grants of land in return for his ser-services, was nevertheless a willing agent for this reason. Whatever may be said about paternalism as an economic policy, as a means of cementing the alliance between the Crown and the aristocracy in the 1560s it was a success.

By contrast the Poor Law of 1563 was something of an ideological measure, and was more equivocally received. Vagabondage had been a recognised problem for almost a century, and at least since 1531 it had been realised that the 'aged poor and impotent' were a different proposition from the idle and recalcitrant. The latter could be, and were, dealt with after a fashion by punishments of varying severity, and no government had difficulty in persuading the magistrates to co-operate in this process. On the other hand the notion that the central government, and particularly the monarch, should be responsible for the welfare of those who were unable to work, won only gradual and reluctant acceptance. For over thirty years after 1531 the duty of providing relief fell upon the parishes, and the incumbents and church wardens had to depend upon whatever funds they could persuade their parishioners to disgorge. Elizabeth's Council recognised that the authority of the Church had declined, and although protestant idealism of the 'commonwealth' kind was rapidly developing a new secular charitable-

[13] E. E. Rich, 'Elizabethan population', *Economic History Review*, 2nd series, 2, 1950, 247.

ness,[14] it was too uneven and unpredictable in its incidence to form the basis of a national system of relief. They therefore introduced, with every sign of hesitancy, a compulsory poor rate which was in fact a parliamentary tax. The unpalateableness of this was reduced by making the justices responsible for assessment, and the procedure of compulsion very roundabout, but nevertheless a new principle of some importance was involved. There was no spontaneous enthusiasm among the gentry for this extension of their responsibilities, and the Council was constantly concerned to prevent negligence and corruption.

Fortunately, under the skilful guidance of Mr Secretary Cecil, that crucial body had recovered a good deal of its Cromwellian efficiency and drive. Cecil was always keenly aware of the necessity to keep a watchful and well informed eye upon the workings of the commissions of the peace, and his tireless energy in the Council and outside it played a large part in transmitting the government's policies effectively to the counties. At a later date he was sometimes to appear in person when the J.P.s of the Home Counties assembled in the Star Chamber at the end of the Law Terms, but during the 1560s the exhortations which were customary on these occasions were normally delivered by the Lord Keeper. Similar exhortations were also directed to the quarter sessions of more distant shires by means of the charge to the grand jury, but the Council remained the main agency both of communication and control, and it is unfortunate that the records are largely missing from May 1559 to 1570. By the time we can again study the day by day workings of this key institution, the formative period of the régime was over and it had also survived its first major domestic crisis.

THE REBELLION OF THE EARLS

The northern rebellion of 1569 was the result of a chain of circumstances stretching back to the beginning of the reign, and involving the political structure of the court, as well as the queen's policy and the regional characteristics of the north. Elizabeth was constantly under pressure to declare her mind on the succession, and as constantly refused to do so. Understandable as her attitude may have been in personal terms it was politic-

[14] W. K. Jordan, in *Philanthropy in England, 1480-1660, The Charities of Rural Eng and,* and other works, has made a definitive study of the growth f secular charities

ally extremely dangerous, since it created an uncertainty which men were tempted to resolve with schemes of their own. When the queen became ill with smallpox in 1562, the future seemed to be a bottomless pit of strife and confusion. If she married and had children the problem would resolve itself, but even so it was desirable to have some acknowledged order to provide security against the hazards of mortality. But Elizabeth was the last of Henry's children, and the existing possibilities were controversial or unimpressive. By the terms of Henry's will, if all his offspring died childless, the crown should have passed to the Suffolk line, but by 1559 that line was represented only by Catherine and Mary Grey, neither of whom was distinguished by character or intelligence.[15] There were a number of lesser claimants, of whom that Margaret Clifford whom Mary had favoured was one, and the Earl of Huntingdon another, but the major rival to the Suffolk claim was inevitably Mary Stuart, and her position aroused the fiercest dispute. Mary was not only a catholic, but also through her mother a member of the militant and ambitious family of Guise, and briefly queen of France. Elizabeth had not striven successfully to persuade the French and Scots to desist from backing Mary's immediate claim in order to recognise her as the heir. In spite of all that the queen could do, however, the claims of both Mary and Catherine were energetically canvassed throughout the decade, the latter naturally finding most favour among those committed to the protestant establishment, and the former among the conservative aristocracy. However, Lady Catherine ruined her credit with the queen by a clandestine marriage to the Earl of Hertford in 1560, and Mary's position was strengthened when she returned to Scotland as a widow in 1561 and established an uneasy, but apparently workable, relationship with the protestant lords who were by then entrenched in power.

At the same time Elizabeth's own marriage continued to be an issue of the first importance. It was not easy to find a foreign prince who could be accommodated by the strongly nationalist and protestant tone of the new régime, and the queen's taste did not run to nonentities. At the same time the factional possibilities of a domestic marriage were daunting, and became

[15] Mary, who was partly deformed, was guilty of a ridiculous *mésalliance* in 1565 when she married Thomas Keyes, a Sergeant Porter of the Court.

more so as Lord Robert Dudley emerged as her personal favourite during the summer of 1559. The queen's real intentions towards Lord Robert have always been a subject of controversy. In 1559 he was already married to Amy Robsart, the daughter of a Norfolk squire, and after her death in suspicious circumstances in September 1560 his elevation to the crown matrimonial would undoubtedly have cost Elizabeth much of her popularity. Cecil was adamantly opposed to the new favourite, both for personal reasons and because he regarded him as a menace to the régime.

The political battle between these two men dominated the court by the summer of 1560, as Dudley did his best to oust the Secretary from his position of trust, and although the latter eventually emerged unscathed there were times when his dismissal or resignation seemed imminent.[16] Dudley was, or believed himself to be, playing for a high stake, and in view of Cecil's known commitment to the protestant party did his best to make himself acceptable to the conservatives. He intrigued with De Quadra, the Spanish envoy and endeavoured to persuade the queen to accept a papal nuncio, and an invitation to send representatives to the Council of Trent. These intrigues the Secretary countered by arresting a number of prominent catholics in 1561, and exposing a net of communications linking several catholic gentry with their co-religionists in exile and with the Spanish authorities in the Low Countries. 'I thought it necessary to dull the Papists expectations,' he wrote, 'by discovering of certain mass-mongers and punishing them. I find it hath done much good.' The Council, of which Dudley was not a member, unanimously advised the queen to reject any overtures from Rome.

By 1564, when he was created Earl of Leicester, Dudley's political role had changed. He was still the queen's favourite, but the possibility of marriage had receded and he was becoming a substantial figure by the exercise of his own abilities. His intrigues with Spain were over, and he had been a member of the Council since 1562. Thus although he was still the enemy of Cecil, he was a less alien and unpredictable element near the centre of power, and their rivalry was becoming an accepted

[16] Wallace MacCaffrey in *The Shaping of the Elizabethan Regime*, has examined the ups and down of Cecil's fortunes during the period 1558-72 when he was clearly much more of a political gambler, and much bolder in his policies, than is usually remembered from his later career.

part of the political scene. At the same time the queen of Scots emphasised her continued interest in the English Crown by taking as her second husband Henry, Lord Darnley, her cousin and consequently a claimant in his own right. Elizabeth's anger at this move was a measure of her alarm, but it also strengthened Cecil's position and alienated her from the pro-Marian conservatives who still hoped for a favourable declaration on the succession. The misfortunes and ineptitude which were to ruin the Scottish queen over the next four years do not form part of this story, but her arrival as a fugitive in the north of England in 1568 was an event of the first importance. Her supporters and sympathisers were aroused to new activity, and this coincided in time with a wave of alarm over England's deteriorating relations with Spain, which seemed to threaten war with the most powerful state in Europe. Cecil was widely blamed for overplaying his hand in the arbitrary seizure of Alva's treasure fleet,[17] and except amongst the most aggressive protestants there was a desire for safer and more conservative policies. Thus by the end of 1568 Dudley was collaborating with the conservative peers on the Council, such as Arundel and Pembroke, to oppose Cecil's foreign policy, and at the same time encouraging a scheme recently mooted by Maitland of Lethington to bring about a marriage between Mary and the Duke of Norfolk.

The Duke was a conformist in religion, and this was sufficient to make the plan acceptable to many moderate protestants, who were acutely anxious over the succession, and worried about the future position of the ex-queen. It was not, however, acceptable to Elizabeth, who refused to countenance any such proposal and was unaware for some time that an extensive 'interest' had been created. Early in 1569 she also came out decisively in favour of Cecil's handling of the Spanish crisis, so that for some time the conservative group did not know which way to turn for fear of her displeasure. It was not until September that Dudley summoned up enough courage to tell her how far the intrigues had

[17] These ships, loaded with Genoese bullion destined to pay Alva's troops in the Low Countries, had put into English harbours for fear of French pirates. Cecil, discovering that the gold did not become Spanish property until it reached its destination, borrowed it in the name of the queen and thus provoked a trade embargo. Cecil in turn seized all Spanish property in England. This episode still further worsened relations which had already become strained on account of the activities of English seamen in the New World.

gone, and by that time Norfolk had become seriously alarmed for his own safety. A few days after Dudley's disclosures, he rashly left the court without licence, and ignored a summons to return. For a short time Cecil was convinced that this defiance would be followed by open insurrection, but Norfolk's nerve failed him. There was no enthusiasm for rebellion among his tenants, or the gentry of East Anglia, and after a week of indecision, during which he made no declaration of intent, he returned to London to throw himself on the queen's mercy, and was lodged in the Tower.

At that point the danger might have ended had it not been for the endemic discontent of the north which had been stirred up by the arrival of Mary and the intrigues which had followed. Protestantism had as yet made little impression north of York, except in a few sizeable towns such as Northallerton and Newcastle. There was little recusancy in the sense of open defiance of the government's religious policy, because little had been done to enforce it beyond the administration of the oath of supremacy. Cecil, with his new ideology and active conciliarism was as disliked and distrusted by the northern aristocracy as Cromwell had been thirty years before. Moreover, the traditional pattern of authority which Henry and his agents had striven so consistently to undermine, had been to some extent revived by the sympathy of Mary, who, as we have seen, had restored the Percies to their ancient dignity in 1557. This made Elizabeth's abrupt resumption of her father's attitude in 1559 all the more resented, especially by the Earl of Northumberland himself who lost the Wardenship of the Middle March and found the icy touch of royal disfavour again freezing his family's wealth. By 1568 both he and the Earl of Westmorland were complaining bitterly of poverty and services unrewarded. It was into this situation that Mary came, expecting to be welcomed and protected by her co-religionists, only to find the English government too quick and clear sighted to allow them any access to her. Nevertheless her coming gave an opportunity to a small and determined group of northern catholics to plot the overthrow of the regime. These men – Richard Norton, a veteran of the Pilgrimage of Grace, Christopher Neville, uncle to the Earl of Westmorland, and a few others – were not interested in the Norfolk marriage project. Their hope was to raise Mary to the throne at once, with foreign help if it could be obtained, and they did their best to engage the interest of the Duke of Alva. Nevertheless the intrigues against Cecil at court and the projects of less radical conservatives were useful to them in that they created an atmosphere of uncertainty in which men might be committed to action for a cause of which they had no real understanding.

Had Norfolk decided upon defiance, the Earls of Northumberland and Westmorland would probably have joined him in an attempt to overthrow Cecil and coerce the queen into a more catholic policy. They had been in communication with the Duke throughout the summer, and although no precise plans had been made, his submission left them in a very exposed position. Extensive disaffection had been stirred up in the north, and although this was probably more the work of Norton and his associates than of the Earls, they would inevitably be suspected when the government took action to pacify the region. It therefore appeared to them almost as dangerous to draw back as to go on, and the extremists succeeded in working upon these fears to commit them to open rebellion. Early in October they were summoned before the Council of the North and apparently convinced the Earl of Sussex that they had no hand in the growing alarm, but the queen was less easily satisfied, and on 24 October they were summoned to give an account of themselves before the Privy Council in London. This action precipitated the crisis, as it may have been intended to do. Although Northumberland was profoundly sceptical about their chances of success, by the beginning of November he was gathering his friends and tenants at Topcliffe, while the Earl of Westmorland did the same at Brancepath in County Durham.

In spite of the leadership of two such substantial magnates, the rising was extremely localised, the vast majority of the known participants being drawn from the Percy and Neville estates in the Bishopric and North Riding. Even in the areas most affected many influential gentry remained aloof, or rallied instead to the loyalist Sir George Bowes at Barnard Castle. Both Sussex and Bowes had difficulty at first in raising men against the insurgents, because their cause was popular with the common people, but their failure to stimulate sympathetic risings outside their immediate reach proved fatal to their chances. By the end of the second week in November the rebels seemed to be firmly in control of the bishopric, and on the 14th they marched to Durham and re-established the mass in the cathedral there, amid scenes of popular enthusiasm. The following day they marched south, raising such sympathisers as they could from the lands around Richmond and Boroughbridge. By the 22nd they had reached Bramham Moor near Tadcaster, with nearly four thousand footmen and about half as many horse. At that point the movement ground to a halt. Mary was far away in Coventry. She had been moved from Tutbury at the first sign of trouble and had in any case expressed her disapprobation of the whole attempt. The staunch catholics of Lancashire and Cheshire were not stirring, and the government had raised substantial forces in the midlands and the south. The Earls realised, even if some of their more fanatical supporters did not, that the attempt to trigger off a major demonstration against government policy had failed, and that discretion was the better part of valour. By the end of the month they were back at Brancepath, and briefly salved their pride by besieging and capturing Barnard Castle. Norton seems to have done his best to keep resolution alive by talking of Spanish aid, but none came and none was intended, since Alva had been justifiably unwilling to commit much needed troops to such an unsound venture. On 16 December the royal army reached the Tees, and the loyalty of the local gentry suddenly waxed and flowered. The Earls fled, first to Hexham, where they were almost intercepted by the Warden of the East March, Sir John Forster, and then into Scotland. By the end of the year the rising appeared to be extinguished, but there was a curious epilogue in February 1570 when an order from the Council to arrest Leonard Dacre resulted in a pitched battle between the wanted man and a royal army under Lord Hunsdon.[18] Over five hundred of Dacre's followers were killed and he himself joined the fugitives in Scotland, having contributed nothing to their cause at the time when his help might have been of great significance.

The rebellion had failed, partly because it was incoherent, and partly because its aims were ill-defined. Significantly, no set of

[18] Dacre had been in London during the autumn, and when he returned to his home at Naworth, near Carlisle, in November, he had begun to assemble men, ostensibly to aid Lord Scrope. For some reason the Council became suspicious of his intentions and ordered his arrest in January 1570.

articles or demands was produced, and the Earl's proclamations spoke generally of 'diverse new set up nobles about the Queen's Majesty', and 'the setting forth of His true and catholic religion'. The religious element was certainly genuine and the main motive of the rank and file, but most of the rebels, the Earls included, seem to have been thinking in terms of reversing the 1559 settlement rather than setting up a new catholic régime with Mary at its head. They spoke of securing Mary's person, and of gaining recognition for her as heir, but not of placing her on the throne. At the same time, whether they knew it or not, a small number of their associates were committed to getting rid of Elizabeth at any price. Confusion and misunderstanding prevailed from beginning to end, fear and desperation playing as large a part in determining their actions as any more positive motive. This is particularly clear in the case of Lord Dacre, but can also be seen in the account which Northumberland later gave of the last debates at Brancepath before the rising began.

They all acted to some extent upon the principle that Sir Thomas Grey was alleged to have enunciated in 1554: 'being in his own country, and amongst his friends and tenants, who durst fetch him?' Grey had rapidly discovered that this old fashioned attitude could not be applied in Leicestershire, but perhaps there was some excuse for thinking that a Dacre, a Neville or a Percy could still evoke it effectively. The outcome proved the contrary, for only a small proportion of their own tenants and dependants joined them. The great Percy estates in Northumberland, for instance, did not stir. For a few weeks the rebels succeeded in paralysing the royal government in Durham and North Yorkshire, but the régime was stronger and less fundamentally divided than they realised – and the traditional autonomy of the north had withered under generations of pressure from Westminster.

By contrast with the great rising of nearly thirty years before, the movement of 1569 was largely contained by local loyalists and royal officials – Sir John Forster in Northumberland, Lord Scrope in Cumberland, and Sir Thomas Gargrave in central Yorkshire. The Earl of Sussex and the Council of the North did not, indeed, succeed in coping with the rising on their own resources, but they never completely lost control of the situation, and were certainly not swept aside as their predecessors had been. The painful process of building up the Crown's authority in the north had paid rather better dividends than might appear at first sight.

The government had been alarmed, but not seriously shaken, and consequently the queen was determined on severity. Instructions were issued for the execution of something like seven hundred of the rank and file by martial law. Some of the intended victims escaped, and others were respited by local officers who had no enthusiasm for such butchery, but it is probable that well over four hundred suffered.[19] Those who had any property were proceeded against at the common law, nearly 150 being indicted before commissioners of oyer and terminer at York, Durham and Carlisle.[20] Most of these were subsequently convicted, but only a relatively small proportion seem to have suffered death. Most were pardoned, at prices which varied from a stiff fine to their entire possessions. 'It is necessary,' wrote Cecil, 'that the lands of the rebels be dispersed by sale and gift to good subjects.' Westmorland lived the rest of his life in exile, while Northumberland was handed over by the Scottish government in 1572 and beheaded. The great families which they represented would never again play a significant role in the politics of the region and the appetite of the northern gentry for gestures of independence was effectively quelled. By comparison with the punishments which Mary had meted out after Wyatt's rebellion (a movement of comparable scale), Elizabeth was brutally harsh in the north, but her policy was a great deal more effective, and in spite of the hardening lines of recusancy after 1570, the political security of the region was never in serious doubt.

With this victory the formative years of the régime came to an end. By 1570 the Queen had really overcome that legacy of dissension which the violent political and religious fluctuations of the two previous reigns had created. Building deliberately upon her father's achievement of the 1530s, like him she had rallied the 'political nation' in support of her national policies. Like him also, however, she had no illusions about the basis of her success. Felt rather than seen (and certainly not defined), the

[19] H. B. McCall, 'Executions after the Northern Rebellion', *Yorkshire Archaeological Journal*, 18, 1887.

[20] The records of these proceedings can be found in the Controllment Rolls of Kings Bench (P.R.O., KB 29/205-6). Much was printed by Sir Cuthbert Sharp in his *Memorials of the Rebellion of 1569*, 226 et seq.

limitations imposed upon her authority by the necessity for aristocratic co-operation were as strong as ever. Expressed through Parliament, or through pressure groups at court rather than through the cruder media of an earlier age, these limitations formed a fine political mesh in which it was Elizabeth's main concern not to tangle her wings.

Part Three

THE DECLINE OF THE TUDOR MONARCHY

1571-1629

These were the years in which success turned sour, and the creative energies of the monarchy declined. Elizabeth and her great councillor Sir William Cecil had met the challenge of shaping a new settlement in the 1560s. During the following twenty years they also met and overcame both the practical and theoretical challenges of militant puritanism and the catholic missions. Coming on top of these complex and exacting tasks, the gruelling war which began in 1585 exhausted the queen's resources, both financial and political. Faced with an aristocracy which was becoming wealthier, more numerous and more sophisticated with every decade, Elizabeth's management continued to depend upon a basic community of interest and the impact of her own personality. After 1590 she was living upon her capital, not meeting, nor apparently perceiving, the increasing need to re-negotiate her agreement with the 'political nation'.

With so many estwhile problems of order and obedience resolved, the constitutional definition of the prerogative was already becoming an issue before Elizabeth died. James, accustomed to the poverty and restricted powers of the Scottish throne, took the imposing position of the English monarchy too much at its face value. Unlike his predecessor, he was only too willing to make definitions, but he lacked political commonsense and became embroiled in a series of legalistic disputes over impositions, and the role of the judiciary. In themselves these disputes were not particularly serious, because the king's critics as yet commanded no powerful body of committed support, but they were symptomatic of a growing malaise.

Corruption in the 'civil service', the erratic and irresponsible use of Crown patronage, and unnecessary quarrels within the Privy Council, all contributed to that decline of confidence of which the constitutional disputes were a symptom. There was little in this situation which was new. English kings had had absolutist pretensions before, had run out of money, and had bestowed too many favours upon unworthy favourites. Nevertheless, by 1620 the prestige of the monarchy was lower than at any time since 1558. In an earlier generation James would probably have been subjected to a series of aristocratic conspiracies and rebellions. It was in a sense a measure of the Tudor achievement that he found himself instead faced with a uniquely recalcitrant House of Commons. Parliament was the residual legatee of all those innumerable limitations upon medieval monarchy which the Tudors had succeeded in removing.

But it was not really James's failure to be a 'constitutional monarch' which annoyed his influential subjects, so much as his failure to be a 'good lord' in the traditional sense. It was for this reason that the position occupied by the Duke of Buckingham was of such crucial importance. George Villiers was a test case. In previous centuries a favourite so impervious to disgrace would have been assailed by insurrection. In the 1620s he was the centre of a political storm of a different kind. His activities did the monarchy untold harm, not, indeed, by provoking civil war, but by further damaging the already difficult relations between the Crown and the political nation and by raising barriers of mutual distrust which were never to be lowered before the revolution.

CHAPTER 10

THE YEARS OF STABILITY

The principal note of her reign will be that she ruled much by faction and parties, which she herself both made, upheld and weakened as her own great judgment advised. (*Francis Naunton*)

REGNANS IN EXCELSIS

The northern rebellion was an event of greater importance than its relatively easy suppression might suggest. As we have seen, the careful dispersal of the rebels' estates strengthened the loyal gentry and destroyed the power of the Dacres and the Nevilles. Henry Percy was allowed to succeed to his brother's Earldom of Northumberland after the latter's execution, but he was not permitted to reside in the north, and his clientage gradually withered away. By a stroke of good fortune the second Earl of Cumberland also died in 1570, leaving his heir a minor, and Cecil was able to grant the wardship to Francis, Earl of Bedford, with the result that young Clifford was brought up as a puritan. In later life his main interests were to be in business and seafaring, and he showed no sign of wishing to re-establish himself as a northern magnate. In 1572 the puritan Earl of Huntingdon began his long and important career as President of the Council of the North, and under his guidance the Council systematically set out to obliterate all those customs and attitudes which preserved the distinctiveness of the region. Also, the greatly augmented military presence in the north which resulted from the rising strengthened the hands of the protestant Anglophile party in Scotland when their ascendancy was threatened by the assassination of the regent, Murray, in January 1570. With judicious English aid so readily available, Murray's successors, Lennox, Mar and finally Morton, were able to defeat the Marian faction, whose last stronghold in Edinburgh Castle fell in May 1573. This not only secured the friendly attitude of the Scottish government, but also made it unnecessary for Elizabeth to take the distasteful step of handing Mary over to her own subjects for trial and execution.

The most far-reaching consequence of the rebellion, however, was the promulgation of the papal Bull *Regnans in Excelsis* in February 1570. Although such action had been long contemplated and was to some extent a gesture of conviction on the part of the zealous Pius V,[1] the particular occasion of its appearance was the desire to strengthen and encourage the northern Earls. Elizabeth was declared to be a heretic and no true queen, so that her subjects' allegiance was annulled. This not only had the effect of making sedition a religious duty to all who acknowledged the papal authority, but of conferring the status of crusader upon any catholic prince whose own interests might incline him to war against England. The reaction from the English Parliament was sharp and immediate. It became treason to import or publish any papal Bull, whatsoever its purpose, to deny Elizabeth's title, or to call her heretic or schismatic. The evangelical thirty-nine Articles of Religion, which had been approved by Convocation in 1563 now received statutory force as the doctrine of the English Church,[2] and the property of those who had gone into exile for religious reasons was confiscated.

In all these measures the queen was yielding to puritan pressure which sought to counter the danger represented by *Regnans in Excelsis* through a campaign of total suppression against the catholics. Such a campaign formed no part of her own intentions, and although she was prepared to countenance severe measures against any explicit rejection of her authority, she refused to regard the old religion as a threat *per se* and would not

[1] It was easy for the English government to represent Pius as the aggressor, but in fact the papacy had endured a great deal of provocation during the previous ten years, and Pius (one of the few popes to be canonised) believed it to be his unavoidable duty to speak out against Elizabeth. Had he been more worldly in his approach he would not have ignored the wishes of Philip II as he did. Nevertheless, he had been advised that many English catholics were prevented from rising through scruples about resisting lawful authority – and he was particularly concerned to remove that inhibition.

[2] The theological content of these articles has been endlessly debated, and cannot be briefly described. The wording of most would have been acceptable to both Lutherans and Calvinists. Some were equally acceptable to catholics, but the intention of Parliament in authorising them was to give the Anglican Church a doctrinal basis which was explicitly protestant, if it was not explicit in any other sense. See E. C. S. Gibson, *The Thirty-Nine Articles*; C. Hardwick, *A History of the Articles of Religion*; C. S. Meyer, *Elizabeth I and the Religious Settlement of 1559*, etc.

allow the recusancy laws to be changed. With this policy neither the majority of her Council nor even the moderate Parker was wholly in sympathy. But Elizabeth understood more clearly than her anxious servants and subjects that Pius's action had in fact created a dilemma of conscience as unwelcome to the majority of English catholics as it was to herself. Although precautions against treason might have to be intensified, there was nothing to be gained from driving the average catholic layman to desperation, or in assisting the papacy to force upon him the kind of political decision which he desired above all to avoid.

Those who looked favourably upon the papal initiative were for the most part already in exile, and the reaction of John Felton, who posted the offending Bull in London in May 1570, was altogether exceptional.[3] It was, however, highly alarming to protestants who did not feel secure in power, and who had no satisfactory means of assessing the scale of the problem with which they had to deal. In fact the danger of a general catholic rising was small and had probably decreased rather than increased as a result of the Bull, since the outright condemnation of Elizabeth had removed any possibility of the kind of conservative pressure which the rising of 1569 had sought to apply. In future any catholic who rebelled in the name of religion could seek no less than the queen's destruction – a radical necessity quite alien to the traditions of English insurrection. On the other hand conspiracy and the threat of foreign intervention had been stimulated, since those who deliberately chose to adhere to their faith in the new circumstances might not scruple to see it reimposed by outside force. *Regnans in Excelsis* thus created deep divisions among the English catholics and virtually destroyed the weighty political power of religious conservatism which had been so important in the first decade of the reign. Understandably, however, the Council did not see the situation in this light, and neither did the enthusiastic Spanish ambassador, Guerau de Spes.

De Spes had allowed himself to be convinced that England was ripe for counter-revolution, and he was inclined to blame the

[3] Felton was a wealthy member of an old Norfolk family which had been closely connected with the Marian régime. He acted entirely on his own initiative, apparently obtaining a copy of the Bull from de Spes. At his execution in August 1570 he claimed that he died for the papal supremacy and refused to recognise Elizabeth as queen.

failure of the Earls on their own hesitancy and incompetence rather than on the weakness of militant catholicism. Consequently, although disappointed at the beginning of 1570, he was not discouraged and saw the Bull as providing exactly the kind of stiffening which the rising of the previous year had lacked. Philip, although indignant at the manner of Pius's action, was strongly influenced by his ambassador's confidence and prepared to encourage his activities. He was also markedly less hostile to Mary than he had been at the height of her fortunes ten years before, when it had seemed likely that she might place the crowns of both England and Scotland at the disposal of the Guises. If de Spes was correct in his estimates of English catholic strength, it ought to be possible to bring Mary to power in England with a minimum expenditure of effort on his part. Consequently he lent a willing ear to the somewhat insubstantial schemes which the adventurer Ridolphi began to weave in the autumn of 1570. Over the next few months a network of communications was established between the Spanish court and the Curia on the one hand and various English malcontents on the other. Mary and her agent, the Bishop of Ross, kept in touch with every stage of the negotiations, and the Duke of Norfolk, released from the Tower in August 1570, was at least aware of what was going on. So also were Cecil's agents, and the speed with which the plot was detected inevitably gives rise to the suspicion that Ridolphi was really a double agent. No proof of this has ever been found, but by September 1571 the government was in possession of the whole story, as far as it had progressed.

As a threat to the régime the 'Ridolphi plot' was negligible, but as a weapon in the hands of the Council it was both useful and important. There was no doubt that both the pope and the queen of Scots had given enthusiastic backing to a scheme to overthrow the English government by a combination of rebellion and Spanish invasion. The propaganda value of these disclosures was great, and was exploited to the full, so that the political implications of adherence to the Roman jurisdiction could no longer be denied, nor easily avoided. Parliamentary pressure upon the queen was renewed, but she would neither sacrifice Mary nor countenance further anti-catholic legislation. Only the Duke of Norfolk paid the price of his muddle-headed and half-hearted treason. He was executed on 2 June 1572, and his status and title became extinct for the remainder of the century. The vast Howard inheritance was broken up, his clients looked for other patrons, and the gentry of Norfolk had to seek elsewhere for leadership and guidance. After the Duke's death there was a significant increase in quarrels and disorders among the Norfolk gentry, which temporarily impaired the efficiency of the local administration.

By the time that Norfolk died, the crisis which had been provoked by Mary's arrival in England four years earlier was over. In spite of the expulsion of de Spes, whose complicity in both the northern rising and the Ridolphi plot had been conclusively demonstrated, there was no open rupture with Spain. On the other hand Elizabeth had been quick to seize the opportunity created by the peace of St Germain to open negotiations with France. The restoration of domestic peace in that country in 1570 brought to an end any lingering English obligation to the Huguenots, and two years of tortuous discussion finally resulted in the Treaty of Blois in April 1572. Short-lived though this was in the form in which it was signed, it was a significant event, for it gave England a catholic ally in defiance of the pope's declaration and marked the end of the Habsburg association as a key concept in English diplomacy. At the same time, Cecil and his colleagues in the Council had formed a pessimistic opinion of the future of Anglo-Spanish relations, and a group had begun to emerge under the leadership of Leicester and Walsingham which advocated a protestant alliance abroad and a decisive initiative against the Counter-Reformation.

At home, the queen was temporarily triumphant, but the problem of Mary had been evaded rather than solved, and the necessity for a clearer identification between the secular state and the protestant religion could no longer be ignored. Although Elizabeth would not permit any explicit rejection of the Stuart claim to the Crown, in 1571 Parliament had taken the unprecedented step of declaring it to be high treason to question the propriety of determining the succession by statute. Had the queen died at this juncture a civil war could hardly have been avoided, and the massacre of St Bartholomew seemed to prove conclusively that the papists applauded murder as a political weapon. 'I learn . . . how they triumph,' wrote Parker of catholic reactions to that bloody event, 'they be full of spite and secret malice. Their imps be marvellous bold and flock together in their talking places, as I am informed, rejoicing much at this unnatural and unprincely cruelty and murder.'

It is against this background that the arrival of the first seminary priests in England must be seen. William Allen had founded his college at Douai in 1568, realising that English catholicism was losing its identity under the sustained gentle pressure of Elizabethan conformity, and that the Marian priests had neither the training nor the character to keep it alive. His aim was to provide guerilla fighters for the Counter-Reformation, men of tireless energy and high morale, who would not shrink from persecution, and who would be equipped to counter attack in those fields of vernacular preaching and scriptural exegesis in which the protestants had hitherto been almost unchallenged. The first ordinations took place from Douai in 1573, and the following year four young priests took up their dangerous duties in England. Seven more followed in 1575, and over a hundred by the end of the decade. By their own account they were superlatively successful. 'The numbers of those who were daily restored to the Church almost surpassed belief,' Allen was to write later. Perhaps this enthusiasm was more the result of small expectations than of great achievements, but they certainly had the satisfaction of worrying the civil and ecclesiastical authorities.

Thanks to their efforts, English catholicism neither withered away nor was killed by the stigma of treason. Instead, it became the faith of an increasingly well defined minority, cut off from their fellow countrymen by civil disabilities and fluctuating persecution. The seminarists were uncompromising in their condemnation of nominal and occasional conformity, with the result that the large numbers whose catholicism consisted in little more than a sentimental or nostalgic attachment to the mass, were shorn away.[4] Those who remained were strengthened and educated in their faith, beyond the point where official persuasions and petty harassment would have any effect. The government was quick to appreciate this fact and understandably

[4] Nominal conformity did not, of course, cease altogether. The heavy financial penalties introduced in 1581 often induced the heads of substantial catholic families to go to church, while their dependents and womenfolk could afford open recusancy. This was, however, a calculated risk and not the result of mere conservatism.

alarmed, so that from about 1574 onwards the Council began to intensify its pressure upon local authorities to enforce the law. Directives were sent to commissions of the peace, and to the Council of the North. Obstinate papists were removed from office, and there was a purge of schoolmasters – for teaching was a favourite occupation among the deprived Marian clergy. In 1577 John Aylmer, the Bishop of London, wrote to Walsingham, lamenting that 'the papists marvellously increase both in numbers and in obstinate withdrawal of themselves from the Church and services of God'. Imprisonment, he urged, was a useless penalty. Only a systematic enforcement of heavy fines would be effective. In October of the same year, instructions were sent to the bishops to make returns of recusants in their dioceses, but Aylmer's suggestion was not finally adopted until 1581.

INTENSIFIED REPRESSION OF CATHOLICISM

The government's main strength lay in its highly efficient intelligence system, and this did not consist only of specialised or professional agents. The Bull of 1570 and the increasing definition of the catholic community after 1574 alarmed Englishmen of all classes, so that information about recusant activities was readily forthcoming except in those areas such as Lancashire where they were numerically very strong. Also, as we shall see, the development of puritanism sharpened the edge of protestant hostility and suspicion. As a result the Council was frequently able to act upon precise information, as in June 1576 when the justices of Hampshire were ordered to investigate a stockpile of 'popish ornaments' known to be in the possession of one Alexander Dering. Local justices and other officials were frequently more zealous than the councillors themselves, and if it had not been so the careers of the seminary priests would have been both longer and more profitable to their cause. On the other hand the queen herself showed nothing but antipathy towards strong measures, pardoning recusants who were able to gain the ear of the court, and persistently refusing to allow her bishops to insist upon suspected papists receiving communion. It was partly in order to tempt his mistress with the prospect of a new source of income that Bishop Aylmer urged the introduction of financial sanctions – but when an initiative came in that direction it came from Parliament and not from the queen.

Elizabeth's complacency over the catholic problem was still to some extent justified. The seminary priests were quite honest in their renunciation of treasonable intent, and those who sought reconciliation and absolution at their hands were not making a political decision in spite of the theoretical logic of their situation. *Regnans in Excelsis* was full of imperfections which could provide loopholes for agile consciences, and in 1580 Pope Gregory XIII issued an 'explanation' of the Bull which absolved even the most zealous English catholic from any obligation to work against the existing government 'things being as they are'. Nevertheless, no priest could deny, if challenged, that he regarded Elizabeth as an heretic and usurper, or that he would be bound to support any invasion or other attempt to overthrow her in the name of the Church. Nor were Gregory's actions consistent with his words. From the moment of his election in 1572 he consistently worked for her destruction, first through Don John in the Netherlands, then through the adventurer Thomas Stukeley,[5] and finally through James FitzGerald, a kinsman of the Earl of Desmond. William Allen, who was consulted about the first of these attempts, not only supported military action but urged the need for haste, a circumstance which did nothing to add to the credibility of his pupils' disavowals. Only the last of Gregory's schemes resulted in action. In 1579, FitzGerald managed to persuade Philip to allow him to go with a small force to Ireland where he quickly stimulated his kinsfolk in Munster to rebellion. The following year he was joined by a Spanish force of about 1500, under a papal banner,[6] and fighting continued throughout the year. The rising was suppressed, but it served to confirm the worst suspicions of the English protestants, and to make the queen appear absurdly careless of her own safety.

The tragedy of the catholic missions was almost entirely the result of this papal attitude. 'My charge,' declared Edmund Campion, the first and one of the greatest of the Jesuit missionaries, who reached England in 1580, 'is . . . to preach the Gospel

[5] Stukeley was an unreliable character who received large sums of papal money in 1578 on the understanding that he was to go to Ireland. Instead he landed at Lisbon and joined King Sebastian of Portugal on his disastrous North African crusade, in which both perished.

[6] Philip carefully refrained from recognising this expedition, although it included about five hundred regular troops. As a result, when Lord Grey of Wilton captured Smerwick he executed the entire garrison as pirates.

... [and] to cry alarm spiritual against foul vice and proud ignorance ... I never had mind, and am strictly forbidden by our fathers that sent me, to deal in any respect with matters of state or policy of the realm, as those things which appertain not to my vocation.' The following year he was executed under the ancient law of 1352, as an adherent of the queen's enemies. Sincere as his protestations undoubtedly were, he could not deny his allegiance to the pope, and the pope was by his own declaration the queen of England's enemy.[7] Campion, like many others, was caught in a confrontation between two totalitarian systems, in which neither was prepared to renounce that association between temporal and spiritual power which had characterised the *respublica Christiana* of the middle ages. To the papacy it was a solemn duty to employ political weapons in the service of the faith; while to the English government, and increasingly to the English people, the identity and security of the nation was embodied in the protestantism of the Anglican Church. Under these circumstances it was disingenuous of Cecil to claim, as he did in *The Execution of Justice in England* (1581), that catholics were punished for sedition or treason only, and not for their faith. Equally, Allen's reply *A True, Sincere and Modest Defence* (1584) was guilty of deliberately begging the question by accusing the English government of arbitrary and unjust legislation on matters of conscience. Both were writing propaganda which by partial statements and wilful misrepresentation added to the bitterness and confusion of the struggle.

The first missionary priest to die at the hands of the English government was Cuthbert Mayne, arrested in Cornwall in 1577. Mayne was convicted of treason under the Act of 1571 because a copy of an old Bull was found in his possession, but this was a somewhat chancy procedure and it was not long before more effective measures were evolved. The Parliament of 1581 saw a renewal of fierce protestant pressure, not only from the House of Commons but also from the Council itself. Sir Walter Mild-

[7] Campion was tried along with seventeen others on particular charges of conspiracy, which were not well founded. He protested rightly that he was only a traitor if his religion made him one, which technically it did not. Legally, Campion's condemnation was highly suspect. On the other hand the purpose of treason laws is to protect the security of the state, and this could be construed as a reason for changing the law – as it was in this case.

may, speaking on 25 January, denounced the pope for 'turning thus the venom of his curses and the pens of his malicious parasites into men of war and weapons to win that by force which otherwise he could not do . . . emboldening many undutiful subjects to stand fast in their disobedience to her Majesty and her laws'. Seminary priests and Jesuits were corrupting the realm with false and seditious doctrine. 'It is time,' he went on, 'for us to look more narrowly and straitly to them, lest . . . they prove dangerous members . . . in the entrails of our commonwealth.'

The result was a ferocious bill, which would have made the singing of mass a felony punishable by death, and imposed the penalties of praemunire for a fourth refusal to attend the worship of the established Church. That the Act which eventually emerged was somewhat less drastic was no doubt due once again to the queen, but it was severe enough to mark a sharp escalation in the war against catholicism. The act of reconciliation itself became high treason, both to the priest and to the penitent, and the penalty for absence from Church was raised to £20 per month. It was now no longer necessary even to prove adherence to the queen's enemies, and the number of executions went up sharply – four in 1581, eleven in 1582, and a further eighty-nine by 1590. Laymen as well as priests suffered, and the heavy economic pressure of the new recusancy fines began to make serious inroads into the catholic gentry and aristocracy.

At the same time, the propaganda war was intensified. It was for this purpose, rather than to provide the basis for legal proceedings, that the so called 'bloody questions' began to be regularly applied after 1580. The suspect was asked whether he believed the pope to have the power to depose Elizabeth, and whether he would assist the efforts of any foreign prince to enforce the Bull of 1570. A negative reply to either question would estrange the victim from his Church, and a positive or evasive reply would create a presumption of treasonable intent. The results of such interrogations were regularly published and helped to stimulate a noticeable increase in anti-catholic feeling in the early 1580s.

The realm seemed threatened by invasion from abroad and conspiracy at home, and it was a relatively easy task to link these dangers with the activities of the missionary priests. For instance, Robert Parsons, the Jesuit, Allen himself, and other English catholic exiles were deeply involved during the years

1581-3 in a scheme to exploit the temporary ascendancy of Esmé Stuart in Scotland by using that country as an entry point for an army under the Duke of Guise. There were constant scares of assassination plots against the queen, and the actual murder of William of Orange by a catholic fanatic in 1584 raised anxiety to fever pitch. The result was further penal legislation, and the Bond of Association – a sworn brotherhood to defend Elizabeth's life and resist any possibility of a catholic succession. Nor were these reactions exaggerated or unjustified, for in December 1580 the Cardinal Secretary of State had written that 'while that guilty woman of England holds the two noble Christian Kingdoms she has usurped . . . whoever removes her from this life with the due end of God's service, not only would not sin, but would even be doing a meritorious deed.'

Catholic propaganda battled valiantly against this increasingly hostile environment. Certainly the recusants were better served by their writers and publishers in the 1580s than the official Church had been under Mary. Apologiae, like Allen's *Defence*, and devotional works such as *An Epistle of Comfort* by the Jesuit Robert Southwell, were produced in large numbers, mainly abroad, and distributed by devoted smugglers. The most prolific press during this period was that of George L'Oyselet at Rouen, which specialised in the writings of the indefatigable Parsons, but there were a number of others, and some books were printed secretly in England. For the most part these writers refrained from direct attacks upon Elizabeth, but strove assiduously to create a martyrology out of the steady stream of executions, hoping no doubt to cause a revulsion of feeling similar to that which their enemies had achieved thirty years before.[8] 'When you persecute us,' Southwell wrote, 'you do but sow seeds that will spring with a more plentiful harvest.' In the event, this forecast was to prove more optimistic than accurate, for the odds were too great. The Elizabethan government was both more efficient and more enduring than that which had persecuted the protestants, and it could call upon a larger measure of popular co-operation. The secret press of Richard Verstegen was discovered in London in 1582. In 1585 Thomas Alfield and Thomas Webley were executed as felons under a statute of 1581 for the possession of seditious literature, and innumerable interro-

[8] E.g. *A Brief History of the Glorious Martyrdom of XII Reverend Priests*, by William Allen, published in 1582.

gations, arrests and punishments for similar offences are recorded. Above all, the Council's own propaganda machinery made full use of the many opportunities which occurred to darken the catholic image.

Cecil himself was an indifferent pamphleteer, but as a patron and organiser he had no equal in the century save Thomas Cromwell. The queen, too, as we have seen, was acutely conscious of the value of propaganda and assiduously encouraged her courtiers in the creation of what might be called the 'Gloriana cult'. This was a literary and somewhat esoteric phenomenon, but it was reflected at the popular level in ballads, 'interludes', catches and all manner of ephemera, which built up her popularity, and especially her identification with national feeling.

Also, the Marian exiles with the encouragement of their political allies had produced at an early stage in the reign one of the great propaganda masterpieces of the century – *The Acts and Monuments of the English Martyrs* by John Foxe. This work had been conceived about 1553 as a general martyrology of the reformed Churches,[9] but by the time the first version appeared in 1559 it had become a specific apology for the English Church, and paricularly for the protestants who had suffered death and imprisonment under Mary. In 1563 the first English edition tentatively embraced the historical myth of the Elect Nation, and this became fully explicit in the expanded version of 1570. The popularity of the work was immense, and shortly after the appearance of the second edition the Council ordered it to be set up in Churches and public places alongside the English bible, so that it became almost a second pillar of the faith. Generations of children were reared on its gruesome woodcut illustrations and colourful stories of popish atrocities.

Building upon this foundation, and upon the actual memory of Spanish domination, it was an easy task for Cecil's pamphleteers to rivet upon the English catholics an evil reputation for tyranny and subservience to foreign interests. *The Execution*

[9] Foxe had published a short sketch of his planned work in Strasburg in 1554 under the title *Commentarii Rerum in Ecclesia Gestarum maximarumque per totam Europam persecutionum a Wiclevi temporibus ad hanc usque aetatem descriptio*. He was not the originator of this polemical use of history, a technique which he probably learned from William Tyndale and John Bale, but he was by far its most successful practitioner.

of *Justice* (1581), the *Declaration of the favourable Dealing* (1584), *The English Roman Life* (1580) and innumerable other similar works formed a part of this campaign. In the face of this barrage, catholic propaganda, like the missions themselves, could exercise little influence on the country at large. Those already within the fold, or strongly sympathetic, were strengthened and encouraged. Those who were indifferent or hostile were not touched, and the great majority of Englishmen believed that the victims of persecution in the 1580s were traitors, not martyrs. By the time that she eventually went to war with the champion of the Counter Reformation, England was a protestant country in a sense which she had certainly not been in 1550, in 1559, or even in 1569. The catholic Church had paid a very heavy price for salvaging a small proportion of its flock.

THE NEW ROLE OF PURITANISM

Elizabeth had done her best to prevent the hardening of ideological lines. For the first ten years she had enjoyed an important measure of success, but the Bull of excommunication and the coming of the missions had taken the initiative out of her hands. As a result it became increasingly difficult to restrain the zeal of the radical protestants, who naturally constituted the vanguard of the attack on 'popery'. As we have seen, these 'puritans' had made a determined attempt to re-direct the policy of the Church in 1563, and had been with difficulty frustrated. After 1570 they returned to the attack with renewed vigour. They did not, however, form a party in the same sense as the catholics, and for that reason their activities are not easy to analyse satisfactorily.[10] The great majority of convinced English protestants were puritans in the sense that they wished to simplify the worship of the Church, to do away with ornaments and liturgical gestures such as the sign of the cross, and to improve preaching and religious education. A rather smaller number were thoroughly dissatisfied with the formal worship of the Prayer Book, as being 'culled from the popish dunghill . . . the mass book, full of abominations', and disgruntled at the queen's refusal to countenance the Calvinist discipline. Those who wished to abolish the system of

[10] The ambiguity of the term 'puritan' has caused considerable difficulty to scholars working on the subject. See Basil Hall, 'Puritanism: the problem of definition' in *Studies in Church History*, II, 283-96; P. Collinson, *The Elizabethan Puritan Movement*, 13-15, 22-8; and P. Lake, *Moderate Puritans and the Elizabethan Church*, 1-24.

government by bishops, and replace it with a Genevan presbytery formed no more than a small core of the puritan movement as a whole – and of this minority only a handful could countenance separation from the established Church.

To all these demands the queen presented a steady opposition, and this in turn revealed a variety of attitudes towards the royal supremacy. No sincere Christian could accept the spiritual authority of an Act of Parliament. All protestants based their faith upon the Scriptures, but in practice this could mean a great many different things. To the vast majority of conforming laity and clergy it meant accepting the whole structure of the Anglican Church as it stood on the vague assumption that it was the queen's responsibility to guarantee the true faith of the realm. Such an attitude was much to Elizabeth's taste, but it was incompatible with any genuine zeal or conviction. The moderate puritan was quite clear that the Scriptures precluded the mass or any other survival of catholicism, but was prepared to give the category of *adiaphora* a generous interpretation. This meant that he did not question the queen's authority to govern the Church within a broadly protestant context, but might feel impelled to campaign within the law for such further reforms as he felt to be desirable. It was to this category that the majority of Elizabeth's councillors, and at least her early prelates, belonged, and although they might differ about the point at which representations should be made, they had no fundamental doubts about the queen's status as a Godly Prince. The parliamentary campaigns of Norton or Strickland for the alteration of the Prayer Book were characteristic of the tactics of this important and influential group, as, in a different way, was the refusal of Archbishop Grindal to suppress the 'prophesying' movement in 1577. Politically there was nothing remotely sinister about these men – they were the pillars of the régime.

This fact, and the somewhat indiscriminate use of the term 'puritan', has sometimes tended to obscure the real danger of radical protestantism – to which Elizabeth herself was so sensitive. Those who felt most strongly the necessity for a full Calvinist establishment, as representing the manifest Word of God, could not indefinitely accept the authority of a ruler who would not submit to their pressure. In fact neither Cartwright, Willcox, Field nor any of the other presbyterians of whom we have knowledge renounced their allegiance in the name of true religion, but the queen could not ignore or condone their ruthless attacks upon her government of the Church. From about 1570 onwards the radicals shifted the emphasis of their campaign from ornaments and vestments to the episcopal structure itself, claiming that it had no scriptural warrant, and therefore no place in a true Church. 'Their tyrannous Lordship cannot stand with Christ's Kingdom,' declared the *Admonition to Parliament*, published in 1572, 'either must we have right ministry of God and right government of his Church, according to the Scripture . . . (both which we lack) or else there can be no right religion.'

To men who thought in these terms the Act of Uniformity was nothing but a stumbling block, and in the 1572 Parliament a group of them took advantage of the anti-catholic scare to introduce a measure which would virtually have nullified it in respect of protestant non-conformity. Elizabeth intervened, not merely to stop this proposal after its first reading, but to give instructions that in future no bills on religion were to be introduced unless they had first been approved by the bishops. The queen treated her bishops badly in many ways, but direct attacks upon their position and jurisdiction were attacks upon her own authority. Neither she nor they were defending episcopacy as *iure divino*, but as a convenient and legitimate system lawfully decreed. The House of Commons was not so radical in its sympathies that it was prepared to defy the royal prohibition, and the parliamentary campaign was temporarily defeated. It may well have been this reversal which determined the radical leaders to publish the *Admonition*, and thus to launch a pamphlet war which was to last for almost twenty years.[11]

The danger of this attack did not lie in sedition – at least not in the obvious sense that catholic conspiracy was seditious – but in its encouragement of contempt for the law. 'Surely if this fond faction be applauded to,' Parker wrote to Cecil in 1573, '. . . it will fall out to a popularity, and as wise men think, it will be the overthrow of all the nobility. Both papists and precisians

[11] *A second Admonition* appeared in the same year, to which Whitgift wrote his *Answer to an Admonition*. There then followed the *Reply to an Answer*, the *Defence of an Answer*, and many other pamphlets. The Marprelate tracts were in the same tradition. P. McGrath, *Papists and Puritans under Elizabeth I*, 135-8. M. M. Knappen, *Tudor Puritanism*, 240 etc.

have one mark to shoot at, plain disobedience.' Thirty years before Stephen Gardiner had written of protestants in general in very similar terms, and many of the nobility did not share Parker's view; but Cecil, in spite of his puritan sympathies, saw the point. In a speech to the judges of the common law shortly after, he warned them against those who sought

> to conceive erroneous opinions, in condemning the whole church and order ecclesiastical . . . and in moving her Majesty's good subjects to think it a burden of conscience to observe the orders and rites of the Church established by law; a matter pernicious to the state of government.

Because of the support which they enjoyed in high places, it was often difficult to bring offenders to punishment – for the Elizabethan bishops lacked the status and confidence to challenge the secular aristocracy as their predecessors had done.[12] Field and Willcox, the authors of the *Admonition*, were imprisoned for a year under easy conditions, and the notoriously radical preacher Edward Dering was no more than briefly suspended from his spiritual functions, in spite of telling the queen to her face that she was sinfully neglecting the welfare of the Church. Proceedings against them were also inhibited by the undoubted fact that they were the most fearless and effective opponents of catholicism and much needed in areas where the old religion was strong, or reviving under missionary influence. Nevertheless the radical movement lost something of its momentum in the later 1570s under pressure from the Council and the queen herself. In October 1573 a royal proclamation ordered the suppression of all 'contentious sects and disquietness', and shortly afterwards special commissions were appointed to ensure compliance. The campaign was concentrated upon the midlands and the south-east where the non-conformists were most troublesome, and according to one recent authority this activity 'delayed the development of English presbyterianism for ten years'.[13] Also it should be remembered that the radicals had no share in the develop-

[12] Their revenues had been decimated during the reformation, and Elizabeth continued a most unscrupulous financial policy towards them (not for the benefit of poor livings, as the puritans would have liked, but for the benefit of her courtiers). Late sixteenth century bishops were also scholars and theologians rather than statesmen, and as a result they ranked with the upper gentry rather than the secular peers, to whom they were often painfully subservient.

[13] Collinson, quoted by McGrath, 145.

ment of the 'national myth', which was closely bound up with the royal supremacy. Their exemplars were 'the best reformed Churches' of the continent, and they therefore also suffered, although to a much lesser extent than the catholics, from the disadvantages of foreign associations. These factors helped to restrict the popular appeal of presbyterianism at a time when the Anglican Church was winning increasing acceptance through its association with the nation-state.

THE IMPACT OF THE NEW STYLE MILITIA

Obedience to the law was no less important for the stability of Elizabethan government than for that of any of its predecessors. Religious non-conformity was dangerous because, under the royal supremacy, it represented a challenge to the Crown based upon conscience. In other words an explicit, although usually partial, refutation of the doctrine of obedience for conscience' sake, which had been built into the foundations of the English Reformation. At the same time, the weapons which were used to combat this threat also built up respect for the secular law. The insistent propaganda of obedience, intensified after the rising of 1569, laid increasing and effective stress upon the patriotic duty of loyalty:

> If that you stick together as you ought,
> This little isle may set the world at nought,

as one pamphleteer expressed it.

At the same time the Spanish and papal threats, and the constant undercurrent of tension and alarm which they created, gave Elizabeth many of the advantages of being at war without the risks and expense of actual fighting. For example in 1573 the militia was re-organised, a development which was to have a lasting and important effect upon the military functions of the aristocracy. Out of the traditional general musters of the shires 'a convenient and sufficient number of the most able' were to be selected for special training. The remainder of the 'able' men were bound to find weapons and to muster as before, but were not required to undertake any training and became increasingly nominal as a military reserve. The trained bands, on the other hand, were to be equipped with up to date pikes and fire-arms, and drilled in their use for ten days in every year at the expense of their shires. Those so selected were exempt from service overseas, which led to considerable competition for membership and guaranteed the military incompetence of any levies sent out of the country. The size of this 'home guard' varied from county to county and was not a fixed proportion of the available men. The exact number was usually the result of a tug of war between the Council, who wished for as large a force as possible, and the local justices who were anxious to save their own and their neighbours' pockets. Somewhere between 10 and 20 per cent was the average. Since these soldiers had to be paid a wage of 8d a day during training, in addition to other provisions, it cost about a £1 a year to drill each man. Consequently a county the size of Norfolk or Devon could be faced with an annual bill of about £500, over and above the capital cost of the equipment. Discontent with the taxation needed to raise such sums was general, but persistent rumours of invasion underlined the need, and on the whole the government was remarkably successful in achieving its aims.

Over a number of years this new system resulted in a significant shift in the balance of power. Since it was no longer necessary to rely upon privately raised forces for defence or domestic security, the system of licensing retainers, which had been used extensively under Edward and Mary, disappeared. Although she might occasionally turn a blind eye to the activities of favoured individuals such as the Earl of Leicester, Elizabeth's expressed policy in respect of retaining was very similar to that of her father and grandfather. A proclamation of January 1572 ordered the existing statutes to be enforced and set up special inquisitions to investigate offences and complaints. Even the commission of array for overseas service was used only occasionally, the Council preferring to rely upon county quotas raised by the Lords Lieutenant, so that the last pretext for private recruiting was reduced to a minimal level at which it safely remained for the next two centuries. The aristocracy remained responsible for arming their own servants, who were exempt from the general musters, but their military capacity nevertheless withered away. Except in so far as they were Lords Lieutenant, or might be needed to decorate a foreign campaign with their rank, the magnates ceased to have any military function – so that already by 1576 only a quarter of the adult peers had seen active service. This represented a sharp contrast with the 1540s, when the great majority of adult peers had seen at least some service in Henry's

French and Scottish wars. By the early seventeenth century the proportion was even lower, in spite of the Anglo-Spanish war and the Irish rebellions. The government preferred professional soldiers, trained in the exacting techniques of modern warfare, and it was men of this kind, Norris, Vere and Mountjoy, who commanded the English forces in the Netherlands and Ireland in the latter part of the reign. Similarly, the drilling of the trained bands required professional Captains and sergeants who were familiar with contemporary tactics and weapons. England was dangerously far behind her continental neighbours, and the local gentry were usually no better equipped than their peers to remedy this situation.

The bow and the brown bill were obsolete, and the new equipment was not only expensive but needed careful maintenance. Consequently the Council pursued a policy of establishing county armouries under the control of the Deputy Lieutenants – who would in practice also be justices of the peace. Gradually, over about thirty years, these central repositories replaced the aristocratic household armouries which had been the universal system before 1570. The last major replenishing of these private stores before the civil war seems to have occurred in the mid 1570s, and it was also at that time that the last great magnate stronghold of the old kind was fortified and equipped. This was the Earl of Leicester's castle at Kenilworth, where he accumulated over 100 guns and enough small arms for 200 horse and 500 foot.[14] Why he thought it necessary to spend over £2,000 on this massive armament is not clear; perhaps it was no more than insurance against loss of favour. No subject had possessed a fortress like Kenilworth since the days of the last Duke of Buckingham, nor was any to do so in future. Many nobles and other aristocrats at this stage possessed arms for a force of a score or two, but only the Duke of Norfolk came near to Leicester in the scale of his preparations, a factor which probably contributed to his downfall. At the time of his attainder he had weapons for 120 horse and 500 foot – and some of his agents, possibly without his knowledge, had attempted to distribute

[14] L. Stone, *The Crisis of the Aristocracy*, 220. Stone quotes numerous figures for other peers, indicating that it was quite common for small quantities of artillery to be in private hands, but neither the Duke of Norfolk nor anyone else approached Leicester in this respect.

these to his tenants and friends in Norfolk during the summer of 1569. By the end of the century most of these private collections had rusted into uselessness, and the warlike attitudes which went with them had disappeared. Some noble families were still cautiously buying weapons as late as the 1590s without this being thought particularly sinister, but by that time it was no longer generally expected that a nobleman or gentleman would be able to appear at short notice at the head of his own 'band'.

The deployment of armed force thus became almost exclusively the prerogative of the state, and those who controlled it did so by virtue of authority delegated by the Crown. The key men in the new system were the Deputy Lieutenants, three or four to a county, who were responsible for the actual work of mustering, the organisation of training and the maintenance of equipment. Occasionally they were professional soldiers with local connections, but usually the heads of substantial country families – the same men who in one way or another controlled every other aspect of local government. Thus although the political power of the nobility remained great, the military reorganisation which began in 1573 resulted in a significant shift towards the Crown on the one hand and the gentry on the other. It also helped to make the aristocracy as a class more amenable to the rule of law.

As we have already seen, early Tudor government had made considerable progress in this direction by its policy of controlling retainder and making the localities more dependent upon the central administration. Private warfare of the kind which had flourished in the middle of the fifteenth century was impossible by the 1530s, and the constant efforts of the Council and the courts maintained a measure of day to day discipline. Nevertheless the habit of casual violence remained, and the comparatively weak government of the mid-century led to a revival of the aristocratic retinue – albeit nominally under licence. In the early part of Elizabeth's reign it was still normal for a nobleman to travel with an escort of scores, or even hundreds, of horsemen. Almost two hundred friends, servants and retainers turned out to welcome the Earl of Aundel when he returned from abroad in 1566, and these displays were not entirely ornamental. There are frequent examples of private quarrels being pursued with the aid of dozens, or scores of servants, who broke fences and weirs, removed cattle and beat up anyone who had the temerity to stand in their way. In 1589 the Earl of Lincoln (who was a notorious offender) led a full-scale assault on Weston Manor at the head of forty armed men – although eleven years later he was reduced to offering 1s a day to induce men to support him against Edward Dymocke. Feuding peers and gentry set upon each other in the streets of London, and even in the semi-sacred precincts of the court. These activities were not pursued with impunity, and most of our knowledge of them derives from the records of legal proceedings, but in spite of its energy the Council in the 1560s did not seem to be getting any closer to a final solution of the problem. Elizabeth herself was surprisingly supine in her attitude, even after the rising of 1569 had demonstrated once again the political threat latent in such unruliness. She was more concerned to keep the quarrelling groups in a state of equilibrium than to put an end to their anti-social behaviour. Perhaps such a reaction was typical of her whole political philosophy, but in the event it turned out to be unnecessarily pessimistic.

For a variety of reasons aristocratic habits, and attitudes towards violence, began to change in the 1570s, although it was to take upwards of half a century to complete the transformation. The development of the trained bands was one factor, and the virtual disappearance of the commission of array was another, but probably the more important reasons were less obvious. Professor Stone has suggested that one of these was the introduction of the rapier, and the accompanying code of the *duello*.[15] The old style of fighting with broadsword and buckler was energetic but not particularly lethal. Such brawling weapons set a premium upon weight of numbers, and their use was not controlled by any code of honour. Consequently attacks in overwhelming numbers, or when the enemy was at a disadvantage, were the order of the day. The rapier, however, was not a brawler's weapon, and in an accomplished hand it could be extremely deadly. The first fashionable fencing school in England was set up in Blackfriars in 1576, and over the next twenty years the style of aristocratic combat was transformed. The surprise assault gave way to the formal challenge to 'gentlemanlike ad-

[15] Stone, 242-50. The French fashion for the 'team' duel never caught on in England, where single combat was always the rule.

venture', in which only the principals were at risk. Thus by the pressure of fashion violence was disciplined, so that by the early seventeenth century the old style of affray was no longer considered becoming for a gentleman, or tolerable in polite society. In England, as in France, one consequence of this code of honour was to diminish factional quarrels and to lessen the danger of oppression and intimidation.

Although a century of constant government pressure had greatly reduced the scale of the problem, there were still instances in the 1580s of local courts being overawed by armed bands – as when Sir James Croft appeared at the Hereford quarter sessions in 1589 with over fifty followers to support his quarrel with the Coningsbys. Such conduct was not to be tolerated, and the usual result was a swift appearance before the Privy Council or one of the two regional Councils. There was nothing that the local justices could do to curb aristocratic disorders of this kind, and some magnates clearly believed themselves to be above the normal course of justice – as when Lord Chandos ignored a summons to appear before the Council of Wales, replying instead, 'I had thought that a nobleman might have found more favour ... than thus hardly to be dealt with ... like a common subject.' It would be wrong to suggest that the Privy Council dealt ruthlessly, even with defiance of this order, unless treason was in question. Usually it preferred to enmesh the offender in the toils of a Star Chamber or common law action, which might be slow or expensive, and would certainly make heavy demands upon his time and energy. It was Cecil's policy to work through the normal courts wherever possible, and certainly by 1600 the gentry, and even the nobility, were amendable to ordinary discipline in a way which they had never been before. In 1626 Lord Keeper Williams could write the epitaph of a way of life which had constantly exercised Tudor governments: 'in ancient times the records of the Court of Star Chamber are filled with battles and riots so outrageous, whereas now we hear not one in our age.' Such a transformation must be credited partly to the unheroic persistence of Tudor administration, and partly to a change of attitude in which official propaganda played no more than a part.

Unlike her father or grandfather, Elizabeth made little personal contribution to the maintenance of order. The Earl of Sussex complained bitterly in 1565 that he was unable to come to Court without danger of personal violence from the Earl of Leicester and his servants – implying that the queen was either unable or unwilling to protect him. In 1582 a court feud between the Earl of Oxford and Thomas Knyvett resulted in the latter killing one of the former's servants, and Elizabeth personally ordered the Lord Chancellor to have the matter heard *in camera* so that Knyvett's plea of self-defence would not be challenged. This particular quarrel produced a series of unsavoury murders, and the queen did nothing to suppress it. She was also easily prone to grant pardons for homicide, being temperamentally unwilling to antagonise any powerful aristocratic group, even in the cause of justice. This was the weak side of that sensitivity to gentry opinion and ambition which we have already noticed as her peculiar asset in attracting loyalty and devoted service. Her practice at court as with the offices of state, was to distribute her favours with a judicious hand, guided not so much by the merits of the case as by her own sense of political balance.

The same attitude can be seen in every aspect of her policy – balancing the cautious Cecil against the more radical Leicester and Walsingham; condoning recusancy, to which her administration was opposed, and sharply checking puritanism, to which it was inclined to be favourable. She loved intrigue and feared commitment, having taken a bold enough step in the first year of her reign to last for the rest of her life. Like her father, she regarded willingness to serve her as the great criterion of acceptability, and in spite of its possible perils her court was open in a sense which her sister's had not been and her successor's would soon cease to be.[16] As long as her nobles and gentlemen were loyal to her, she did not much mind how they conducted themselves, leaving it to her servants to enforce the law as best they could. As long as her authority was acknowledged, she did not 'make windows into men's souls', and her bishops complained with justice of her failure to support their efforts.

In many ways this was a successful policy, partly because of the queen's gift for choosing able servants, and partly because she reigned for forty-four years, but it carried the seeds of its

[16] Elizabeth expected all her peers to spend some time at court each year, to demonstrate their loyalty and to enable her to keep an eye on them. The queen also lived an extremely public life, with innumerable progresses, pageants and other festive appearances. This was all a calculated part of her brilliantly successful public relations, but it created security problems which drove her Council to despair.

own destruction. Francis Naunton may have believed that ruling by faction showed Elizabeth's 'great judgment', but it led to constant tension and uncertainty, and eventually to shameless gerrymandering which undermined the integrity of the administration. In the last decade of the reign it was to be shown up in the worst possible light by the confrontation between Sir Robert Cecil and the Earl of Essex.

CHAPTER II

THE STRESSES OF WAR

> My good lord, advancement in all worlds be obtained by mediation and remembrance of noble friends. (*Anonymous suitor*)

THE WORKINGS OF ELIZABETH'S GOVERNMENT

From 1585 until the end of Elizabeth's reign, England was at war with Spain. Like all sixteenth century warfare, it was a desultory struggle, brief periods of strenuous campaigning being interspersed with long intervals of inactivity or half hearted negotiation. It was fought more or less continuously in the Netherlands and upon the high seas; intermittently in France in the interest of Henri of Navarre; and after 1595 in Ireland, where the extensive Tyrone rebellion attracted Spanish intervention.[1] The progress of the fighting need not concern us here, but the fact of being at war had important effects within England which we must briefly consider. Catholic opinion became more sharply and openly divided on the subject of political allegiance. Large numbers of men had to be recruited for foreign campaigns, and some reabsorbed into civilian life on their return.

Above all the government faced steadily mounting financial difficulties, which inevitably affected its relations with the aristocracy by necessitating more frequent recourse to Parliament, and cutting down the scale of royal patronage. The maintenance of a force in the Netherlands cost £2 million over eighteen years, and the suppression of the Irish revolt almost twice as much. Even the small scale campaign in Brittany absorbed nearly £300,000, and the cost of the war at sea was certainly

[1] Hugh O'Neill, Earl of Tyrone, was the first man to put an organised Irish army into the field against the English in 1594. Spanish attempts to send an expedition to Ireland in 1596 and 1597 were frustrated by the weather, but in 1601 a force of four thousand infantry was landed at Kinsale. Mountjoy besieged the town in December 1601, and broke the rebellion by defeating Tyrone's relieving army. The Spanish expedition being a recognised act of war, there was no repetition of the massacre of 1579.

very much greater than the occasional profits which resulted from plunder or privateering. To set against this the annual ordinary revenue of the Crown was about £300,000, most of which was absorbed by ordinary expenditure. By careful management over a number of years, in anticipation of such a need, Cecil had built up a reserve of about £300,000 by 1585. This lasted for three years, and thereafter the government was forced to live from hand to mouth, as Henry VIII had done in the 1540s.

Six Parliaments over sixteen years granted the queen the unprecedented sum of £2 million in direct taxation and extraordinary revenue of other kinds. Members grumbled, and so did the tax-payers they represented, especially after 1593, but there was no serious opposition. The House of Commons did rather well out of the situation. It confirmed its right to initiate financial measures, developed its procedures, and made several advances in the definition of privilege – notably to gain a measure of control over election returns, which properly speaking belonged to Chancery.[2]

Above all the members were given an increasing sense of being a part of the regular machinery of government – of belonging to a powerful institution upon which the Crown was unavoidably dependent. Partly to avoid increasing this impression, and partly because she genuinely feared the reaction to a demand of such magnitude, Elizabeth resorted to all manner of expedients to avoid presenting a realistic bill to Parliament. The customs were farmed at augmented rents; Crown lands were sold; forced loans and benevolences were revived. At the same time, military expenditure was cut back wherever possible, and naval operations were financed upon a joint stock basis which placed the Crown in the position of a shareholder. No method existed whereby the wealth of the country could be accurately assessed, because although the political classes broadly supported the war policy, they had no intention of being fully honest about their resources. As a result, by 1603 the Crown was reduced to financial exhaustion, while the burden fell very unevenly upon

[2] After the Norfolk election case of 1586, it became customary to appoint a standing committee of privileges at the beginning of a new Parliament, and to commit all election disputes to it. In this manner Chancery lost the initiative, although the matter was not finally settled in favour of the House until Goodwin's case of 1604.

its subjects, many of the richest of whom had contributed comparatively little.

The consequences of this were of the greatest importance. Over the next twenty years it became clear that the balance of power between the Crown and the parliamentary Commons had shifted decisively in the latter's favour. More immediately a storm blew up over one of Elizabeth's fiscal devices – the monopoly – and her desperate economies produced ominous discontent among those courtiers and office holders who were largely dependent upon the royal bounty. The monopolies issue was fought out in the Parliaments of 1597 and 1601, culminating in the famous surrender of the queen's 'golden speech'. In origin the monopoly was a device to protect and foster domestic industry and enterprise, but it could easily become an artificial restriction the only purpose of which was to enrich the holder by enabling him to raise prices and force merchants to trade under expensive licences. The potential profits from a flourishing trade were great, and the value of the monopoly to the Crown was two-fold. It might be used as a means of conferring a generous reward on a servant at the expense of the consumer; or it might be leased to a company or an individual for a substantial rent as a commercial speculation. In either case the consumer was paying an inflated price for what often became an inferior commodity. Elizabeth made considerable use of these grants to reduce pressure upon the Exchequer, but they were not worth a serious political quarrel, and eventually she agreed to extensive curtailment. In spite of this, monopolies survived to be an even more burning issue under her successor.

The queen's inability to reward her servants and officers, of which this dispute was a partial reflection, was a matter of the utmost gravity. Patronage was one of the greatest pillars of monarchical authority, and disappointed expectations of place and preferment one of the swiftest begetters of aristocratic discontent 'Little gain there is gotten in this time,' lamented one courtier in 1594, while in 1597 another spoke more ominously of 'this time that no man is rewarded to his desert.' Elizabeth was not given to being apologetic, but in 1600 she felt bound to explain to a disappointed petitioner that the cost of war had forced her to 'restrain her bountiful hand from rewarding her servants'. Of course, this 'freeze' was relative and did not much affect the number of routine offices available, or the regular fees and perquisites attached to them; but all placemen expected some occasional bounty in return for their efforts, and this was not forthcoming. Nor was this a small scale problem, affecting only the court and the upper reaches of the administration.

Altogether the Crown disposed of about 1,200 places which were worth a gentleman's having, besides a great many lesser posts. In 1587 there were 1,500 justices of the peace over the whole country, and the 'upper gentry' probably numbered around 2,500 adult men.[8] So, even allowing for a considerable amount of pluralism, it is evident that a large proportion of the aristocracy were attached to the Crown in this way. The positions involved varied from the stewardships of royal manors to the highest offices of state, and many were sought rather for their prestige value than for profit. For instance Sir Robert Sidney held the royal park of Otford in Kent and esteemed it 'of great value, not for the profit but because it was of Her Majesty's gift and of reputation in his country'. Unfortunately there were always more men desirous of such reputation than there were places to satisfy them, and the accelerated sale of Crown estates caused by the war created something of a famine. Military and naval operations created new posts and offices, but the resources available to finance them were always inadequate, which meant that the butter had to be spread more thinly on existing bread, and thus made the situation worse rather than better.

Apart from a growing discontent, which was to contribute significantly to the Essex 'rebellion', these circumstances also greatly increased the temptation for those who held offices to exploit them beyond the limits which had hitherto been regarded as proper. Earlier in her reign Elizabeth had distributed profitable grants and concessions, annuities, and even outright gifts of cash to those who had served her or pleased her well. Sir Christopher Hatton received an annuity of £400 over and above his fees in 1576, while the prime favourite, Dudley, had received £1,000 a year out of the customs at the beginning of the reign.

Such generosity was exceptional, even at that date, for the queen was always more judicious than lavish with her gifts, but after 1585 it would have been impossible. In the latter part

[8] These were the county élites, mostly knights and esquires, although the division between them and the 'mere gentry' is necessarily an arbitrary one.

of the reign such gifts as are recorded tended to be charged against uncertain sources of income, such as recusancy fines – or virtually left for the recipient to collect for himself, such as concealed lands.[4] This would have mattered less had Tudor officials been adequately salaried, but apart from the judiciary very few were. Fewer than 200 of Elizabeth's servants received more than £50 a year from this source, which on its own would not have been sufficient to support even a modest gentleman. On the other hand, not even the most stringent moralist expected a civil servant to live on his salary. Every officer was entitled to charge fees for the services which he rendered to the general public, who thus bore directly the cost of administration, instead of paying through taxation to the central government. In many cases these fees were charged upon a fixed scale, as was the case for sealing writs issued out of Chancery; but there were always services to be rendered which could not be so charged, and in such the official himself exercised considerable discretion. Inevitably the borderline between a fee and a bribe was indistinct, and office holders showed great ingenuity in devising possible sources of profit. The magnitude of some such opportunities can be judged from the fact that the Earl of Leicester paid the Crown a rent of £2,300 a year for the right to make writs of covenant and alienation fines in the Court of Common Pleas – and he certainly expected to make a profit.

Partly because of the queen's poverty, and partly through a change of attitude which is not easy to account for, customary restraints upon exploitation of this kind relaxed in the last twenty years of the century. So also did restraint upon the exercise of the private patronage which high office conferred. The queen's Remembrancer of the Exchequer was allowed eight clerks; in fact he had twelve. The Council of Wales was supposed to be served by eighteen similar functionaries; in 1591 it had over one hundred. The disposal of such minor posts might be useful in local politics, or they might even be sold.[5] For what-

[4] These were lands which should have been surrendered to the Crown by escheat or forfeiture, but had been overlooked. The recipient of a grant of this kind would have to employ a legal agent to discover the titles, and then prosecute in the courts before gaining his reward.

[5] The sale of offices was not much practised in England before the seventeenth century, and even then did not reach the scale it achieved in contemporary France where it formed a regular source of royal income. Nevertheless minor posts were sometimes distributed in this way, and

ever reason they were created, it was not normally to improve the efficiency of the administration, and the chief effect was to create an army of underpaid functionaries, each seeking to devise some pretext for living at the public expense. At a higher level the great officers of state might use their patronage (as they always had done) to build up their own clientage, but there was an increasing tendency to offer it for sale. This was often done through intermediaries. Lord Buckhurst used his daughter, Lady Anne Glemham; Sir John Carey sold army appointments through his wife; even Lord Burghley used his wife to sell profitable wardships. Just after Elizabeth's death Sir Robert Cecil instructed his secretary to offer the Lord Treasurer £100 through Lady Anne Glemham in return for a favour to his protegé Fulk Greville. 'For the £100,' he concluded, 'I will find a ward to pay it.' In spite of precautions such trafficking did not remain secret, and the result was a dangerous decline in public respect for those closest to the queen's person.

The rapacity and corruption of royal servants had been a favourite fifteenth century grievance of which little had been heard since the 1530s. Significantly, in the 1590s, such complaints began to appear again, referring both to the ingenious extortions of minor officers and concessionaries, and to the general conduct of high politics. The queen had always been reluctant to thwart the ambitions of the aristocracy, unless they indulged in treason, and at this time she seems to have felt bound to allow her servants to help themselves to the rewards which she was unable to give. As a result she did nothing to check such practices and left a demoralised administration to her successor.

In other respects, Elizabeth used her patronage with great astuteness. Like her father, she was always prepared to recognise real merit, and avoided the danger of allowing political control to fall into the hands of personal favourites. Above all (and in this she differed somewhat from Henry) she never allowed any minister, however trusted, to monopolise access to her favour. In spite of her high regard for Cecil, and the skill with which he built up his clientage, his position at court was never unchallenged. Leicester, although he became a politician of no mean

it was normal to regard an office as a piece of property. The Six Clerkships of Chancery were valuable freeholds, for example, and were normally granted for life. Although the reversion of offices might be granted or sold, it was not normal in England for such grants to be heritable.

stature, was first and foremost a courtier, and his influence there was always great. Indeed the court had its own network of patronage, dependent less on office than on grants of other kinds, such as monopolies, export licences and similar marketable privileges. The queen's control was always strict and personal, so that her councillors, household officers, and others who enjoyed access to her could make claims upon her bounty with some chance of satisfaction independently of either of the major brokers. Although the Duke of Norfolk and the Earl of Northumberland had complained bitterly in the 1560s about their exclusion from favour, Elizabeth was careful not to antagonise conservative interests at large, and several peers of the old school did receive tokens of her esteem – which might well not have happened had either Leicester or Cecil been in complete control. However, Leicester died in 1589, Walsingham in 1590, and Sir Christopher Hatton in 1591. Which left Lord Burghley, the last of the older generation of the queen's advisers, in a position of lonely eminence which he had never enjoyed before.

THE EARL OF ESSEX'S REVOLT

At this juncture, when the Council was considerably weakened by its recent losses, and the Secretaryship vacant by the death of Walsingham, Burghley began his long campaign to secure the latter office for his second son, Robert Cecil. Success would have given his family an almost unshakable grip upon the administration, and there was no statesman of stature to oppose him. However, in 1587 the twenty-year old Robert Devereux, Earl of Essex, had taken the court by storm, and he had no intention of conceding such a vital preferment. Essex was a man of passionate ambition and considerable gifts, but totally lacking in discretion or diplomatic skill. Although the queen rapidly came to regard him as a favourite nephew, and bestowed upon him the kind of largesse which was being conspicuously withheld from the majority of her servants, her political judgement did not desert her. She would not make Essex Secretary. On the other hand she did not wish to thwart him openly, or to give the Cecils so much power. Consequently the office remained vacant for over five years, although during that time Robert Cecil in fact did most of the work.

In these circumstances it is not surprising that the two young men became first rivals, and then enemies. The Earl's position at court naturally gave him the disposal of a valuable patronage, and attracted to his service young, able and ambitious men who saw him as the rising star. This clientage Essex was anxious to use for political purposes to extend his power from the court to the government, as Leicester had done. He was not conspicuously successful and blamed his failure, with some justice, on the opposition of the Cecils. The quarrel came to a head in 1594 over the appointment of a new Attorney General. Essex made no secret of the fact that he wanted the position for Francis Bacon, and it was important for him to demonstrate that his influence extended to such valuable promotions. When Cecil expressed doubts about Bacon's suitability, the Earl burst out,

> The Attorneyship for Francis is that I must have; and in that will I spend all my power, might, authority and amity ... and whosoever getteth this office out of my hands for any other, before he have it, it shall cost him the coming by.

This was a declaration of war, and when, shortly after, the office in question was given to Sir Edward Coke, relations between the two sides deteriorated rapidly.

The climax of the Earl's career came in 1596, when his advocacy of more active campaigning seemed to be justified by success and his own participation in the Cadiz expedition made him a popular hero. This acclaim was sweet to him, and probably increased his following, but it did not satisfy his political ambitions. On the 5 July, while Essex was at sea, Robert Cecil was at last sworn as Principal Secretary, and this setback to his influence robbed the Earl of much of the satisfaction of his triumph. By the end of the year his animosity towards the Cecils was more intense than ever, since they not only continued to frustrate the promotion of his protégés, but had subjected him to a damaging inquisition into the finances of the Cadiz expedition. After this exposure of his mismanagement, Essex sulked furiously and even went so far as to complain of his treatment in correspondence with leaders of the Scottish kirk who had solicited his good offices. Thereafter, although he retained his hold upon the queen's affections, and continued to build up his own wealth and clientage, he was unable to make any real impression upon the political supremacy of the Secretary. His support could not even secure the Mastership of the Rolls against Cecil's opposition. This situation was not much affected by Lord Burghley's death in 1598. For some time the great statesman had been in failing health, and although the queen felt his loss keenly, in fact his son had been bearing the family fortunes for some years and was perfectly capable of sustaining them unaided.

In the event it was not Cecil who ruined Essex but the Earl himself. When the situation in Ireland became desperate as a result of Tyrone's victory at the Yellow Ford in August 1598, he pressed the queen to appoint him to the vacant Lord Lieutenancy, characteristically hoping to win a dazzling victory in that graveyard of reputations. Elizabeth hesitated, not wishing to lose his company, and not altogether sharing his own confidence in his abilities. Nevertheless eventually she yielded, and he arrived in Dublin in April 1599 at the head of the largest and best equipped English army which had ever crossed the Irish Sea. The result was a fiasco, in spite of his charm and personal courage. He ignored his instructions, wasted his resources, and was duped into fruitless negotiations with the wily Tyrone, who thereby gained a much needed breathing space. The queen was furious, and wrote to him in stinging terms which he immediately construed to be the result of Cecil's influence. Pathological suspicion of the Secretary completely destroyed his sense of proportion, and in September he abandoned his post without permission to return and confront his supposed detractors. But instead of rehabilitation, disgrace awaited him at Elizabeth's hands, and he was placed in close confinement under the custody of Sir Thomas Egerton.

The accumulated evidence of his incompetence and indiscretion had at last broken down the queen's affection, and replaced it with a growing distrust. In June 1600 he was arraigned before a special commission sitting in private and charged with misconduct under five heads: desertion of his post, failure to carry out his instructions, the presumptuous tone of his letters, his unauthorised negotiations with Tyrone, and his lavish distribution of knighthoods. With some difficulty he was induced to throw himself on the queen's mercy and thus avoid public disgrace. Nevertheless he was deprived of most of his offices, and confined to Essex House in the Strand. Elizabeth had at first wished to bring him to trial in Star Chamber, but wiser counsels prevailed, for a potentially dangerous situation was developing as a result of his imprisonment.

The grinding effort of the war, the parsimony and caution of an ageing ruler, and the inevitable feeling that the reign was drawing to a close had produced widespread restlessness and dissatisfaction. This feeling was particularly strong among the younger gentry, many of whom had attached themselves to Essex as the man of the future. Such men were only too willing to believe that their patron was the victim of factional malice – and those personal qualities which at one time had endeared him to his sovereign had also given him a popularity with the common people, especially in London, which survived his fall. Consequently Essex House became the headquarters of a faction, and a resort for all those who felt deprived of office, favour or employment by the ascendency of Cecil and his allies – deserters from the army in Ireland, impecunious younger sons, disgruntled young peers such as Rutland and Southampton, and disappointed place-hunters of all descriptions. For the best part of a year the Earl did little or nothing to encourage this development, but his own sense of grievance and the promptings of some of the extravagant adventurers who surrounded him led him by stages into a fatal maze of conspiracy.

By this time his hatred for Cecil had become an obsession. He became convinced that the Secretary was intriguing with Spain to secure the succession of the Infanta,[6] and endeavoured to persuade Mountjoy to bring his Irish army into England to secure the protestant cause. He expressed opinions of his enemies which stirred up some of his followers to plot murder, and opinions of the queen which went to the very brink of treason. This wild behaviour was not merely the result of injured pride, or even of disappointed ambition. The Earl's finances also tottered on the brink of collapse, and in spite of his great estates by the summer of 1600 he was well over £25,000 in debt. Consequently the queen's refusal to renew his lucrative monopoly for the import of sweet wines contributed significantly to his mood of desperation. Similar difficulties, the results of idleness and gross extravagance, seems to have afflicted all his more important associates. Rutland's debts stood at £5,000, Southampton's at £8,000, and others had been forced to sell or mortgage large parts of their estates.

For all of them, the overthrow of Cecil seemed to be the key

[6] His evidence for this seems to have been based upon a misunderstanding of some words spoken by Sir William Knollys. When challenged at his trial, he was unable to produce any corroborating evidence. P. M. Handover, *The Second Cecil*, 226-8.

which would unlock the golden door of the queen's bounty, and place the fruits of power and office in their own hands. As a result, by the end of 1600 Essex stood at the head of a great 'connexion' which was none the less powerful for being so discreditably motivated. It consisted not merely of the swordsmen and bravos who gathered at Essex House, but of the wide ramifications of his own and his associates' clientage throughout the country. The Devereux interest, for example, was strong in the west and in North Wales, where even at this late date some justices of the peace wore the Earl's livery, despite explicit laws to the contrary. In 1597 at least a dozen members of Parliament had recognised Essex as their patron, and he could command the loyalty and service of a large number of lesser dependents, servants and friends. His Irish knights were also principally a personal following, and it was for that reason that the queen had looked upon their creation with such misgiving. In short, Essex had many of the makings of an 'overmighty subject', and had it been more efficiently managed, his stroke against Cecil could have caused a dangerous insurrection.[7]

In the event it was scarcely managed at all. By his insinuations against the Secretary he succeeded at length in persuading James to send a special embassy to know the queen's mind on the succession. The intention was to cement an alliance between Essex and the Scottish king at Cecil's expense, which would assure the Earl of first place among the councillors of the next reign. However, James became suspicious and delayed sending his ambassadors, which made Essex more reckless with the tension of waiting. A vague plan had already been conceived for seizing Whitehall palace and forcing the queen to dismiss her 'evil councillors'. This would have been followed by the summoning of a Parliament, the elections for which Essex seems to have imagined he could control. At the beginning of January 1601 he decided not to go ahead with this scheme but to await the outcome of the Scottish negotiations. By the end of the month his wilder followers were crazy with impatience and hopelessly indiscreet. On 7 February Essex was summoned before the Council to explain the rumours and suspicions which were focusing

[7] It has been pointed out (Elton, *England under the Tudors*, 473) that in trying to exploit the military potential of his 'connexion', Essex was acting in the pure tradition of bastard feudalism – the last occasion upon which this was done, except in the context of the civil war.

upon him, and he refused to attend on the grounds that there was a plot against his life. This reaction precipitated a crisis. The following morning four members of the Council visited Essex House to demand an explanation, and the Earl knew that he must either strike or surrender.

By this time he had almost three hundred gentlemen and several peers around him, thirsting for action, and determined, as one of them put it 'to be their own carvers' in the commonwealth. The four councillors were imprisoned, and Essex led a furious, but not particularly warlike cavalcade up Fleet Street and into the City. His hope was clearly to stimulate a great demonstration in his support and by that means to gain control of London. But he had miscalculated wildly, if he had calculated at all. There was a world of difference between the citizens turning out to cheer him as he went about his lawful business, and risking their necks in support of this madcap enterprise. No one stirred in response to his frantic cries: 'For the queen! For the queen! A plot is laid for my life!' And hard on his heels came a royal herald and a troop of soldiers, proclaiming him traitor. Seeing that he was making no progress, Essex made a final attempt to arouse a patriotic alarm: 'The Crown of England is sold to the Spaniard!' By this time his own party was melting away, and his new appeal met with no more success than the old. With a much diminished following he took to the water and returned to Essex House, where he found that his hostages had already been released. Several forces of royal troops converged upon the house under the direction of the Council, and the inmates hastily fortified themselves. The Earl talked of fighting to the death, and had he remained in that frame of mind a bloody siege might have ensued, but by the evening he had thought better of his resolution and surrendered. Along with his principal supporters he was sent to the Tower, while his lesser followers were distributed to other prisons to await trial.

Most of them escaped formal proceedings, and after a period of imprisonment were allowed to purchase their pardons as best they could. Even the Earl of Rutland, who had been conspicuous throughout, escaped with a heavy fine. But a few of the more active spirits such as Sir Christopher Mount and Sir Gelly Meyrick paid the full penalty, and there could be no question of mercy for Essex himself. He was tried, along with Southampton, on 19 February, and both were convicted. Southampton eventually escaped with his life, but in spite of Elizabeth's last minute reluctance to sign the warrant, the 'wild Earl' was brought to the block on 25 February and died with considerably more dignity than he had lived. Once his own disturbing presence was removed, the mischief which he had stirred up was soon appeased. His followers denounced one another with a frantic energy which robbed them of all credit, and Cecil was easily able to rid himself of the pro-Spanish imputations which had been made against him.

The impression which remains is of a selfish and irresponsible conspiracy which stood no chance of disturbing the established political order. This, however, is not quite just. Had the movement in the capital succeeded, even temporarily, it would certainly have been reflected in those areas where Devereux, Manners or Wriothesley influence was strong. The completeness of its failure was due partly to the Earl's error of judgement in seeking to raise the city, rather than heading straight for the court, where he had many sympathisers. It was also partly due to the speed and efficiency of the government's reaction. Tudor monarchy was always more vulnerable to sudden stirs close to London than it was to much larger risings in distant provinces – and the Essex revolt had many of the characteristics of a palace revolution.

But Cecil was ready; his intelligence was good, and his own position was at stake as well as the security of the state. He had troops in readiness, and his immediate proclamation of the Earl's treason gave the latter no chance to exploit a confused or ambiguous situation. In fact, he had judged the threat accurately and snuffed out the attempted *coup d'état* with deceptive ease. But the Earl's fate did not remove the problems which he represented – an aristocracy starved of favours and rewards, and a faction estranged from the court by the narrowing circle of political power. Not only had the war drained away the queen's resources, but age had sapped her resilience, and weakened her sense of balance. At the end of her reign the Council numbered only twelve, and Sir Robert Cecil enjoyed a monopoly of power which had always been denied to his father.

THE MISSIONARY MOVEMENT CONTAINED

By contrast to these somewhat ominous developments, the war years also saw the partial resolution of those conflicts which had disturbed the security of the régime before 1585. The Parry plot in that year, followed by the more extensive and puzzling Babington Plot in 1586,[8] brought anti-catholic feeling to a head, and sealed the fate of Mary Queen of Scots. A new Act against Jesuits and seminary priests made the mere fact of Roman ordination treasonable, and removed any necessity to prove either deeds or intentions hostile to the state. Not surprisingly, the vast majority of those subsequently executed were arraigned under this statute, rather than under the less accommodating laws which had existed previously. At the same time the enforcement of recusancy fines was tightened up, and although the majority of catholic gentry continued to avoid prosecution, those who were proceeded against were very heavily mulcted. The total received went up from an average of about £1,800 a year to over £6,000.

These measures might not in themselves have made much difference to the catholic community, for the missions continued with undiminished zeal, but the execution of Mary in 1587 and the 'enterprise of England' in the following year brought a significant shift in the political position. Philip now brought forward his own claim to the English throne, based upon his descent in the female line from Philippa, the daughter of John of Gaunt, and there could not be the slightest doubt that any catholic who allowed his faith to affect his allegiance would be bound to adhere to him. Acting on this assumption, and evidently in complete ignorance of the real state of opinion, William Allen wrote to the Spanish King in 1588: 'I think there can be very few indeed who love their country and religion who do not from their hearts desire to be once more subject to your most clement rule.' In the same spirit Allen also drew up the *Declaration* which was to be issued by the invading army, justifying its actions, and an 'Admonition to the nobility and people of England,' which contained a vitriolic attack upon Elizabeth as 'an incestuous bastard, begotten and born in sin of an infamous courtesan'.

These words, coming from the Cardinal of England, the acknowledged leader of the English catholics, not only appeared to

[8] Anthony Babington had been a household servant of Mary's, who had listened too readily to the schemes of one John Ballard for the assassination of Elizabeth. Ballard was a renegade priest and may have been an *agent provocateur*. The net result of the conspiracy was the production of conclusive evidence against Mary. Babington and twelve others were also executed.

justify every stringent precaution which the government had taken in the previous twenty years, but significantly increased the estrangement between the faithful in England and the exiles who claimed to speak for them. Since no Spanish army actually landed in England, it is impossible to be sure whether or not it would have received any support – but every English catholic who expressed an opinion upon the subject was most earnest in his profession of loyalty to the queen. Over thirty priests and laymen were executed in the crisis year, and the alarm did not subside with the passing of the Armada.

For another decade the possibility of a Spanish invasion was constantly present, and the government's restraint in the enforcement of recusancy laws was noticeably reduced.[9] Early in 1589 Sir Christopher Hatton delivered in Parliament a denunciation of the papacy which might have come straight out of the puritan repertoire of a few years before. He also denounced 'that shameless atheist and bloody Cardinal' Allen, and 'those vile wretches, those bloody priests and false traitors here in our bosoms'. In 1591 a lengthy proclamation rehearsed all these dangers to the realm, and announced the establishment of special commissions to track down priests and their abettors. At the same time open dissent began to be expressed by clergy working in England against the political views of their ecclesiastical superiors. The Jesuit Robert Southwell in his *Humble Supplication to her Majesty*, written early in 1592, declared 'we do assure your Majesty that what army soever should come against you, we will rather yield our breasts to be broached by our country's swords than use our swords to the effusion of our country's blood.' A secular priest named Wright went even further. In a paper dealing with the question 'is it lawful for catholics to take up arms to defend their queen and country against the Spaniard?', he concluded that it was, on the grounds that Philip had not taken up arms for the faith but to further his own interests.[10]

[9] It is interesting to notice that in 1593 the government introduced a very severe bill against recusants, which the House of Commons moderated. Of course the increasing severity of enforcement was relative. Professor Neale has remarked with justice that such laws 'were often intended to be held *in terrorem* over offenders, and were neither expected to be, nor capable of being, rigidly enforced.' *Elizabeth I and her Parliaments*, II, 281.

[10] *An licitum sit catholicis in Anglia arma sumere et aliis modis reginam*

These disagreements and tensions were not conducive to the good discipline which was essential to a movement under persecution, and other disputes followed in their wake. In spite of Southwell's words the Jesuits in England were more closely associated with the views of the expatriates than were the secular priests. This was partly because they were subject to the control of their order, and partly because of the energetic political activities of Robert Parsons, which continued until his death in 1610. Consequently the jealousies which already existed between Jesuits and seculars were given a new edge in the 1590s and speedily emerged into the open. The first clear sign of trouble came in the outbreak of a protracted wrangle among the priests imprisoned in the government's special 'top security gaol' at Wisbech castle. The full story of the 'Wisbech stirs' need not concern us here, but they originated with the arrival there of William Weston, the Superior of the English Jesuits in 1588. Weston wished to improve the discipline of the prisoners and resist demoralisation by the imposition of a Rule. In this he was strenuously opposed by a group of seculars, who accused him of hubris, and the dispute came to a head in 1594.

By this time the wider quarrel between the Jesuits and the seculars was common knowledge, and the situation was aggravated by two further developments in 1594 and 1595. The first was the death of Cardinal Allen, which necessitated fresh arrangements for the government of the Church of England, and the second was the appearance of a book entitled *A Conference about the next succession to the Crown of England*, which was a political manifesto of the Allen-Parsons group. This pamphlet, which bore the name of R. Doleman, was apparently written by a syndicate of exiles, headed by Parsons. The first part consisted of a general discussion of the nature of government, similar in purport to the Leaguer pamphlets against Henri IV of France. Divine right arguments, which had regularly featured in the catholic armoury while Mary Stuart was alive, were now rejected. The obedience which subjects owed to their prince was conditional upon his ruling in accordance with the law – which of course included the law of God – and the advice of his councillors. The succession should be determined not by blood alone,

et regnum defendere contra Hispanos. Translated in J. Strype, *Annals of the Reformation*, III, ii, 583-97.

but also by the choice of the commonwealth. Thus the position taken up by the authors of the *Conference* was very similar to that adopted by the Parliament in 1571. Each was concerned to modify the hereditary principle, and each regarded 'true religion' as an essential qualification. The second part of the pamphlet surveyed the prospects of ten possible contenders for the English throne[11] and came down firmly in favour of the Infanta of Spain. Appearing at this juncture, when Elizabeth had just forbidden all discussion of the subject, the *Conference* infuriated the English government, embarrassed the catholic rank and file, and added fuel to the rage of the anti-Jesuit party among the English clergy.

Four years were allowed to pass after Allen's death before any fresh provision was made for the rule of the English province, and when the pope at last acted in 1598 his decision made the already turbulent situation worse. Instead of providing a bishop or bishops with full diocesan authority, an Archpriest was appointed with limited disciplinary power over the seminary trained priests, but no jurisdiction at all over either the laity or the Jesuits. Worse still the man appointed, George Blackwell, although a secular, was strongly sympathetic to the Jesuits and was specifically instructed to consult the Jesuit superior in England on all matters of importance. 'All catholics must hereafter depend upon Blackwell, and he upon Garnet, and Garnet upon Parsons, and Parsons upon the Devil who is the author of all rebellions, treasons, murders, disobedience and all such designments as this wicked Jesuit hath hitherto deigned against her majesty, her safety, her crown and her life.' The writer of these savage words was not a government pamphleteer, but an English catholic named William Watson. Parsons became convinced that an anti-Jesuit conspiracy was afoot in England and the Netherlands, and when the high feeling resulted in a petition against Blackwell in December 1598, he had the bearers imprisoned in Rome and their case dismissed without a hearing.

Eventually wiser counsels were to prevail, and in 1602 the 'appellants' gained some success, at least to the extent that Blackwell was instructed to modify his attitude. However by that time considerable damage had been done. The two sides had

11 Philip II, his daughter the Infanta; the Duke of Braganza; the Duke of Parma; James VI; Arabella Stuart; Edward Seymour; Lord Beauchamp; Henry Stanley, Earl of Derby; and Henry Hastings, Earl of Huntingdon.

abused each other in print, and the appellants had entered into negotiations with the government, which resulted in their second appeal being forwarded by the secret assistance of Bancroft, the Bishop of London. The Council naturally welcomed these divisions, and hoped to exploit them to the extent of persuading the appellants to renounce the pope's power of deposition in return for a limited toleration. However, in this they failed. The appellants were sharply called to heel by the Holy Office in October 1602, and the government felt constrained to issue a proclamation in the following month reaffirming the principle that there could be only one authorised religion in England.

Nevertheless, distinctions were to be made. The proclamation went on to point out that not all papists were equally guilty. The Jesuits and their adherents were to leave the realm at once, on pain of death under the existing law. Such seculars as did not share their treasonable purposes but nevertheless persisted in maintaining the pope's power of deposition were to be given until the end of the year. Such as should submit, on the other hand, and acknowledge their allegiance to the queen, were to be allowed to remain on some unspecified terms. In the event thirteen secular priests took advantage of the offer and issued a statement affirming that they acknowledged her lawful authority in all temporal matters, 'as that no authority, no cause . . . can or ought . . . to be a sufficient warrant to us more than to any protestant, to disobey her majesty in any civil or temporal matter'. They were only a small minority of the four hundred or so priests working in England at the time, and they did no more than to make explicit the views which had been held implicitly by most lay catholics throughout the reign, but their submission was nevertheless an important event.

By 1603 the missionary movement had been contained, and any chance that it might have turned the English catholic community into a politically dissident minority had been defeated. At the same time the violent quarrels between the Jesuits and their opponents had to some extent confused and demoralised the laity, and diverted energies which could have been more profitably employed. The will to resist was weakened, and the unrelenting pressures of propaganda and the law began to increase their toll. At the end of Elizabeth's reign the catholics were probably less of a danger to the state and to the established Church than at any time since 1570.

THE PURITAN CHALLENGE

Over forty years of consolidation and development had also given the Anglican Church a strength and a distinctive character which in its early days it had seemed unlikely to acquire. The war, and the divisions of the papists after 1590 had contributed to this, but more important was the failure of the militant puritans to secure the further reformation which they so earnestly desired. In 1581, undaunted by earlier rebuffs, they had returned to the attack in Parliament, backed by the widespread and carefully organised 'classical movement', which consisted of quasi-presbyterian meetings of local clergy. By the end of the century they were in disarray; deeply divided, uncertain of their objectives, and much less widely supported by the thinking laity.

The fundamental reason for this was the unrelenting hostility of the queen herself, but her resolute defence of the 1559 settlement took on a new dimension as a generation of churchmen emerged who could match conviction with conviction, and defend the Church not merely in obedience to the queen's will, but because they believed it to be a unique embodiment of divine truth. How deeply Elizabeth felt this is uncertain, but it is perhaps significant that in the parliament of 1588 she took her stand not upon her ecclesiastical supremacy and the inconvenience of innovation (as she had done in 1585), but upon her conscience 'by the word of God, that the estate and government of this Church of England, as it now stands in this reformation . . . both in form and doctrine is agreeable with the Scriptures, with the most ancient General Councils, with the practice of the primitive church, and with the judgements of all the old and learned fathers'. This was not a view which would have been shared by Grindal, Cox or even Jewel, but it was fully endorsed by John Whitgift, who had received the see of Canterbury in 1583.

To some extent such confidence was the natural result of thinking of England as an Elect Nation, but it was equally the result of success. Over twenty years of peace and relative prosperity, the defeat of papist conspiracies at home and abroad, and finally the victory over the great Armada, had set a seal of Divine approval upon the régime. The medals struck in 1588 were careful to reflect this mood: *Afflavit Deus et dissipati sunt.* God had raised up a mighty salvation for His people. In these circumstances the carping criticisms of the puritans seemed less plausible; apparently the Almighty did not think as poorly of the English Church as His self-appointed spokesmen. Significantly, the last great puritan assault in Parliament came in 1584-5, on the eve of the war.

Whitgift's immediate campaign against protestant non-conformity had stirred up something of a hornets' nest. On 19 October 1583 he issued three articles to which all clergy were required to subscribe. These affirmed the royal supremacy and agreed that the whole *Book of Common Prayer*, the Ordinal and the thirty-nine Articles were consistent with the Word of God. After much angry discussion, between three and four hundred ministers refused to subscribe and were suspended from their cures.[12] Consequently, when Parliament met in November 1584 a powerful attack upon the Archbishop and his methods was rapidly mounted, in spite of the queen's explicit instruction that 'the cause of religion [was not] to be spoken of amongst them'. Several councillors, notably Sir Francis Knollys, were openly critical of Whitgift for choosing a moment when the popish danger was so acute to set the protestants wrangling among themselves. The puritan strategy was to muster a collection of petitions, drawing attention to the poor state of the Church, and protesting against the silencing of good preachers – hoping thereby to present an irrefutable case for a reform of Church government.

This reform would not have been presbyterian. An individual presbyterian member, Dr Peter Turner, attempted to bring in a bill for a new Prayer Book (probably the Genevan *Form of Prayer*) and failed to secure a hearing. No doubt some form of diocesan synods would have been established had the puritan campaign succeeded, but in spite of the growth of organised presbyterian opinion during the previous fifteen years, it was far from dominating the movement as a whole. The petitions came in with well organised promptness, although from re-

[12] The great majority of these were soon reinstated, having agreed to sign a slightly modified subscription which Whitgift was prepared to offer. By doing so they greatly weakened their own position and made it harder for their lay supporters to represent them as martyrs for the truth. McGrath, 217, comments: 'Like the papists in the 1560s, the puritans in the 1580s had made a dangerous mistake. They had failed to make a stand.'

latively few localities,[18] and the House seized upon them eagerly. A committee of enquiry was set up, and discussion passed back and forth between the Commons and the Lords. Elizabeth was not impressed, and at the beginning of March 1585 she intervened to forbid any further reading of the bills which were by then under consideration. Far from restraining the energy of her Archbishop, she clearly wished to encourage it and took a number of his colleagues to task for not being sufficiently enthusiastic. 'You suffer many ministers to preach what they list, and to minister the sacraments according to their own fancies . . . ,' she complained; 'I wish such men to be brought to conformity and unity.' At the same time the Parliament was sharply reminded that the proper procedure for airing ecclesiastical grievances was through the bishops, and she would undertake to see that they did their duty.

Although Anthony Cope was to make a further bid two years later to bring in a radical Genevan prayer book, after 1585 parliamentary opinion moved steadily against the puritans, until by 1593 it was possible for the government to promote successfully a bill 'against seditious sectaries' which imposed upon protestant non-conformists penalties similar to those long used against the catholics. Frustrated in Parliament, the puritans once again turned their main energies to propaganda. The secret press of John Waldegrave produced a steady stream of pamphlets, while the energetic John Field organised the nationwide collection of evidence designed to demonstrate how scandalous the state of the clergy had been allowed to remain. In 1587 Walter Travers produced his *Disciplina Ecclesiae Sacra*, which was intended to be the new textbook of English presbyterianism. It circulated widely in manuscript and was partly put into effect, both in individual 'classes' and in the convening of a 'General Meeting' which was to all intents a national synod. There seems to have been a real danger in the late 1580s that the presybyterians would become a separatist movement – although they never abandoned their conviction that a national Church was both necessary and proper.

By 1590, however, the movement was past its peak. Field

[18] Warwickshire, Lincolnshire, Essex, Sussex and Leicestershire. Presbyterian support was concentrated in these regions, and much less widespread than its leaders claimed.

died in 1588 and was never really replaced. The last 'General Meeting' in 1589 broke up in disagreement, and in October 1588 appeared the first of the extremely two-edged 'Marprelate Tracts'. These pamphlets were a series of savage and witty attacks upon particular bishops, and upon episcopal government in general. They seem to have been produced by a group of men organised by John Penry, and were widely read and enjoyed. At the same time the more weighty presbyterian leaders, such as Cartwright and Travers, disowned them, and their fierce invective did not meet with the approval which its authors must have expected. Most important of all, they alienated that sympathy in high places which had been the chief strength of protestant radicals since the beginning of the reign. The Earl of Hertford, who had always looked favourably on the puritans, concluded that such attacks upon the bishops would soon lead to similar attacks on the nobility. And in 1590 Lord Burghley wrote 'Care is to be taken to suppress all the turbulent precisians who do violently seek to change the external government of the Church'.

This important change, coming almost simultaneously with the deaths of Leicester and Walsingham, two of the puritans' principal patrons, greatly weakened their position. The 'Marprelate' press was discovered, and the authorities began a systematic drive against the puritan leadership which resulted in a series of prosecutions before the ecclesiastical court of High Commission and the Star Chamber. By 1600 the days of political pressure and agitation seemed to be over, and the main strength of radical protestantism was flowing in quieter channels, building up its own distinctive brand of piety and its ideals of the Christian ministry.

This process was aided by a sharp new emphasis upon radical separatism. Small separatist congregations had existed since the day of the Marian persecution, basing themselves upon the doctrine of the 'gathered' church which was totally opposed to all forms of ecclesiastical establishment.[14] Such doctrine was as repugnant to the presbyterians as it was to the Anglicans, and persecution was always the lot of those who held it. Their numbers were so small that it is difficult to see them as a threat to the

[14] A 'gathered' church was one which was defined by those who confessed its faith. Consequently it could not include children as full members and could not be co-extensive with any society which might include the reprobate as well as the saved.

state, but nevertheless in 1593 the government decided to administer a sharp lesson to such dissenters and executed two of their leaders, Barrow and Greenwood, for sedition. Both had been in prison for several years, and their deaths at this juncture must have been connected with the actions of John Penry. Penry had fled to Scotland after the discovery of the 'Marprelate' press, and when he returned in 1592 he joined the ranks of the London separatists and wrote in their defence. In 1593 he was captured, and the opportunity of associating the 'Marprelate' authors with so disreputable a group was too good to miss. Thomas Cooper, replying to the first of the tracts, had deplored the attitude of men who flouted the queen's laws and sought to bring her officers into contempt, almost in the face of the Spanish enemy, and this was a view which gained considerable credence. Penry was executed along with the earlier leaders, and the reaction against them helped to pass the Act against seditious sectaries in the same year.

It would be unjust, however, to accuse Whitgift and his associates of mere repression. They counter-attacked vigorously, and the quality of their arguments was much improved from earlier years. In a significant sermon, preached at Paul's Cross in February 1589, Richard Bancroft challenged the puritan interpretation of Scripture, and justified episcopal government by reference to the earliest practices of the Church. The enemies of the establishment, he claimed, were not only setting up their private judgements against the Church, but were motivated by a base desire for gain. 'The clergy factions do contend that all the livings which now appertain to the church ought of right to be employed for the maintenance of their presbyteries . . . The lay factions . . . that our preachers ought to conform themselves to the example of Christ and his Apostles . . . to the intent that they may obtain the prey which they look for.' Bancroft came very close to asserting a *iure divino* episcopacy which neither Burghley nor the queen would have tolerated, and in the process absorbed a good deal of the catholic tradition. In his sermons and writings the Anglican Church took a long step forward in the development of a distinctive, non-puritan protestantism.

Shortly after, in 1594, Richard Hooker published the first four books of the *Laws of Ecclesiastical Polity*. It is beyond the scope of this study to do justice to Hooker as a thinker, but he gave to the Anglican position an intellectual respectability which it had never before possessed, and to which the puritans could offer no effective reply. The roots of Hooker's work went back not merely to Jewel but to the *De vera obedientia* of Stephen Gardiner, expounding with subtle and penetrating logic the co-extensiveness and interdependence of Church and state. 'We hold that . . . there is not any man of the Church of England but the same man is also a member of the commonwealth; nor any man a member of the commonwealth which is not also of the Church of England.' Hooker's view of the Scriptures – the heart of his argument against the puritans – was basically similar to Gardiner's. Men may lawfully do that which the Scriptures do not forbid, and in matters upon which the Word of God is silent a variety of practices may exist. Unlike Bancroft, Hooker was not interested in the Apostolic succession, but he was deeply concerned about the sacramental life of the Church, and there was much in his writings upon which the later Arminians could draw. By the end of the century the naked Erastianism of the early Elizabethan Church was being clothed with a new spiritual and intellectual life, which, ironically enough, was to commend it only too effectively to Elizabeth's successors.

The Anglican victories against both papist and puritan, which characterised the years after 1590, were bought at a price. The importance of the new 'high church' position of Bancroft and his friends was still unclear when Elizabeth died, but the constitutional quarrels between Whitgift and the common lawyers were well known, and boded no good for the monarchy. No sooner had the Archbishop been enthroned in 1583 than he had sought, and obtained, a new ecclesiastical High Commission under his own presidency. This commission, which had first been established under the terms of the Act of Supremacy, had evolved gradually over twenty years into an ecclesiastical court, and this development Whitgift rapidly completed. The authority of this court rested directly upon the queen's ecclesiastical supremacy, and it was in effect a spiritual equivalent of Star Chamber. As such it was extensively used after 1584 and became one of the principal instruments against the puritan leadership. Naturally this earned for it a good deal of abuse and criticism, because its victims were articulate and not accustomed to mince their words.

In particular they objected very strongly to the procedure which was known as the oath *ex officio*, whereby suspects were sworn in advance to answer truthfully questions of which they were still in ignorance. This oath immediately became the target of a strong parliamentary attack, in which the puritans were joined by the common lawyers. There is no reason to suppose that the lawyers were more infected with religious radicalism than any other profession, but the *ex officio* oath was not a procedure of the common law and was therefore mistrusted. More important the High Commission itself was seen as a rival jurisdiction. The old rivalry between the common law and the canon law had come to an end before 1560, because the moribund ecclesiastical courts of the Elizabethan period offered no serious challenge. But this vigorous new tribunal was a different proposition. Not only did it threaten the lawyers' professional interests, it also revived the fears of the 1530s that the spiritual jurisdiction of the Crown might be used to bypass the restraints traditionally imposed by Parliament and the common law. In 1585 it was proposed in the Commons that all proceedings under the oath should be declared illegal, since it rested neither upon statute nor the common law, and shortly after its use was denounced as a breach of Magna Carta.

The success of the Church in general, and of the High Commission in particular, thus created the possibility of a serious political clash. This danger was intensified by the poor public image of the late Elizabethan civil service, which, by attracting much justified criticism, had brought the whole administration into a certain disrepute. As a result the conciliar jurisdiction of the Crown, which had been such a popular bulwark of law and order in previous years, began to be regarded with suspicion. Star Chamber was as yet little affected, but Requests was seriously undermined by a decision of Common Pleas in 1598, when it was 'adjudged upon solemn argument that this which was called a Court of Requests or the White Hall, was no court that had power of judicature, but all the proceedings thereupon were *coram non judice*.' The common lawyers had no power to destroy their rival, and it continued to function, but they did succeed in bringing the validity of its decisions into doubt, and thus greatly impairing its attractiveness to litigants. Between the professional interests of the lawyers, lack of confidence in the integrity of the Crown's highest servants, and the ancient fear of ecclesiastical jurisdiction, a first class attack upon the prerogative was building up by 1600. In a sense Elizabeth had done her job too well, to bring her subjects to the point at which they could afford the luxury of such relatively sophisticated discontents. They did not press their attack against the aged queen, partly out of respect for her achievement and partly in awe of her formidable personality, but their grievances constituted an explosive legacy.

CHAPTER 12

THE NEW KING AND THE OLD PROBLEMS

Diverse other rights and preeminences the prince hath which he called prerogatives royal . . . which be declared particularly in the books of the common laws of England. (Sir Thomas Smith *De Republica Anglorum*)

THE KING AND THE COMMONWEALTH

The Divine Right of Kings was a theory of ancient origin; or, more accurately, parts of it were, for it was made up of a number of related but distinct ideas which had grown up in response to different circumstances. The medieval papacy had claimed its authority by divine right and thereby compelled its opponents to do likewise. Most of those who did so confined themselves to claiming that kings derived their temporal jurisdiction directly from God, and not through the Church. A few writers, such as the publicists of King Philip the Fair of France, or Dante in his *De Monarchia*, made very extensive definitions of temporal jurisdiction, but none went so far as to claim the *potestas ordinis* for the Crown. Had they done so, Henry's propagandists in the 1530s would not have had to grope for a theory, or make reluctant use of the radical Marsilius. But medieval divine right was only partly directed against the intrusions of the spiritual authority. It was also aimed against the rival claims of feudal magnates and estates, because to assert that the king derived his authority directly from God was to place him upon a different level from those who challenged or sought to limit his jurisdiction. In England the monarchy had made little progress in this direction.[1] The exalted theories of Richard II had been effectively countered by feudal rebellion, and the mystique of the coronation had been answered by the limitation of the coronation oath. As we have seen, the characteristic political

[1] The corollary of this was a very diffuse concept of authority. Not only the king, but his lords, the lesser aristocracy in their 'countries', corporations and heads of households at all levels were thought to possess an authority which was divine in origin. This 'natural' authority was not derived from any human superior, but it might (in the case of the aristocracy) be held alongside a delegated authority from the king until the two became virtually indistinguishable.

writer of the fifteenth century had been the lawyer Sir John Fortescue whose firm belief in limited monarchy continued to dominate English thinking throughout the period with which we have been concerned.

In looking at Tudor England, however, it is necessary to distinguish between different aspects of divine right. Legitimism – the belief in an indefeasible hereditary succession – was one such aspect. The Yorkists had used it to support their claim to the throne in the 1460s, and it remained a popular concept. Henry VII was not in a position to make much use of it, and neither Henry VIII nor Edward was seriously challenged, but we have seen what an important part it played in the defeat of Jane Grey, and how persistently it nagged at Elizabeth in the person of Mary Queen of Scots. Mary's execution in 1587 and the fact that her son James was a protestant enabled it to re-emerge in the 1590s as a respectable political doctrine. The alternative, 'constitutionalist' view of the succession was simultaneously discredited by the appearance of Doleman's *Conference*, and even if James's ideas had been other than they were he would have been compelled to rely heavily upon legitimist arguments in advancing his claim to the throne. The Stuart line had been explicitly excluded from the succession by Henry VIII's will, confirmed by a statute which had not been repealed; yet in the changed circumstances of 1603 his accession was unchallenged and almost undisputed. James rightly attributed the relief and enthusiasm which greeted him in England to the fact that he was the heir by hereditary right, and understandably concluded that other aspects of the divine right philosophy would be equally popular.

To this belief he was also led by his understanding of the royal supremacy, a doctrine which contrasted so sharply with the theocratic presbyterianism of the Scottish Kirk. Logically the ecclesiastical supremacy of the Crown implied a theory of the monarchy so exalted that even the absolutism of Spain would have paled into insignificance by comparison. It was also an authority upon which Elizabeth, no less than her father, had placed great emphasis. However, as we have seen, in practice the situation was not logical, and although the queen had upbraided her Parliaments on numerous occasions for trespassing upon her jurisdiction, they nevertheless enjoyed an undefined right of participation in ecclesiastical affairs. In fact the government of the Church approximated to the government of the state, in that the executive authority rested in the proper person of the monarch, while the legislative authority was vested in the sovereign assembly of king, Lords and Commons. Although the royal supremacy had always been regarded as a sacred trust, it was also a convenient means of keeping the clergy in their place and laying hands upon a large proportion of their wealth. Both Henry and Elizabeth had been realistic enough to understand that the popularity of the doctrine depended upon the last two factors rather than the first, and had been content to see the Church fall increasingly under secular control. James, with his keen eye for first principles, took the concept of the Godly Prince too much at its face value.

There was, of course, every excuse for the new king as an outsider to make this kind of mistake about England's 'peculiar institution', since much of the royal propaganda from the 1530s onward had emphasised the unique responsibility of the monarch for the spiritual welfare of his subjects. However, there was much less excuse for him to make the same kind of mistake about his secular jurisdiction, because divine right had never made any impression upon what might be termed English constitutional theory.[2] Although all the Tudor monarchs had been prepared to tamper with the law in their own interests, only Mary had not been consistently respectful of its forms, and none had ever claimed to stand above it. The civil law had made no progress in England, while the common law had flourished exceedingly and before the middle of the sixteenth century had replaced the Church as the high road to success in the royal service. Writers such as Sir Thomas Smith, William Stanford[3] and John Aylmer who had discussed the royal prerogative had insisted unanimously upon its limitation by the law. Only William Tyndale appeared to make no such reservation, and he imposed instead the strictest conditions of religious allegiance, which no Tudor monarch ever accepted without heavy qualification.

There was thus no reason why a studious and thoughtful man

[2] The use of the word 'constitution' presents some difficulties in this connection. Contemporaries spoke of 'the first frame and constitution of the realm', meaning the form of the law, and political arguments were conducted in terms of 'fundamental law'. The word does not seem to have been used to mean a set of related institutions. From the modern standpoint it was precisely the need for a constitution which was being discovered during these years.

[3] The author of *An Exposition of the King's Prerogative* (London 1567).

such as James should not have realised that any claim on his part to be *legibus solutus* would be flying in the face of all custom and established opinion. The king did not see this, partly because he had pondered the problems of royal authority himself and come to different conclusions, and partly because of the existence of those other aspects of divine right which we have already noticed. James had published the results of his own studies in 1598 under the title *The True Law of Free Monarchies*, and although this had appeared anonymously, he had all the academic's dislike of being proved wrong. More seriously, he was also unable to appreciate that the legal or 'constitutional' relationship between the English monarchy and its subjects was not static but dynamic. Divine right, in the full form in which James accepted it, was an extremely static and uncompromising doctrine, whereas in England the relationship between theory and practice was constantly changing, and the latter was setting the pace. To be fair to the king, it is also true that very few of his contemporaries understood this; but Elizabeth had done so to some extent, which was why she was so extremely chary of definitions and issues of principle. Any attempt to anchor such a fluid situation by rigid definitions was bound to result in violent disagreements.

Even if James had been a more imposing personality and a more tactful politician than he was, there would still have been quarrels. Elizabeth had left too many discontents, and too many issues unresolved, for her successor to reign as peacefully as he had succeeded. For nine years, until his death in 1612, Sir Robert Cecil[4] retained the first place in the king's confidence. Careful and indefatigable, he did his best to diminish the effects of his master's dogmatism by skilful and patient negotiation, but he was unable to provide the statesmanship and vision which the king lacked. A fit councillor, Sir Francis Bacon is alleged to have remarked disparagingly, to prevent the affairs of the kingdom from getting worse. Cecil's political qualities were best appreciated when his restraining hand had been removed, because he was the last great civil servant to have been trained in the Tudor tradition. He did not think in terms of sovereign authority, but of working arrangements and realistic compromises.

James quarrelled on these latter grounds both with his

[4] Cecil was created Earl of Salisbury on 4 May 1605, but for convenience I have continued to use this form of his name.

judiciary and with his parliaments, but the quarrels were always about specific issues and should not be seen as evidence for the existence of a generalised 'constitutional opposition'. Sir Edward Coke, appointed Chief Justice of Common Pleas in 1606, had strong views about the jurisdiction of the Court of High Commission, and made extensive use of writs of prohibition to confine it to what he considered to be its proper sphere. Richard Bancroft, who had succeeded Whitgift as Archbishop of Canterbury in 1604, endeavoured to counter this move by representing prohibitions as a threat to the king's prerogative, but the judges were unanimous in rejecting the imputation. The nature of the High Commission court had been tested by the common law in 1591, when an ejected minister by the name of Cawdrey had challenged his dismissal in Queen's Bench.[5] It had then been pointed out that High Commission did not derive its jurisdiction from the Act of Uniformity of 1559, which had been purely declaratory, or from any other statute, but from the prerogative of the Crown, and Cawdrey's suit had been rejected. The problem lay in the very general terms of the Letters Patent under which the Commission operated, and in the sensitivity of the common law courts to encroachments upon their profitable business, rather than in any deliberate attempt by the judges to set limits to the prerogative. It seems to have been James rather than Coke who wished to conduct the dispute at the level of high principle, when he intervened personally in 1607. According to the latter the king was greatly offended with his arguments 'and said that then he should be under the law, which [it] was treason to affirm', to which Coke claimed to have responded 'that Bracton saith *quod rex non debet esse sub homine, sed sub Deo et lege*'. However, since Coke was writing many years after the event the authenticity of this exchange in 1607 may well be doubted. During the next few years prohibitions became increasingly frequent, and were occasionally directed against the Councils in the north and the marches of Wales as well as against High Commission. The death of Bancroft in 1610 and the issue of more precise Letters Patent in the following year reduced the temperature of the controversy, but did not

[5] Coke, *Fifth Report*, 334–5.

resolve it, particularly since the hated *ex officio* oath continued to be used.

The Chief Justice did not confine himself to prohibitions. In 1610 he issued a celebrated opinion denying the right of the Crown to alter the law or create new offences by proclamation. In 1615 he denied the right of the king to consult individually with the judges about cases which were pending before them, and in the following year refused to admit the validity of the writ *de non procedendo rege inconsulto*, whereby cases at common law could be stayed. For this last piece of obstruction he was dismissed from office and replaced by Sir Henry Montague. Coke was undoubtedly an indomitable champion of judicial independence, but he was also a member of the Privy Council, to which he was restored in 1617, and by 1620 was sufficiently in favour to entertain realistic hopes of appointment as Lord Treasurer.[6] His conduct as Chief Justice can be at least partly explained by his implacable hostility to Sir Francis Bacon, the Attorney General and also a Privy Councillor. Bacon took the opposite view to Coke on the independence of the judiciary, as upon most other things, describing them in a famous phrase as 'lions under the throne'. Both Bacon and Coke were active councillors, and their antagonism provides an important clue to many of the more notable controversies of the reign, which took place, not between the king's opponents and his servants, but within the court and the royal service between groups and individuals who held different views as to the best method of promoting the king's interests and their own. The fact that he had been dismissed from office because judges held their positions *quamdiu se bene gesserint* signified that Coke had been defeated on the issue of judicial independence, but it did not alienate him from the court, and his subsequent obstructiveness in the House of Commons was more the result of disappointment over the Lord Treasurership than of any decision to choose new ground for his opposition to the prerogative.

James's disagreements with parliament have to be seen in a somewhat similar light. He had managed its Scottish

[6] B. Coward, *The Stuart Age*, 133. When Montague was appointed to the vacant Lord Treasurership in 1620, Coke was doubly affronted.

equivalent with considerable success, but the Scottish parliament had neither the same political muscle nor the same sense of its own importance. This latter characteristic was crucial and the more so for being extremely insecure. The members of the House of Commons were keenly aware of their responsibilities to their constituents, and of the fact that the development of Tudor government had left them in a position of isolated splendour when it came to imposing limitations upon the Crown. They also realised, with a mixture of pride and apprehension, that they were the last effective Estates in Europe, and that the contemporary tendency was towards greater absolutism. This awareness was not suddenly born in 1604, it had certainly existed in Elizabeth's last parliament, but it was heightened to an acute pitch by the king's clumsiness. Neither he nor his ministers had prepared properly for the session which opened on 19 March 1604. Cecil, as Principal Secretary, was already a baron and sat in the Lords, while those Privy Councillors who remained in the Commons lacked both personal status and proper briefing to defuse controversial issues as they arose. The session was barely a day old before this weakness began to be exposed by the Commons' insistence upon adjudicating the disputed election for Buckinghamshire. Before 1580 such disputes had belonged to the jurisdiction of Chancery, which issued the writs; but a series of cases between 1581 and 1586 had, as we have seen, given the Commons a legitimate interest in them. Consequently, when it was discovered that the Buckinghamshire election had been overturned on the ground that the successful candidate, Francis Goodwin, was an outlaw, the Commons promptly reinstated him. Instead of treating this as an isolated problem, James then compounded his difficulties by using the case as an occasion to lecture the Commons upon the nature of their privileges, which were in his view '. . . from him and by his grant'. Having thus quite unnecessarily raised an important issue of principle, and struck a raw nerve in the Commons' susceptibilities, the king then went on to concede the substance of their claim over Goodwin, thus giving himself the worst of both worlds.

To James's logical mind the power of the monarch to summon and dismiss parliaments at his discretion conclusively proved that they functioned by grace and not by right, and historically he was quite correct in claiming that privileges such as freedom from arrest and freedom of speech originated in the king's need to have his business discharged efficiently. Freedom from arrest, which extended only to private suits while parliament was in session, had been specifically granted by Henry VIII, who encouraged the House itself to release members so detained by 'warrant of mace', a custom which had been established since 1542.[7] Similarly, freedom of speech derived from the fact that the king needed to know the true opinion of the House on matters placed before it, otherwise there was little point in summoning the members from their distant constituencies. In the early sixteenth century the Speaker petitioned for the House collectively, but by the beginning of Elizabeth's reign the privilege had been extended, without any specific decision, to cover individual members speaking to any issue that was 'before the House'. Since issues came before the House via the Speaker, who was a royal nominee, this meant in effect that private members could initiate matters for discussion, but only with the consent of the government. It was against this situation that Peter Wentworth had made his protest in 1576, when he had claimed 'there is nothing so necessary for the preservation of the prince and state as free speech, and without it is a scorn and a mockery to call it a parliament house'. Wentworth was complaining that the queen's management prevented members from offering her such advice as they thought fit. Quite apart from his unflattering reference to Elizabeth, this was an opinion for which the Commons were not yet ready, and Wentworth was imprisoned by order of the House itself. In 1593 Lord Keeper Puckering reasserted the traditional view without serious protest:

> The very true liberty of the House [is] not, as some suppose, to speak there of all causes as himself listeth and to frame a form of religion or a state of government as to their idle brains shall seem meetest.

By 1610, however, the climate was changing, and many members had convinced themselves that their privilege of free

[7] The key case was that of George Ferrers. Prior to that time a member arrested could only be released by writ of privilege, issued from the Chancery at the Speaker's request. Elton, *Tudor Constitution*, 261.

speech meant precisely that right to offer unsolicited advice that Wentworth had proposed. In that year it was claimed as 'an ancient general and undoubted right of parliament to debate freely all matters which do properly concern the subject and his right or estate'. The king was fully justified in rejecting this as an innovation, but in doing so he failed to perceive both that the relationship between Crown and Commons was dynamic rather than static, and that the Commons were becoming ever more anxious about their function in the commonwealth. At the same time, there was no unanimity about how that anxiety should be brought home to the king. Members spoke and voted in accordance with their consciences, their perception of the interests of their constituents, and their own or their patrons' personal inclinations. There were *ad hoc* groupings, as there always had been, but no semblance of a 'country party'. Consequently the *Form of Apology and Satisfaction*, drawn up in 1604, should not be seen as a 'party manifesto', but rather as an attempt by a few of the more aggressively minded members to draw attention to their fears. This document attempted to maintain that the House was a court of record, that their privileges were of right, and that the king could not alter the state of religion without parliamentary consent. Technically, they were wrong on every count, and the *Apology* was not endorsed by the House, but the king made no attempt to offer the reassurance which was clearly sought.[8] As with the judiciary, the tendency to veil insecurity in a cloak of medieval precedent confused James's literal mind and disorientated his reactions. It was done partly because of the extreme conservatism of prevailing habits of thought, and partly because of the genuine relevance of some medieval legal concepts. A better knowledge of English history might have prompted the king to realise that those rights and privileges which had originally been diffused among territorial lords, corporations, franchises and liberties had now come to repose almost entirely with the county aristocracy, and particularly with the institution through

[8] Properly the whole parliament, not the Commons alone, formed a court of record, but the point was conceded implicitly over the return of election writs. For the debate over the *Apology*, see G. R. Elton, 'A high road to civil war?' in *Studies in Tudor and Stuart Government and Politics*.

which they were represented at Westminster. As it was he tended to respond with irritation and with pedantic logic.

The king, however, was seldom entirely to blame for these misunderstandings and disputes. As we have already seen, English government was basically underfunded, and in spite of his initial tendency to regard England as *El Dorado*, James was quick to grasp this fact. He recognised that English taxation did not in any real sense reflect the wealth of the community, and consequently took the view that it was his subjects' duty to provide him with the ordinary revenue necessary for the expenses of administration. The members of the House of Commons did not dispute this in principle, but had a very different notion of what was needed. In the eyes of the political nation, who were the taxpayers, their *entente* with the Crown required them to undertake all manner of offices in local and central government for little or no pay, but not to provide revenue for the normal processes of government. They had little notion of what government actually cost, and clung to the traditional view that ordinary expenses were met out of the king's 'own', with taxation in reserve for particular emergencies. James inherited a debt of some £400,000, which was partly the result of war and partly of Elizabeth's failure to solve the same problem, so he was fully justified in seeking for means to augment his income. Unfortunately he aggravated his difficulties very much by being generous to the point of prodigality. It could have been politically wise to relax the late Elizabethan austerity, and he had a family to keep, but James's largesse exceeded all bounds of sense or moderation. In the first four years of his reign he dispensed nearly £200,000 in gifts and annuities, and his household expenditure was more than double that of his predecessor. There was consequently much justification for the observation of John Hoskyns in the parliament of 1610, that 'the royal cistern had a leak, which, till it were stopped, all our consultations to bring money unto it was of little use'.

Robert Cecil, first as Secretary and after 1608 as Lord Treasurer, was the man who embraced the unenviable task of royal plumber. The case of John Bate in Exchequer Chamber in 1606 had reaffirmed the Crown's traditional right to levy import duties, and Cecil seized upon this as an opportunity to increase ordinary revenue. In 1608 he introduced a new book of rates, designed to bring in an additional £60–70,000 a year. The rates had not been changed for sixty years, and the Marquis of Winchester's rates of 1558 had been designed for the same purpose. Nevertheless, there was a major political storm, and James Whitelocke's comment in the House of Commons in 1610 explains why:

> If this power of imposing were quietly settled in our Kings, considering the greatest use they make of assembling of parliaments, which is the supply of money, I do not see any likelihood to hope for often meeting in that kind, because they would provide themselves by that other means . . .

Cecil persisted, and over the specific issue of impositions he was successful, but he realised perfectly well that this would not solve the king's problem. At least two other things were necessary; one was to persuade James to curb his generosity and cut back on his personal spending; the other was to gain the consent of parliament to a long-term arrangement for increased ordinary revenue. His efforts in the former direction produced many promises, but little fulfilment, while the latter failed after being apparently brought to the brink of success. The Great Contract, as it was called, was a sensible proposal to exchange the surrender of the Crown's obsolete feudal revenues for a fixed income of £200,000 a year. In the discussions over this measure, Cecil's success over impositions turned out to be a serious handicap, and although James handled the parliament of 1610 with considerable skill, the Commons' fear of obsolescence eventually induced them to make unacceptable demands, and the project failed. Two years later Cecil died and the king's finances, with a debt running at over £600,000, sank from difficulty to disaster.

Cecil's death ended the first period of the reign. On balance, he had lost more battles than he had won; not only the Great Contract, but also the king's cherished project for the union of the realms, and the need to maintain a pragmatic approach to politics in face of the king's ideological enthusiasm. Nevertheless, in 1612 there had been no serious breakdown. In spite of quarrels and misunderstandings, the first parliament of the reign had gone through five sessions, and had functioned normally as a legislative institution. In spite of the unpopularity of Scottish courtiers and favourites, they had not been allowed any significant influence over policy, and the main effect of their presence had been to increase the king's financial embarrassment. It is easy with the benefit of hindsight to see ominous developments in these early years, but the temptation to do so should be resisted. It may be that the king's apparent failure to appreciate the nature of the Commons' anxieties was the result of deliberate misinformation by his own advisers, or that the Lords rather than the Commons was the true source of opposition to the union of the kingdoms; the fact remains that while James reposed his chief confidence in Cecil, the parameters of normal political behaviour as these had been established during the previous hundred years were not transgressed.

After 1612 the situation deteriorated sharply. The emergence of Robert Carr, early attempts to negotiate a marriage alliance with Spain, and a sharp decline in administrative efficiency associated with the rise to power of the Howard family,[9] all provided an unpromising background to the second parliament of the reign, summoned in 1614. Impositions remained a contentious issue, and James's prodigality reached new heights, but the session was in effect sabotaged by the Howards, who were responsible for spreading the extravagant reports about 'undertakers' which aroused the Commons to obstructive fury. These 'undertakers' were supposed to be royal agents briefed to secure a compliant House by gerrymandering elections. That a group of Privy Councillors should react in this way when parliament was called against their advice, and should have retained favour and power, is a serious indictment of the king's competence. It may also have been as a result of Howard intervention that the Crown was so poorly served in the House of Commons in this session, and that the initiative in debate in consequence so frequently rested with the opposition. Nothing went right. James expressed his disapproval of the habit which the Commons had recently developed of collecting their grievances into general petitions. Such representations, he

[9] The Howards, particularly the Earls of Suffolk and Northampton, had begun to acquire considerable influence before Cecil's death, and were the principal supporters of the king's negotiations with Spain. Their financial corruption was notorious even by the lax standards of James's court, and their careers provide important insights into the processes of patronage brokering which went on there. L. L. Peck, *Northampton; Patronage and Policy at the Court of James I* (1982).

complained, were designed rather to bring his government into discredit than to secure reformation. The correct procedure was for each member to present the troubles of his own constituency – a method which would inevitably have weakened the impact of any parliamentary campaign by fragmentation. In response, and smarting from their failure to force a retreat over impositions, the Commons began to demand explicitly that redress of grievances should precede supply – a tactical development with a considerable future ahead of it. Unsure of their way, they became sidetracked into an attack on Bishop Neile of Lincoln, who had accused them of sedition and disloyalty, and in exasperation the king dissolved the parliament without a subsidy, and without any legislation.

It was in the aftermath of the fiasco of this 'Addled Parliament' that James made his celebrated remark to Gondomar about being obliged to put up with what he could not get rid of. There is no reason to suppose that he had any serious intention of dispensing with it,[10] but the walls had ears in the English court, and the king's obvious anger, combined with the Howard ascendancy, generated still further fear and suspicion among those who looked upon the House of Commons as the protector of their liberties. In many ways the Addled Parliament marked the end of that partnership which the Tudors had gradually and painfully built up. For the first time in any session since 1485 a sense of common purpose was completely lacking. Not even when Lord Paget had sabotaged Gardiner's programme in April 1554 did divisions within the Privy Council have such a deleterious effect, and on that occasion Paget had been lucky to escape the Tower. James, even more than Mary, had proved unable to impose his authority upon disruptive agents, and the credibility of his government had suffered a serious blow.

[10] The fact that no further parliament was called until 1621 has caused it to be argued that James had at least a shortlived determination never to call another. Recent research has shown, however, that he seriously contemplated a fresh parliament several times before it happened. A gap of seven years between sessions was in any case not particularly remarkable by sixteenth-century standards.

THE DEBASEMENT OF THE ARISTOCRACY

The House of Lords had so far played no significant part in these controversies, and there is a natural temptation to underestimate its power. On the whole, both under Elizabeth and at first under James, the Lords had created few problems for the monarchy, and tended to ally with the Crown against the Commons in the event of a clash. There were various reasons for this. The bishops, who formed almost a third of the nominal roll by the end of the sixteenth century, were royal nominees, economically and socially weak. At first they tended to be puritanical, and later Erastian. By 1603 they were beginning to reflect the new 'High Church' Anglicanism of Bancroft, and this rapidly developed into an outspoken sympathy with divine right. Their opponents suggested that this was pure opportunism, but it was not without intellectual justification. James saw his supremacy as personal rather than parliamentary and was happier to share that authority with a *iure divino* episcopacy than with a purely secular institution. At the same time some Anglican divines saw in the exaltation of a divine right monarchy the means to rescue the Church from the degrading and indefensible position of a department of state for ecclesiastical affairs. Hence the arguments of Bancroft and Neile which so annoyed the lower House and the common lawyers. The lay peers had no such vocational preoccupation, and their religious opinions were diverse. They were, however, much more closely linked with the court than were either the bishops or the Commons. Elizabeth expected them all to attend upon her for at least a short period in every year, and many spent long months in residence. The queen had been as sparing with titles as with all other rewards, and the number of peers declined from fifty-seven to fifty-five in the course of her reign. During that time fourteen families became extinct by failure of male heirs, and six titles lapsed by attainder. New creations thus narrowly failed to keep pace with wastage. This meant that the House of Lords was not receiving the due measure of new blood and new wealth necessary to preserve its political vigour.

Economically, the peers had been hard hit between 1560 and 1600 for a variety of reasons which included Elizabeth's parsimony and their own tradition of conspicuous consumption. Taking into account the profits of office and the liabilities of debt, the average income of each peer in 1559 was about £2,200 net, while two families (the Howards and the Talbots) received more than £5,000 each. By 1603 the equivalent average was a little over £3,000, but the cost of living had risen by something like 70 per cent in the interval, so in real terms this represented a decline of over 25 per cent. Nor were there any families left in the top bracket, the highest being the Talbots with £7,500 (£4,100 in the money of 1559). Generalisations are extremely dangerous in this controversial field, but the size of noble estates was also tending to contract.[11] This was partly because changing fashions made lucrative properties more attractive than large ones, and partly because the hazards of inheritance and the expensiveness of life at court was forcing many noble families to sell. Competent estate management also became increasingly important as the pressure of inflation built up. Careful scrutiny and strict control of leases, exploitation of mineral resources, and building upon urban property (particularly in London) could make crucial differences to the fortunes of noble families. Skilful or fortunate marriage settlements and commercial investment could salvage incumbered estates, while rash speculation or courtly extravagance bred debt and disaster, as we saw in the cases of Rutland and Southampton. At the same time it must be remembered that the situation in 1603 was artificial. Lord Burghley and others had made repeated representations to Elizabeth to replenish the peerage with fresh creations, and shortly before he died the Lord Treasurer had drawn up a list of seventeen commoners who were qualified by wealth and distinguished service for such promotion. Even allowing for this, however, it seems that the peerage, like the Church and the Crown itself, had suffered a relative decline in wealth during the second half of the sixteenth century.

The class which gained, by and large, was the gentry. Figures are much more difficult to obtain, particularly at the lower level, but it is clear from the large number seeking the honour of

[11] Figures for the gain and loss of manors are relevant in this connection, although the manor was a legal and not a territorial unit. In the period from 1485 to 1547, and dealing with 90 families, the holdings of 69 per cent remained fairly static; 27 per cent gained ten or more manors, and only 4 per cent lost a similar number. Between 1558 and 1641, and dealing only with 74 families that were in the peerage before 1600, 35 per cent were static, 10 per cent rose and 55 per cent fell. In spite of the technical imperfections of the sampling, these figures are sufficiently different to be significant. Stone, *op. cit.*, 129-98.

baronetcy after 1610 that the incomes of many commoners matched or outstripped those of the peers. Candidates were supposed to have land in possession or reversion worth £1,000 per year, and there were far more at that level than the ninety-nine who actually benefited from the initial distribution. At the same time, the gentry class was expanding rapidly. This was partly the result of social ambition and snobbery, which stimulated the creative imaginations of the Elizabethan heralds, but it was also a reflection of the fact that more and more erstwhile yeoman or merchant families could afford to support an aristocratic standard of living.[12] 'What is nobility but ancient riches?' Burghley once asked in a moment of candour. He might have added that the true test of gentility was present riches, whatever social theorists might say. Approximately 2,300 grants of arms were made between 1560 and 1600, a figure which must have increased the armigerous class by almost 50 per cent. The title of esquire, which theoretically implied a precise status, also underwent a process of inflation during the period and by 1620 signified no more than a gentleman with rather more than average means. Knighthoods, like peerages, were in short supply under Elizabeth, and in 1600 there were probably no more than 550 knights in the whole country – many of whom had been created by the Earl of Essex and lacked the means to support their status. The economic fortunes of individual gentry families might rise or fall, but there can be no doubt that the men who were primarily represented in the House of Commons were, both relatively and absolutely, more numerous, more wealthy and more self-confident in 1600 than they had been in 1560.

James had already acquired in Scotland a reputation for being generous with honours, and he speedily proved this to have been well earned. In a burst of prodigality which even he never subsequently approached, almost 1,000 knighthoods were created in the year after his accession. This was over-correction with a vengeance, and was accompanied by much abuse. Some gained the honour for little more than a tip to a courtier friend, and the king deliberately revived the long obsolete requirement for all those worth £40 a year to come forward. In view of the changed

[12] It is significant that this was the period of 'the great rebuilding' in lowland England, and a period when household inventories from the yeoman and artisan class upwards show a considerable increase of material possessions.

value of money this was absurd, and fortunately the vast majority of those qualified concealed the fact. Nevertheless the ancient and honourable status of knight was brought into contempt, to the fury of those who already held it and the disgust of conservatives of all ranks.

> At this time the honour of knighthood . . . was promiscuously laid on any head belonging to the yeomanry (made addled through pride and a contempt of their ancestors' pedigrees) that had but a court friend, or money to purchase the favour of the meanest able to bring him into an outward room

wrote Francis Osborne half a century later. In fact a large number of these knights were not dubbed by the king himself, but by such of his courtiers and favourites as he bestowed the right upon, either as a favour or reward. This set a pattern which continued (although at much reduced rate) for knighthoods, and was subsequently adopted for other dignities. The rank of baronet was frankly created to turn the king's position as the fount of honour to financial advantage. In the first instance the cash price was £1,095, in three instalments, but by 1615 the right of creation itself was being sold, or used in lieu of a cash reward – not only courtiers, but even civic corporations being among the recipients.

At first the peerage proper escaped this degrading process. The numerous creations of the first three years of the reign were justified by the earlier famine, and the choice of recipients was judicious. No reasonable complaint could be made against the elevation of such men as Sir Robert Cecil and Sir Thomas Egerton. Even here, however, there was a suspicion of jobbery, and Cecil certainly received a number of *douceurs* from hopeful courtiers. The somewhat desperate bribery by which men like Sir Edward Wotton had striven to undermine Elizabeth's exclusiveness had left its mark. Although there were cases of outright corruption as early as 1605, for the most part the new peers were well qualified and there was no serious debasement of the dignity. After 1615, however, a change of policy occurred. Peerages, like baronetcies, were openly sold for cash, and the right of nomination granted indiscriminately to court favourites – notably that rising young man George Villiers. The result was a rapid inflation, from 81 peers at the end of 1615 to 126 at the end of 1628, and a comparable change of character. Whereas the pre-1615 nobility had received their titles for the most part by inheritance or acknowledged public service, the later creations were mostly determined by relationship to Villiers or to some member of his family. This caused great bitterness among the existing peers, which was to be reflected in the Parliaments of 1621 and 1624 and deprived the Crown of the vital support of the upper House at a time when its relations with the Commons were particularly difficult.

There was more to this situation, however, than parliamentary politics. The whole social hierarchy was shaken in the most disconcerting fashion. A parvenu baronet like Sir Thomas Harris could be declared and pronounced 'no gentleman' by the Earl Marshal's court, but his patent of creation was not invalidated. Since England did not possess the kind of caste system which was isolating the French nobility by legal and fiscal privileges, the preservation of customary deference was extremely important.[13] In the last analysis this deference depended partly upon wealth, and partly upon prestige and respect. On the whole the readjustments of the early seventeenth century improved rather than diminished the correlation between wealth and status, but the changes were too rapid and too large in scale. All ranks of the aristocracy were more accustomed than they would readily admit to recruitment from below, but theory was all against it and time and tact were necessary for successful assimilation. The obvious exploitation of titles of honour by an impecunious king and his upstart favourite offended against a very deeply held sense of propriety, and disturbed the social confidence of the whole aristocracy. It was felt (more strongly than the facts justified) that every status from knight to duke had been brought into ridicule, and that as a result the subordination of the lower orders had been weakened in a manner which undermined the whole fabric of the commonwealth. Looking back upon this period from the lean days of the 1650s, Sir Edward Walker could write, 'It may be doubted whether the dispensing

[13] The English peerage enjoyed very limited legal privileges, such as immunity from arrest for debt. The aristocracy as a whole had no such privileges, but were by custom immune from corporal punishment. Thus, in spite of the strict theoretical stratification of society, it was possible to move downwards as well as upwards, because there was no great incentive to cling to a status which could not be supported and might impose intolerable economic burdens. This comparative flexibility, however, increased the importance of the protocol surrounding the aristocracy *in situ*.

of honours with so liberal (I will not say unconsiderate) a hand, were not one of the beginnings of general discontents, especially among persons of great extraction.' The Marquis of Newcastle was blunter in the same vein: 'Noble men were pulled down, which is the foundation of monarchy – monarchy soon after fell.'

The prestige which suffered most severely was that of the king himself, and James was not the kind of man who could afford this tarnish upon his public image. Not only was he personally unimposing and lacking in dignity, but he was an intellectual, which meant that most of his subjects were unable to follow the workings of his mind and consequently distrusted him. Also his court became increasingly squalid as the rewards of successful intrigue increased. Where Elizabeth had been consistently mean, James was erratically generous and distributed his favours arbitrarily according to the fancies of the moment. He also failed to distinguish between his personal feelings and his political judgement, and this became particularly obvious after Cecil's death when key offices were granted to favourites, or put into commission. The amoral attitudes of the court thus came to dominate the royal administration, completing a process which had begun in the previous reign. There were also odious scandals, such as that over the murder of Sir Thomas Overbury which finally ruined Robert Carr in 1613. Overbury had originally been a friend of Carr, but when the latter persuaded James to arrange a divorce for the Countess of Essex, for the purpose of securing her hand himself, Overbury objected. Carr induced James to imprison him, and the Countess had him poisoned in 1611. It was two years before the story came out, and then both Carr and the Countess were tried and convicted. Both were pardoned by the king, and their disgrace did nothing to restore his reputation in the public eye.

This whole unworthy edifice was supported by those revenues which the taxpayer was constantly being called upon to augment, and although extravagance was not in fact the key to James's financial problems, his disapproving subjects clearly had every incentive to think that it was.[14] Thus the court became increasingly unpopular, and the aristocracy began to divide into

14 In the Parliament of 1610, during the debate over the 'Great Contract', one member declared 'he would never give his consent to take money from a poor frieze jerkin to trap a courtier's horse withal'.

those who were associated with it and those who were not. This was in itself a dangerous development, because the Tudor court had always served a constructive political purpose – and had been both a focus of loyalty and a means of communication. By 1620 the Stuart court had lost these functions, and in spite of its occasional magnificence was becoming isolated by distinctive thought and behaviour from the majority of the ruling class.

POPULAR UNREST

At the opposite end of the social scale there was also discontent, and although this was not the fault of either the king or the court it added another element of tension to the deteriorating political situation. The peers had not been the only class to suffer particular economic difficulties in the late sixteenth century. While the cost of living rose by about 80 per cent between 1550 and 1600, wages had risen by only 50 per cent. At the same time the expanding population, and the necessity for landlords to exploit their estates more efficiently, were multiplying the numbers of the rural poor. As we have already seen, copyhold tenures were much better protected by the law than used to be supposed, but this only served to increase pressures upon short lease tenants and tenants at will. Outright depopulation was not common, but the numbers of cottagers and wage labourers increased; and they tended to become poorer as those with secure tenures or long leases flourished. Even in good years these people lived close to the subsistence level, and bad years might see a third of the parish receiving poor relief. Also the fact that the local magistrates fixed the maximum wage rates meant that there was a standing temptation for employers to use the poor rate as a regular means of subsidising their inadequate payments. The decreasing cost of labour was a factor of some significance in the prosperity of the middle and upper classes.

One consequence was the problem of vagabondage, which greatly exercised Tudor governments in the second half of the century. After 1585 many of these 'sturdy rogues' seem to have been discharged soldiers, who moved about in gangs terrorising villages and small towns. Such men were instinctively drawn towards London, where an extensive underworld developed, living by violence and 'cozenage' off an increasingly wealthy and populous city.[15] This 'anti-society' was a nuisance, but it never became a threat because the property-owning classes combined to enforce the law, and its very nature made it incapable of large scale organisation. Nevertheless its existence helps to explain the contemporary conviction that England was overpopulated, a conviction which stimulated Richard Hakluyt, John Dee and others to advocate colonial projects in the 1590s.

A series of bad harvests from 1595 to 1597 had aggravated the general distress of the poor, and produced one of the sharpest periods of inflation in the whole century. All figures are controversial, but there is general agreement as to the magnitude of the rise in the 1590s. According to the Phelps Brown index (1500=100) in 1594 the cost of living stood at 381, and by 1597 it had soared to 685. Thereafter it dropped to 459 in 1600, but was never again below 500. As a result, after a long period of relative calm, there were a number of agrarian riots in 1596, the most serious of which were in Oxfordshire. As usual, enclosures were the ostensible cause, and 1597 saw the last of the long series of Tillage Acts by which the Tudors had endeavoured to check economic self-interest in the name of social responsibility. There is no reason to suppose that it was any more effective than its predecessors. In the early part of James's reign real wages sank even lower. It has been estimated that a labourer born in 1580 would never have enjoyed more than half the real earnings which his great-grandfather would have received in about 1500. At the same time ready cash became more important because a higher proportion of the lower classes were now landless, or virtually so.

In 1607 this distress erupted in a number of midland counties in the form of quasi-religious riots of an egalitarian nature, led by groups resembling early Levellers and Diggers. The most serious outbreak occurred in Northamptonshire where a certain 'Captain Pouch' appeared, claiming a divine mandate. Several thousand peasants took part in disorganised risings which were suppressed without great difficulty by the local gentry – the 'garrisons of good order', as Sir Walter Raleigh called them. These

[15] The population of London in the 1590s was probably about 100,000 and growing rapidly. The City had by then secured an economic dominance in England unequalled by the capital of any other European state. For an account of criminal activities see A. V. Judges, *The Elizabethan Underworld*.

were not the last disturbances in which anti-enclosure sentiment played a part; there were to be demonstrations in the south-west in the late 1620s, and all over the south of England in 1640-3; but the climate of opinion was nevertheless changing. It began to be recognised that the blanket prohibition of enclosures might not only be ineffective, but might also be the wrong way of endeavouring to protect the poor.

In 1608 an Act was passed specifically authorising the enclosure and conversion to pasture of certain lands in Herefordshire on the grounds that they were more suitable for that purpose. Eleven years later it could be admitted in a royal proclamation that the statutes for the protection of arable land might be harmful to agricultural development, and in 1621 a general bill was presented to Parliament for the facilitating of enclosure, although it was rejected after long debate. In the Parliament of 1624 Sir Edward Coke denounced the Tillage Acts as mere devices to enable the Crown to extract large sums in fines from enterprising landlords, and the actions of the Council after 1630 to some extent bore him out. The same Parliament repealed the bulk of the Tudor legislation against enclosure,[16] and thus removed the main obstacle to capital investment in agriculture. It could perhaps be argued that this was merely the triumph of aristocratic self-interest over the social conscience of a government which was losing its grip. On the other hand it was vitally important to the poor that the price of grain should be reduced, and the best method of doing this was to encourage agricultural improvement, and to attract investment. The moral stigma of enclosure was only slowly conquered. It was still strong on the eve of the civil war, and was to revive in the eighteenth century. Nevertheless a more objective attitude was developing among the peasantry themselves, so that the villagers of Eagle in Lincolnshire could reply in answer to an enquiry that 'most of the land now tilled is more proper for grass, and that moor ground now eaten as common is fitter for corn, as it proved by experience among our next neighbours'. This was not until 1656, but such views did not appear overnight, and other examples could be cited.

By about 1620 real wages were beginning to improve, in spite

[16] Enclosure of arable land became legal, enclosure of commons remained forbidden.

of the sharp crisis which afflicted the clothing industry after the collapse of the Cockayne project.[17] A gradual expansion of urban employment began through the connivance of justices who refused to enforce the restrictive clauses of the Statute of Artificers and virtually ignored an Act of 1621 which was designed to prevent the poor from gravitating into the towns. This attitude was not the result of benevolence so much as the desire to obtain an exploitable labour force unprotected by the traditional regulations. It was not uncommon for monopolists to be given the right to conscript labour, and in 1618 a hundred young paupers were rounded up in London and shipped off to Virginia. Little humanity was shown to such unfortunates, and James's Council made only feeble attempts to enforce the charitable provisions of the great Poor Law of 1601. As we have seen, justices had always been inclined to drag their feet over the provision of relief, and this reluctance was now intensified by the spread of what was basically a puritan attitude to poverty among the well-to-do. The poor were seen, rightly enough, as improvident, but instead of regarding improvidence as the consequence of poverty, it was interpreted as the cause.[18]

To be poor thus acquired a stigma, and the 'idleness' and 'luxury' of the lower classes became a favourite topic of conversation. Hypocritical and irresponsible as such a view may seem, especially in the economic circumstances of the early seventeenth century, it nevertheless implied a refusal to accept mass poverty as inevitable and irremediable – a revolutionary change essential if such conditions were ultimately to be conquered. A far sighted man like Francis Bacon could even express the possibility of such a consummation. Although the Tudor Poor Law was feebly administered and the poor were frequently treated with great callousness and brutality, they were cer-

[17] An unsound scheme for the creation of a new monopolistic company to market finished cloth, known by the name of its originator, Alderman William Cockayne.

[18] This attitude seems to have sprung originally from the Calvinist conviction that it was the responsibility of every man to labour in his calling for the glory of God, and as a sign that he was among the Elect. There was consequently a tendency to regard poverty not as misfortune, but as evidence of divine disfavour or reprobation. On this interpretation of the situation the truest charity became not relief, but Conversion. There is a vast literature on this subject, to which one of the most important contributions is R. H. Tawney, *Religion and the Rise of Capitalism*.

tainly less vulnerable economically in 1640 than in 1600. Significantly less is heard of vagabondage and over-population after 1620, and the almost daily reports of minor agrarian riots which are found in the records of the mid-sixteenth century have largely disappeared by the reign of Charles I.

Fear of popular violence – the 'many headed monster' of contemporary literature – normally tended to bring the Crown and aristocracy together. The seriousness of the crisis of 1548-9 had been largely due to Somerset's failure to respond intelligently to aristocratic fears. James certainly had no intention of countenancing social disorders, but the activities of 'Captain Pouch' and his like were not sufficiently menacing to draw attention to the permanent background of unrest, or to convey any warning of the possible consequences of the political quarrels already beginning in Parliament. A more serious agrarian crisis, necessitating repression upon a national scale, might have served to emphasise the continued need for a strong executive. As it was, the more obvious conclusion seemed to be that the local aristocracy could cope with any emergency unaided. At the same time the traditional economic policy of the Crown fell further into discredit as its professed paternalism became less effective. The unpopular activities of projectors, patentees and monopolists appeared to be no more than fiscal devices, placing burdens and restrictions upon trade and industry which no longer could or should be justified in terms of craft standards or social benefit.[19] Informed opinion in the City of London and elsewhere was beginning to move towards a less restrictive policy – a parallel development to the gradual abandonment of moral objections to enclosure – so that by 1620 it was clear that if the Crown insisted on maintaining its existing attitudes a new field of political friction would rapidly develop.

INCREASING RELIGIOUS TENSIONS

The Crown did insist, partly in expectation of fiscal advantage, but partly also out of a sense of duty, and this element of principle was to make negotiation a great deal more difficult. The same could be said of the religious tension which James inherited. As we have seen the king found ideological allies in his bishops,

[19] It was alleged in 1621 that aulnagers' seals (which were supposed to guarantee that cloth had been inspected and found up to standard) could be bought by the bushel.

which gave him a political motive for reinforcing the jurisdiction of the Anglican hierarchy. On the other hand he also believed it to be his solemn duty to preserve his people in the true faith, which to him was protestantism of a non-puritanical kind. His response to the mildly puritan Millenary petition of 1603 was thus predictable both in terms of interest and principle. Elizabeth's reaction would no doubt have been similar, but James exacerbated the situation by inept tactics. Instead of simply shelving the petition, or rejecting it out of hand, he called a conference with the puritan leaders at Hampton Court. This naturally raised their expectations and made their eventual disappointment and indignation sharper.

If the king had intended to dazzle his opponents with theological argument, or even overawe them with his divine authority, he failed totally. Instead they came away with an impression of weak petulance, and the threat of stiffer measures for legal conformity which seemed to indicate a complete lack of spiritual conviction. Coming at the same time as James's initial pronouncements on the subject of divine right, the Hampton Court conference reinforced the existing alliance between the puritans and the common lawyers and contributed to a rapid revival of puritan influence in the House of Commons. The limited victory which the Church had achieved under Whitgift was soon overturned, not because of any lack of determined ecclesiastical leadership, but because the new identity of Anglicanism was too closely associated with novel and unpopular political ideas.

These developments were also encouraged by new fears of popery, which at first found a traditional form in the Gunpowder Plot of 1605. Apparently a small group of catholic gentry were driven to desperation by the fact that the new reign saw no amelioration of their position and attempted what can only be described as an act of political terrorism.[20] They had no coherent plans for the exploitation of possible success, and the only result of the plot was to intensify hostility and produce a fresh crop

[20] As with most of the Elizabethan catholic plots, it has been suggested that the Gunpowder Plot was largely invented by the government to discredit the catholics. This view was advanced by John Gerard in 1897, and refuted by S. R. Gardiner in the same year. *The Gunpowder Plot* by H. R. Williamson (1951) tends to support Gerard, but the debate is never likely to be resolved.

of penal legislation in 1606. The king's attitude towards his catholic subjects, however, was even more ambiguous than Elizabeth's had been. The existing recusancy laws were re-enacted in 1604, and the Acts of 1606 extended the obligation of church attendance to include receiving the sacrament – a move which the queen had never permitted. At the same time a new oath of allegiance was imposed upon all recusants which involved the explicit repudiation of the papal power of deposition.

On the other hand, James quickly made it clear that he had no time for old-fashioned denunciations of the papacy and the catholic Church. In his first speech to Parliament he acknowledged that he regarded Rome as the mother of Churches, 'although defiled with some infirmities and corruptions'. His mind, he declared, was free from persecutions. This view did not commend itself to those who had come to regard the pope as Anti-Christ. In theory James attempted to adhere to the traditional distinctions between the Jesuits and their followers on the one hand, who were actual or potential traitors, and the bulk of the catholic laity on the other. In practice what happened was a vacillation of policy far more marked than that of the previous period, or even of the 1560s. Sometimes the king permitted the recusancy laws to be enforced severely, as he did for a while after the Gunpowder Plot. Sometimes he deliberately inhibited them. As a recent scholar has observed, 'he treated catholics according to dynastic or personal rather than national or religious consideration'.

One consequence of this was the development of a fashionable catholicism at court, centring upon the queen, Anne of Denmark, who was a catholic convert. The dangers of this did not become fully apparent until the following reign, but the isolation and unpopularity of the court were immediately increased. Since 1570 at least the court had been strongly protestant and nationalistic in its flavour, and James's toleration of catholicism so close to his person appeared a most sinister change to the majority of his subjects. It was also, and quite unjustifiably, linked with the growth of High Church opinions and the king's patronage of them.

For all these reasons puritan mistrust of James's religious policy became steadily more plausible and influential as the reign advanced and contributed largely to the growth of political opposition. At the same time, partly for financial and partly for ideological reasons, the king was unable to achieve any formal or lasting improvement in the position of the catholics and thus failed to win their confidence or to impress the seriousness of his desire for toleration upon outsiders. This last factor was of some importance, because James had very sensibly ended the Spanish war in 1604, and by about 1610 was much less sensibly pursuing a project of European pacification through alliance with that country. This was far too abrupt a change for English opinion to accept and naturally awakened the fear that the papists were going to attempt by diplomacy and infiltration what they had failed to accomplish by conquest. The king's unwillingness to accept any kind of criticism of his foreign policy produced, as we shall see, an important reaction in Parliament. But while the House of Commons became convinced that he had been seduced by popish conspirators, the Spaniards understandably looked upon the recusancy laws as proof that he was not serious in desiring their friendship.

CHAPTER 13

THE ASCENDANCY OF THE DUKE OF BUCKINGHAM

It behoveth without doubt his Majesty to uphold the Duke [of Buckingham] against them [the Commons], who, if he be decourted, it will be the cornerstone upon which the demolishing of his monarchy will be builded. (Anonymous commentator, 1628)

NEGOTIATIONS FOR THE SPANISH MARRIAGE

On 14 February 1613 the Princess Elizabeth, James's only daughter, married the Elector Frederick V of the Palatinate, the leading Calvinist prince in the Empire. To most Englishmen this was a hopeful sign of a firmly protestant commitment in foreign policy, and their rejoicings were inspired by that conviction. To the king, however, the marriage was one half of an ambitious scheme to place England in a key diplomatic position through dynastic alliances with the leaders of both sides in the potential religious conflict. In 1611 an embassy had been sent to Madrid to suggest the possibility of a match between the Infanta and the Prince of Wales, but it had met with a discourteous reception and Prince Henry had declared himself flatly averse to a catholic marriage. However in 1612 that promising young man had died, and his brother Charles was too young to offer similar objections, having been born in 1600. Consequently discreet overtures began to be made towards the court of France, and these advances, followed as they were by the Palatine marriage, produced a change of heart in Madrid. Whether the Spanish governments – first Lerma and later Olivares – were seriously interested in an English marriage is highly questionable, but they deemed it expedient to appear so. In 1614 Lerma specifically raised the matter with the English Ambassador, Sir John Digby, and the Spanish envoy in England, Diego Sarmiento, began to trail the same bait in conversations with the king. Sarmiento (better known by the title of Count Gondomar which he received in 1617) gained a considerable influence over James, which coincided with the ascendancy at court of a catholic faction led by Northampton and Suffolk. These circumstances, combined with the fact that Digby was an anti-puritan of conciliatory views, may have persuaded the Spaniards initially that they would have no difficulty in bringing about the repeal of the recusancy laws as the price of alliance. At any rate, in 1615 Sarmiento put this forward as one of the three conditions upon which Philip III was prepared to proceed; the other two being that the princess's household should consist exclusively of her co-religionists, and that she should control the education of her children up to the age of twelve.

The negotiations dragged on inconclusively for several years. English opinion was completely hostile, and the Spaniards became increasingly sceptical of James's ability to honour any undertaking which he might make. Probably Gondomar had no real intention of reaching a settlement, and the main purpose of the discussions from his point of view was to prevent any further English approach to France. James was easy to keep in play. Quite apart from the fancied diplomatic advantages of such a marriage, a dowry of some £600,000 was in question. In 1618 Raleigh's expedition to the Orinoco caused a temporary suspension of negotiations but the outbreak of war in Bohemia shortly after induced Spain to take a fresh initiative in the hope of distracting English attention from the continental struggle. By 1620, however, the progress of events in Germany had placed both sides in embarrassing positions. James could not ignore the catastrophic decline in his son-in-law's fortunes[1] without a complete loss of face, and English opinion was almost unanimous in demanding military intervention upon the protestant side.

The Spaniards, on the other hand, were apprehensive lest the defeat of the Elector should bring into existence an anti-Habsburg coalition which would include not only England and France but also the Sultan, who showed signs of renewing active hostilities. Since Spain was in no financial position to undertake a major war on behalf of the Emperor, the continuation of the English negotiations acquired a new importance, and Philip's Council was prepared to welcome almost any initiative which

[1] Frederick had been foolish enough, in 1619, to accept the crown offered to him by the Estates of Bohemia, who were in rebellion against their designated king, Ferdinand, who was almost simultaneously elected Emperor. On 8 November 1620 the Bohemian army was shattered at the battle of the White Mountain, and Frederick was left without allies or resources.

would prevent a breakdown of relations. Consequently they listened with professions of interest to James's proposal that the king of Spain should bring pressure to bear upon his uncle to restore the Palatinate to Frederick as part of a family settlement accompanying the Anglo-Spanish marriage. At the same time Gondomar had become virtually convinced that no religious concessions of any significance would be acceptable in England, and without such concessions Philip could not entrust his daughter to a foreign land.

By the time that this *impasse* had been reached, James had been forced to resort to Parliament once more. Between 1616 and 1620 his financial position had been significantly improved by the overthrow of the Howards and the rise to favour of the London merchant and financier Lionel Cranfield. The Howards fell primarily because they were supplanted in the king's favour by George Villiers, but their removal from public office and the trial of the Earl of Suffolk on charges of corruption undoubtedly led to an improvement in financial administration. The grip which Villiers rapidly acquired upon royal patronage, and the manner in which he used this in the interests of his family, were ultimately to have disastrous effects, but in the short term his régime appeared to be a distinct improvement, and his friendship with Cranfield brought the latter offices and preferments which for once were thoroughly deserved. The Customs, the Household and the Wardrobe were all reformed under his direction, and a large measure of retrenchment achieved, while his contacts in the City restored a measure of confidence among the mercantile community. At the same time the Admiralty administration was reformed, the incompetent Nottingham being squeezed out by Villiers who became Lord Admiral in his place. The latter, who had been created Earl of Buckingham in 1617, was all-powerful by 1620, and under his influence the Naval Commission became a permanent board which considerably improved the condition of the fleet. Nevertheless, Buckingham was not the man to sustain an attack upon corruption and peculation once it had served his immediate ends, and without a prolonged campaign there was no prospect of any permanent improvement in the integrity of the civil service. Consequently, in spite of the reforms there was no general recovery of confidence, and the king's appeal for a benevolence to enable him to help Frederick fell flat. James could no more afford an active foreign policy in 1621 than he could in 1614. Although he was in the unusual position of being able to balance his ordinary budget, only Parliament could provide the resources necessary for intervention in Europe.

Unfortunately, the king was not in a position to be perfectly frank about his intentions. Although he desired to raise a mercenary force to go to Frederick's assistance,[2] he continued to pin his real hopes of a favourable settlement upon the good offices of Spain obtained through a marriage treaty. These were not compatible objectives, and the pursuit of the second was not only unrealistic, but also ruined any chance of achieving the first. Initially feeling in Parliament was unanimously in favour of intervention in the Palatinate, but James mistakenly decided to take a lofty tone and to demand subsidies without offering any explanation as to how they were to be used. Consequently the Commons voted only the most perfunctory supply before turning to their own grievances, and putting forward their own foreign policy, in defiance of the king's express prohibition. To the opposition leaders Spain, not the Emperor, was the real enemy. In spite of contrary assurances from the privy councillors in the House, they insisted on regarding the Spanish king as the paymaster of the catholic armies and proposed to rescue the Palatinate by waging an Elizabethan sea-war against the treasure fleets. This point of view they expressed in a petition which James refused to receive on the grounds that it was an attempt to infringe his prerogative of making war and peace. The Commons denied any intention of usurping the prerogative, which they recognised, but defended their right to give such advice if it seemed to them to be justified. After a further angry exchange, the Parliament was dissolved in December 1621, and James tore the Commons' 'protestation' on free speech out of the Journal. All that the king had gained was an interim subsidy designed to keep Frederick's existing army in the field for about two months while a more permanent arrangement was negotiated. Gondomar, whose promptings had certainly influenced James's attitude, was delighted with the quarrel and dissolution, which served his purposes admirably. At the same time the king's policy had become wholly dependent upon a

[2] Such an army was, in fact, already in existence under the command of Count Ernst von Mansfeld, but it could not be kept in being without English financial help.

successful outcome to the marriage negotiations.

The collapse of the protestant position in Bohemia and the Palatinate, which could have provided at least a temporary basis for co-operation between king and Parliament, thus became the cause of further estrangement. Englishmen in general had become passionately interested in the continental struggle which they naturally saw in simple terms of black and white. Sermons and early newsbooks all painted the same gloomy picture of religion in mortal danger and built up considerable popular resentment against James's incomprehensible attitude. The king seems to have been quite unaware of the strength of the 'Black Legend', which had been a fact of English political life for about seventy years, and contented himself with the conviction that because his subjects were necessarily ill-informed their opinions were of no significance.

GROWTH OF POLITICAL FACTION

This pent-up resentment found a partial if not particularly relevant outlet in a renewed storm over monopolies. These unpopular concessions had not been ended by Elizabeth's famous surrender of 1601, nor by the unanimous judicial decision (in the case of Darcy v. Allen) that they were *prima facie* contrary to both common and statute law. Parliamentary agitations in 1606, 1610 and 1614 had achieved little, and the situation had deteriorated still further since 1616 with the rise of the Villiers family.[8] In 1621 the wrath of the Commons exploded against two notorious monopolists, Sir Francis Mitchell and Sir Giles Mompesson. In their enthusiasm the members forgot that the House did not, in itself, constitute a court of law, and that they had no power to sentence offenders, other than their own number in cases of privilege. Even the most fertile brain could not discover a favourable precedent, but rather than remit Mitchell and Mompesson to the common law they appealed to the House of Lords. As a result the long obsolete procedure of impeachment was revived, whereby the Commons acted as accusers and the Lords as judges. In spite of the implied criticism of himself and

[8] One of the reasons for the savage outburst of 1621 was the economic crisis which had begun to develop in the previous year, and which many people blamed upon the activities of the monopolists. In particular the shortage of bullion was blamed upon the existence of monopolies in the manufacture of gold and silver thread (which were held by Buckingham's brothers).

his favourite, James raised no objection to this, contenting himself with a solemn charge to the Lords that they should examine the accusations with proper care. Mompesson was not an intimate member of the court, and the procedure, although long out of use, was perfectly legal. Nevertheless the willingness of the Lords to gratify the Commons in this way was a sinister portent which the king would have done well to heed.

The chief reason for this was the flourishing of what a contemporary called 'temporal simony' – that trade in honours of which Buckingham was the acknowledged master. Although the worst excesses of this system were seen in the sale of Irish peerages (which did not carry membership of the upper House) fierce quarrels nevertheless broke out in the Lords. Peers of ancient lineage, such as the Earl of Arundel, mocked the bourgeois ancestry of parvenues like Lord Spencer, and new peers of longstanding gentry families, such as Lord Digby, hurled insults at those of baser blood, even though, like the Earl of Middlesex,[4] they enjoyed both higher rank and the king's favour. These disparagements were not meekly accepted, and the result was bitter feuds and factions, in which the new men commonly enjoyed the support of the all-powerful favourite. The conservatives, being in a majority, were thus doubly driven to express their resentment through political action in Parliament.

The first important victim of this tension between the king and the Lords was the Lord Chancellor, Francis Bacon. At the beginning of the session a committee had been set up to examine complaints of abuse in the administration of justice, and one of the grievances presented to this committee concerned the issue of bills of conformity out of Chancery whereby that court could be persuaded to extend protection to insolvent debtors. This was particularly resented in the City of London, and Bacon came under heavy fire. The Chancellor's belief in the importance of equity jurisdiction as an aspect of the prerogative turned this into a political attack, but a direct confrontation with the king was avoided by the discovery of evidence to convict Bacon of ordinary corruption. He was impeached on charges of bribery and the misuse of office which he did not attempt to refute. This surrender made it impossible for James to take a stand and although his fine was remitted, he had perforce to be dismissed from office,

[4] Lionel Cranfield, who had been created Baron Cranfield in July 1622, and Earl of Middlesex in September of the same year.

and his fall created a precedent which threatened every royal servant.

The parliamentary session of 1621 thus marked an important stage in the growth of the 'country' opposition. Already procedural devices like the Committee of the Whole House, and the development of concerted tactics by the 'country' spokesmen had deprived the Crown of most of its powers of management.[5] Now the opposition leaders were deliberately taking the initiative, formulating their own statement of foreign policy, and, with the co-operation of the Lords, converting the obsolete judicial process of impeachment into a political weapon over which the Crown could have no control short of the dissolution of Parliament. Several members were imprisoned at the end of this session for their refractory conduct, and the Earl of Southampton, although a privy councillor, was accused of consulting with members of the lower House to further the purposes of the opposition. The 'privy conventicles and conferences' in which members like Sir John Eliot and William Hakewill had long taken part now embraced the upper House as well, and although it would be anachronistic to call the 'country' a party in the later sense, at least opposition to the court had produced an extensive community of interest. The 'country' was not a religious faction like the puritan 'choir' of the 1560s, nor was it a connexion, linked by ties of patronage and dependence to one or more great men. The involvement of members of the peerage was mainly significant in the parliamentary context, not because their resources gave them a capacity either to resist or to take over the local operations of royal government. The 'country' was not even united by a common exclusion from favour and the fruits of office, but rather by a broad, if somewhat negative, political philosophy of 'mixed' monarchy and the rule of law.

In intention it was a highly conservative opposition, whose object was to defend the traditional system of government against the innovations of divine right. In 1629 John Pym declared that the law which required the consent of Parliament for

[5] It is now thought unlikely that procedural changes, such as the development of the Committee of the Whole House, had the constitutional significance which Professor Notestein attributed to them when he wrote *The Winning of the Initiative by the House of Commons*, although concerted action outside the House was probably becoming more important. S. Lambert, 'Procedure in the House of Commons in the Early Stuart period', *English Historical Review*, 1980.

direct taxation 'was not introduced by any statute, or by any charter or sanction of Princes, but was the ancient and fundamental law issuing from the first frame and constitution of the kingdom'. Such views were axiomatic, and although, as we have seen, they were mistaken in many particulars, they were held with a sincerity which was later to cause great difficulty and confusion. The monarchical framework of government was never called in question, nor was it ever suggested that the Lords and Commons in Parliament could exercise any authority without the participation of the king. Indeed, even the *de facto* sovereignty which the whole Parliament had acquired during the sixteenth century seems to have been held in some doubt, since the 'country' members were unable to conceive of any circumstances in which the fundamental laws, by which they set such store, could be legally altered or abolished. They regarded what they believed to be the ancient constitution of England rather as Sir Thomas More had regarded the catholic Church. Consequently they not only respected the royal office, but had a strongly developed sense of the responsibility of the monarch for the welfare of the commonwealth. The executive power of the king, and with it the prerogative, was therefore recognised as both lawful and necessary.

Where his opponents usually disagreed with James was over the distinction between 'ordinary' and 'absolute' prerogative. The latter had long been acknowledged as an emergency power, to enable the king to act for the general good and safety of the realm. Since the king alone was judge of the appropriate circumstances in which it should be used, however, and James was not trusted to exercise the traditional degree of self-restraint, the very existence of such a power began to seem unacceptable to the 'country'. Also James was inclined to exalt the 'absolute' prerogative above the 'ordinary' and hence above the law, a position which was defended in a number of judicial decisions after the fall of Coke. By 1614 members of Parliament had come to see in the 'absolute prerogative' the same kind of threat that lawyers of an earlier generation had seen in the royal supremacy. Impositions, for instance, could be levied on the pretext of emergency, as Edwin Sandys pointed out, in which case 'no man could know his right and property in his own goods'. This was the fundamental point. To concede the 'absolute prerogative' in the forms in which James was claiming it was to give the king a means of access to his subjects' property without their consent.[6]

The function of the 'ordinary' prerogative presented no such threat, nor did the king ever claim to be above the law in the normal routine of government. A real control over policy, however, as distinct from administration, depended upon some measure of 'absolute' power. By rejecting this the opposition were implying that the ultimate control over decisions of policy should lie with the Parliament rather than the king. For all their self-conscious conservatism, the 'country' members were in effect seeking to place the monarch in the position of an executive officer who would be allowed only a limited discretion in the exercise of his duties. Lord Chancellor Ellesmere had perceived something of this danger as early as 1610, when he wrote:

> The popular state . . . hath grown big and audacious, and in every session of Parliament swelled more and more. And if way be still given unto it . . . it is to be doubted what the end will be.

The 'country' itself was not yet prepared to face the logic of its own attitude to the prerogative, but it did display a heightened awareness of Parliament's function as the representative and trustee of the commonwealth. By long tradition 'all the whole body of the realm, and every particular member thereof . . . are by the laws of this realm deemed to be personally present'. But speeches in the Commons in the 1620s were going further than that. 'When the king says he cannot allow our liberties of right,' declared Coke in 1621, 'this strikes at the root. We serve here for thousands and ten thousands.' 'We are entrusted by our country,' protested another member. 'if we lose our privileges, we betray it.' Other speeches rehearsed the fall of representative estates in other European countries and tapped a rich seam of nationalism in support of their cause. Should the privileges of the Commons be impaired, warned Edward Alford in 1621, then 'farewell Parliament and farewell England'.

This tendency to equate the realm with Parliament, rather than the king, and to look to the Lords and Commons (and particularly the latter) to defend the common weal was a change of the greatest importance. The 'commonwealth men' of the sixteenth century had looked to the king to defend his people

[6] C.f. the opinions of John Ponet in 1556. See above, p. 247.

against the 'conspiracy of rich men', and the development of Tudor government had made this possible to a limited extent. Their successors in the 1620's saw the king as the principal threat and thus sought to throw the whole process of political and administrative evolution into reverse, looking back to the middle ages to undermine those Tudor achievements which now seemed to threaten rather than defend their interests. This whole campaign they had perforce to concentrate in the defence of parliamentary privilege.

> That which is more than lives . . . than all our goods, all our interests and faculties [is] the life, the liberty of the Parliament, the privileges and immunities of this House which are the bases and support of all the rest,

as Sir John Eliot expressed it.

The 'country' could afford the luxury of political opposition because Tudor government, and the social changes which had accompanied its growth, had largely overcome those forces of provincialism and magnate ambition which had so disrupted the kingdom in the fifteenth century. By 1620 the pallid ghosts of Lancaster and York had no power to terrify. Under the protection of the Tudor monarchs the English gentry had grown to a wealth and political maturity which enabled them to challenge that very authority which had fostered them and freed them from dependence upon their social superiors.

The 'country' formed a complete cross section of the ruling class, distinguished only by the strength and articulateness of their opinions. Except for that small group which was intimately associated with the workings of the court, the 'country' leaders spoke in a measure for the whole aristocracy, and it was this fact which gave substance to their identification of the realm with Parliament. The 'country' peers were a minority group and were motivated at least as much by private grievances as by public conscience, but they included the very wealthy (such as the Earl of Warwick) and the relatively poor (Lords Saye and Mandeville). They were more puritan in religion that the peerage as a whole, and naturally hostile to Buckingham, but they cannot be identified simply as an 'interest group', whether political, religious or economic. Some contemporaries thought their hostility to the court the most significant feature of the whole opposition movement. The herald Sir Edward Walker later wrote, 'if the nobility had been unanimous to have defended the just rights of the king . . . it had never been in the power of the Commons to have begun their rebellion'. To the modern observer, however, their role seems less decisive, since the most outspoken leaders of the 'country' were among the Commons, and the patronage of the opposition peers was relatively insignificant.

Predominantly the 'country' was a gentry movement, strong among those families which dominated the commissions of the peace and controlled the government of the shires. It included some, like Sir Robert Harley, who were prominent royal officials, and many who held minor posts of profit in the localities. John Pym, for example, was a receiver general of royal revenues for three counties from 1607 to 1636. Like the peers, the leading 'country' gentry tended to be more puritan than their neighbours, but they cannot be distinguished by wealth or ancestry, or geographical location. As the beneficiaries of the existing system they were socially conservative, and when they spoke of 'the people' they meant themselves, the propertied class whose 'liberties' they genuinely believed safeguarded the welfare of the whole commonwealth. The 'country' was therefore not so much a party as a state of mind, impossible to define precisely in terms of membership or antecedents, and identified chiefly as a degree of alienation from its much more tangible opposite, the 'court'.

THE ISOLATION OF THE COURT

The court was first and foremost the royal household, and those great offices of state which carried with them the privilege of regular or frequent access to the king's person. In its wider sense it was the whole staff of the central administration, and embraced both those who held such posts and those who aspired to them. The latter formed a floating population as individuals either achieved their objectives or fell away. Because of the contemporary attitude towards office as a form of negotiable property, the court in many respects resembled a market, where prices and profits were both high and the competition fierce and unscrupulous.

> The Court is fraught with bribery and hate,
> with envy, lust, ambition and debate . . .

as one of its critics wrote.[7] It was, notoriously, a world of intrigue and unstable friendships in which success or failure

[7] G. Wither, *Britains Remembrancer* (1628), 195-6.

might depend upon the merest trivialities. It was also the hub of the executive, where councillors and civil servants gathered around the monarch, where decisions of public policy were made, and meritorious service was supposed to receive its due reward. There was always a tendency for the private affairs of the courtiers to exercise an undue influence upon their public functions. As long as place and preferment depended upon patronage, and patronage was accessible to wealth and personal considerations, such influence was inevitable, and neither Elizabeth nor any ruler before her had succeeded in eradicating it.

However, the ascendancy of Buckingham – raised to a Dukedom in 1623 – transformed abuse into a scandal of systematic exploitation. The court was Buckingham's chess board, and he dominated it completely from about 1617 to his death in 1628, enjoying the unwavering confidence of both James and Charles. No office could be obtained but by his gift or mediation. The kind of feuds which had brought Carr and the Howards into disgrace could not touch him. His advice governed royal policy, and his favour made and unmade fortunes, both at court and in the City. As a result those who were Buckingham's enemies, whether for personal reasons, like the Earl of Essex, out of contempt for his ancestry, like the Earl of Arundel, or simply out of jealousy of his success, were forced to withdraw from the court. In many cases this meant moving into the political ranks of the 'country', so that by 1628 many of those who would seem to be natural members of the 'court' were in fact alienated from it. This was particularly true of the 'civil service', many of whom held their offices by life patents or in reversion from an earlier period, and who feared the favourite's brokerage as a threat to their established interests. Such administrative dynasties as the Fanshawes, Osbornes and Crokes were not necessarily enthusiastic supporters of royal policy in the 1620s, in spite of long and faithful service to the Crown.

There was consequently a dangerous tendency for the circle of the court to diminish and consist only of those who already enjoyed Buckingham's patronage, or were prepared to compete in seeking it. This placed a barrier between the king and the bulk of the aristocracy which further increased misunderstanding and distrust. On the one hand this was reflected in the constant literary denigration of the courtier's life. 'There is no Machiavilian policy he diveth not into . . . nor sordid actions which he doth not accomplish . . . [courtiers] nourish oppositions and factions to make the path more facile for their ends . . . their motto is: Qui nescit dissimulare nescit vivere . . . ,' wrote Edward Payton. This was contrasted with the simple and peaceful virtue of the country life, so that to be a country gentleman or lord was virtually in itself a guarantee of integrity and public spirit. A speaker in the Parliament of 1625 described himself as 'neither a lawyer nor a courtier, but a plain country gentleman', clearly expecting this description to stand as a warrant of his candour.

On the other hand, the court withdrew increasingly into artificiality and isolation, Charles's refined tastes lacking even the extravagant vulgarity which had retained a measure of extroversion in his father's amusements. The worst effects of this were not to be seen until the following decade, when drama, painting and poetry alike combined to produce a 'precious' and sentimental atmosphere which insulated Charles, his family and his most intimate friends from the world of political reality. But as early as 1630 the court poet Sir Richard Fanshawe was sufficiently unaware of the outside world (or sufficiently dishonest) to celebrate the king's pacific reign:

White Peace (the beautifull'st of things)
Seems here her everlasting rest
To fix, and spreads her downy Wings
Over the nest.

The occasion of this ode was a royal proclamation commanding the gentry to reside upon their estates – but it was not a love of Charles's irenic court which was causing indignant gentlemen to foregather in the capital.

The court also became increasingly isolated by its religious atmosphere. Queen Anne had died in 1619, but the catholic group continued to exist and James, preoccupied with his Spanish negotiations, could not afford to be overtly hostile. When the Spanish marriage at length collapsed in 1623, the king at once turned his attentions to France, and the wedding of Prince Charles and Henrietta Maria in 1624 set up another and much more influential catholic sanctuary within the court. This in itself was bound to cause resentment, but the situation was made worse by Charles's peculiarly conscientious churchmanship. In spite of his sympathy with the High Church party, and his quarrel with the puritan leaders at the Hampton Court conference James had never completely lost touch with English puritanism. A number of the reforms demanded at that conference had subsequently been implemented through royal instructions to the bishops, and when the zealous Bancroft died in 1611 he was replaced by the latitudinarian George Abbott. The pressures which Whitgift and Bancroft had applied were relaxed, and the fierce controversies of the early years of the reign died away.

Although the king would not tolerate any challenge to episcopacy as such, and rightly regarded the High Church party as the group most sympathetic to divine right, he was never an Arminian,[8] and he shared with many of his puritan subjects the millenarianism of an older generation. Consequently, although the puritans were highly suspicious of James, most of them did not feel it necessary to abandon their deeply engrained faith in the Godly Prince. The vision of Foxe and Aylmer remained authentic, and the link between scripture and the royal supremacy still held. By contrast, Charles was an Arminian; not an ally of the High Church party, but a member of it. James had tolerated, and sometimes encouraged, the concept of *iure divino* episcopacy, but had not lost sight of the fact that it implied a diminution of his own supremacy. Charles was prepared to accept the arguments of Anglican divines such as George Downame for the spiritual autonomy of the clergy:

> The Magistrates, indeed, having the keys of an earthly kingdom, have also power to loose and bind the bodies of their subjects and to commit the same to a gaoler or executioner, but the ministers having the keys of the Kingdom of Heaven, have power to bind and loose the souls of men.[9]

After 1625 the personal piety of the new king made him positively anxious to promote the authority and jurisdiction of

[8] Jacobus Arminius, after whom this theological attitude was named, was a Dutch Reformed minister who had died in 1609. His views were set out in the *Remonstrance*, published after his death, which rejected the determinism of predestination and maintained that divine sovereignty was compatible with a real free-will in man. The *Remonstrance* was condemned at the Synod of Dort (1618-19). The extent of his influence in England is uncertain, since the views of the High Church group, although very similar may have evolved independently. The term 'Arminian' was applied to them by their enemies, but not unjustly.

[9] George Downame, *An Extract of a Sermon . . . Of the Dignity and Duty of the Ministry* (1608). The first systematic exposition of the High Church position came in George Carleton, *Jurisdiction, Regal, Episcopal, Papal* (1610).

the clergy in the interests of the Church.

The full impact of this renascent clericalism was not felt until the period of personal rule, but the advance of the Arminians to favour was noticeable from the first. William Laud, the most dynamic and one of the ablest divines of that persuasion, whom a distrustful James had reluctantly promoted to the minor see of St David's, was chosen to preach at the opening of Charles's first Parliament. The king, he declared, 'is God's immediate lieutenant upon earth; and therefore one and the same action is God's by ordinance and the king's by execution . . .' This sermon set the tone for many Arminian pronouncements upon the subject of royal authority in the later 1620s. The High Church party may have been more concerned with the Godly Bishop than they were with the Godly Prince, but they remained within the boundaries laid down by the Act of Supremacy, and both interest and principle led them to exalt a king who was so responsive to their ideals. This can be seen in its crudest form in the sermons of Robert Sibthorpe and Roger Mainwaring in 1627, which raised the duty of obedience above all law and limitation, for the purpose of inducing compliance in the king's financial demands. Charles, with characteristic obtuseness, wished to have Sibthorpe's oration published, and when Archbishop Abbot refused to license it, he sequestered him from his jurisdiction. William Laud became Bishop of Bath and Wells in 1626, and in 1628 was translated to London where he was virtually primate during Abbott's eclipse. Theologically Arminianism was a Calvinist deviation and bore little resemblance to post-Tridentine catholicism, but to the uninformed and prejudiced English observer the two appeared almost identical. The clericalism of the High Church, its rejection of strict predestination, and above all its emphasis upon liturgy and ceremonial aroused the bitterest hatred and suspicion. In fact both Laud and the king were resolute opponents of Rome, but the 'beauty of holiness', which flourished in the secluded atmosphere of the court looked remarkably like the mass when viewed across the ever widening gulf which separated the monarch from his people.

GROWING STRIFE BETWEEN CROWN AND PARLIAMENT

For a short time at the end of James's reign political tension had eased. The strange and perilous expedition of Charles and Buckingham to Madrid in 1623 had not only given the *quietus* to the marriage negotiations, but brought the travellers back thirsting for war with Spain, and thus briefly in substantial agreement with English public opinion.[10] As a result, the Parliament which met in 1624 was a good deal more amicable than its recent predecessors. It had good reason to be, since the king had been forced to abandon the foreign policy to which he had clung at such heavy cost for ten years, and virtually handed over the control of war finance to a committee of the House of Commons. 'I shall then entreat your good and sound advice,' James had declared in his opening speech, '. . . Never a king gave more trust to his subjects than to desire their advice in matters of this weight.' Of course, the king was perfectly entitled to change his mind, and welcome the counsel which he had previously repudiated. In doing so he was not abandoning his prerogative, but in the circumstances his change of attitude looked remarkably like a surrender of principle.

Perhaps because he was old and weary, James also allowed this Parliament to strike a solid blow against the prerogative by impeaching the Lord Treasurer, Lionel Cranfield, Earl of Middlesex. The fall of Middlesex was a direct result of the temporary *rapprochment* between court and country. It was promoted by Charles and Buckingham, with small-minded and shortsighted animosity, and eagerly taken up by a House of Commons which was only too anxious to remove a royal official whose competence constantly threatened to rescue the king from their clutches. James warned his son and his favourite of the probable consequences of such irresponsible action, but lacked the willpower to forbid it. Middlesex did not admit to being guilty of any ordinary offence, as Bacon had done. He was accused of extortion and the misuse of his office, charges which on this occasion were specifically framed by the Commons and not simply handed on to the Lords for investigation. Some of the accusations were probably justified, and he had made enough enemies to ensure his conviction, but the reasons for his downfall were political and not legal. By failing to stop the proceed-

[10] The most complete account of this expedition, which was an acute embarrassment to Olivares, is contained in Roger Lockyer, *Buckingham: the Life and Political Career of George Villiers, First Duke of Buckingham* (1981). Charles and Buckingham significantly chose, on their return, to deliver a report to a joint sitting of the Committees of both Whole Houses.

ings, James had tacitly conceded that his servants might be called to account by Parliament for the execution of their duties. Whether they were aware of it or not, the Commons had revived another fifteenth century practice, that of using impeachment as a crude method of enforcing 'ministerial responsibility'.

From Cranfield the scent of this kind of hunt led swiftly and inevitably to Buckingham, as James had foreseen. When Charles met his first Parliament in 1625 he found the relative complaisance of the previous year ebbing fast. The government's elaborate military plans were not accepted as the inevitable consequences of the decision to make war, and the king's marriage, which had taken place in the interval, was viewed with great suspicion. At the end of 1624 the recusancy laws had been suspended, a move which was generally, and rightly, attributed to French pressure. Consequently the Commons were not in a co-operative mood, and Buckingham's decision to undertake the defence of royal policy himself did not improve the atmosphere. After making a very perfunctory grant, the members returned to the question of grievances, and in a number of speeches hinted broadly that the real trouble with the realm lay in the ancient problems of official extortion and evil counsel. The signs of an impending attack upon the favourite were unmistakeable, and Parliament was hastily dissolved.

However, both the military and the financial position deteriorated in the second half of 1625. An attempt to raise a Privy Seal loan met with no response, and Parliament had to be recalled at the beginning of the following year. The disastrous expedition to Cadiz had put a fine edge on the anger of the Commons, and with only the briefest preliminaries the members took up their cudgels at the point where they had been forced to lay them down. A leader of eloquence and determination emerged in the person of Sir John Eliot. His demands that those responsible for the conduct of the war should be called to account met with an immediate response, and placed the conflict upon the highest level of political principle. The Council of War refused to be interrogated, and Charles upheld them, commenting, 'It is not you that they aim at, but it is me upon whom they make inquisition.' Once the king had made it clear that he would not purchase subsidies by sacrificing the Council of War, the Commons changed their tactics and moved directly against Buckingham, ignoring Charles's warning that he would not allow such an attack to be pressed home.

For a variety of reasons the upper House was ready to welcome this initiative. On 4 March the Earl of Arundel was committed to the Tower for countenancing the clandestine marriage of his son with Elizabeth Stuart, sister of the Duke of Lennox and a kinswoman of the king. In fact this harsh treatment seems to have stemmed from a quarrel between Charles and Henrietta Maria, but Buckingham was widely blamed. The Lords petitioned three times for Arundel's release, and the king yielded when it seemed likely that they would refuse to transact business in the Earl's absence. At the same time the Earl of Bristol, lately Ambassador in Spain,[11] who had been kept under house arrest since his return, seized the opportunity to petition the House for its intercession with the king. He had been charged with no offence beyond an error of judgement, and the Lords declared that it was contrary to their privileges that his writ of summons had been withheld. As soon as he appeared in London, Bristol made haste to level accusations against Buckingham which Charles attempted to parry by accusing the Earl of treason. By this time the peers were thoroughly aroused and insisted upon hearing the two cases simultaneously, suspecting rightly that the main purpose of the charges against Bristol was to prevent him from making damaging revelations about Buckingham's conduct in Madrid three years before.

At this juncture, in early May, the Commons submitted their articles of impeachment against the Duke, and it was abundantly clear that only the king's intervention could save his favourite from conviction. The ten year old grievance of his abuse of patronage, a welter of personal animosities, and the blatant nature of the attempt to silence Bristol, not only made the outcome a foregone conclusion, but meant that it would reflect directly upon the king's own honour. On the 11 May the promoters of the impeachment, Digges and Eliot, were imprisoned, and the Commons refused to transact any further business until they were released. Both were freed within a few days, but there was no longer any chance of the session reaching a fruitful conclusion. A stormy debate in the lower House on 12 June produced a strongly worded remonstrance, renewing the attack upon Buckingham:

We protest before your Majesty and the whole world that

[11] Sir John Digby, created Earl of Bristol in September, 1622.

> until this great person be removed from intermeddling with the great affairs of state, we are out of hope of any good success; and do fear that any money we shall or can give will, through his misemployment, be turned rather to the hurt and prejudice of this your kingdom than otherwise, as by lamentable experience we have found in those large supplies formerly and lately given.

Three days later the Parliament was dissolved.

During 1627 Charles made strenuous efforts to finance his policies by extra-parliamentary means. A free gift was demanded by royal letters to selected gentlemen; ships were commandeered from certain maritime towns on the grounds of emergency; and a forced loan equivalent to five subsidies (£300,000) was levied by special commissioners. Meanwhile the military situation deteriorated still further, Danish intervention on behalf of the German protestants collapsed, and a personal quarrel between Charles and his queen resulted in a breach with France. Fortunately the Spaniards lacked either the resources or the inclination for a direct attack. An expedition was launched to relieve the rebellious Huguenots of La Rochelle, but by the end of September it had to be abandoned in confusion and disgrace. Buckingham received most of the blame for this last misfortune, not without cause, and general exasperation with his mismanagement stiffened resistance to the king's fianancial demands. The High Church pulpits expounded the duty of obedience, as we have seen, but the unpopularity of the Arminians themselves did nothing to commend their cause. The 'free gift' which had been demanded in 1626, before the La Rochelle fiasco, was refused outright by the great majority of those to whom it had been addressed, and many gentlemen were removed from the commissions of the peace in consequence.[12] The government had slightly more success in raising ships, an action for which there were good precedents, but the City of London refused a loan on the security of the crown jewels, and much of the king's plate had to be sold.

The greatest controversy raged over the forced loan, both be-

[12] These suspensions were for the most part of very short duration, as with the refusers of the forced loan (see below pp. 376-7). There was, however, some overall reduction in the numbers on the commissions, which had been growing steadily for over a century, and not all those excluded were restored. J. H. Gleason, *Justices of the Peace in England, 1558-1640.*

cause of the magnitude of the sum involved and because of the principles it raised. In a number of counties the commissioners themselves refused to serve. Twelve of the twenty-five named for Gloucestershire took this stand, and a number in Norfolk and other counties. Much larger numbers of those assessed declined to pay, and many made explicit protests against the illegality of the levy. A score of gentry and over two hundred freeholders in Northamptonshire were reported to the Privy Council as refusers, and there were also numerous groups in Yorkshire, Lincolnshire, Essex and Warwickshire. In several London parishes there were riots, and six hundred tax-payers in Hertfordshire signed a letter of protest to their Lord Lieutenant, the Earl of Salisbury.

Some of the nobility shared the commons' indignation, and a servant of the Earl of Lincoln was apprehended while distributing anti-government propaganda among the freeholders around his master's estates. The Lord Chief Justice, Sir Randolf Carew, was dismissed for refusing to uphold the legality of the loan, and when Privy Council pressure failed to secure compliance, a number of recalcitrants were imprisoned. This caused a further 'escalation' of the struggle, because the king's right to imprison his subjects in this fashion was almost immediately called in question. Technically he was quite correct in claiming this power. The writ *habeas corpus* was designed to protect individuals from incarceration by their private enemies, not by the public authority. No writ ran against the king, and he did not have to show cause why offenders had incurred his displeasure. A test case brought by four of the imprisoned 'refusers' in 1627 resulted in the correct (but by no means final) decision that prisoners so committed could not be bailed by *habeas corpus*.[13] Public opinion promptly magnified this decision into a general statement of the legality of the loan, and of the king's power to imprison his subjects indefinitely without legal redress. At the beginning of 1628 nearly eighty knights, gentlemen and substantial citizens were in prison or under restraint for disobedience, and the recipients of almost universal sympathy and support.

[13] Usually known as 'the five knights case', but one of the defendants refused to proceed after the initial refusal of the writ. The judges seem to have intended their decision to be an interim one, while the position was clarified but it was generally taken as final.

Faced with similar resistance a century before, Henry VIII had abandoned the 'amicable grant' without resorting to imprisonment. Charles persisted, and it is some tribute to the efficiency of the administrative system which had evolved in the interval that, in spite of all resistance, he managed to raise £245,000 in fourteen months. But the political price which he paid was heavy, and the sum was nowhere near sufficient to enable him to survive without recalling Parliament. Although the prisoners were released at the beginning of 1628, they and their cause dominated the subsequent elections. 'All the counties,' one observer reported, 'have uniformly rejected candidates who had even a shadow of dependence upon the court, electing members who refused the late subsidies . . . now everywhere called good patriots.' Crown and court patronage proved almost totally ineffective, and loan refusers or other known oppositionists were returned in overwhelming strength, making the task of managing the Commons impossible from the start. Some contemporaries thought that the only outcome of such overt hostility would be a speedy dissolution, but this did not prove to be so. Perhaps the king had hopes of renewing his alliance with the Lords. Certainly Buckingham had been busy trying to soothe the tempers of his fellow peers, not altogether without success, and the bishops were becoming ever more solidly in favour of the court.

When the Commons, led by Eliot and Sir Thomas Wentworth, launched their expected attacks against the forced loan and arbitrary imprisonment, the Lords did not respond with the enthusiasm of 1626, and after long debate attempted to tone down the vehemence of the protests from the lower House. The Commons, realising that the peers were not prepared to make an explicit declaration against the 'extraordinary prerogative', changed their tactics and attempted to proceed by means of a declaratory Act, embodying their own interpretation of the existing statutes. This the king would not countenance, saying that he was prepared to observe the statutes themselves, but not to allow his subjects to remake the laws in their own interests. Rather than proceed with legislation which was bound to prove abortive, the Commons thereupon resorted to the method of petition, embodying their grievances in a comprehensive document which became known as the Petition of Right. The main points of this petition were four: that no tax, gift, loan or other exaction should be levied without consent of Parliament, that no free man should be imprisoned without lawful cause shown;[14] that soldiers should not be billeted upon civilians without the latter's consent; that martial law should never be extended to the civilian population. The last two articles were the result of a strong suspicion that the king was using the state of war as a pretext for imposing extra-legal sanctions upon those who displeased or resisted him.

The Lords hesitated, particularly over the question of imprisonment, but the Commons were adamant and eventually had their way. The petition was presented in the names of both Houses, and after several attempts to evade the issue, Charles assented to it, although it was not clear either then or later exactly what legal force this assent conferred. Such a limited success was by no means sufficient to satisfy the 'country'. Two strongly worded remonstrances were prepared and passed, one against the Arminians and the other against the collection of tonnage and poundage to which, it was alleged, the king was not entitled without specific grant.[15] Articles of impeachment were presented against Roger Mainwaring, the indiscreet advocate of divine right, and there was talk of reviving the impeachment of Buckingham.

There could only be one end to such proceedings, and on 26 June the king announced his intention to prorogue the Parliament in a speech to both Houses which contained a succinct summary of his own view of the session. After condemning the remonstrances as presumptuous, Charles went on,

> The profession of both Houses, in time of hammering this petition [of Right] was no ways to entrench upon my prerogative, saying they had neither intention nor power to hurt it: therefore it must needs be conceived I granted no new, but only confirmed the ancient liberties of my subjects; yet to show the clearness of my intention . . . I do here declare that

[14] The term 'free man' was used with specific reference to the 'liber homo' of Magna Carta, presumably in ignorance of the fact that this had been a description of a specific status in the early thirteenth century. The bondman of condition had disappeared from England before 1628.

[15] It was customary for parliament to make a life grant of these dues to each monarch in his first parliamentary session. In 1625 the Commons, alarmed by a reminder of the impositions issue, had proposed to offer them to Charles for one year only. The Lords had rejected this, and consequently the king had no statutory grounds for their collection.

> those things which have been done whereby men had some cause to suspect the liberty of the subjects to be trenched upon . . . shall not hereafter be drawn into example to your prejudice . . .

Many of the Commons felt that such assurances were no substitute for legal obligations, but for the moment there was no more to be done.

The 'country' leaders were now in an exposed position as their radical distrust of the king became increasingly clear. During this session they had not confined themselves to the relatively firm ground of 'evil counsel', but had attacked royal policy itself upon a wide front. The majority of the Lords no longer supported them, and indeed had not been consulted over the later remonstrances. Even their own ranks showed signs of cracking as the full implications of their actions began to be visible. Sir Thomas Wentworth abandoned the opposition before the end of the session, and shortly after entered the royal service – a defection of considerable significance for the future.

Towards the end of August 1628 the Duke of Buckingham was assassinated. His death was the work of an unbalanced individual, not of a political conspiracy, but nevertheless it was widely and openly welcomed with rejoicing. Charles's personal distress at the loss of his friend was greatly intensified by this demonstration of popular feeling, which so sharply accentuated the gulf dividing the court from the remainder of the nation. Buckingham's death brought to an abrupt halt the 'inflation of honours', and ended his family's virtual monopoly of court favour. The king soon began to cut down the traffic in offices and to make a more equitable distribution of rewards. Nor did he ever again give his whole confidence to a single man. Neither Laud, nor Juxon, nor Wentworth ever approached Buckingham's stature as a courtier.

All this was to the good, and resulted in an appreciable improvement in Charles's relations with the secular peers, but it came too late to check the headlong decline in his relations with the 'country' at large. Buckingham's position had already ceased to be the centre of the political storm before he died, and his disappearance from the scene carried no guarantee of an improved attitude on the part of the Commons. Nevertheless, when Parliament reassembled in January 1629 the king seems to have been optimistic, in spite of recent friction over his continued attempts to levy tonnage and poundage. He was speedily disillusioned, for the complaints of the merchants who had been prosecuted were immediately taken up by the lower House who protested that the Petition of Right had been violated. Moreover within a few days Sir John Eliot had once again raised the temperature of discussion by introducing the subject of religious grievances. The promotion of Richard Montague,[16] the royal pardons given to Sibthorpe and Mainwaring, the translation of Laud to London, and above all the king's declaration of December 1628, gave him an abundance of ammunition. This last document, while laying great emphasis upon the king's responsibilities as supreme head, also explicitly confirmed and extended the jurisdiction of the Convocations:

> Out of our princely care that the churchmen may do the work that is proper unto them, the Bishops and Clergy, from time to time in Convocation, upon their humble desire shall have licence under our broad seal to deliberate of and to do all such things, as being made plain by them, and assented unto by us, shall concern the settled continuance of the doctrine and discipline of the Church of England now established; from which we will not endure any varying or departing in the least degree.

Eliot had an easy task, not merely to convince his hearers that all their anti-Arminian representations had been ignored, but that the king was planning a fresh assault upon the puritans, and was yielding step by step to the pressure of the Roman Anti-christ.

At the end of February the king felt obliged to intervene. In spite of their strong feelings, the 'country' leaders seem to have had no clear programme in mind beyond a further series of remonstrances, and their proceedings were becoming both pointless and abusive. On 2 March the Speaker declared the king's pleasure that the House should stand adjourned, nominally until the 20th. The result was the unprecedented and celebrated scene in which the opposition leaders prevented Finch from leaving his chair until a series of resolutions against catholicism, Arminianism, and tonnage and poundage, had been passed by acclamation. After a sharp disagreement within the Council, Charles decided that the only answer to such conduct was a dissolution, and

[16] Author of *Appello Caesarem* (1625), the classic statement of the alliance between Divine Right monarchy and High Church theology, promoted to the see of Chichester in 1628.

eight of the Commons' leaders, including Eliot, were committed to prison.

The king's action may well have prevented the 'country' leaders from losing touch with their supporters in their radical enthusiasm. As it was, he turned them into martyrs of a popular cause which was rapidly losing its political bearings, and gave them a chance to draw breath and assess the situation. The general atmosphere was bitterly hostile to the court, and a number of observers, both English and foreign, thought that rebellion was imminent. At the end of 1628 Salvetti, the agent of the Grand Duke of Tuscany, reported to his master that the 'growing and daring opposition of the people' would certainly result in serious disorders. Perhaps if the 'country' leaders had believed that they possessed the right of armed resistance, he would have been justified, but as yet they would not go so far. Englishmen no longer expressed their discontents in action with the spontaneity of the previous century, and the aristocracy continued to believe in the efficiency of civil or 'constitutional' action long after their grandfathers would have taken to their swords. This was partly because they were justifiably confident of their power in the localities. Court influence in the shires was at a very low ebb, and although resistance to the forced loan had not been unanimous, there was no sense of a real division of opinion among the country gentry. Nor does there seem to have been any significant increase in ordinary lawlessness, such as had often characterised periods of acute political tension in the past. The government's policy of disafforestation and enclosure in some western counties caused riots between 1628 and 1631, but there was no return to the high level of agrarian violence which had prevailed in the previous century. This was partly because, in spite of the rising tide of opposition, the king did not attempt a radical purge of the commissions of the peace. Individuals were removed for political reasons, notably for resistance to the forced loan, but their exclusion was seldom of long duration. For example, the resistance in Somerset was led by Robert Phelips, John Symes and Hugh Pyne. All three were removed from the commission, and Pyne was imprisoned in King's Bench. Phelips was pricked as sheriff to keep him out of the 1626 Parliament, and Symes followed him in that unwelcome but by no means disgraceful office. Both Phelips and Symes were restored to the commission in 1628, and in 1629 Pyne's son succeeded both to his father's estates and to his position on the bench. Similar examples could be quoted from other counties. Respect for the monarchy had declined during the decade, and the prestige of the nobility had suffered both from the 'inflation of honours' and from the association of many of their number with Buckingham and the court. But the grip of the county hierarchies upon local administration was unshaken.

It was not until the king began to rule without Parliament that these gentlemen came to regard the machinery of conciliar government as a threat to their interests and authority, and the fear of the prerogative extended to embrace the traditional equity jurisdiction of the Crown. When that happened, during the 1630s, one of the fundamental achievements of the Tudors had been undermined. Henry VII, Henry VIII and Elizabeth had all taught the gentry to look to the monarch as their leader and champion, and they had done so with only brief and local intermissions since the end of the fifteenth century. By the time the Long Parliament met that policy was in ruins and the politics of conflict had spread to the counties.

Part Four

THE COLLAPSE OF TRADITIONAL GOVERNMENT

1630-1660

During these years the traditional monarchy was demolished by a combination of political circumstances and personal incapacity, leaving a void which neither soldiers, saints nor constitutional engineers were able to fill. It was not, in the first instance, Parliament which made Charles I's personal government unworkable, but the refusal of the 'political nation' to pay prerogative taxes. Apart from its legal pretext, this refusal was not very different from the rejection of the 'amicable grant' in 1525, but Charles was much less alert to evidence of aristocratic exasperation than Henry VIII had been. A man of high principle and low intelligence, he had contrived by 1641 to offend almost every interest and susceptibility which commanded any general support. Staunch protestants believed that he had betrayed his trust as a 'Godly Prince'; lawyers and parliamentarians were convinced of his absolutist ambitions; and the county hierarchies feared that the persistent intrusions of the central government were intended to undermine their local authority. When the king also succeeded in provoking the Scots to open rebellion by his rash attack upon the Kirk, he was faced with a political opposition of overwhelming strength. In these circumstances he was forced to make concessions, but did so in such a manner as to create no confidence in his sincerity, and consequently no basis for future trust and co-operation. This grudging and inflexible attitude brought some advantages, as it may have been designed to do. The king's opponents were not revolutionaries. Monarchy was the only form of government they understood and approved, and monarchy was intimately associated with those ideas of social hierarchy and discipline which they had no intention of abandoning. When forced to the point of decision, many of them preferred an unsatisfactory king like Charles to the destructive possibilities of continued opposition.

As a result the united front of 1641 began to disintegrate.

Charles's position was at least coherent. He was the lawful king, and it was his duty and responsibility to rule and to suppress disobedience. None of this could his opponents deny, and their sole programme consisted of seeking to make him rule in accordance with their wills rather than his own. What would eventually happen if both sides continued recalcitrant, no one could imagine, and it says a great deal for the strength of the feelings which Charles had aroused that a large proportion of his opponents were prepared to face the unknown rather than trust to his 'good lordship'. From the king's point of view there were distinct advantages in driving his enemies into open rebellion, but they stood to gain nothing from a military arbitration. If they lost they would face a traitor's death; if they won they would have done no more than recreate the political situation of 1641. Three years of inconclusive fighting resulted, until a group emerged within the parliamentary ranks who were prepared to face up to the logic of victory, and to work for it wholeheartedly. Charles never grasped the significance of this development until it was too late. Although his armies were defeated, and he himself a prisoner, he continued to believe that the 'political nation' could not frame a government without him. In a sense he was right, but the men whom military success had placed in command of the situation did not really belong to the 'political nation'. They did not share its assumptions, and had other criteria of judgement. Although reluctant to do so, in the last analysis they were prepared to destroy both the king and the traditional machinery of royal government, if these could not be made to serve their purposes.

Charles therefore ended, like Samson in the Temple; by bringing down the whole political order in his own fall. To bring about his defeat, his opponents had called up a demon in the shape of the New Model Army, which they could not control and which destroyed their own power as completely as the king's. Fortunately, Cromwell and his officers were to some extent reluctant revolutionaries. In cutting down the Tudor monarchy, they left the social and administrative roots in the ground, so that when their own creative efforts had failed in turn, a modified form of the old order was able to grow again after 1660.

CHAPTER 14

THE FAILURE OF COMMUNICATION

Princes are to be indulgent, nursing fathers to their people; their modest liberties, their sober rights ought to be precious in their eyes . . . Subjects, on the other hand, ought with solicitous eyes of jealousy to watch over the prerogatives of a crown; the authority of a king is the keystone which closeth up the arch of government and order, which contains each part in due relation to the whole, and which, once shaken, infirmed, all the frame falls together into a confused heap. (Sir Thomas Wentworth at his installation as President of the Council of the North).

CHARLES'S FINANCIAL EXPEDIENTS

The dissolution of Parliament in March 1629 was probably a mistake, although an understandable one in the circumstances. After the Petition of Right the opposition had manifestly run out of ideas, and the disadvantages of having put all their eggs in the parliamentary basket had become clear. In spite of all their clamour and efforts, the Commons had not progressed beyond the concept of using their traditional functions to limit and direct the king's government. Having led their horse to the water, they could not make him drink. A ten year lapse caused this failure to be conveniently forgotten and preserved the high prestige of Parliament as the defender of the common weal. At the same time, without the constant and exhausting struggles at Westminster to draw attention to his subjects' discontents, Charles was able to persuade himself that these much discussed grievances had no substance outside the minds of a few seditious troublemakers and need not seriously affect his dealings with the faithful majority.[1]

[1] It was a feature of this whole period of tension and crisis that Charles continued to blame 'the peevishness of some few factious spirits' for all his troubles. This made him ultimately unable to distinguish between the criticism of the 'country' in the 1620s and the radicalism of the 1640s. By treating all alike he played into the hands of the extremists. For this lack of perception the artificial and cloistered atmosphere of the court was largely to blame.

The king still had the power to govern, and this might yet prove sufficient if he could divide his opponents and defeat them in detail. During the session of 1629 the Lords had been at odds with the Commons, and the latter had been at odds among themselves. In a confused exchange with his judges during April and May, Charles insisted on the imprisoned members being refused bail, an action which would certainly have caused a storm had another session been in prospect. In the circumstances it was not challenged, except by the prisoners themselves.[2] At the same time he defeated a trade boycott by the Merchant Adventurers, who had suspended operations in March 1629 as a protest against the continued collection of tonnage and poundage. A London merchant named Richard Chambers was fined £2,000 in Star Chamber for denouncing the dues and was sentenced to imprisonment until he acknowledged his fault. By the end of May trade was flowing normally, and the dues continued to be paid.

These successes appeared to confirm the view that only Parliament could offer any real challenge to the prerogative and encouraged the king to believe that the political crisis which had seemed imminent in the previous year could be indefinitely evaded. In fact the suspension of Parliament, while it checked the operations of the 'country' as a constitutional pressure group, strengthened rather than weakened its hostility to the court, and increased the probability that hostility would find more direct methods of expressing itself. At the same time the viability of prerogative government depended very largely upon adequate finance. Charles had prudently ended the futile Spanish war in 1628 and patched up his relations with France. As long as he could continue to avoid foreign entanglements there was some prospect of managing successfully on his ordinary revenue, for the precedent of Cranfield's administration was hopeful. On the other hand, in spite of a comparatively sober court, costs continued to rise and the ordinary revenues themselves were a source of constant friction with his subjects. Moreover, a régime

[2] They were charged in King's Bench with conspiracy, defamation of the king's ministers, and assault on the Speaker. Eliot took the lead in refusing to acknowledge the jurisdiction of the court. He was fined £2,000 and remained in prison, refusing to admit his guilt, until his death from consumption in November 1632.

which could do no more than survive by abdicating its foreign policy for the foreseeable future did not satisfy the Stuart concept of monarchy. Inevitably Charles attempted to make himself genuinely independent of Parliament by exploiting traditional sources of revenue far beyond the traditional limits. This coloured every aspect of his policy and administration between 1629 and 1640 and eventually produced among the propertied classes a unanimity and determination in opposition greatly in excess of anything that the 'country' leaders had succeeded in creating during the previous decade. It also germinated a small seed of genuine radicalism, which despaired of the existing political structure altogether.

In theory, as we have seen, the government's economic and social policies were paternalistic, based upon protection and stability. In practice they were based upon vested interest and financial necessity. Thus while the Privy Council made strenuous efforts to enforce the Poor Laws and control the price of grain, royal patentees and monopolists pushed up their prices without scruple and individual ministers such as Wentworth sold their grain in excess of the permitted prices with complete impunity. The Tudor enclosure commission was revived in 1633 to protect small tenants against enclosing landlords. But while a number of landlords were proceeded against in Star Chamber and fined, the Crown itself was carrying out extensive enclosures on its own estates in an effort to improve their profitability. In the royal forests of Braydon, Gillingham and Dean hundreds of armed commoners rioted on a number of occasions between 1628 and 1631 to defend their customary rights against enclosures. In these circumstances the landlords fined by Star Chamber felt a legitimate sense of grievance, and there was nothing to prevent them from raising their fines by intensifying pressure upon their tenants.

The interests of the commoners in fact received scant consideration from either the aristocracy or the Crown. Apart from the activities of his own officers, Charles was prepared to sell the right to enclose commons to a wealthy man such as the Earl of Worcester, and the practical effects of the enclosure commission were negligible. The erratic attempts of the Privy Council and the conciliar courts to enforce the protective elements of the Poor Law similarly proved to be of little benefit to the poor, but aroused among the justices a grave suspicion that the central government was attempting to undermine their social power.[3]

An equally ambivalent attitude can be seen in relation to trade and industry. Mercantilist theories about national self-sufficiency caused certain industries to be encouraged, notably ship-building, alum processing and the making of gun-powder. At the same time official reactions to most industrial enterprise were hostile or indifferent. It was feared that social mobility and change would cause violent unrest, and that the amassing of capitalist fortunes would disturb the social hierarchy and impoverish the aristocracy. There was an element of pure snobbery about this, which was supported by such antiquated laws as that which laid down the principle that it was disparagement for a ward in chivalry to marry a *burgensis*. It also reflected the decaying economic morality of the middle ages – the concept of the 'just price and the condemnation of usury. Archbishop Laud was speaking with the voice of Latimer when he claimed during a Star Chamber case against a group of land speculators that 'this last year's famine was made by man, and not by God'.[4] Consequently the government continued to put its weight behind that complex system of regulation and control which had put over two hundred and fifty statutes on the rolls during the sixteenth century. In part this anxiety was perfectly genuine. When the clothing industry was depressed (as most of it was throughout the 1620s) the government did its best to prevent employers from laying off their workers, and some attempts were made to improve working conditions.

On the other hand the Tudor system had also created an immense variety of vested interests and fiscal opportunities. Privileges, patents and monopolies were all means whereby the Crown and the beneficiaries were able to turn the artificial restriction of trade and industry to profitable account. A statute of 1624 had forbidden the issue of monopolies to individuals but Charles

[3] The ministers of the prerogative government entertained ambitions of centralising the administration which were beyond their resources and succeeded only in irritating opinion in the counties. It was this conciliar interference, as much as anything else, which made 'thorough' appear tyrannical to the gentry.

[4] There is a strong echo of Protector Somerset about the social and economic policy of the government in this period, but the fact that it was associated with the High Church party no doubt strengthened puritan inclinations towards free enterprise. These inclinations had not been manifested by the protestants of the 1540s.

evaded this without difficulty by making his grants to chartered companies. Some of these were genuinely mercantile concerns, such as the East India Company or the Merchant Adventurers. Others, like the holders of the soap monopoly, were just cover organisations for groups of courtiers. In 1638 the king chartered a new company of beaver makers which was controlled by a small group of capitalists with court connections who virtually ruined the actual craftsmen by forcing them to trade through the company and charging exorbitant sums for membership.

It has been estimated that the king derived about £100,000 a year from monopolies in the late 1630s, which largely explains his attachment to the system. Nevertheless, as a means of taxing economic activity they were extraordinarily inefficient. For every shilling raised by the customs, tenpence reached the Exchequer. For every corresponding price increase caused to the consumer by a monopoly, 1½d went to the king, and 10½d to the monopolist. Had their purpose been wholly fiscal, it is hard to see why the king should have persisted with them in the face of so much criticism. But they were also an important part of the general defence of economic privilege. Interlopers were discouraged by prosecutions and fines in which the privileged organisations themselves co-operated with the royal courts and officials. Similar policies were applied at the local level by upholding guilds in their attempts to enforce apprenticeship regulations, as the Privy Council did with the glovers and shoemakers of Chester, or in upholding the rights of corporate towns such as Wigan and Preston against the new clothing villages of Lancashire.

This conciliar activity, with its doctrinaire basis, aroused a great deal of resentment among those whose prosperity depended upon a measure of freedom, such as the clothing workers of East Anglia and the metallurgical craftsmen of Birmingham. In some places the local justices shared this hostility. In 1634 the commissioners in Lancashire refused to prosecute middlemen for not buying their flax at Preston, nor would they enforce apprenticeship among the producers of the 'new draperies' – alleging that such regulations only resulted in unemployment. The whole policy of close control was coming to be questioned, and many contemporaries doubted whether it provided the best protection for the economically vulnerable. 'This strict looking to the markets is the reason why the markets are smaller, the corn dearer,' claimed the Hertfordshire justices in 1631, and their colleagues in Dorset agreed with them. There were so many laws, protested one merchant, that they contradicted each other and could not be enforced. Not surprisingly, the government's good faith came to be doubted, and it was claimed that such rules only existed to provide the king with revenue by selling permission to break them.

Apart from the courtiers the only men who undoubtedly gained from this policy were the privileged corporations. The great London based companies received the full support of the Crown in putting down unlicensed rivals and deemed this support to be worth the large sums which they had to pay for their Charters.[5] The city fathers of Newcastle or Norwich or Bristol were similarly protected. For example, the monopoly of selling coal in London made the fortunes of Newcastle hostmen and merchant venturers such as Sir Henry Anderson and Leonard Carr. The implications of this also extended into urban government, where the handful of wealthy men, who formed the ruling oligarchy in each place, were consistently backed against any challenge from the unprivileged citizenry. Norwich was ruled by twenty-four aldermen, Bristol by twelve, Exeter by twenty-four, and these small groups were self-selecting and self-perpetuating. The mayors and aldermen were sheriffs and justices within their own jurisdictions, and the government's attitude was an aspect of its general concern with order and discipline, since the closely packed masses of the towns were notoriously prone to riot and mayhem. In 1628 the Privy Council communicated to the magistrates of Norwich its anxiety that 'the orderly government of city and corporations should be maintained, and that popular and factious humours that trouble the same should be suppressed and punished'. Such a policy naturally inclined the favoured municipalities towards the court, but sharpened the antagonism of those who hovered on the fringes of the ruling groups. There were many such, men of substance and often minor office holders or leaders of inferior guilds, whose aspirations to local power were frustrated by the exclusiveness

[5] Theoretically the high price of these Charters was supposed to cover the cost of protecting the companies' ships from piracy, but in fact the government was extremely inefficient at providing this service, and most companies preferred to organise their own convoys. Political and diplomatic protection within the state system was rather more real.

of those in possession. Every city had a long history of conflict between 'in' and 'out' groups of this kind, but in the political atmosphere of the 1630s it was natural that they should take on the guise of 'court' and 'country', although this equation cannot be pursued too far because of the complicating factor of religion. Puritanism frequently weakened the 'court' allegiance of those who stood to gain from the king's policies economically, although the converse was not so often true.

For the most part urban politics played only a minor role on the national stage. Even cities like Newcastle and Norwich had fewer than 15,000 inhabitants and correspondingly small resources, so that their influence was local and their outlook predominantly parochial. London, however, was a different matter. A great city by any contemporary standard, its population in the 1630s stood at about 350,000, and in 1633 the Lord Mayor, Sir Ralph Freeman, boasted that he and his twenty-six aldermen could buy out any hundred burgomasters of Amsterdam. The resources of London, and of its leading citizens, were vast (the property qualification for the status of alderman stood at £10,000); and its population was turbulent and outspoken. In 1598 John Stow had written, 'London is a mighty arm and instrument to bring any great desire to effect, if it may be won to a man's devotion; whereof . . . there want not examples in English history'. It handled by this time almost seven-eighths of the national trade, and although this overwhelming predominance was lamented by many it provided a great market without which much of the prosperity of southern England and much of the lively coastwise trade would have languished. Able young men from the provinces sought their fortunes there, and later endowed schools and hospitals in the towns and villages from which they had sprung, or returned to buy landed estates and hope that their sons would be accepted into the local aristocracy.

London was a national institution, and a political power of the first importance. It was also, inevitably, a major factor in royal finance, being constantly called upon to lend, or to underwrite the king's obligations. In 1617 the City had guaranteed a loan of £100,000 subscribed by the wealthier citizens, which was supposed to be repaid within a year at 10 per cent interest. James defaulted, both upon the capital and the interest, although fair words and promises kept hope alive for several years. Hopefully, another £60,000 was raised for Charles I shortly after his accession, but in spite of renewed promises, this was never fully repaid either. By 1628 the City would lend only upon ample security and received an extensive grant of Crown lands which were supposed to cover the king's outstanding debts in addition to a further loan of £120,000 raised in that year. Unfortunately disputes arose over the disposal of these lands; Charles unwisely accused the City of malpractices and compelled the Corporation to compound for its alleged offences. In the circumstances this was to add insult to injury, and for the next ten years the government's credit was so impaired that no further attempt could be made to raise loans from this source.

Another substantial source of friction and bad feeling was the Ulster plantation, in which the Corporation had taken part most unwillingly on the king's insistence. This project had begun in 1610, and various livery companies had contributed large sums levied upon their members. By 1630 a net loss of about £50,000 had been incurred, but in spite of this in 1631 the Attorney General entered a bill in Star Chamber accusing the Corporation of fraud and excessive profit. The case did not come to trial until 1635, when the City was fined £70,000 and forfeited its Irish lands.[6] Charles's intention seems to have been one of intimidation, following his decision to call no more Parliaments. According to Sir John Coke he hoped to 'break the confidence of the times that have encroached upon him, and increase his royalties and revenues in an ample and fair manner'. In other words to use the Star Chamber to extract, under cover of litigation, those large sums of money which he could no longer obtain either by taxation or by commercial loan. As some compensation for this dubious proceeding, the king in 1638 granted London a new Charter, amplifying some of its privileges. This, together with the fact that he consistently supported the oligarchic Court of Aldermen,[7] and defended the privileges of the liverymen against the unenfranchised, prevented any open

[6] The bulk of this fine was eventually remitted, but the City had to pay £12,000 in addition to its earlier losses and the loss of the lands.

[7] London's government worked in three tiers: at the top the Lord Mayor and the Court of Aldermen, which possessed the full executive authority; next the Common Council of about 250, nominally chosen by all freemen, which was the legislature; and finally the Court of Common Hall, which elected the four City M.P.s, nominated to various other offices, and was restricted to the liverymen – the élite of each company.

breach with the Corporation. At the same time those elements within the city which were discontented with its government, and this included a number of wealthy and influential men, were naturally encouraged to side with the 'country' – and it was such people who protested against the forced loan, suspended their trade in 1629, and later resisted the imposition of ship money. When the crisis of the reign came in 1641, these political struggles within the City were to play a crucial part in determining the national balance of power.

Relations between the Crown and the Corporation during the 1630s were delicate and inclined to be cool, but never hostile. The ordinary population of the City, on the other hand, became increasingly antagonistic to the court and apt to the hand of the religious or political agitator. This animosity can to some extent be attributed to London's own political tensions, but it was undoubtedly stimulated by the presence in their midst of so many of those great capitalists and monopolists who were the subjects of such universal execration. Sir Paul Pindar, Sir Nicholas Crispe, Sir William Russell and many others were men who had succeeded in turning the financial exigencies of the Crown to their own advantage. As individuals or in *ad hoc* groups they frequently advanced the substantial sums which the king could no longer obtain from the Corporation itself. In return they might receive titles, as Sir Baptist Hicks did in 1628, additional privileges or exemptions for their companies, or offices of profit. Sir William Russell became Treasurer of the Navy and recouped his loans out of the opportunities which that position put in his way. Such an arrangement clearly suited the king better than having to make repayment in cash, but it did not make the administration either more efficient or more popular.

The most conspicuous example of this kind of transaction was the General Farm of the customs which enabled the Crown to anticipate its largest single source of revenue and placed immense opportunities for profit in the hands of the farmers. The General Farmers were a syndicate of very wealthy City merchants and bankers who paid the Crown a fixed rent in return for the right to collect dues at the ports. This rent was constantly reviewed, and in 1638-9 stood at £172,500. How much profit the farmers actually made is uncertain because they were all men with numerous interests, but they were well able to anticipate their rents and to make additional loans when these were called for.[8] Their intimate relations with the court exposed them to particularly fierce animosity, and led to the ruin of their fortunes in the years after 1641.

OPPOSITION TO THE ECCLESIASTICAL REVIVAL

The position of these great entrepreneurs was thus analogous to that of the bishops, whose advancement also involved them in a particular relationship with the monarch. As we have already seen, puritan hatred of the episcopate had a long history, going back to the origins of English presbyterianism in the 1570s. Whitgift and Bancroft had virtually killed presbyterianism in the 1590s, but it had left behind a seed of animosity which the High Church party awakened to new and vigorous life. After 1600 the bishops were criticised not so much because their office was unscriptural as because they resisted the puritan programme of reform and became involved in the political pretensions of divine right. Parliamentary leaders such as John Pym and Sir Simonds D'Ewes spoke for the great majority of their followers when they 'allowed ancient and Godly bishops', but attacked the claims and practices of the current incumbents. There were thus three distinct elements in the anti-episcopal agitations of the 1620s and 1630s. The first, which was genuinely radical and sectarian, was of very small importance before the meeting of the Long Parliament. The second belonged to a century-old tradition of protest and complaint: the bishops were indifferent to parochial discipline and the shortage of good preachers, too fond of ceremonial and blind to the abuses of pluralism and low clerical standards. The third sprang directly from the growth of 'Arminianism' and its patronage by the Crown. This was partly doctrinal and partly Erastian in its inspiration, expressing itself in suspicions of 'popery' and in violent objections to ecclesiastical jurisdiction. The king's support for this jurisdiction, and the consequent revival of clerical power in the state, eventually helped to turn a deep rooted religious tradition into political opposition and make puritanism one of the dominant features of the 'country'. 'What was it,' asked the presbyterian divine Thomas

[8] There was a considerable growth of trade during the 1630s, when England benefited economically from the government's inability to intervene in the European conflict. This growth was probably not fairly reflected in the increase of the farm, since increasing demands upon the farmers had to be compensated for by better opportunities for profit.

Edwards in 1646, 'that ruined the Bishops and that party, but their grasping and meddling with all at once, Church and Commonwealth both, provoking all sorts of persons against them, nobility, gentry, City ministers, common people . . . ?'

Puritan attitudes had been strong in the English Church since the 1560s, and had been expressed in countless petitions, bills and pamphlets. Although the majority of puritan leaders were clergy it was not, except in its presbyterian form, a clerical movement. Lay patronage had always been important, and continued to be so. 'If the patron be precise,' wrote Robert Burton, 'so must his chaplain be . . . or else be turned out.' Puritan gentry and nobility controlled large numbers of advowsons and were frequently able to provide for and protect those clergy whose views they shared. Also, poverty had afflicted the majority of English livings since before the Reformation, so that the willingness of puritan patrons to provide some augmentations, and of puritan companies and corporations to endow lectureships, were other factors which increased their influence. Similarly in 1625 there came into existence that *ad hoc* group of puritan laymen known as the Feoffees for Impropriations. The aim of this body was to buy up and restore to parochial use those rectorial tithes which had been originally acquired by monastic houses and had subsequently passed into secular hands. The ecclesiastical authorities naturally regarded the activities of these Feoffees with suspicion, and they were eventually suppressed upon the grounds that they were also purchasing advowsons (in the puritan interest) which was *ultra vires* by their terms of association.

In spite of the logical implications of a faith based upon the scriptures alone, there was nothing revolutionary about the bulk of this puritanism. The royal supremacy was built into its foundations, and, as the authors of the Millenary Petition had told the new king in 1604,

> divers of us that sue for reformation have formerly, in respect of the times, subscribed to the Book [of Common Prayer], some upon protestation, some upon exposition given them, some with conditions, rather than the Church should have been deprived of their labour and ministry.

This was very much the advice which Bullinger had given to the first generation of Elizabethan bishops, and in spite of his quarrels with the puritan leaders James had never really striven to create a situation in which it could not be followed.

Laud and his followers had different ideas. This 'occasional conformity' was not sufficient to satisfy the strenuous Bishop of London, and he began to deprive incumbents whose subscriptions did not convince him of their sincerity. As Archbishop of Canterbury from 1633 onwards he strove to tighten up the whole administration of the Church, and although some bishops continued to be latitudinarian, their number steadily decreased. Whereas Archbishop Mathew of York had taken virtually no action against conscientious nonconformists between 1606 and 1628, Archbishop Neile carried out a number of deprivations after 1632. At the same time the nature of conformity changed, becoming harder for puritan consciences to accommodate. In addition to the surplice and the Prayer Book which had satisfied the Elizabethan and Jacobean authorities, Laud demanded the sign of the cross in baptism, kneeling at communion, and a number of other liturgical gestures. Above all he insisted upon the eastward position of the communion table and its isolation by rails. To most Englishmen, whether puritans or not, this turned the table into an altar, and by implication revived the intercessory function of the priesthood. It was this, more than any other single fact, which caused the Arminians to be accused of popery. In truth the general conclusion was incorrect, because the Laudians came nowhere near to a doctrine of transubstantiation. but the Archbishop reacted to criticism with irritation and did not deign to explain his views in a way which the majority of his opponents could have understood. Moreover it was substantially true that the High Churchmen had abandoned the fundamental reformed doctrine of the priesthood of all believers. *Iure divino* episcopacy and the apostolic succession cut right across the main Anglican tradition. As a recent scholar has written; 'in place of the Elect Nation, Laud offered the Elect Church'.[9] In place of the Godly Prince he raised up the Godly Bishop, with the king's full approval, and in place of the indifferent Erastianism of Elizabeth an ecclesiastical régime which took its spiritual and moral jurisdiction with the greatest seriousness. Laud opposed the puritans, not out of a sense of loyalty to the Crown, but out of faith in the Church as he saw it, conscience to conscience, integrity against integrity. In such a position there was no room for flexibility, and in such a conflict no

[9] J. P. Kenyon, in *The Stuart Constitution*, 147. For a full consideration of this point, see W. M. Lamont, *Godly Rule*.

opportunity for negotiation.

In these circumstances the revival of clerical authority was inevitable. This brought a new lease of life to the ecclesiastical courts, and many allies of convenience to the puritan cause. The Archbishop was no respecter of persons and proceeded impartially against cottager and gentleman alike. The gentry, who had long been accustomed to have their moral peccadilloes overlooked by an indulgent (not to say subservient) clergy, now found themselves subjected to humiliating censures and damaging fines which could be enforced by the full power of the king's prerogative. In fact Laud carried out the majority of his important prosecutions not in High Commission but in Star Chamber. It was there that Bastwick, Leighton and Prynne were sentenced and the lay Feoffees proceeded against. This brought a bitter unpopularity to the court which had been for over a century regarded as a powerful instrument of justice, and which even Sir Edward Coke had described as being of high honour and integrity. Not only did Star Chamber lose much of its prestige by being used for ecclesiastical purposes, it also damaged its reputation by a severe use of corporal punishment. William Prynne, John Lilburne and a small number of other puritan agitators were pilloried, whipped and mutilated by order of the court. Such punishments were very commonly inflicted upon the lower orders, but these men were gentlemen and by tradition exempt from such humiliations. Although there were only about ten such cases out of 236 heard by Star Chamber between 1631 and 1640, they aroused an extraordinary degree of indignation, and the victims hastened to seek redress from Parliament as soon as it met. Hostile observers noted that an unusual number of bishops were now sitting upon the board, and that they were more inclined to severity than their lay colleagues, even when the issues were not ecclesiastical.

By 1635 Star Chamber had, in effect, taken the place of High Commission as the supreme tribunal for religious offences as well as dealing with Crown cases of a secular nature, while the proportion of private business fell away. In 1633 a certain Allen, parson of Sudbury in Suffolk, sued a group of his parishioners for riot when they refused to kneel for the communion and, having found the High Commission ineffective, brought the case to Star Chamber. At the same time the vast majority of cases going before the Commissioners were party issues, and such 'office' cases as there were tended to be of small significance. The Church had to some extent recovered from its long political eclipse. On 6 March 1636 William Laud noted in his diary, 'William Juxon, Lord Bishop of London, made Lord High Treasurer of England. No churchman had it since Henry VII's time . . . And now if the church will not hold up themselves under God, I can do no more.'

The puritans objected both to the way in which this power was used, and to the power itself. Their concept of spiritual discipline was congregational rather than episcopal, the 'good bishop' being a co-ordinator and guide rather than a ruler. For them there was only one machinery of authority, and that was the secular hierarchy of king, Parliament and magistracy to whom belonged all authority of a public nature in Church and state. There was nothing democratic about this view, and no hint of 'toleration' in the modern sense. Like Cranmer in 1555, they were defending a concept of the royal supremacy which the monarchy had abandoned. Charles had seen fit to restore a measure of the *potestas jurisdictionis* to the Church which the puritans maintained was an inalienable part of his own office. Moreover, since he shared that office with the Parliament, which represented the realm, he had doubly offended against the fundamental laws of the kingdom. The House of Commons had objected to his programme in the most explicit terms, but its protests had been ignored. Many Englishmen who were not puritans in any deep religious sense could share their belief that the king had betrayed his God-given responsibility and handed over the Church of England to a group of quasi-papists who would 'sell out' to the Roman Antichrist at the first available opportunity. Fears of this nature cut across family connections and economic interests, and they also allied powerfully with other fears of a legal and constitutional nature to strengthen the 'country' during the early 1630s when it was seeking for a new method of expression.

Puritanism had always been a potentially dangerous solvent of that ideology of obedience which the Tudors had striven so hard to create. As we have seen, the puritan view of political obligation was basically functional and depended upon the Calvinist concept of the Will of God. This had been apparent in the work of Christopher Goodman, and to a lesser extent of John Ponet, both of whom had been concerned to provide grounds for resistance to a catholic ruler, and who had led the protestant retreat from passive obedience in the 1550s. Consequently the puritans were inclined to reject any image of the state which implied that unquestioning submission was the proper or unavoidable lot of the subject. This applied particularly to the traditional metaphors of the human body and the family. While to Sibthorpe the prince was a head, in relation to which his subjects were hands and feet, even to so moderate a puritan as William Pemberton, writing in 1619, the magistrates were the 'masters and pilots of the ship of the commonwealth, who sit at the stern and guide it forward through their wisdom and fidelity . . . unto the desired haven of peace and prosperity'. Although both would have regarded obedience as a means rather than an end in itself, the practical implications of these two images were widely different. The hands and feet have neither the will nor the means to challenge the mastery of the brain – the very suggestion is unnatural, or 'monstrous'. The crew of a ship, on the other hand, may have a very good idea as to whether it is steering a true course, although it may not be their normal function to navigate. The puritan, possessing a clear vision of the divine purpose, felt himself qualified to declare whether the ship of state was being steered in a Godly direction or not. The success which Elizabeth had enjoyed in harnessing puritan eschatology to the service of the Crown had created a precedent which men were slow to forget. But by the 1630s puritan disillusionment with Charles as a 'Godly Prince' in the Elizabethan tradition had reached that level at which serious erosion of political obedience began. Those who did not wish to take refuge in the New World or in the outer fringes of sectarian separatism, sought a programme of political action in their calling to the service of God.

POLITICAL DEADLOCK

It was religion, more than anything else, which divided the civil service and makes it impossible for the historian to equate office with devotion to the court. Professor Aylmer has shown that there were numerous catholics in high positions during the 1630s, although most held their beliefs in secret or avowed them only on their death-beds.[10] The Earl of Portland (Lord Treasurer 1628-35), Lord Francis Cottington (Chancellor of the Exchequer 1629-42) and Sir Francis Windebank (Secretary of State 1632-40)

[10] G. E. Aylmer, *The King's Servants*, 357.

were merely the most obvious of a numerous group who aroused the anger and suspicion of the protestants by the influence which they were supposedly exercising over royal policy. In fact the catholics seem to have been divided upon most political issues, but they were bound to uphold the prerogative in self-defence, and they symbolised the estrangement of England from the suffering and striving protestantism of continental Europe. Most of the diplomats who served Charles abroad during these years seem to have wished for a more protestant foreign policy, and while this argues a lack of sympathy with the king on their part it also argues a lack of any conscious partisanship on his, since he could easily have removed them from their posts.

In fact it is impossible to speak of 'parties' among the king's servants, except for the known catholics, since the attitudes of most are not clearly known. Those who were obviously puritans must have been hostile to Laud, and those who were closely associated with the Providence Island Company, like Sir Gilbert Gerrard, were presumably sympathetic to the opposition, since that Company provided the 'cover' organisation which kept the 'country' leaders in constant touch with each other during the years without a Parliament. However, this did not prevent the puritan Earl of Northumberland from being appointed Lord Admiral in 1638 and filling the Admiralty with his religious associates. Nor does the hostility of numerous middle-ranking civil servants to the court prove any more than the fact that their hopes of promotion had been frustrated. Whilst the king occasionally deprived notorious enemies of the prerogative like Sir John Eliot of offices of profit, there was no systematic exclusion of puritans or others with suspect antecedents. The officials remained a fair cross section of the aristocracy, which was not as paradoxical as it sounds since neither hatred of catholics, hostility to Arminians nor dislike of the prerogative government as yet implied any radical attack upon the king's authority. Consequently, to say that numerous civil servants were antagonistic to the court and critical of its religious attitudes is not to represent them as a 'pre-incarnation' of the parliamentary party of the civil war.

The same is true of those who opposed such other manifestations of prerogative government as the Council of the North which, under Wentworth's presidency, acquired a new energy and purpose. Wentworth was the prime architect of the policy which he called 'thorough' and which involved a steady and unrelenting administrative pressure to break down the resistance of those who either opposed the government's financial demands or objected to its emphasis upon religious conformity. He ruled the north with a strong hand, but after 1633, when he became in addition Lord Deputy of Ireland, the effectiveness of the Council was somewhat impaired, and Wentworth's local enemies were able to turn his high handed methods to the discredit of the court. Without a professional bureaucracy on the French model, 'thorough' was not a realistic conception. Without a consensus of aristocratic opinion to support them, neither the provincial Councils nor the Privy Council itself could be more than spasmodically effective. In view of the historical development of English local government and the relative weakness of Charles's Privy Council, it is remarkable that the early 1630s did not see more resistance, at least to his financial devices. The fact seems to have been that the opposition lacked organisation at the county level, and that individuals or small groups were reluctant to challenge the power of Star Chamber. Lacking any coherent theory of resistance,[11] and accustomed for many years to express their opinions on national issues through the House of Commons, the gentry were temporarily at a loss to know how to deal with 'thorough'.

This may have induced a sense of security in the isolated atmosphere of the court, but time was not on the king's side. Although he was able virtually to ignore a debt of over £1 million which had piled up by 1629, it still required constant application to sustain the ordinary revenue at an adequate level. From 1630 to 1635 the king's income averaged £600,000, leaving a trifling deficit of no more than £20,000 a year. In order to achieve this, however, the Lord Treasurer, Richard Weston (created Earl of Portland in 1633), was forced to resort to methods which might have been designed to cause the maximum irritation to the aristocracy. The activities of the Court of Wards were intensified; the price of wardships rose, and the chances of

[11] The first open advocation of armed resistance to the king seems to have been made in a sermon preached in September 1639 by Dr Calybute Downing to the Artillery Company of London. His conclusion was that the government was under the control of a 'Jesuitical faction', and might lawfully be overthrown in the cause of true religion. After his oration Downing felt it wise to leave London and retire to the Earl of Warwick's house in Essex. Zagorin, *Court and Country*, 145.

evasion diminished. The obsolete forest laws were revived, and large numbers of land-owners were heavily fined for technical encroachments on lands which had not in fact been used as forest for centuries. The fourteenth century statute requiring all men worth £40 a year in land to receive knighthood was invoked in order that large sums could be collected in compositions for default. With the possible exception of the forest fines there was nothing remotely illegal about these exactions which stemmed from the traditional feudal and military relationship between the Crown and its vassals.

On the other hand the resentment which they caused made it extremely likely that any sudden crisis would shatter the eroded shell of acquiescence. That crisis came, in the first instance, over ship money. Ship money was a traditional composition levied upon the coastal towns in lieu of their obligation to supply vessels for coastal defence. The first writs sent out for this purpose in 1634 were in strict accordance with precedent and met with no objection. Almost 99 per cent of the sum demanded was collected. The following year writs were sent out again, this time to the inland counties as well, and still resistance was negligible. In 1636, however, when a third writ was issued requiring contributions from all, numerous voices were raised in protest. In theory ship money was an emergency device, levied by the king in virtue of his 'absolute prerogative', yet in practice it was clearly becoming a regular tax. The fact that, at this stage, most of the money raised was actually spent upon the navy was not really relevant. If the king could tax by his emergency power in this fashion, no doubt the ingenuity of his servants would discover other methods by which he could do so. The monarchy had such deep rooted resources of authority and obedience that even a temporary affluence on Charles's part could have made a decisive difference to his long term prospects.

It was therefore of the first importance that a test case was fought in Exchequer Chamber in 1637. This arose from the refusal of John Hampden (a very rich man) to pay his assessed levy of £1. The court decided against him by a very narrow margin, but it was a Pyrrhic victory for the government since Chief Justice Finch in giving judgement stated explicitly that no Act of Parliament could 'bind the king not to command his subjects, their persons and goods'. The decision was, and was generally understood to be, a statement of principle; 'no more looked upon as the case of one man, but the case of the kingdom,' as Edward Hyde was to write later. The effects were immediate, and politically disastrous for the Crown. Charles's whole hope of success had lain in preventing the opposition to his régime from crystallising. Hampden's case raised a standard to which the propertied classes rallied, since the judges' logic 'left no man anything which he might call his own'. In 1636 ship money had raised almost £190,000 or 96½ per cent of what was demanded. In 1637 89 per cent was collected, but by 1638 the proportion had fallen to 39 per cent and in the following year to 20 per cent. Receipts from other sources also fell away, although not so dramatically. The tax-paying classes were on strike, and the fragile balance of the king's finances was destroyed.

How long Charles might have held out against the inevitable demand for a Parliament is uncertain. In the event the situation in Scotland added a new element of crisis in 1639, while at the same time offering a flimsy hope of distracting the English aristocracy from their own grievances. James had succeeded in curbing the Kirk by breaking the alliance between the nobility and the presbyterian ministers which had been the foundation of the Scottish Reformation. By 1618 he had succeeded in imposing a precarious episcopate, and in that year persuaded the General Assembly to accept the Five Articles of Perth which provided for a modified form of Anglican ceremonial. In 1619 a Scottish Prayer Book was prepared, but the obvious unpopularity of the Articles caused its introduction to be postponed indefinitely. Charles seems to have been quite unaware of the nature of his father's achievement in the northern kingdom, or of its precariousness. In 1625 he shattered the *entente* with the Scottish aristocracy by re-annexing all the Crown and Church land which had been alienated since 1542. This was certainly an effective answer to the problem of ecclesiastical poverty, but hardly a single substantial family was unaffected, and there was no longer any possibility that the nobility would assist the king against a recalcitrant Assembly. In 1633 he visited Edinburgh for the first time since his childhood and was solemnly crowned at the royal palace of Holyrood. If this was intended to stimulate the loyalty of his Scottish subjects, it failed disastrously since the Arminian ritual used by Laud and the other English divines was regarded with incredulous horror, and the natural suspicion of English interference and domination merged with a passionate hatred of Roman catholicism. In spite of this hostility, which did not lack powerful and articulate expression, in 1637 the king revived his father's scheme for a Prayer Book, and insisted upon putting it into effect.

The result was the National Covenant, a document which proclaimed unswerving loyalty to the presbyterian form of religion, the laws and liberties of the kingdom, and the authority of the king. Subscription was almost universal, but it soon became apparent that professions of loyalty to the Crown would be no more than pious platitudes unless Charles abandoned the Prayer Book. This he steadfastly refused to do, in spite of urgent representations from his advisers on the spot, and by November 1638 Scotland was virtually in a state of rebellion. The General Assembly which met in that month simply ignored the king's commissioner, the Duke of Hamilton, when he attempted to dissolve it, and proceeded to sweep away episcopacy, the Articles of Perth, the Canons of the Church, and the order of service hitherto in use. This stand was resolutely supported by all classes, and provides a revealing contrast with the hesitant attitudes of contemporary English puritans. Here was no tradition of a Godly Prince, and no habit of 'tarrying for the magistrate'. The trappings of the Jacobean period had flattered the royal supremacy only to deceive it. In Scotland the king was 'God's silly vassal', and the political doctrines of the Kirk were theocratic. Consequently there was no trace of the English reluctance to defy the king, and no self-doubting debates about the correct course to take with a ruler who had betrayed his trust.

By the beginning of 1639 the Scots were 'busy preaching, praying and drilling'. Alexander Leslie, a veteran of the Thirty Years War, was appointed commander in chief, and a number of other experienced Scottish officers returned from the continent to serve under him. The king's response was feeble. The northern trained bands were summoned and might have been inspired to fight by their long traditions of border warfare, had they been adequately led. But the aristocracy were disaffected; some, like Lord Brooke, because they were puritans, others through hatred of Wentworth or estrangement from the court. There was no money to pay the levies, and no competent officers to train them. To have risked battle with such troops would have been suicidal, and the king had no alternative but to give way. By the treaty of Berwick, signed on 18 June, he agreed that all ecclesiastical matters in Scotland should be determined by the General Assembly; in return the Scots were to disband their army. Charles seems to have been under the mistaken impression that time was on his side. Certainly the *de facto* government of 'the Tables' was not uniformly popular with the Scottish aristocracy,[12] and there were some signs of disaffection in the highlands, but the grip of the General Assembly was not seriously shaken, and the Parliament of 1639 gave it whole hearted support. At the same time the Scottish committee of the Privy Council advised the king that if he wished to reimpose his authority in the north, it could only be by calling upon the English Parliament for financial backing. A group of councillors, led by Wentworth, were prepared to advance the substantial sum of £230,000 out of their private resources, but they knew well enough that this would not be adequate to support a prolonged campaign. A Parliament would at least have the merit of forcing the opposition to a showdown so that

> if his people should not cheerfully according to their duties meet him in that [supply], especially in this exigent, when his kingdoms and person are in apparent danger, the world might see he is forced contrary to his own inclination to use extraordinary means, rather than by the peevishness of some few factious spirits to suffer his state and government to be lost.

In March 1640 the writs were sent out, and the country went through the by now unfamiliar process of an election. Surprisingly enough, there does not seem to have been great excitement. Court candidates fared badly,[13] and most of the surviving leaders of the 1628-9 Parliament were returned, but the majority of the members were novices and by no means uniformly committed to opposing the king's policies. However, Charles had learned nothing by his earlier mistakes and opened the session with a bald demand for generous subsidies. The mood of the Commons was

[12] 'The Tables' was a select committee appointed by the General Assembly which became the *de facto* government of Scotland late in 1638. Montrose disliked the 'bourgeois' element among the covenanting élite, and the traditional feuds, such as that of Huntly and Gordon, began to reappear in contemporary colours.

[13] For instance the four men chosen for the City of London were all oppositionists, Cradock, Vassall, Soame and Pennington. Sir Roger Twysden noted that the Kentish voters were 'very averse to courtiers', and only one of the ten Duchy-backed candidates in Cornwall secured a seat.

unresponsive, and John Pym was able to seize the initiative with an extremely able speech which marshalled all the grievances of the last fifteen years in a calm and compelling argument. What Pym was proposing was, in effect, the legislative programme of the first nine months of the Long Parliament – the demolition of prerogative government – which he offered as a remedy 'to make the king great and his people happy'. His speech gives no hint of any realisation that such action would bring about a profound change in the traditional pattern of monarchical rule, nor does its reception suggest that his audience were aware of any radical implications. The Commons at once set up a series of committees and started translating Pym's proposals into draft bills. However, Charles had different ideas about what constituted his people's happiness, to say nothing of his own greatness. He succeeded in persuading the Lords that subsidies must take precedence over reform, and the intervention of the upper House challenged the opposition leaders in the Commons. A conference between the Houses failed to resolve their differences, and the proposal for a second conference was only defeated after a division which revealed a substantial minority in sympathy with the king's demands; 257 to 148, a split which a contemporary regarded as having 'fully discovered the temper' of the House. Had Charles been prepared to make voluntary concessions at this point his whole subsequent fortune might have been different, but such a course was never contemplated. Hearing a report that the Commons were likely to petition him against the Scottish war, he dissolved the Parliament abruptly on 5 May, a bare three weeks after it had met.

Nothing was resolved by this action. The king had gained no money, and his opponents had gained no redress. Wentworth, near to despair, urged resort to the money and troops which his strong rule in Ireland had placed at his disposal.[14] It was essential to break the vicious circle of poverty and weakness in which the government was caught. 'Go on with a vigorous war, as you first designed,' he urged, 'loose and absolved from all rules of government, being reduced to extreme necessity; everything is to be done that power might admit.' This argument that neces-

[14] It was this suggestion, to use the Irish army 'to reduce this kingdom', which was later quoted against Wentworth at his trial. His accusers interpreted him to mean the subjection of England, whereas it is fairly clear from the context that he was referring to Scotland.

sity knew no law appealed to the Council, but Wentworth was soon to find that although the Irish Parliament might be willing, its financial resources were quite inadequate for such an undertaking. Meanwhile resort was made to the great London financiers, some of whom were prepared to respond (at double interest), and to the clergy. Against all precedent the Convocation of Canterbury had continued to sit after the dissolution of Parliament, and contributed its mite in the form of an annual grant of £20,000 for six years. At the same time, however, it passed the most provocatively Arminian set of Canons ever to be promulgated, which might have been deliberately designed to inflame protestant opinion in the tense summer of 1640. Through these months wild rumours of Spanish landings circulated, and the government threw out helpless appeals for money in all directions – even to the Roman Curia. The Scottish Parliament declared itself capable of legislating without the king's consent,[15] and the Scottish army moved into Northumberland almost unopposed.

By the end of August the Scots were immovably entrenched around Newcastle on Tyne, and their effective propaganda, identifying their own cause with that of the English opponents of 'thorough', paralysed the natural reflexes of the northern counties. So satisfactory was this situation from the viewpoint of the 'country' leaders that it is natural to suspect collusion. Certainly both Charles and Wentworth believed that they had enough evidence to convict Pym and his friends of treason for their negotiations during this period – and knowledge of that fact was to exercise a powerful effect upon the subsequent actions of the opposition leaders. The exact extent of Pym's involvement with the Scots may never be known, but he was certainly in close communication with his allies among the peers and within the City of London. At the end of August the former produced a petition, enumerating the evils from which the realm was suffering and asking for a Parliament. A few days later this was backed up by a second petition, signed by several thousand citizens. Charles strove unavailingly to avoid the in-

[15] This decision seems to have been reached relatively painlessly, perhaps because the kingdom was already in armed revolt. The straightforward radicalism of the Scots provides an illuminating contrast to the proceedings of the English Long Parliament and makes it clear how different the traditions of the two kingdoms were.

evitable. In October he appealed to ancient and long disused precedent by calling a Great Council at York. Such a body had not met since the reign of Henry VII, and there was grave uncertainty as to how it should conduct its business. In the event, it could do little, and the extent of its powers was never tested. The peers advised the king to make peace with the Scots and call a Parliament.

Charles had now played his last card, and the terms which his commissioners were forced to accept at the Treaty of Ripon delivered him into the hands of his enemies. The Scots were to remain in possession of Northumberland and Durham, and to receive £850 a day until all outstanding disputes were resolved. Only Parliament could conceivably supply such a sum beyond the first few weeks, and this was presumably the intention of the Scottish commissioners. News of the treaty was greeted in London with triumph, and the Scots were hailed as the saviours of English liberty. With this guarantee against sudden dissolution, it seemed that the long political deadlock might at last be broken. When the writs were at length sent out the country prepared for its second election of the year in a spirit of high excitement and expectation.

CHAPTER 15

CONSTITUTIONAL STALEMATE AND CIVIL WAR

I never dreamed that we should remonstrate downwards, tell stories to the people, and talk of the king as a third person. (Sir Edward Dering on the Grand Remonstrance.)

RESTRAINTS ON THE ROYAL PREROGATIVE

Only forty days elapsed between the issuing of the writs and the meeting of Parliament on 3 November. There was little enough time for electioneering, and probably none was attempted on the national scale.[1] Popular opinion was now thoroughly awake – more thoroughly than many members of the aristocracy thought healthy – and no one who had a part to play could have been unaware of the issues involved. Nevertheless, there was little hint of the radical developments to come. The vast majority of returns were determined by the exercise of local patronage, and where there were contests they tended to spring from local and personal rivalries, as they had done in every Parliament during the previous two hundred years. Court interests suffered heavily, but always at the hands of rival patrons or interest groups, not at the hands of outsiders armed principally with a programme of national reform. In Huntingdonshire those ancient rivals, the Hastings and the Greys, 'fought the public quarrel with their private spirit and indignation', and similar situations existed elsewhere. In the south-west the Earl of Bedford's influence completely overcame that of the Duchy of Cornwall, while the Duchy of Lancaster suffered in the same way at the hands of local gentry and corporations. In South Wales the Herberts managed to return some members more favourably disposed to the court, and Sir Henry Vane, the Comptroller of the Household, secured the election of three out of his twelve candidates, but the overwhelming temper of the House of Commons

[1] There was plenty of local electioneering, in some cases four or even five candidates appearing for a contested seat. A lot of beer seems to have flowed in these local contests, but Anthony Wood's story of Pym stumping round the countryside is unsupported by evidence.

was fiercely critical of the prerogative government and amenable to the leadership of John Pym and his allies.

Although many of the members had not sat at Westminster before, it was a House full of political experience, particularly at the county level, and well-educated, especially in the common law. It was at least as representative of the 'political nation' as any previous assembly and in the early stages of its existence proceeded with an unusual unanimity and sense of purpose, accurately reflecting the alienation of the 'political nation' from the king. Pym, Hampden and St John in the Commons, Bedford and Brooke in the Lords, worked as a team and met with little organised resistance as they set out to destroy the instruments of 'thorough'. Prynne, Lilburne, Burton and other victims of Star Chamber were released at once and received a tumultuous welcome in the streets of London. At the same time articles of impeachment were drawn up against Laud, Wentworth (who had become Earl of Strafford in January 1640), Windebank, Finch, and other leading ministers, some of whom were arrested while some fled abroad.[2] Although this attack was much more sweeping than any which had been launched before, it did not represent a new political or constitutional approach. The emphasis was still upon 'evil counsel', as it had been in the days of Cranfield and Buckingham. In other ways, however, the Parliament did begin to show significant signs of re-appraising its role in the government. There was now no point in refusing or delaying subsidies, since the Scots were patently earning their ransom. Also, although tonnage and poundage was so much disliked, the revenue was obviously needed, and only Parliament could now guarantee loans which would have to be raised in London. Consequently parliamentary committees began almost at once to take over control of these funds, to negotiate with the farmers of the customs and to allocate money for the payment of the armies in the north. Their lack of relevant experience made them clumsy and slow, but there does not seem to have been any unwillingness to shoulder such responsibilities. On the contrary, the Commons showed a new earnestness in

[2] Laud was one of those arrested, but his impeachment was not proceeded with until 1644. In October of that year it was dropped, and attainder resorted to, for the same reasons as in the case of Strafford. He was executed in January 1645 – a perfectly futile gesture against a man whom events had left behind.

tackling their labours. Whereas by immemorial custom the House had sat only in the mornings, it now met in the afternoons as well, and occasionally the members would labour on into the night. The Lords were less enthusiastic, but their work also increased. Thus even before the king was forced to surrender his right of dissolution, the Houses had become accustomed to act as though they were a permanent part of the government in the same sense as the Council or the Exchequer.

The steady encroachment of parliamentary committees upon the work of administration attracted little attention outside the Houses themselves. Pym and his friends manœuvred patiently and skilfully to maintain control of these committees, and to extend their operations, while the eyes of the country were fixed upon the impeachment of the Earl of Strafford. Strafford was the most hated man in the three kingdoms. Autocratic by nature, he had been living on his nerves for the past two years as the fabric of royal government crumbled. In that time he had uttered many irritable and ill-advised words, aggravated existing enmities, and created fresh ones. He was also by far the ablest and most resolute of the king's advisers, and if he succeeded in defeating his accusers, they would receive short shrift at his hands. There was a mountain of 'evidence' against him in the form of complaints about his activities, particularly in Ireland, but little that could be construed as treason in the existing state of the law. The most important of the articles were extremely vague; 'endeavouring to subvert the fundamental laws and government . . . and to introduce an arbitrary and tyrannical government against law'; seeking to 'set a difference' between the king and his subjects, and to rob him of their affection. This last charge was supported by a number of sixteenth century precedents, particularly the cases against Edmund Dudley and Elizabeth Barton, in which similar constructions had been put upon the Statute of 1352. The others depended upon acceptable definitions of the terms 'fundamental law' and 'arbitrary government', which were inevitably political rather than legal in their nature. Although Pym might declare, with good reason, that 'to alter the settled form and constitution of government is treason in any state', it was another matter to bring such a charge home to Strafford with unequivocal legal proofs. There was, of course, a certain flexibility in the definition of treason, which could be swayed by political circumstances, and it was in that debateable ground that the prosecution was operating.[8] Had Pym and his allies been concerned merely to bring about Strafford's dismissal and disgrace they could probably have accomplished their ends without difficulty by accusing him of corruption and misuse of office, as the 'country' leaders of 1624 had done with the Earl of Middlesex. But that was not sufficient. 'Stone dead hath no fellow,' declared the Earl of Essex, voicing the fear of many that as long as 'Black Tom Tyrant' was alive their own heads would sit loosely on their shoulders.

On 23 March 1641 Strafford was brought to the bar of the House of Lords, and John Pym opened the case against him. It was an uneven case and the Earl's cogent and forceful defence won him unexpected sympathy and support. The most dangerous single weapon in the Commons' armoury, the younger Vane's notes of the Council meeting at which Strafford was alleged to have proposed the use of the Irish army, misfired badly. None of the other councillors who had been present at the meeting would uphold Vane's evidence, or admit that any such suggestion had been made at any time. By the beginning of April it was beginning to seem likely that the impeachment would fail, and Pym's prestige was severely shaken. As a result, a more radical group led by Sir Arthur Hasilrige gained a temporary ascendancy in the lower House and managed to introduce a Bill of attainder against the Earl, which passed its first reading on 12 April.

Pym would have preferred to press the impeachment to a conclusion but circumstances conspired against him. The northern army was becoming discontented over the delays in its pay, which contrasted starkly with the prompt and full payments being made to the Scots, and a group of officers entered into direct negotiations with the court. At the same time it became known that the queen was endeavouring (albeit unsuccessfully) to raise money for her husband in France; and Charles pointedly ignored a petition from both Houses to disband his forces in Ireland. An atmosphere of panic began to prevail in the Commons, and after a fluctuating contest the advocates of attainder had their way. The Bill received its third reading on 21 April, and

[8] For a discussion of the grounds upon which treason was alleged against Strafford, see Conrad Russell, 'The theory of treason in the proceedings against Strafford,' *English Historical Review*, 312, 1965.

passed by 204 votes to 59 in a division from which many members absented themselves.[4] The Lords were similarly alarmed and allowed their fears to overcome their judicial scruples. Attainder was a political weapon and had the great advantage of not requiring legal proof for the charges which it advanced. Peers who might have hesitated to convict Strafford as judges were prepared to condemn him as legislators, and the bill passed.[5]

This placed the king in a most unenviable dilemma. Twice he had been convinced that his minister had escaped, and his own questionable moves, such as reinforcing the garrison of the Tower, had helped to create the panic which had frustrated his hopes. He declared that he was prepared to accept Strafford's disgrace, but not his death. The opposition was not placated, and the ominous crowds whose demonstrations had helped to hasten the Lords to a decision, virtually besieged the palace of Whitehall, shouting for the death of their enemy. Sometimes these crowds consisted of more or less respectable citizens, stirred up by their preachers, sometimes they seem to have been just mobs. How far the parliamentary leaders were responsible for their appearance is not known, but they were a portent of the greatest significance for the developments of the next six months. They were also immediately effective. Exhausted by the strain, and fearful for the safety of his family if an actual attack should develop, Charles gave way and assented to the Bill of attainder on 11 May. The following day Strafford went to execution on Tower Hill, with exemplary courage and in the presence of one of the largest crowds ever to rejoice at such a grisly ceremony.

Charles had never felt for Wentworth the kind of personal affection which he had lavished upon the Duke of Buckingham and to that extent was less moved by his death. But in sacrificing

[4] In 1640 the total membership of the House of Commons numbered 507, which casts an interesting light on the voting figures in all these important divisions.

[5] At the beginning of May the Lords sought the help of judges, submitting to them a list of the points of fact which they had already accepted against Strafford. The judges ruled that, given that the accepted facts were true, Strafford was guilty of treason. It was almost certainly this opinion which finally persuaded the upper House to accept the Attainder, and it leaves the possible outcome of the impeachment an open question. How large a part political pressure played in producing this opinion cannot be calculated. Russell, *op. cit.*

him he had relinquished the last possibility of defending the policy of 'thorough', since no man would undertake to defy popular opinion in the service of a master who was so incapable of protecting, not merely his interests, but his very life. In the shadow of this event the legal and institutional fabric of the prerogative government was dismantled, without resistance and almost without objection. The existing Parliament was not to be dissolved without its own consent, and machinery was created for the automatic convening of future assemblies if the king should allow more than three years to elapse between one dissolution and the next summons.[6] By these crucial measures the prerogative of dissolution was temporarily suspended and permanently reduced to the status of a delaying tactic. No measures of such importance had been passed since the 1530s, and by comparison the remaining legislation of 1641 was a mere matter of administrative re-arrangement. It is hardly surprising that the king's acquiescence was soon to cause suspicion and justifiable fears that his supine attitude concealed a determination to regard all such revolutionary changes as *ipso facto* invalid. Henrietta Maria was certainly urging him to such a course and declared to at least one foreign diplomat that any concession extorted under compulsion was null and void by the laws of England. For a few weeks, however, the Parliament proceeded with apparent confidence and substantial unanimity in its remedial programme. In July Star Chamber was abolished, and the judicial functions of the Privy Council were 'regulated' so that it was unable to touch the property rights of the subject. Requests, the regional Councils and High Commission also disappeared in a series of somewhat doctrinaire measures which, in their enthusiasm for the common law, neglected to provide any substitute for the useful work of administration and arbitration which these courts had performed. Before many years had passed the northerners, at least, were to look back upon their Council with regret.

Provision was also made for the specific grievances of the previous decade. 'No part of the king's government but was inveighed against by one or another,' as a contemporary wrote. Tonnage and poundage was re-affirmed to be a parliamentary tax; ship money was declared to be illegal, and the verdict against

[6] 16 Charles I c.1, 'An Act for the preventing of inconveniences happening by the long intermission of Parliaments'.

Hampden reversed. Forest boundaries were pegged at the limits of 1623, and composition for knighthood abolished. More important, monopolies were cut back severely, so that they consisted of little more than a temporary protection for new developments. Only the great London companies, who had influential friends in both Houses, managed to salvage their interests from this reform, which effectively abolished economic patronage as a weapon of the court. At the end of August those few weary members who had stuck to their posts through the hot and plague-ridden London summer voted an adjournment, and the 'constitutional' phase of the Parliament was over. The 'country' interest of the 1630s, which had been so sweepingly successful in the elections of the previous year, had now brought its programme to fruition. The Commons had not always been unanimous over what they had done, and there had been a number of disagreements with the upper House, but legislation of the utmost importance had been successfully carried through. The structure of the central government had been re-modelled with the intention of embodying in laws and institutions those intangible limitations which the Tudors had always observed. The result had been to revolutionise the relationship between the king on the one hand and the Lords and Commons on the other, and to define the functions of the monarchy with unprecedented strictness.

The weakness of this 'constitutional settlement' was that it depended entirely upon the co-operation of the king who retained the executive power, albeit in a modified form. Only if he could be induced to work within the new framework could political stability be preserved, and, as we have seen, the omens were not particularly good. Certainly during the course of the year Charles had added a number of 'opposition' peers to the Council, and he was prepared to confer office upon Pym, St John and others, but this was rather out of a mistaken assessment of their intentions than a genuine desire to embrace their view of his position.[7] He had done nothing to check his wife's dangerous negotiations with the catholics, or her clumsy diplomatic ven-

[7] Charles remained convinced, right up to the end of 1641, that the opposition leaders were motivated by the desire to secure office for themselves. St John accepted the post of Solicitor General, but Pym rebuffed all offers including the Chancellorship of the Exchequer. The incredulity with which news of this was received at court is another example of its isolation.

tures abroad, both of which had contributed to a rising tide of anti-papal emotion. Also he had refused to accept parliamentary representations against his intended visit to Scotland in the summer of 1641 and had thus provoked the first Ordinance of the Lords and Commons – taking order for certain aspects of the government during his absence. The king went north in the middle of August, and in September, much to everyone's relief, came the news that the Scottish army had withdrawn from Northumberland and Durham. The immediate fear that Charles would win over his northern subjects and turn them against the English Parliament had proved to be unfounded, but that it should have been entertained at all was significant of an atmosphere of mistrust which boded no good for the future peace of the country.

THE GROWING POLITICAL STORM

At the same time Pym's position in the Commons, although apparently triumphant, was in fact precarious. As soon as the pressure of business relaxed, many members began to be alarmed by the course which they had taken and to share in the mildly conservative reaction which built up during August and September. Parliament, the Venetian Ambassador wrote in early September, was losing the credit which it had recently enjoyed. One of the reasons for this reaction was the withdrawal of the Scots, and another was the disbanding of the northern army, which removed the source of those convenient 'plots' with which Pym had been bolstering up his position since February. But the largest single factor was probably the growth of vociferous religious radicalism after the collapse of Laudian censorship. This appeared in a great many forms, from the extravagant preaching of self-appointed apostles to the fierce but disciplined rhetoric of more sober puritans such as John Milton. It had appeared in the House of Commons as early as March in the form of a bill for the exclusion of the bishops from the House of Lords, and in an early 'root and branch' motion introduced by Sir Edward Dering. Even the most conservative members were no friends to the Laudian episcopate, but these proposals had alarming implications. In a significant speech, George Digby urged his fellow members 'not to be led on by passion to popular and vulgar errors . . . we all agree upon this; that a reformation of Church government is most necessary . . . but . . . not to strike at the root, to attempt a total alteration . . . I am confident that instead of every bishop we put down in a diocese, we shall set up a pope in every parish.' Other members, such as Sir Benjamin Rudyerd and Edmund Waller, supported this line of argument, pointing out that the abolition of episcopacy would mean 'a popular democratical government of the Church', which would inevitably be reflected in the organisation of secular society. The institution of episcopacy was an integral part of the traditional order, and bishops were always useful for disciplining recalcitrant clergy. Pym, who was not a radical in this context, nevertheless felt that it was necessary to keep up a 'head of steam' for possible use against the king and consequently he supported exclusion, although not abolition at this stage. Partly as a result of this attitude a sharp rift opened between the Lords and Commons at the beginning of September, and this was to prove virtually the end of united parliamentary action.

Had it not been for the equally strong fear of catholic conspiracy, fostered by the indiscreet activities of the queen and courtiers such as Sir John Suckling, it is probable that the reaction among the propertied classes would have left Pym and his followers high and dry. As it was, a painful uncertainty prevailed, rumours of popish plots and of the king's activities in Scotland contending with a mounting dread of popular disorders and social revolution. By October Charles had come to terms with the Scottish Parliament, and although these amounted to almost total surrender on his part, they meant that for the time being at least he would not have to fight on two fronts.[8] His English opponents did not know whether to rejoice at his defeat or fear the consequences of his disengagement. When Parliament reconvened at the beginning of the month, Pym and his friends do not seem to have intended any clear-cut initiative, preferring, perhaps, to wait for the king's return.

However, within a few days the whole situation had been transformed by the news of the Irish revolt, in which the spectre of popish atrocities became suddenly and dramatically real. There is no space here to go into the background of this revolt, which lay in the Ulster plantation, the dispossession of Irish landholders, and the sudden removal of Strafford's harsh but

[8] Any chance of a real alliance with the Scots at this stage was ruined by 'the Incident' – an obscure plot to kidnap the covenanting Duke of Argyll – in which royal agents were suspected of complicity.

effective government. There were many causes for anger among the Irish catholics, and in the latter part of October this exploded in a series of savage attacks upon the colonists, which swept away their settlements and resulted in thousands of deaths by massacre, hunger and exposure.

The consequences in England were immediate and profound. At the conscious political level men were alarmed at the apparent loss of the colony and fearful lest Ireland should become a bridgehead for the militant Counter Reformation, as it had almost been at the end of the previous century. More fundamentally, they were enraged by what protestant propaganda represented as a treacherous and unprovoked attack, and convinced that this was merely the first stage in a universal catholic conspiracy of blood and terror. The king's position was affected in two ways. In the first place his catholic associations, which had already been exaggerated by fear and rumour, caused it to be widely believed that he was actually a party to the plot. It was even reported that one of the rebel leaders possessed a commission under the Great Seal to restore the old religion in Ireland. Secondly the necessity to take urgent military action against the rebellion raised the crucial question of who was to control the operations, which in the circumstances inevitably meant a fresh demand for accountability to Parliament.

At the beginning of November Pym resolved to grasp this nettle and put before the Commons an 'additional instruction' to the parliamentary commissioners with the king in Scotland. This amounted to a demand for control over the executive, asking 'His Majesty to change those counsels from which such ill courses have proceeded . . . and be graciously pleased to employ such councillors and ministers as shall be approved by his Parliament'. If this should not be granted, the Instruction went on, '. . . in discharge of the trust which we owe to the state . . . [we shall] resolve upon some such way of defending Ireland from the rebels as may concur to the securing of ourselves'. This radical ultimatum was put to the vote on 8 November, and passed by 151 votes to 110. Although this success was a great tribute to Pym's parliamentary skill, it signified a parting of the ways. The members had now come to the point at which they must either trust the king to carry out the reforms which had been embodied in the legislation of the summer, or press on into an unknown future of political innovation. The division was not really one of principle, for Pym and his friends did not see themselves as radical innovators; it was a disagreement over means rather than ends – a choice of risks. Those who pressed on feared the king's deceit more than they feared any foreseeable consequences of trying to forestall it. Those who held back feared social revolution more than they feared popish conspiracy.

The celebrated debates over the Grand Remonstrance between 8 and 22 November thus deepended and perpetuated a split which already existed. The Remonstrance had been under discussion since the summer, but Pym's decision to re-introduce it in the wake of the Irish rebellion was an opportunist move designed to rally his wavering supporters. It was, as its name suggests, a manifesto of grievances rather than a political or ecclesiastical programme; a deliberate attempt to undermine confidence in the king's good faith by emphasising the danger from unspecified 'malignants'. It passed by the narrow majority of eleven votes in a House exhausted by long debate and exasperated by half articulated fears and animosities.[9]

There was no chance that this Remonstrance would pass the Lords, the majority of whom were by now thoroughly alarmed at the attitude of the Commons, and after a furious altercation its sponsors succeeded in passing a resolution that it should be published as it stood – a move which its opponents justifiably represented as subversive of the good order of the kingdom. By the time that Charles returned from Scotland in late November, Pym's position was becoming increasingly isolated. The king was studiously gracious, and laid careful emphasis upon the legality of his position. In reply to the Remonstrance, which was presented as a petition on 1 December, he declared his intention to abide by the reforms already passed and his willingness to 'grant what else can be justly desired for satisfaction in point of liberties, or in maintenance of the true religion that is here established'. He had no knowledge of any malignants, but would give the Remonstrance such attention as it deserved.

By contrast, the Commons continued to be aggressive. On 6 December they passed a resolution to nominate a Lord General with full military powers – a flagrant breach of the prerogative – and at about the same time placed on record the view that

[9] The voting figures were 159 to 148 – a total of 307 or three fifths of the House.

they alone represented the kingdom 'their lordships being but as particular persons',[10] and consequently that the true function of consent was vested only in themselves. Had Charles been able to maintain his position, his opponents might well have discredited themselves completely, but he was unable to do so. In mid-December the courtier Lord Mayor of London, Sir Richard Gurney, who had welcomed the king back from Scotland with such a lavish demonstration of loyalty, was shaken by the defeat of his associates in the Common Council. Thanks to some hard campaigning, the City legislature was now dominated by men committed to support Pym.[11] The king's reaction was to appoint a notorious adventurer, Thomas Lunsford, to command the garrison of the Tower, a move which undid overnight the good effects of his earlier moderation. At the same time he definitively rejected the Remonstrance as presumptuous and thus strengthened Pym's hand in pressing the further stages of the militia bill.

At the end of 1641 the country was gripped by an atmosphere of crisis. It is impossible to understand the events of these winter months without taking account of the emotional context. Following a tense and expectant summer, the Irish rebellion had caused a wave of panic in which no tale of popish conspiracy was too improbable to be believed. On 12 November, for example, Sir William Acton (an alderman of London) brought to the House of Commons one John Davis, a servant, who claimed to have guided a party of unknown gentlemen to Raglan Castle, the seat of the catholic Earl of Worcester. Davis's story was that he had seen at Raglan vast stocks of arms and munitions, 'enough for two thousand men', kept in underground store houses, and that a servant of the Earl had told him that his master had seven hundred men in his pay. Within a few days this extravagant and probably fictitious recital was published as a pamphlet, with the question 'whether we have not as just cause to fear the Papists in England as they had in Ireland'? On 15 November the Commons heard an even more hair-raising revelation from an out of work tailor named Thomas Beale who claimed to have overheard a plot to assassinate over one hundred puritan members and lords. 'There was 108 men appointed to

[10] *Commons Journals*, II, 330.

[11] For a full consideration of the circumstances surrounding this vital success, see V. Pearl, *London and the Outbreak of the Puritan Revolution*, 210-36.

kill 108 persons of the Parliament, every one his man', the murderers' zeal being stimulated by cash rewards. The date appointed for this massacre, according to Beale, was 18 November, and a general catholic rising was intended to take advantage of the confusion.

These wild stories were believed, not merely by village gossips but by the substantial and responsible men who governed the shires. On the night of 19 November a rumour spread through Herefordshire, Worcester and Shropshire that the papists had risen. At Brampton Bryan in Herefordshire, Sir Robert Harley's wife armed his servants, and the villagers retreated into the castle as their ancestors would have done in the days of the border wars. At Ludlow, Bewdley and Bridgnorth the townsmen set watches and patrolled the streets. This particular panic passed, but the general atmosphere of tension remained. Lady Harley was typical of many when she wrote to her husband,

> I have, according to your directions caused a good provision of bullets to be made and the pieces charged. There are no men at Brampton except Samuel and another . . . If we should be put to it, I do not believe we should be able to stand siege.

By comparison with their great-grandfathers, or even with their grandfathers, the gentry of 1641 were unaccustomed to violence, untrained in war and unprepared for self-defence. They were consequently a prey to false alarms and prone to over-react, like nervous men in any age and place.

It was against this explosive background that the dramatic events of January 1642 took place. At the end of December the bishops, who dared not attend the House of Lords for fear of the London mob, attempted to claim that the work of the House was invalidated by their absence. Angered by this pretension, the lay peers fell in with the Commons' desire to impeach them and thus severely weakened the king's position in the upper House. Consequently, when Charles resolved to strike at his enemies in the first week of January, his ability to do so was greatly impaired. Apparently a rumour reached the king that Pym intended to impeach Henrietta Maria, and he decided to get his blow in first. On 3 January he presented articles alleging high treason against Pym, four other members and one peer,[12] for raising tumults against the public order and levying war in collusion with the Scots. Instead of receiving these at once or

[12] Hampden, Holles, Hasilrige, Strode and Lord Mandeville.

ordering the arrest of the accused, the Lords merely resolved to consider them, and Charles was left to secure his prisoners as best he could. Duly warned, the wanted men took refuge in London, and the king's attempt to arrest them in person on 4 January was frustrated. This catastrophic blunder destroyed his credit at a blow and crippled the efforts of those members of Parliament who had been striving to represent him as the only sound bulwark against a rising tide of innovation and disorder. Not only had Charles assaulted the treasured privileges of the House of Commons, but he had also gathered together an armed force several hundred strong. The presence of these troops in the vicinity of London gave substance to those fears of 'malignants' which were already strong, and caused an alarm to be raised on 6 January 'that the king and cavaliers, with fifteen hundred horse were coming to surprise the city' and to seize the five members by force. This panic brought thousands of armed men into the streets, and its after effects drew the Commons and the City together as never before. Common Council refused to consider surrendering the fugitives, and the trained bands were placed under the command of Philip Skippon, with responsibility to the Commons.

By this time political tension had virtually put an end to the commercial activities of the capital, and the result was widespread unemployment and distress. During January and February tens of thousands of demonstrators marched to London from all over the south of England bearing petitions to the Parliament against papists and malignants—and complaining of the universal decay of trade and industry. 'We find the trade of clothing . . . upon which the livelihoods of many thousands . . . in this town do depend, to be almost wholly decayed, and poverty abundantly to grow upon us', declared the mayor and aldermen of Colchester. The unemployed 'express sad intentions of disturbing our public peace', warned a petition from Suffolk, and the burgesses of Exeter similarly feared that poverty would 'stir up many thousand persons to insolent and outrageous actions'. These petitions, as their tone implies, were the work of local authorities, and they were presented in disciplined demonstrations frequently led by the gentry of the neighbourhood.[18] Their pur-

[18] An observer described the Northamptonshire petition, presented on 10 February as being 'the best attended by gentlemen of quality of any

pose, declared or undeclared, was to bring pressure to bear upon the upper House to co-operate wholeheartedly with the Commons in a united front against the king, since the general impression seems to have been that it was mainly disagreements within the Parliament which were preventing a solution to the political deadlock. The Venetian ambassador observed that the 'ignorant people' were 'persuaded that these calamities proceed from the presence of the bishops and catholic lords in Parliament'. Pym wished the Lords to join in a petition to the king to put the Tower and other military strongholds 'into the hands of such persons as your Parliament may confide in', and his supporters in the upper House represented this as 'absolutely necessary to the settling of the present distempers'. Presumably it was felt that Charles was in no position to refuse (he had left London on 10 January and was wandering rather aimlessly in the midlands), and once the vital question of military control was settled enough confidence would return to breathe life into the economy. Before these very explicit threats 'of tumults and insurrections of the meaner sort of people' the Lords gave way at the beginning of February. But nothing was accomplished because the king, helpless though he was, would not budge an inch on what was, after all, a fundamental issue of principle.

THE DRIFT TOWARDS WAR

During the next few months the situation drifted towards war, not because anyone regarded war as the best method of arbitration, or even a possible one, but simply because the machinery of government had ground to a halt. At the beginning of March Parliament converted the militia bill into an 'Ordinance' when it became apparent that the king would not surrender control of the army, but confidence was not restored. Unwilling to depart from their traditional stance of defending precedent and the 'ancient laws', the parliamentary leaders grasped only half-heartedly at the sovereignty which the logic of their position now demanded. A pamphlet war developed as they strove to justify their position to the country at large, and probably to convince themselves. Charles had the better of this exchange

petition that hath yet been delivered'. The Kentish petition was also well supported.

since, sensibly advised by Hyde and Falkland, he stood pat upon his legal rights and accused his opponents of making the country ungovernable. Pym and his allies could think of nothing better than to go on demanding that the king should make a complete and explicit surrender of his executive functions and convert the monarchy into a Dogeship. In this situation they were handicapped by their sense of political vocation because, although they regarded the defence of their own interpretation of the constitution as a sacred trust, they had also embraced as a part of the divine order a concept of the monarchy which they were powerless to enforce. Like Charles himself, they regarded the king as a servant of the Will of God. But while this gave him the comparatively straightforward task of invoking the traditional theories of obedience for conscience' sake, they were faced with the impossibility of having to persuade him in advance to accept the validity of their own vision. Understandably, they hardly tried, but attempted instead to compel him to exercise his rule under the permanent surveillance of men who would stand *in loco Dei*.

Meanwhile the civil order was disintegrating. There were widespread riots in Essex and Suffolk as mobs attacked the houses of recusant gentry and others who were suspected of favouring the king. The home of the catholic Countess Rivers at Long Melford was sacked, and unpopular landlords such as Sir John Lucas found themselves accused of 'malignancy'. Similar disorders occurred in Somerset and in the West Riding of Yorkshire. 'This fury,' observed a contemporary, 'was not only in the rabble but many of the better sort behaved themselves as if there had been a dissolution of all government; no man could remain in his house without fear, or be abroad with safety.' Others, particularly those inclined to the court, felt that 'popery' and 'malignancy' were merely excuses under colour of which the 'many headed monster' worked off its grudges against the aristocracy in general. Certainly by the autumn of 1642 many gentlemen who had wholeheartedly supported the 'country' in the 1630s had come to feel that the Parliament was stuck in an *impasse*, and that the urgent necessity to preserve order must take precedence over the niceties of constitutional law. At the same time others, equally alarmed, were so convinced of the king's perfidiousness and of the reality of the popish threat that they felt their only hope of security to lie in upholding the members assembled at Westminster, no matter how ambiguous their political position might be.

In spite of this deepening division within the ruling class, and the temporary paralysis of the executive, spontaneous violence remained upon a comparatively small scale. No Jack Cade marched on London at the head of an army of malcontents; no Duke of York marched his private resources against a debilitated Crown; and no Kett or Robert Aske attempted to turn economic or religious grievances into large-scale revolts. In many ways this crisis revealed how well the long pressure of Tudor centralisation had done its work. The authority of 'great men in their countries' counted for less than at any time in the past. In spite of some alarmist reports, no magnates appeared with armed retinues to take advantage of the confusion. Nor was there any revival of the provincialism of 1549 in the south-west, or 1569 in the north. At the same time the greatly diminished importance of magnate initiative in local government heightened the paralysing effects of the divisions among the gentry. In almost every county the local leaders were at odds among themselves, and unable to take any effective disciplinary action without risking the kind of political commitment which most of them were so anxious to avoid.

During the summer of 1642 the king's cause gradually recovered as it became apparent that the parliamentary leaders had again run out of ideas. From May onward a steady trickle of peers and members of the Commons who could no longer stomach the implications of the conflict were leaving London, and some of the more resolute joined the court at York. Thither in June came the Lord Keeper bearing the Great Seal, and other officials with the apparatus of their departments. Faced with the possible defection of the whole central administration the Commons, on 6 June, resorted to a somewhat desperate expedient. Taking advantage of the traditional distinction between the king in Parliament and *in propria persona sua*, they declared and placed on record that 'the King's supreme and royal pleasure is exercised in this High Court of law and council after a more eminent and obligatory manner than it can be by personal act or resolution of his own.'[14] In other words the will of Parliament

[14] Gardiner, *Documents*, 257: 'Declaration in defence of the Militia Ordinance'.

must be deemed to be the will of the king, no matter what Charles Stuart might do or say. Ridiculous as this expedient might appear to the royalists at York, it gave the men in London a tattered fragment of theoretical justification which was disproportionately valuable to them at the time. If the essence of the royal office was to defend the commonweal, then those who were so defending it must by definition be serving the king's true will, and if he in his own person opposed them it could only be because he was misled or coerced by wicked men. 'Tis to preserve his majesty that we against him fight,' the cavaliers were later to mock. But the idea, fragile as it was, did yeoman service in the confused and panic-striken atmosphere of 1642.

In a way Charles played up to it by going through the anachronistic ceremony of raising his standard at Nottingham on 22 August. His intention was to make a public declaration of the fact that he now considered the parliamentary leaders to be rebels, and that a state of war existed in the realm. Unfortunately for the symbolism of his action, rebels could also raise their standards (Sir Thomas Wyatt had done so at Maidstone in 1554). Charles was in exile from his capital and thinly attended. It was not difficult for his opponents to produce a convincing line in propaganda which represented him as the helpless puppet of the 'malignant faction', waging war upon the state and upon his own true subjects. Charles, already rebuffed from Hull, had no army with which to fight a war, and his commissions of array, unsupported by financial resources, met with a poor response. By contrast the parliamentary commissions, backed by grants for equipment and pay underwritten by the City of London, were immediately successful, and by October the Earl of Essex had an army which nominally consisted of 5,000 horse and 25,000 foot. Unfortunately, the Parliament sacrificed its chance of a bloodless victory by issuing an aggressive declaration on 6 September, demanding that the king surrender to 'justice' all those whom the Houses might vote to be 'delinquent'. This vague category could be held to include anyone who had ever expressed the slightest approbation of bishops or any aspect of the prerogative government, and drove a whole host of waverers to seek security in the victory of the king. His coffers filled with loyal contributions, and by the end of the month he had almost 10,000 men under arms, including 2,000 good horsemen commanded by his nephew Prince Rupert of the Palatinate.[15]

With this force at his disposal, the king's objective was straightforward – to defeat his enemies in battle and reimpose his authority. His opponents had no such simple concept of their task, and for them the outbreak of war offered no solutions. The fundamental problem remained, as it had been since the spring of 1640, to make the king accept a considerable reduction of his constitutional powers. Had there been a plausible alternative claimant for the throne to conceal the nakedness of their political aggression they might well have used him, but there was none. All they could hope and fight for was a bargaining position of irresistible strength, but they had had Charles by the throat before without being able to enforce his co-operation. Negatively, of course, they had to defeat the king to protect their own lives and property, but this was no help in creating a policy for victory. On the other hand, time was on their side. If Charles was going to win, he must do so quickly, before the volatile enthusiasm of his younger supporters burned out and his resources, derived mostly from private backers, were exhausted. The Parliament not only controlled London, but also the fleet and a solid bloc of counties in the wealthy south-east of the country.

The main problem facing the parliamentary leaders, and Pym in particular, was how to fight and win a war against their lawful king without destroying the social and political order in which most of them still believed. Pym worked tirelessly. Whether they liked it or not, parliamentary committees now had to take over all the functions of the executive in those areas to which their control extended. New sources of revenue had to be devised, of which the excise was the most important, and the trade of London had to be set in motion again. Equally vital was the preservation of morale. There were those among the rump of two hundred and fifty or so members of the Commons who were so alarmed at finding themselves in an actual state of war with the king that they were prepared to advocate peace on almost any terms. On the other hand, an increasingly vocal party of extremists led by Sir Arthur Hasilrige and Sir Henry Marten were pressing for bolder and more radical action. It was during these months, from the outbreak of war in September

[15] The second son of Charles's sister Elizabeth.

1642 until his death in December 1643 that Pym earned his nickname 'king'. He was, declared the Venetian ambassador, 'the promoter of the present rebellion and director of the whole machine'. The first part of this statement may be open to doubt, but the second is undeniably true. By his skilful manœuvring and indefatigable organisation he held a diverse group of apprehensive men to the unpromising task which they had set themselves, and kept 'the cause' united at a time when it seemed only too likely to break up.

CIVIL WAR

The first year of fighting was inconclusive. The Marquis of Newcastle secured most of the north of England for the king, and Sir Ralph Hopton the south west, but important towns in both areas – notably Hull and Plymouth – held out for Parliament, and the royal army was unable to make any real impression on the south-east. The first pitched battle at Edgehill on 23 October 1642 exposed the limitations of Essex's generalship and enabled the king to occupy Oxford and Banbury. The possibility of following this up with an attack on London was, however, frustrated in a bloodless confrontation with the trained bands at Turnham Green. By the early summer of 1643 the royalists seemed poised for complete success. Newcastle defeated the Fairfaxes in Yorkshire at the end of June and occupied the West Riding clothing towns. In the south-west Hopton routed a parliamentary force under Sir William Waller at Roundaway Down and captured Bristol.

Charles, who was a good strategist, resolved to follow up these successes with a three-pronged advance upon the capital from the north, west and south-west. This sensible plan was defeated, not by the parliamentary forces but by the provincialism of the royalists themselves. The northerners refused to advance south with Hull untaken behind them, and Hopton's forces, exhausted by a hard campaign, settled down to besiege Plymouth. Lacking an effective central command, and inadequately supported by *ad hoc* administrative and financial arrangements, the king could do nothing but acquiesce, and his own army turned to the siege of Gloucester. That city held out resolutely from 10 August to 5 September, when it was relieved by the advance of Essex, with the main parliamentary force. Dislodged from the siege, Charles then moved behind Essex to cut him off from his base, and intercepted him at Newbury in Berkshire. Again the actual fighting was inconclusive, but the royalists seem to have suffered the heavier casualties and drew off during the night, leaving Essex free to resume his march.

By the end of 1643 the war had developed a logic and momentum of its own. Reluctant as most men were to choose sides in a conflict which they regarded as an unmitigated and incomprehensible disaster, they were commonly forced to do so by circumstances. For every man who joined the king out of conviction, ten contributed money, arms and plate to his cause because they were under the surveillance of a royalist army, or because the king's supporters were more resolute in their particular neighbourhood. Except for the Marquis of Newcastle, the influence of great men seems to have counted for little in this process, although in the royalist areas, which tended to be more conservative, it was the practice of the more determined gentry each to enlist a small number of followers for the king's service. The motivation of those who did deliberately choose sides naturally varied. On the royalist side the principle of loyalty to the person of the king was a strong factor, even among those who were not threatened with parliamentary sequestration for their earlier attachment to the court. On the parliamentary side adherence to the self-appointed defenders of law and liberty was probably less important than religious puritanism. Positive commitment to both sides was encouraged by the desire to restore political stability, and at a lower level by the alignments of local feuds and family relationships. Thanks to the influence of London and the fleet, the seaports were mostly for Parliament. Catholics and Arminians sided with the king for the sake of self-preservation, and merchants with Parliament out of self-interest. For the rest, the division was determined by geography rather than ideology, and because of the peculiar importance of the capital geography favoured the Parliament. This being so, local alignments changed as the war progressed, relatively few men being prepared to abandon their homes and property for the sake of either cause. In Cheshire the two parties were so equally poised at first that they made a local compact of neutrality. Elsewhere ordinary people with no interest in the conflict banded together in vigilante groups to protect their houses and crops from the attentions of both sides.

Relatively little is known about the way in which the royal

government worked in those areas which it controlled. The king raised troops by commission of array and probably collected taxes and other revenues in a similar manner, or through such local receivers and officials as were still functioning. Civil order was preserved by suitably purged commissions of the peace, in the traditional manner, and there may well have been a temporary revival of magnate influence in the further north and west. The Parliament, by contrast, had to develop new methods, and because of the eventual outcome of the war these were important for the history of the subsequent period. Troops were raised by invoking the Militia Ordinance and placing the trained bands under the control of reliable lieutenants who were appointed for each county and major town. These lieutenants were normally nobles or substantial gentlemen, and they appointed their deputies from among the other gentry of the shires. These deputy lieutenants formed the nucleus of the 'County Committees' which gradually came into existence during the winter of 1642-3, being joined in the spring of the latter year by the commissioners appointed to operate the new fiscal system, established by ordinance. This system included the excise, a direct tax called the 'weekly pay', forced loans and the sequestration of royalist estates. These devices were unpopular and form an ironic comment on the 'country' grievances from which the parliamentary party had sprung, but they were undoubtedly necessary. The actual constitution of the County Committees varied, since they were not so much established as evolved, but typically they consisted of such of the local gentry as were most enthusiastic for the cause, reinforced by other men of substance, such as merchants.[16] In some counties, such as Sussex, the traditional government, including the work of quarter sessions, was carried on with little disruption. In other more disturbed areas the Committees administered justice by a sort of rough and ready method of arbitration, as the Committee of Staffordshire did when it resolved to compensate one Abberley whose cows had been taken in a royalist raid, by giving him a few unclaimed beasts which they happened to have on hand. These bodies tended to be local in outlook, and to improve the military aspect of their work the Parliament endeavoured to band them to-

[16] D. H. Pennington, 'The County Community at War', in *The English Revolution*, ed. E. W. Ives.

gether in 'Associations', with common funds and wider jurisdiction. In East Anglia this worked fairly well, and the army of the 'Eastern Association' was a respectable force by 1644, but elsewhere the idea proved abortive.

The greatest single problem facing each of these Committees by the end of 1643 was the collection of revenue, and in 1644 the Parliament resolved to split off this aspect of their work and to set up new committees specifically for that purpose. Since these finance committees were deliberately appointed from among those who were not already serving, there tended to be a shift towards the lesser gentry families and townsmen with particular financial skill. Quarrels with the established powers naturally resulted, and Parliament tended increasingly to side with the 'new men' who were less conservative in their outlook and less afraid of upsetting the stability of propertied society. The more work local government had to perform, the more influential such men became, until the balance had shifted decisively in their direction, just as the military balance shifted to the New Model Army.

> We had here a thing called a committee, [Sir John Oglander later wrote of the Isle of Wight] which overruled deputy lieutenants and also justices of the peace; and of this we have brave men: Ringwood of Newport the Pedlar, Maynard the Apothecary, Mathews the Baker, Wavell and Legge farmers . . . These ruled the whole island and did whatever was good in their eyes.

A royalist exaggeration, perhaps, but a significant one nonetheless. By the time that the traditional ruling class was fully awake to what was happening, the whole of England and Scotland was in the efficient grasp of a professional army, and there was nothing they could do to remedy the situation.

Even before Pym's death removed his stabilising and conservative influence it was clear that the demands of war were undermining the traditional attitudes of the parliamentary leaders. In September 1643 the king negotiated a cessation of hostilities with the catholic rebels in Ireland. All he gained from this virtual surrender was the disposal of those English troops which had been serving in Ireland, and they turned out to be unreliable; but it was commonly believed that he had entered into a pact with the 'wild Irish' for the extermination of protestantism.[17] Not only did this revive something of the panic atmosphere of November 1641, but it also drove the English Parliament and the presbyterian Scottish Kirk into alliance. 'Most of all the Irish cessation made the minds of our people embrace that means of safety,' wrote Robert Baillie. They were uneasy allies, since the English purpose was primarily political and the Scots' purpose religious. But the parliamentary leaders felt that their need of military support was so urgent that they accepted the Solemn League and Covenant which bound them against their will and better judgement to establish a presbyterian form of Church government in England, '. . . that Popery and Prelacy should be extirpated'. In the days to come this agreement was to be a source of great bitterness and strife, but it served its immediate purpose beyond all hope.

In January 1644 the Earl of Leven led his forces across the border and transformed the military situation in the north of England. While the Marquis of Newcastle manœuvred to intercept the invasion, the Yorkshire royalists were routed in his rear by the Fairfaxes, and Newcastle had no option but to retreat to York. There he was blockaded by the Scots, and a stalemate of several weeks ensued. At the end of June a royalist force under Prince Rupert and the army of the Eastern Association commanded by the Earl of Manchester and Oliver Cromwell also converged on York. Rupert, believing that he had positive orders to fight, challenged battle at Marston Moor on 2 July, in spite of being at a numerical disadvantage. He was defeated by the superior discipline of Manchester's cavalry, and the whole north passed under parliamentary control. Newcastle and most of his officers retreated to the continent, and the royalist strongholds fell one by one over the next twelve months.

In the south the balance was more even. A powerful thrust by Hopton into Hampshire was defeated at the end of March, but on 6 June the king himself overcame Waller and the latter's army mutinied. More important, incompetent generalship by Essex resulted in most of his force being driven into Cornwall and compelled to surrender at Lostwithiel. The Earl himself, with part of his cavalry made good his escape, but his credit as a commander was severely impaired. By this time a crisis was brewing in the parliamentary armies. Manchester, thoroughly

[17] The Irish 'confederation' agreed to pay the king £30,000, but there is no evidence that they ever did so.

alarmed by the growth of religious radicalism in the Eastern Association, was at odds with many of his best officers, including Cromwell. The House of Commons, similarly apprehensive, went out of its way to avoid blaming Essex for the Cornish fiasco, but at the same time (much to the indignation of the Scots) issued a declaration promising relief for tender consciences in the matter of Church government – a gesture specifically intended to conciliate the army radicals.

These issues were brought to a head by the messy and inconclusive battle at Newbury on 27 October, in which divided command and hesitant tactics enabled the king to get the better of an army with almost twice his numbers. In the Council of War which followed, the whole political dilemma of the Parliament was brought into the open. 'If we beat the king ninety and nine times,' declared Manchester, 'yet he is king still, and so will his posterity be after him; but if the king beat us once we shall all be hanged and our posterity made slaves.'[18] This was a declaration of political bankruptcy. The war had brought no new counsel to the existing leadership and seemed to offer no promise of an acceptable outcome. Pym, Hampden and Brooke, the three ablest and most respected moderate leaders, had all died in 1643. They had never really been replaced, and the conservatism of those who remainded had betrayed them, revealing to the rank and file that they had been fighting for two years under the command of men who did not want victory because they had no idea what to do with it.

The opposition to this defeatism was led by Oliver Cromwell, who emerged at this time as a political leader of skill and determination. He very cogently pointed out that if his colleagues had no real intention of winning the war, the only sensible thing to do was to sue to the king for whatever terms he would grant. At the beginning of December he carried his battle into the House of Commons. Distrustful of local forces, and hostile to the rigid presbyterianism of the Scots, he argued forcefully for the establishment of a new army with a unified command, proper technical services and efficient administration. In the circumstances his proposals could not be gainsaid. Worried as many members may have been by the creation of a professional army on a semi-permanent footing, the logic of the situation demanded nothing less. Consequently the establishment of the New

[18] Gardiner, *Civil War*, II, 59.

Model Army was authorised on 17 February, and a few weeks later, in spite of the justifiable suspicions of the House of Lords, all members of the Parliament were required to lay down their commands by the terms of the Self-Denying Ordinance.[19] During the opening weeks of 1645 the high command was recreated to consist of men who were first and foremost committed to winning the war. In this way the initiative passed from the traditional leadership, with its roots in the 'country' opposition of the 1620s and 1630s, to a group which was differently constituted and potentially much more radical.

These men were not consciously revolutionaries, but the long accepted theories of political obligation naturally did not weigh so heavily with them. Manchester's statement had revealed that in spite of his puritanism and the exigencies of his situation his thinking had never really moved from the non-resistance doctrines of the previous century. The new commanders were more logical. Ultimately the welfare of the state as they saw it must take precedence over traditional allegiance, and the inadequacies of the monarch himself faced without equivocation. The puritan writer John Goodwin was to express their position succinctly a few years later:

> When the pilot or master of a ship at sea, be either so overcome and distempered with drink, or otherwise disabled . . . so that he is incapable of acting the exigencies of his place, for the preservation of the ship, being now in present danger . . . any one or more of the inferior mariners having skill, may, in order to the saving of the ship and of the lives of all that are in it, lawfully assume and act according to the interests of a pilot . . .

Such theories had good Calvinist foundations and derived much of their strength from that sense of 'calling' which was so strong in Cromwell and his associates. As yet there was no need to contemplate the question of Charles's ultimate recalcitrance, but these men were equipped to do so in a way which their predecessors had not been. As we have already seen, similar men were moving into positions of responsibility at the local level. In

[19] The decision to create the new army and the operation of the 'Self-Denying Ordinance' were not, of course, as neat as this brief summary suggests. The Ordinance was at first rejected by the Lords (13 January), but Fairfax and Skippon went ahead with the creation of the New Model, so that by March such of the previous commanders as had neither resigned nor been given new responsibilities were left 'in the air'.

fact this change of leadership marked a crucial breakthrough in the process which gradually transformed the deferential opposition of the late sixteenth century into the revolutionary movement of 1648-9.

The king, poorly informed and slow to grasp even the superficial significance of what was happening, failed to seize the opportunity of negotiation which the worried moderates were offering at the beginning of 1645. Prevarication lost him the chance to exploit conservative fears, and by the beginning of April rumours of the queen's activities in France had once again closed the ranks against him. On 3 April the House of Lords at last accepted the *fait accompli* of the Self-Denying Ordinance.

Once the New Model Army had taken the field, the issue was not long in doubt. After two months of indecisive campaigning the king's main field army was brought to battle at Naseby near Market Harborough on 14 June and virtually destroyed. The royalist cause no longer had the resources to recover from such a disaster. Cut off by the parliamentary fleet from possible foreign relief, and penned in a diminishing area of the west of England, the king's agents had already alienated such sympathy as they had among the ordinary people by their financial demands, and by extensive requisitioning which was little short of plunder. On 10 July a second royalist force under Lord George Goring was smashed by the New Model at Langport, near Bridgewater. 'The Lord hath wrought for us,' declared Cromwell characteristically, and 'God will go on.' Montrose's royalist rising in the highlands of Scotland was defeated at Philiphaugh in September, and by the end of the year only mopping-up operations remained. Not only had the king's armies been wiped out, but the Scottish alliance had been virtually declared redundant, a matter of considerable and ominous significance in view of the obligations of the Solemn League and Covenant. There must have been many men in England who looked with apprehension on the emergence of the political and religious force which the New Model represented, albeit it was as yet nominally in the service of that established body which still called itself a Parliament. Sir Jacob Astley did not need to be a prophet, when, after leading the last fragment of the king's army to defeat in March 1646 he declared, 'You have now done your work and may go play, unless you will fall out among yourselves.' Play did not come naturally to the leaders of the New Model Army.

CHAPTER 16

THE FALL OF THE MONARCHY, AND MILITARY DICTATORSHIP

> We were not a mere mercenary army, hired to serve any arbitrary power of a state, but called forth and conjured by the several declarations of the Parliament to the defence of our own and the people's just rights and liberties. (*Declaration of the Army*, 16 June 1647)

THE ARMY IN CONTROL

Negotiations between Parliament and the king had gone on intermittently throughout the war, but had always failed because Charles refused to abandon the Church and the militia. As late as January 1645 the Uxbridge talks had broken down for these reasons, and thus at a crucial moment strengthened the hands of those who were building the New Model Army. When the king gave himself up to the Scots in May 1646 it still remained to be seen whether total military defeat had brought him to a more compliant frame of mind. There were several reasons why it might not have done so. In the first place Charles himself and the vast majority of his opponents (including Cromwell and Ireton at this stage) believed that his participation in any settlement was essential. It was still unthinkable to establish any permanent form of government without the king. Secondly, he shared Astley's expectation that his enemies would soon quarrel among themselves, and this was one reason why he had chosen to surrender to the Scots rather than to Parliament or the army. Thirdly (although there is no means of knowing whether he was aware of this) the chances of war had left the vanquished more popular than the victors. With the Parliament committed to presbyterianism, and the army increasingly influenced by the views of Levellers and other advanced revolutionaries, only the king still represented the comfortable world of custom and tradition which the great majority of the 'political nation' now wished most earnestly to re-create.

In these circumstances the parliamentary 'Propositions of Newcastle', submitted to the king in July 1646 offered no prospect of agreement. They demanded his submission to the Covenant, surrender of the militia for twenty years, and his consent to the punishment of all his leading supporters. Charles prevaricated, confident that Parliament's position was growing steadily weaker and that the members would soon be forced to make a more acceptable offer. His first assumption was correct, but the immediate consequence was not a reduction of their demands but a settlement with the Scots, whereby the latter withdrew their army from England and handed over their royal prisoner, who was lodged at Holmby House in Northamptonshire in February 1647. Nevertheless, if it had not been for the army the king would probably have been able to dictate terms within a matter of months. His long delayed reply to the Newcastle Propositions, made in May 1647, was studiously moderate. He would surrender the militia for ten years and was prepared to negotiate a religious settlement along presbyterian lines, but he would not allow the arbitrary prosecution of his friends.[1] At this point, sensing that a common front was forming against them, the soldiers intervened. On 4 June a troop of horse removed the king from Holmby and brought him to the army headquarters at Newmarket.

There were many reasons for dissatisfaction with the parliamentary régime, some general and some peculiar to the army. The financial expedients necessitated by the war were bitterly unpopular. Constant riots against the excise produced, in February 1647, a declaratory ordinance promising to abolish it as soon as the army was demobilised. The sequestration of royalist estates was causing a major upheaval in the countryside, and the weekly assessment ordained in 1643 soon became that most resented of impositions, a land tax. Government by committee was relatively efficient, but by 1647 the House of Commons had lost all credibility as a representative assembly. Royalist defectors had been formally expelled in 1644 and their places filled by bye-elections, but the necessity to uphold the Solemn League and Covenant had cut the House off from the sympathies of conservatives and radicals alike.

[1] The king would never accept the permanent loss of military command, or the end of his freedom to choose his own advisers. The only treaty which he actually signed (the Engagement) did not make these demands. He seems to have been less adamant about episcopacy than his later Anglican admirers claimed.

Indeed, the religious situation satisfied nobody. Although an Ordinance of August 1642 had abolished 'all monuments of superstition and idolatry' – notably altars – and the Houses had developed an increasing taste for sabbatarianism, public fasts and other puritan joys, progress towards a new Church order had been slow and hesitant. An Assembly of ministers, nominated by Parliament, had been set up in June 1643, but it was allowed no initiative and beyond an unfulfilled commitment to the abolition of episcopacy had accomplished nothing until the autumn of 1644. At that stage, with the cause in disarray, the combined pressure of the Scots and the presbyterian ministers of London had produced a quicker tempo. The Assembly drew up a *Directory of Worship* to take the place of the *Book of Common Prayer*, and in January 1645 this had been authorised for use, the Tudor legislation enforcing the Prayer Book being repealed. However, the Directory had not been specifically enforced until August 1645, so that for several months England had had two authorised forms of public worship, neither of them prescribed by law. Also, although 1645 had seen a steady progress towards the official establishment of a presbyterian system of Church government, little attempt had been made to implement it outside London,[2] and it had not been until October 1646 that the offices of bishop and archbishop had finally been abolished.

Consequently at the beginning of 1647, when the Scots alliance virtually ceased, there was no effective system of ecclesiastical government. On the other hand, there was no toleration either. As Scottish pressure weakened, its place had been taken by pressure of a different kind. As we have seen, anxiety about religious radicalism in the army had been a major factor in the quarrels of 1644, but the fears then expressed had given way to military necessity. By April 1645 Parliament had felt it necessary to prohibit preaching by laymen, and from then on it became clear that many of the members were looking upon presbyterianism mainly as a means of preserving order. To this the army reacted with natural suspicion. Cromwell and several other senior officers were 'classical' Independents; that is, they asserted the right of each congregation to discipline itself and appoint its own minister without the controlling authority of either presbytery or bishop. This was not incompatible with a national Church of

[2] Presbyteries were organised elsewhere, notably in Lancashire, but these owed little to initiatives coming from the centre.

a loosely federal kind and did not deny that the magistrate had a function to perform in the suppression of blasphemy and the wilder kinds of heresy. The men who held such views have been called 'decentralised Calvinists' for they firmly maintained that each congregation contained both the elect and the reprobate, and that there was no certain means in this world of telling one from the other. At the same time the army had also fostered the growth of a more radical Independency of lower-class origin. The main characteristic of this movement was that its adherents not only believed that they were of the Elect, but that they were the whole Elect, opposition to them in any form being the mark of the Beast.[8] Time was to reveal a deep rift between these two groups, but in 1647 they were united by a common fear of religious authoritarianism, and a common demand for toleration. Faced with a Parliament which was politically aimless and irresolute, while ineffectually committed to an unpopular ecclesiastical system, the army could plausibly claim to be more truly representative of the people.

In fact the majority of the soldiers were not idealists, let alone saints. They had enlisted for pay rather than to fight for religious toleration or civil liberties. Nevertheless, the myth of a sort of 'people's crusade' for political and religious freedom was of contemporary origin and served many useful purposes. The senior officers subscribed to it because it gave them a pretext for using the army as a political weapon in pursuit of their own ideals; the sectaries propagated it with similar hopes, and both in a measure believed it. The ordinary rank and file, with no religious axe to grind, nevertheless accepted it, partly out of natural loyalty to their leaders and partly because they had their own grievances against the Parliament. With incredible ineptitude the latter proposed in the early part of 1647 to draft a proportion of the army to Ireland and to disband the remainder without any guarantee of indemnity, or any security for the many months of back pay which were owing. Parliament did not wish to pass an Act of Oblivion in case the king should seek to have his own supporters included, and it dared not increase taxation to meet the soldiers' demands, but neither of these points was explained.

[8] Most of these sects drew their millenarian schemes from imaginative interpretations of the Apocalypse and the Book of Revelation. The mystical arithmetic of the Beast was called into service in many ways.

The various regiments appointed representatives or 'agitators' to negotiate with the parliamentary commissioners, and only the intervention of Cromwell and Fairfax prevented an open mutiny. The motives of these generals are in some doubt. Both were genuinely concerned for the welfare of their men, but apprehensive at the potential breakdown of discipline. After mediating and negotiating with some success from March until May, Cromwell at least then seems to have made up his mind that the Parliament was incorrigible and determined to direct the grievances of the army into more constructive channels. At the beginning of June the regiments came together at Newmarket in a general rendezvous, seized control of the king and issued their first political manifesto, the *Declaration of the Army*. This document was based upon the claim that the army, as the true defender of the commonweal, possessed a mandate superior to that of the outworn parliamentary junto. It demanded the immediate expulsion of those members hostile to the soldiers, provision for regular future parliaments, and an early dissolution of the existing assembly.

From this point onwards the army dominated the political scene, its overwhelming physical force tempered only by the self-restraint of its leaders and disagreements within its own ranks. A Council was formed, representing both officers and men, and during July this body drew up its own terms for a settlement with the king (the *Heads of Proposals*) apparently seeking to cut the ground from under the Parliament's feet. However, Parliament clung to its rags of constitutional legality and made it perfectly clear that it would yield only to coercion. This Cromwell was reluctant to employ, in spite of any justification which the *Declaration* might have given him. At the end of July the London mob rioted against the Independents,[4] and a military occupation of the City was necessary to enforce the expulsion of the presbyterian leaders from the Commons, but no attempt was made to terminate the Parliament, and the attitude of most of the members continued to be hostile and unyielding. Meanwhile Charles had rejected the *Heads of Proposals*, with the significant remark, 'you cannot be without me; you will fall to

[4] All sorts of contradictory elements can be found in the City in this period. It was the only major stronghold of popular presbyterianism, and at the same time the chief headquarters of the civilian Levellers. The mobs who came out at this time did so in support of the presbyterian members.

ruin if I do not sustain you'. His reaction is not surprising, but it was becoming less realistic. The *Proposals* were more moderate than the parliamentary demands in their attitude to 'delinquents' and put forward no positive scheme of Church government, but they did demand reform of the law and the franchise, both of which reflected the influence of the Levellers in the Army Council. While the senior officers still clung to the necessity for a monarchical form of government, the rank and file were being increasingly influenced by more radical voices. Some of these were religious sectaries who cared nothing for constitutional forms and looked for the coming of the millenium. Others, of which the Levellers were the most important, were mainly concerned to bring about a social revolution of an egalitarian kind, and although not yet specifically hostile to the monarchy, certainly regarded it as dispensable.

The king's rejection of the *Proposals* thus strengthened the position of the radicals and increased the influence of extremists such as John Lilburne who were already calling for the end of the kingship and denouncing Charles as a man 'of bloody and tyrannical spirit'. This development represented a serious threat to Cromwell's control. His continued negotiations, both with the king and with the hated presbyterians, exasperated the ideologists and made even the ordinary soldiers wonder whether he was quite the resolute leader they had taken him for. One radical tract accused the generals of making the king an idol and urged the rank and file, 'ye have men amongst you as fit to govern, as others to be removed, and with a word ye can create new officers'. By October the spirit of mutiny was strong. Fresh agitators were elected, many of them Levellers, and Cromwell had to call a full meeting of the Army Council at Putney on 28 October. The discussions that followed, which are fully documented, brought forth some of the most remarkable social and political speculation of the century.[5] Religious illuminists such as Goffe, and democrats like Rainborough confronted, and sometimes denounced, the more conservative views of Cromwell and Ireton, who continued to believe in the monarchy, a propertied franchise and social hierarchy. In the event, in spite of the

[5] See particularly *The Clarke Papers*, ed. C. H. Firth. The records of these debates are most frequently quoted on the origin of democratic ideas, such as the famous remark by Rainborough, 'I think that the poorest he that is in England hath a life to live as the richest he.'

polemical tracts issued by the radicals and the publicity won for their views by *The Case of the Army truly stated* and the *Agreement of the People*, the conservative leadership prevailed. Cromwell succeeded in getting the production of a new army manifesto referred to a committee. The result was the relatively moderate *Second Agreement*, which was not very different from the *Heads of Proposals*. By the end of November Cromwell felt strong enough to reassert regular military discipline. The agitators were sent back to their regiments, and the Army Council was dissolved.

Had the army fallen apart in this crisis, or its leadership failed, a powerful royalist reaction would certainly have taken place. Every shade of opinion, and every interest which had been of the smallest political significance before 1645 was thoroughly alienated by the social and religious radicalism which had been manifested at Putney. Apart from the sects, who formed only a minute proportion of the population at the artisan level, the army's only civilian support was to be found among those small gentry, lawyers and merchants who were represented by the 'Independent' members of Parliament. These men were not necessarily Independents in the religious sense. Indeed, some of them (such as Sir Arthur Hasilrig) were 'as to religion perfectly presbyterian'. But they were prepared to accept a form of toleration and looked to Cromwell and Ireton as the only men capable of providing a solution to the apparently interminable political deadlock. Those members of Parliament (the majority) who still hoped to make a settlement without the army and to get rid of their overweening foster-child, are in this period confusingly labelled 'Presbyterian'. Many of them were not religious presbyterians, although they had supported that establishment in 1646 when it had briefly seemed likely to provide a remedy for further disintegration. They were united by a common abhorrence of toleration and by conservative social opinions which now clung to the monarchy as being the only familiar landmark still standing above the rising tide of revolution. The great majority of the old political nation was in this sense 'Presbyterian' at the end of 1647.

For these men Cromwell's victory at Putney was a disaster, since it placed him in an unassailable position, and they rightly believed that the continued loyalty of his soldiers would be of greater consequence to him than the life of the king. Charles also saw the explicit threats of the army radicals with growing alarm, and without waiting for the final outcome of the discussions he escaped from custody on 11 November and made his way to the Isle of Wight. There, although he was treated as a prisoner by the parliamentary governor, he was able to complete a secret negotiation with the Scots, whereby he accepted the constitutional position of 1642, agreed to a presbyterian establishment for a trial period of three years, and undertook to suppress the sects. The fact of this Engagement, although not its terms, became known at the end of December when the king rejected a further set of proposals from Parliament. In mid-January negotiations in that quarter were formally broken off,[6] and a Committee of Safety was set up with full executive powers – an ominous warning that the future of the royal office itself was in doubt. By this time Cromwell was personally much more hostile to the king than he had been six months before, but he does not seem to have had any positive course of action in mind. Within two months the progress of events had made his decision for him. Exasperated by heavy taxes and the bad harvest of 1647, hatred of the army and the County Committees flared up in spontaneous revolts all over the country. Royalist groups quickly appeared to take advantage of this situation, and within a few weeks the whole of South Wales, parts of Kent and Essex, and a number of northern towns had fallen under their control.

This crisis looked more dangerous than it really was. The various insurrections were ill-co-ordinated and poorly led. Presbyterian support was only half-hearted, and neither the Parliament nor the City of London would take the risk of breaking with the army. Scotland, enmeshed in the endless complexities of its own politics, could produce only a force of raw levies in defence of the Engagement, while the veteran covenanters led by the Earl of Leven played no part.[7] All that these warlike disturbances really accomplished was to heal the divisions in the army and create among the soldiers a great wave of hostility to the king which swept their leaders along with it and convinced

[6] By the so called 'Vote of No Address', which was repealed in the autumn of the same year.

[7] The covenanters held aloof from this campaign because the king had not actually subscribed to the Covenant. The so called 'Engagers' were mostly members of the nobility and their followers.

them that Charles would have to be removed. In a great prayer meeting at Windsor just before the army went into action in April, it was urged and generally agreed 'to call Charles Stuart, that man of blood, to an account for that blood he had shed, and mischief he had done to his utmost, against the Lord's cause and people in these poor nations'. Over the next four months disciplined forces under Cromwell, Fairfax and Lambert made short work of the royalist rebels, who in spite of their courage had for the most part neither military experience nor proper arms. Only a mutiny in the fleet caused real embarrassment by temporarily blockading London's trade. The king failed to escape from custody, and the Earl of Hamilton's dilatory invasion from Scotland was decisively crushed at the battle of Preston in August. Although a few pockets of resistance held out until March 1649, the war was effectively ended by this blow, and in October the army commanders at last decided to take the political future of the country into their own hands.

THE ENGLISH REVOLUTION IN GOVERNMENT AND RELIGION

Step by step, Charles had destroyed the imposing edifice of obedience and subordination which his predecessors had created and brought the monarchy itself to the verge of destruction. He had done this fundamentally because he had failed to understand the nature of his political inheritance. Partly on account of the divine right ideas which he derived from his father, and partly because he took too literally the royal propaganda of earlier generations, he lived in a deceptively simple world of first principles. The obligation of obedience on the part of his subjects was absolutely binding. The corresponding obligations upon himself to rule in accordance with law and to the glory of God, while equally binding, were more amenable to interpretation. When examined closely, the theoretical limitations upon the English monarchy tended to dissolve. It was consciousness of this fact which sometimes made early seventeenth century common lawyers so perverse in their interpretations of legal history. At the same time the real limitations, although they might be almost equally intangible, were eminently practical. No late medieval king, except the simple minded Henry VI, had been unaware that his obligation to be a 'good lord' to the aristocracy meant an equable distribution of favours and a willingness to listen (at least) to self-important advice. The effectiveness, or even the very existence of his government might depend upon this simple political awareness. The Tudors had succeeded in modifying this obligation and increasing their own freedom of action. But their flamboyant self-confidence concealed an acute awareness of its continued existence. When Charles had entrusted his patronage to the Duke of Buckingham, or ruled through a small faction of courtiers who were cut off from the attitudes of the majority of their class, he had committed one of the most ancient and basic of political sins. By the time he ascended the throne, the traditional methods of calling attention to the need for 'good lordship' – bands of retainers, aristocratic violence, and the ostentatious independence of great provincial families – had withered away. But they had been replaced by the clamorous voices of privilege in the House of Commons, which now represented that class best placed to demand consideration, and Charles never appreciated the significance of that fact.

Nor did he ever understand the extent to which protestant 'godliness' had become an essential characteristic of his office. When medieval kings had needed to be reminded of their obligation to obey the law of God, that task had been performed by the Church, and commonly by the pope. Henry VIII had emancipated himself from such limitation, but in setting up a protestant establishment his daughter had by implication accepted new criteria of 'Godly rule'. Throughout her long reign she had managed to keep the obligations which this involved flexible and ill-defined, but she had nevertheless remained sensitive to that body of moderate puritan opinion which had constituted itself as a sort of national conscience.[8] James, with different assumptions, and without the advantages of his predecessor's anti-catholic record, had largely frittered away the immense advantages which the royal supremacy and the concept of the 'Godly Prince' had given him, and had handed on to his son a situation in which the religious prestige of the monarchy was already heavily undermined. Consequently when Charles had committed himself to the Arminians and ignored the desperate plight of continental protestantism, he had finally cut himself off from the powerful support of Elizabethan protestantism.

[8] This was an achievement which became magnified by time and distance, to her successors' discomfort. *Oliver Cromwell and the Elizabethan Inheritance*, by C. V. Wedgwood (Meade Lecture, 1970).

Thereafter there had been an increasing tendency for puritans to regard such convincing evidence of the king's reprobation as dissolving the bonds of their allegiance. By his actions between 1645 and 1648 Charles had forced many of his opponents to take this way of escaping from the political deadlock, with the result that he placed the initiative in the hands of those with the toughest puritan consciences. By this means the potential radicalism of the puritan movement was released, and constitutional reform and armed rebellion eventually became revolution.

The final determination of the army leaders to take effective political control was probably less the result of victory in the field than of the negotiations which Parliament had been endeavouring to conduct behind their backs. Their allies in the House of Commons had been outnumbered and outmanœuvred by the presbyterians in a desperate bid to convince Charles of the hopelessness of his position and induce him to make a graceful capitulation before it was too late. The news of this attempt made the council of officers more amenable to Leveller pressure and resulted in another *Remonstrance of the Army* which was presented to Parliament on 20 November. In this document, for the first time, the senior officers accepted and expressed the radical view that ultimate sovereignty lay in the people, and that the power of both king and Parliament existed only by delegation. Cromwell was not present at the meetings in which this decision was reached, but he concurred in a letter to Fairfax, and there is no reason to suppose that his presence would have made any substantial difference. The Parliament with astonishing ineptitude paid no attention to the Remonstrance and continued their attempts to come to terms with the king. This was a direct challenge to the army to put its principles into effect, and at the beginning of December Ireton arrested the king and re-occupied the City of London. Logically he should then have dissolved the House of Commons by force and ordered fresh elections, but there were cogent reasons why this could not be done. The army had no practical plan of electoral reform ready for implementation, and even if it had had, the delays and confusions which must have intervened before a fresh House of Commons could meet would have been intolerable in such a tense situation. Any election conducted according to the existing franchise would have produced a House fundamentally hostile to all that the army stood for; and such a house would inevitably have sought an understanding with the king, whom the officers were now determined to bring to a reckoning. Consequently Ireton was reluctantly compelled to purge the House rather than dissolve it, and on 6 and 7 December one hundred and forty members were arrested or excluded, leaving a remnant of about sixty who were regarded as reliable 'Independents'.[9]

The constitutional position of this Rump had neither principle nor practical sense to commend it. It existed only because the army leaders could not bring themselves to overthrow the monarchy and put the king on trial by the naked use of the sword, which was their true mandate. In spite of their willingness to use the language of divine retribution, they did not show that lofty disregard for legal forms which such a conviction should have given them. The Levellers had always been quite prepared to regard the army itself as a representative institution, but Cromwell and his colleagues could never quite stomach such a fiction. Instead, they resorted to the even more implausible device of treating the handful of discredited minor politicians who had been allowed to linger at Westminster as though they were a National Assembly, combining the authority of the sovereign people with the traditional functions of the ancient Parliament. On 4 January 1649 the Rump formally arrogated these powers to itself, declaring

> that the people of England are, under God, the original of all just power . . . that the Commons of England in Parliament assembled, being chosen by, and representing, the people, have the supreme power in this nation . . . that whatsoever is enacted, or declared for law, by the Commons in Parliament assembled, hath the force of law; and all the people of this nation are concluded thereby, although the consent and concurrence of king, or House of Peers be not had thereunto.

This last clause was rendered necessary by the fact that the few peers who had remained at their posts had made it clear that they would not be party to any further change. Two days later another resolution set up the High Court of Justice which was to

[9] These numbers refer only to the members who actually attempted to take their seats on those days (well under half the nominal strength). Altogether 186 were excluded by the army, and 45 arrested, leaving about 250 eligible to sit, but many never did so. D. Underdown, *Pride's Purge*, 208-56.

try the king. Tactically, this move was a blunder and, had the power of the army not been invincible, might have had serious consequences. Theoretically, the Court existed in the name of the people of England, but it had obviously been established by a clique of nonentities who commanded neither allegiance nor respect. It attempted to employ the procedures of the common law, but no law existed for the required purpose. An unconvincing mixture of *ad hoc* improvisation and traditional forms, its erection profited no one but the members of the Rump, who had now unassailably constituted themselves as the chief legal authority in the land.

Charles, inevitably, refused to recognise the jurisdiction of his judges. With an unerring skill which he had never shown in practical politics, he exposed the weaknesses and contradictions in their position and pointed out the ominous significance of allowing justice to be defined by power and not by law. It was a fine performance. Unavailing, of course, for the saving of his own life, but a major contribution to his personal legend, which was to be expressed shortly after his death in the *Eikon Basilike*, a tract so popular that it went through fifty editions in a year. It was no doubt this factor which a recent historian had in mind when he wrote 'They (the army) would have done much better to have tried him by Court Martial and shot him'.[10] Certainly it would have been a more honest expression of the nature of the power at work, but many of the regicides believed in the validity of their mandate both from God and the people (even if they were not very happy about its transmission) and were proud of the openness and publicity of their dealings. Eventually the king was condemned as a traitor for levying war upon his own people and was executed at Whitehall on 30 January 1649. The Rump had now burned its boats. On the day of Charles's death, an Act was passed and promulgated against the proclamation of any successor, and by the middle of March both the royal office and the House of Lords had been abolished.

In a sense revolution could go no further. The whole traditional structure of political obligation built upon the royal office, the 'keystone which closeth up the arch of government and order', had been destroyed. A uni-cameral legislature and a Council of State were the irreducible constitutional minimum, and as far as could be imagined from the traditional machinery

[10] Kenyon, *Stuart Constitution*, 294.

of king, Lords and Commons. At the same time, in other ways change was strictly limited. Over three quarters of the new Council of State which was set up to wield the executive authority of the Crown were members of the Rump, and the remainder were mostly senior army officers. A narrower and more oligarchic government could hardly be conceived than this which operated in the name of the sovereign people. Theoretically rather more than 250 men were entitled to sit in the Rump, but many of them never attended at all, and an average sitting consisted of fewer than eighty. They were of varied status and background, but overwhelmingly men of property and substance, and the majority belonged to the lower or middle ranks of the gentry. Their Independency was of a piece with that of Cromwell and Ireton, and their social attitudes were closer to those of the excluded 'Presbyterians' than they were to those of the Levellers. Hostility to the king had held the Rump, the 'high command' and the true radicals in an uneasy alliance and exaggerated the influence of the last. Men such as Lilburne had been prepared to stomach the unrealistic pretensions of the Rump only as long as it had seemed to be a necessary expedient for bringing Charles to justice. As soon as the trial was over they looked for the implementation of a genuinely democratic constitution, and were bitterly disillusioned.

At the end of February Lilburne presented a petition, subsequently published under the title *England's New Chains Discovered*, in which he called upon the self-styled representatives of the people to face a greatly augmented electorate. The civilian Levellers, who were few but vocal, kept up a constant barrage of protest and criticism throughout the spring of 1649, and this soon began to be echoed by their supporters among the soldiers and junior officers. There were demands for the election of fresh agitators. Cromwell and Ireton were denounced as hypocrites, and an appeal to democratic violence hinted at. This dangerous development quickly stirred the senior officers to action. A number of soldiers were court martialled, several being cashiered and two shot. Although the disaffection was widespread, the discipline of the army as a whole stood the strain, and Cromwell caught and crushed the main body of mutineers at Burford in June.

This final and definitive break did not end the Levellers' vision, or their agitation, but it did end their influence on the English revolution. Whatever republican constitution might eventually emerge, it would be based no less firmly than the monarchy had been upon the sanctity of property. The gentry who had clung to their estates through thick and thin, and the new men who had gained land and wealth during the war, could alike breathe more easily. They might not like Cromwell, but he now seemed to be their only safeguard, and for a little while they were not disposed to be too critical. In fact the political upheavals had created less disturbance in society at large than might be imagined. Some outright royalists fled or were killed in the war, and their estates passed into new hands, but many sequestered properties were sold back to agents of the original owners, who eventually resumed possession. So although confiscated estates to the value of one and a quarter million pounds were disposed of by the government, this did not represent a comparable turnover of personnel.

A more important re-distribution was the sale of Crown and Church lands, which amounted to four and a quarter million pounds in capital value over the whole interregnum, a change which has been compared not unfairly with the dissolution of the monasteries. However, the bulk of this property, like that of the monasteries, was bought by those who were already substantial 'possessioners', so that although the existing gentry were augmented they were neither swamped nor overthrown. What did happen, as we have seen, was a shift of balance. Minor gentry families suddenly became wealthy and important, while men who had been powerful were hard hit by 'compositions' and excluded from office. Royalists were forced to sell lands which were then bought up by their more adroit or fortunate neigbours. All this amounted to a severe shaking, but it was not a revolution. War-time fears of local government dominated by tradesmen and other members of the 'lower orders' turned out to be exaggerated, and when the alarms caused by Leveller influence in the army were finally set at rest, the pattern of authority which had emerged in the counties was not so very different from what had been there before.

This relative stability is well reflected in the fortunes of the common law. Legal reform was undoubtedly needed and had been demanded by conservative oppositionists for many years, but the emphasis placed by both sides upon the preservation of the law during the crisis years caused this need to disappear from sight. It was one of the greatest grievances against Strafford that he had overridden the common law in Ireland, and the destruction of the prerogative courts had ostensibly been undertaken to protect the ancient system from arbitrary interference. The radicals, on the other hand, had no respect for the existing law. Against those parliamentarians who maintained that they were defending the ancient liberties of the Anglo-Saxons against a revival of Norman tyranny, they claimed that, on the contrary, the common law was an invention of the Norman oppressor.

> It is the usual cry and saying [wrote William Cole] both among the masters of oppression, the lawyers, and the ignorant people that know no better, that the laws of England are the safest and best laws in the world; and whosoever shall alter the said laws will unavoidably introduce a mischief instead of a benefit. But to those it is answered, that the major part of the laws made in this nation are founded upon principles of tyranny, fallacy and oppression for the profit and benefit of those that made them.

The defence of property and the defence of the common law went hand in hand. 'Nolumus leges Angliae mutari,' Charles is supposed to have quoted, and the vast majority of those who made the English revolution agreed with him. The Levellers wanted not reform, but a new legal system. They sought the abolition of charters, privileges and titles, the reduction of the law to a simple rulebook, written in English, and the revival of a primitive system of hundred courts in which local juries would have arbitrated on principles of natural justice. This was not the programme of a propertyless rabble, and it was no less self-interested than that which it sought to replace. The Levellers were moderately prosperous peasants and artisans and, like egalitarians in all ages, they wished to destroy the social hierarchy above them while protecting themselves from the pressures of the rootless and destitute. However, this did not make their proposals any more acceptable to those who felt themselves threatened. The lawyers and gentlemen drew together and defended the existing order, abuses and all, as though they were defending their very lives.

With the destruction of the army Levellers in 1649 the most serious danger disappeared, but the feeling of shock remained and impeded all efforts at sober and responsible reform. Without the co-operation of the legal profession reform, as opposed to revolution, was impossible. The Nominated Parliament of 1653, in which some radical notions raised their heads again, tried to abolish the Court of Chancery as 'a mystery of wickedness and a standing cheat'. But neither the members nor Cromwell knew what to put in its place, and it had to go on functioning because its business continued unabated. A few improvements were introduced, such as the use of English in legal records, but on the whole the traditional courts continued unchanged. King's Bench became the Upper Bench, but its termly sittings were never interrupted. As soon as the war itself was over the assizes were resumed, and quarter sessions picked up the threads again in those places where they had snapped.[11] The continuity of personnel was less well maintained. All the high court judges resigned when the monarchy was abolished and refused to serve again. But they were replaced from within the existing system, and the same was true of other officials who resigned for conscientious reasons.

Throughout the period of revolution the law and the property interests which it protected remained untouched, and from that root the traditional system of government was able to grow again with great rapidity in 1660. These important elements of stability also helped to preserve political obedience. In spite of the revolutionary foundations of his power, Cromwell was nevertheless able to inherit much of the social and political discipline which his royal predecessors had so painfully established, and which neither the war nor the unpopularity of Charles's government had wholly uprooted. He was, so to speak, the residual legatee of the political assets of the monarchy, and although he never enjoyed the active co-operation of most of the traditional ruling class, they nevertheless accepted his *de facto* authority. For the most part they confined their active opposition to such constitutional channels as were open to them, and this relative acquiescence cannot be entirely attributed to the effectiveness of the army. This continued to be true even after the rule of the Major Generals had added a particularly

[11] After the abolition of the monarchy, justices of the peace continued to be appointed by the Commissioners of the Great Seal, but their work was much more strictly judicial than it had been before, most of their administrative functions having been taken over by the County Committees.

sour grievance to their discontents in 1655.

While social conservatism was thus winning important victories, the religious conservatives were in full retreat. The reason for this lay largely in the personality of Cromwell himself. The members of Parliament whom Colonel Pride had been instructed to admit in December 1648 had been those who shared his views, both on the defence of property and on religious toleration. Consequently, while the Levellers were fiercely suppressed, the sects flourished. Baptists, Seekers, Ranters and Muggletonians[12] were all free to propagate their gospels in the ecclesiastical vacuum left by the collapse of the presbyterian experiment. After 1650 it was no longer even theoretically compulsory to attend one's parish church. There was no system of government, and no discipline above the congregational level. Cromwell, who depended so heavily upon his own sense of divine inspiration, and 'who waited upon the Lord day and night' before any important decision, was always reluctant to deny the authenticity of another man's vision of God. There was nothing logical about this, for some of the sects held views, for instance on adult baptism and the emancipation of women, which were subversive of the social order which he was anxious to maintain.

The doctrine that Christ died for all men was as democratic in its implications as any aspect of the Leveller programme. Nevertheless Cromwell held firmly to the opinion that many of his soldiers had fought for the freedom of their consciences and must be allowed to enjoy the fruits of their labours. Even the emergence of the Quakers and Ranters after 1652 did not cause him to abandon this principle. The Quakers and Ranters were millenarian extremists, and the most political of the sects. In the days of the Rump many disillusioned radicals took refuge in the hope of an immediate Second Coming and regarded themselves as inspired by God to overthrow the existing order. 'Lord, wilt thou have Oliver Cromwell or Jesus Christ to reign over us?' prayed Vavasour Powell in 1653. Fifth Monarchist risings, such as that led by Thomas Venner in 1657, were effectively suppressed, but no general attempt to proscribe these sects was made (except by implication through the treason laws), and their excesses were never used as a pretext to reimpose religious uniformity. Successive Parliaments and assemblies continued to

[12] The followers of Ludovic Muggleton, one of the more cheerful of the self-appointed messiahs who appeared at this juncture.

legislate on sabbatarianism and the suppression of moral offences, but the enforcement of these laws was entrusted to the secular government. Almost the only central ecclesiastical machinery to be set up under the Protectorate were the committees of 'Triers' and 'Ejectors' who pronounced upon the fitness of ministers and candidates for the ministry – but the criteria of 'fitness' were moral and educational rather than doctrinal.[13]

Within this extremely loose framework both Anglican and presbyterian worship continued in an attenuated form. Groups of ministers formed *ad hoc* presbyteries, particularly in London where their movement was strong, although the discipline which they were able to impose was entirely voluntary and unofficial. The Prayer Book continued to be used, although privately and with discretion, and the great majority of parishes continued to be served by men episcopally ordained. Although the lack of central control distressed authoritarians so much and drove strict men like Baxter into regarding episcopacy as a small price to pay for order, the Church under the Protectorate never dissolved into anarchy. The parochial system remained intact, and the rights of lay patrons very largely so. It was characteristic of Cromwell that, in spite of radical pressure, he should have refrained from interfering with the property rights of patrons. Tithes also remained, in spite of numerous pledges to the contrary, partly for the same reason and partly out of a realistic understanding that a system of voluntary contributions would have left many learned and Godly men in penury. Consequently, although the religious changes were much more radical than those which affected secular society, there too a solid foundation remained upon which an authoritarian superstructure could easily be reimposed.

Unsatisfactory as it was in many ways, the government of the Rump nevertheless survived for over four years. This was partly because Cromwell was reluctant to sever his last link with the traditional legality of the Long Parliament, and partly on account of the other preoccupations which distracted him until the early part of 1652. Shortly after the suppression of the Leveller mutiny in July 1649, he set off for Ireland, and in a series of ferocious battles and sieges over the next ten months reduced that intract-

[13] Local commissions of investigation were also set up on the lines of the traditional episcopal visitations, operating under the control of the central committees.

able country to obedience. Never had the New Model Army fought better, or more savagely, than against the confederate Irish, whom the soldiers genuinely regarded as children of Satan and emissaries of Antichrist. Not only did this bloodthirsty campaign give great encouragement to the apocalyptic orators in the ranks, it also strengthened Cromwell's own sense of mission in a manner which the modern mind is bound to find barbarous.[14]

In May 1650 he was recalled to face a threatened renewal of hostilities from Scotland. The situation in the north was both more straightforward and more dangerous than it had been in 1648, although the basic cause of discontent was the same – fear and hatred of the sects. The English army, wrote Alexander Jaffray, was 'likely to set up a lawless liberty, and toleration of all religions', and for the defence of the Kirk 'no means was thought to be so fit as to bring home our king'. Charles II was more amenable (or less scrupulous) than his father and swore to the Covenant after prolonged negotiations in the spring of 1650. Thus instead of 'the rag and tag of engagers', Charles was supported by a seasoned covenanting army under Alexander Leslie when he arrived in Scotland from the Netherlands in June. The support of the Kirk was not an unmixed blessing, since the ministers insisted on purging some of Leslie's best troops on grounds of ungodliness, but at first the king's position seemed to be greatly strengthened by the element of crusade. After a disagreement with Fairfax which hastened the latter's retirement from public life, Cromwell led his forces north and the two armies spent a debilitating month manœuvring for position along the south shore of the Forth. By the beginning of September the English were bottled up in Dunbar, with Leslie in a commanding position across their line of retreat. Since the Scots were also the more numerous and the better supplied, Cromwell seemed to be faced with total defeat. Such might indeed have been his fate had it not been for the intervention of the men of the Kirk, who, in their anxiety to smite the godless, overcame Leslie's professional objections and insisted upon immediate attack. As a result the Scots abandoned their strategic advantage and were

14 The Protector's policy in Ireland, particularly the massacres at Drogheda and Wexford, has left a permanent blot upon his reputation. The explanation must lie partly in religious fanaticism, but it seems that he was also ill in the course of the campaign, and this may have impaired his judgement. He certainly acted very differently in Scotland – but then the Scots were not catholics.

totally defeated in a pitched battle.

Cromwell naturally, and perhaps with more justification than usual, saw the hand of God in this remarkable reversal of fortunes. Within a few days he had taken Edinburgh and most of the central lowlands, but the war was very far from won. With a political skill remarkable for his twenty years, Charles continued to rally support, now distinctly more royalist than presbyterian in flavour, and was crowned at Scone on New Year's Day 1651. Cromwell was ill in the spring and the English campaign hung fire, while Charles gathered a new army, free from doctrinal distractions. By the summer the results of Dunbar had almost disappeared. At this juncture, in July 1651, the king decided to take a bold and, as it proved, disastrous step. Without waiting to try conclusions with the main English army, he resolved to strike south, expecting little opposition from a disaffected northern militia and a rapturous welcome from the English royalists. He was disappointed. Seasoned troops under Harrison and Lambert commanded the north-east, while Fleetwood with another army waited in the midlands. Some English royalists joined Charles but barely enough to replace the numerous Scots who deserted as they got further from home. By and large the gentry, reassured by the suppression of the Levellers, reacted as their ancestors had reacted when confronted with problems of conflicting allegiances and did nothing, so that Charles was forced to turn towards Wales in search of a more enthusiastic reception. Cromwell, after a remarkable march from Perth, caught up with the royal army at Worcester on 3 September and won the hard fought battle which he later described as 'God's crowning mercy'. Charles escaped to France, leaving his conqueror the undisputed master of what had once been three kingdoms. Scotland, denuded alike of troops and leaders, was effectively won by a small army under George Monk, who had overcome all organised resistance before the battle of Worcester was fought. A sensible scheme of union was put into effect within a year, and Monk behaved with studied generosity and moderation, but the Scots never became reconciled to Independency. By 1653 royalist revolts were again breaking out, and an army of occupation had to remain in the north, with significant results in the crisis of 1659-60.

INSTRUMENT OF GOVERNMENT

By the end of 1651 Cromwell was thus free for the first time to pay serious attention to the problem of a permanent constitutional settlement. The Rump had never been intended as more than a temporary expedient, but the task of replacing it with something more satisfactory had not grown any easier since December 1648. The army naturally wanted to get rid of it and hold fresh elections, but there were many disagreements over the nature of the franchise which should be employed. The Rumpers equally wanted to get rid of the army now that the war was over, to create a new citizen militia, and to use their existing legal position to guarantee the survival of the traditional social structure. In November 1651 a rough bargain was struck, whereby the Rump agreed to dissolve itself on 3 November 1654, in return for a reduction in the army establishment. Shortly after, the long awaited Act of Oblivion was passed; but the soldiers, with time on their hands, were soon agitating again for an immediate dissolution.[15] Cromwell, with whom the initiative now lay, seems to have remained in a state of chronic uncertainty. He had no illusions about the Rump as a representative assembly and knew that it must be replaced, but he was a prey to conflicting ideas. A tolerant and loosely federated state Church, on the lines of a scheme proposed by John Owen, the Dean of Christ Church, was a *sine qua non*. But he was also quite sincere in wanting a Parliament which would be genuinely representative of the propertied classes. These aims were simply incompatible. Religious toleration commanded no general acceptance at any social level and could only be maintained by armed force under one disguise or another. No elected assembly would be as amenable to Cromwell's religious programme as the Rump, but the army either could not or would not appreciate that fact. 'I am as much for government by consent as any man,' he is alleged to have declared, but if you ask me how it is to be done, I confess I do not know.'

The last seven years of Cromwell's life were a commentary upon this text. In August 1652 the Council of Officers again petitioned for a dissolution, and a Committee on Elections was at

15 By this time England was at war with the Dutch, but since this was a naval war the army remained unemployed.

length set up. However, when the next step came it was not by deliberation, but by the kind of dramatic action with which Cromwell had cut Gordian knots in the past. Exasperated by the Rump's delays, and realizing that he could not both continue to negotiate with them and retain the confidence of the army, he went to the House, on 20 April 1653, accompanied by a file of musketeers, and put a forcible end to their prevarication. He and his colleagues were now face to face with the fact that, whatever theoretical position they might adopt, they were the sovereign power in the state, 'The Parliament is not the supreme power,' Cromwell had earlier told the Council of Officers, 'but that is the supreme power that calls it.' The only justification for such a position must lie in an appeal to the will of God, and it was upon this basis that the next experiment in government was conducted. Cromwell had been considering the idea of a nominated assembly before he put an end to the Rump, and in May a request was sent out to the Independent congregations of England and Wales to submit lists of God-fearing men who might serve in such a body. In the circumstances this concept had a certain logic. If traditional representation was to be abandoned for the pursuit of a religious ideal, then the participation of those who shared that ideal was both just and reasonable. If England was going to be subjected to the 'rule of the saints', then the gathered congregations were the right places to look for consent. On 4 July 1653, 129 chosen men from England and Wales, 5 from Scotland and 6 from Ireland met in the Council Chamber at Whitehall. Although not summoned under that name, this assembly at once designated itself a Parliament and removed the scene of its deliberations to Westminster.[16]

The experiment did not work. Although it contained a surprisingly large number of traditional 'parliament men', the House was (not unexpectedly) dominated by inexperienced idealists who immediately attempted to implement a programme of advanced reform. To save taxation, the army's pay was to be reduced; ecclesiastical patronage was to be abolished, and the common law heavily pruned. All these were explosive issues, into which the members rushed, heedless of the implications.

[16] The nickname 'Barebones' Parliament' (derived from the name of one of the members, the London Baptist and leatherseller Praise-God Barebones) was only invented later. The best account of this experiment is contained in A. Woolrych, *Commonwealth to Protectorate* (1982).

This wild career was checked, not by Cromwell, but by the soberer members of the assembly itself who contrived by a subterfuge to vote their own dissolution on 12 December and surrendered their power to the Lord General, from whom it had been received. The Council of Officers was clearly expecting the *dénouement*, since within a few days it had an alternative plan ready to put into operation. On 16 December this plan was published as the *Instrument of Government*, and Cromwell was sworn in as Lord Protector.

The *Instrument* was a fully fledged written constitution, offering for the first time a rational attempt to create a permanent government along the lines laid down in 1647. Unfortunately it was the work, not of constituent assembly (a device which never seems to have been considered), but of a group of men determined to cling to power. Cromwell may have been quite sincere in believing that his own position must be preserved as a divine trust to protect his policy of religious toleration, but from the constitutional point of view he might just as well have been clinging to power for its own sake. The *Instrument* appeared to be nothing but a compromise of interests. The executive was vested in the quasi-monarchical office of Protector which was endowed with a guaranteed revenue of £200,000 a year, the remaining Crown lands, and other perquisites of royalty. The Protector had to choose his officers of state 'with the approbation of Parliament', but he was given extensive powers to legislate by decree while Parliament was not sitting. These decrees could not become permanent without ratification, but Parliament was only required to sit for five months in each period of three years. The legislature was to consist of a single chamber of 400 members which was to be called 'Parliament'. 340 of these members were to represent constituencies in England and Wales, and 30 each were to be drawn from Scotland and Ireland. The English and Welsh seats were to be so extensively redistributed that they bore little relation to the composition of the traditional House of Commons.[17] The franchise was now uniformly based upon the substantial property qualification of £200 in real or personal estate.

[17] 264 were to be county seats, as against 90 in the traditional Parliament. This had the effect of keeping up the number of country gentry being elected, in spite of the fact that they partly lost their hold upon the boroughs.

The *Instrument* proved to be unworkable because Cromwell's attempt to obtain the co-operation of the traditional ruling class failed. When the first assembly to be elected on the new franchise met in September 1654 it proved to be as recalcitrant as the Commons of the Long Parliament, and for much the same reasons. The members represented the wealth of the nation, but they were given no real power and immediately suspected with justice that their function was merely to add an appearance of constitutional consent to a self-perpetuating military dictatorship. They attacked Cromwell's control of the army, his income, and his veto on legislation, in the true spirit of 1641. The Protector was more fortunate than Charles in that he was able to resort to dissolution as soon as the five months were up, and on 22 January 1655 he closed the session with a turgid and emotional denunciation of their obstructiveness. There is no doubt that Cromwell was bitterly disappointed by this rebuff, and he made no further attempt to face a representative assembly until September 1656.

In the meanwhile there was much to be done, and if the problems of administration and local government could be solved effectively, the problem of Parliament might solve itself. There were constant rumours of a royalist conspiracy, and early in 1655 a small rebellion occurred in the south-west, normally known as Penruddock's rising. It was a feeble affair and soon suppressed, but it served to draw attention to the security problem and to justify the continuation of an inflated military establishment. Cromwell knew well enough how unpopular the cost of the army was, and how impossible it would be to maintain himself without it. If only the professional soldiers could be made less obtrusive they might become proportionally less obnoxious. Consequently a new militia scheme was evolved early in 1655, whereby groups of professional officers and N.C.O.s were to be sent into the regions to raise and train local levies, along the lines of the traditional trained bands. The remainder of the professional establishment was to be gradually diminished, and would finally 'wither away' when the new militia was ready to take its place. This scheme had many attractive features. It guaranteed employment to the leaders of the existing army, promised financial retrenchment, and seemed to offer a way back to civilian government which would not issue an open invitation to counter-revolution. The first area to receive the benefit of the new plan was the south-west, where Penruddock's rising gave a pretext for the despatch of John Desborough as 'major general of the west' in March 1655. By October England had been divided into ten regions with a Major General for each, and although the principal instructions of these provincial commanders were concerned with the militia it soon became apparent that they were being treated as a new device for centralising control of local government. No attempt was made to replace the existing machinery of sheriffs, J.P.s, County Committees and other special commissions, but the Major Generals were superimposed upon them, rather like Richelieu's Intendants.[18] Within a few months the government in London was deluging them with instructions, largely of a disciplinary nature, as the Tudors had deluged their J.P.s. Apart from the militia itself, their chief responsibility soon became the collection of a 'decimation tax' to maintain it. This was supposed to be levied upon 'known royalists' of proven wealth, (£100 per annum in land, or £1,500 in personal estate) but its application in practice was flexible, and was both bitterly unpopular and a sad disappointment to those who had looked forward to a period of 'healing and settling'.

Assisted as they were by their military aides, there was no gain-saying these masterful newcomers, and far from making the military dictatorship less conspicuous, they crammed it down the throats of the county gentry as never before. Non-co-operation was widespread, but much less effective as a sanction than it had been in earlier years, when the government lacked other resources. The Major Generals chose such agents as they needed, and if the old ones would not serve they chose new. They were reluctant, usually, to look outside the ranks of the gentry, but within that class they could still find many who were anxious to climb the county ladder, even in such unpopular company. They were for the most part hard working administrators and men of integrity, but some of them were censorious puritans and all were of relatively humble origin. They were uniformly hated and seem to have been genuinely distressed by their own unpopularity. In 1657 these agents of the new 'thorough' were sacrificed to the Protector's renewed need for a

[18] Officials appointed by, and directly responsible to, the central government of contemporary France. Cardinal Richelieu did not invent the position, but he did revive it and made it effective, so it is normally associated with him.

measure of parliamentary co-operation,[19] but by then they had probably contributed more than any other single factor to the mounting desire for a return to the old ways and the old inefficiencies.

By the terms of the *Instrument*, the Protector could both tax and legislate by decree. But whereas reluctant taxpayers could be persuaded by the army, there was no means of forcing the legal profession to administer unratified laws. The legal validity of the *Instrument* itself was not called in question, but a serious attempt was made to compel Cromwell and his advisers to abide by its principles. Many judges and other officials resigned in 1655 and 1656, protesting that they were prepared to accept the constitution for the sake of good government, but would not accept its constant manipulation by the executive. Consequently in September 1656 a new Parliament was summoned. The Major Generals did their best to influence elections, and the Council of Officers excluded one hundred members before they could take their seats, but the hostility of the assembly was not noticeably diminished. Consequently a well intentioned group led by James Ashe petitioned Cromwell to accept the Crown. A monarchy seemed to be the most acceptable form of government, and Cromwell could not be got rid of, so there was much sense in this suggestion. To the Protector, however, it would have been little short of apostasy, and the reaction from republican elements in the army was strong enough to convince him that a mutiny would result. So the *Humble Petition and Advice* was rejected in April 1657.

Nevertheless, amendments to the *Instrument* were accepted which placed the Protectorate upon a semi-hereditary basis by giving the holder for the time being the right to nominate his successor. A 'Second House' was also authorised, and the government's permanent finances were placed upon a fresh footing. The constitution as thus amended came into operation with the reassembly of Parliament in January 1658, but its life was short. Those members who had been excluded in 1656 were now admitted after swearing a simple oath of loyalty to the Protector, but many of them were deeply incensed by the high-handed

[19] In January 1657 the Parliament refused to ratify the decimation tax, thus cutting the ground from under the new militia, and other evidence of their unpopularity persuaded the Protector to cut his losses.

attitude of the executive and resented the constitutional changes which had been enacted without their consent. They consequently launched an immediate attack upon the 'Second Chamber', which had been carefully selected from among the staunchest upholders of the regime. After less than a fortnight, on 4 February, Cromwell dismissed the House in a towering rage. He never faced another, for on 3 September he died with the constitutional problem still unresolved, and with his death the last element of justification departed from a government which was essentially his personal creation.

Cromwell had been an able man, feared and respected. Above all he had been a man whose formidable integrity was bound up with an ideal which depended upon power. When he was gone the spell was broken, and his ideal appeared a petty and sectarian interest. His son and successor, Richard, had neither the character nor the ability to sustain his position, and the Council of Officers broke up into quarrelling factions. Within a few months the Protectorate had collapsed in political bankruptcy, a ruin only preserved from dissolution by the swords of an increasingly bewildered and frustrated army. By the autumn of 1659 many of the soldiers felt with justice that they were merely being used as pawns in a power game played by their officers under the pretext of the 'good old cause'. Consequently when the sane and intelligent voice of George Monk, backed by the financial resources of the City of London, offered them a means of escape from this increasingly meaningless charade, most of them were only too glad to take it. Once the doctrinaire resistance of the army had been overcome, the restoration of the monarchy was only a matter of time and negotiation. The wise and moderate Declaration of Breda, issued on 4 April 1660, determined the final form of the settlement by basically accepting the constitutional changes of 1641. At the end of May Charles landed at Dover, in the middle of what was officially regarded as the twelfth year of his reign.

Within a few months there were few traces of the long interregnum to be seen. Indeed the 'English revolution' in a sense had been only skin deep. Had the concept of popular sovereignty, so freely canvassed, been rigorously applied, the situation might have been very different. But it proved to be little more than a theoretical expedient to justify the execution of Charles I whose continued existence had become a political impossibility. Consequently, the republican constitutions had lacked conviction, depending upon nothing more than the *de facto* position of Cromwell and the army. Thanks partly to the alarming experience of the revolution itself, the normal patterns of political behaviour and obedience had been largely restored by 1650, and it was only Cromwell's puritan scruples which prevented a traditional form being given to his authority, as the *Humble Petition and Advice* makes clear.

The various regimes of the interregnum had not been without their positive achievements, particularly in foreign policy and in the encouragement of economic development. They had failed to produce a stable constitutional or ecclesiastical settlement, but the execution of the king and the abolition of the Anglican church could never be forgotten or ignored. The political situation in England could never be quite the same again. Although Divine Right theory and an intolerant Laudian hierarchy both returned in 1660, the Tudor monarchy, as it had been wielded by Elizabeth and adapted by James and Charles, perished in the civil war. Charles II may have entertained absolutist ambitions, but he was in no position to execute a policy of 'thorough', even if he had had the energy and application to try. The powerful equity jurisdiction of the prerogative, feudal revenues, and that paternalistic fiscal system which had briefly seemed to offer an alternative to parliamentary taxation, had all disappeared.[20]

The search for a stable settlement was not over in 1660. The next thirty years were to reveal that both the Crown and the church could still reflect the authoritarian attitudes of continental absolutism. Yet parliament met almost every year until 1681, and represented the full weight of the landed

[20] During the interregnum, in spite of the heavy taxation, wealth by trade and industry increased because the government was prepared to listen to the advice of those who had most experience of the markets. The new excise and other taxes, much as they were disliked, also removed the incentive for monopolies and other similar devices – which were no longer worth the trouble they caused. Whether Charles II or James II could have financed their governments for any length of time without occasional parliamentary grants must remain an open question. The intention in 1660 was to give the king an adequate ordinary revenue, along the lines proposed in the Great Contract of 1610, and it was not deliberate meanness which prevented that from happening. At the same time the fear of parliamentary obsolescence, so strong in the early seventeenth century, is not noticeable after 1660.

and propertied interests without which no English government could function. Thanks to Cromwell's fundamental conservatism, the landed interest emerged in 1660 much less changed than the monarchy which was so ostentatiously restored, but the final constitutional balance between the two was still to be struck.

Significantly, it was the defence of property rather than indefeasible right which was to form the basis for the political thinking of the next generation. The institutions of English government, both political and ecclesiastical, were to be defended upon grounds of good sense and convenience rather than by invoking the first principles of an earlier generation. The bitter ideological strife of the 1640s produced a reaction which lasted many years and was not repeated in the next crisis of 1689–90. At the same time, the aristocracy had received a sharp lesson. 'Posterity will say,' a royalist writer had declared in 1649, 'that we overthrew the king to subject ourselves to the tyranny of the base rabble.' Thanks to Cromwell this had not happened, but it had come close enough to constitute an unmistakable warning of the dangers which could follow if the 'lower orders' were called in to settle quarrels within the ruling class. The experience was never to be forgotten and was not to be repeated in this country until the eve of the present century.

In 1660 no less than in 1450, the aristocracy were in command of the political situation. But whereas the feudal magnates of the fifteenth century had been individuals whose power lay in their own resources, the squires and politicians of the Restoration were the masters of a sophisticated constitutional and administrative machine. That machine was primarily the creation of the Tudor monarchy, which, by a long slow process of unification and centralisation had made England the governable entity which it was in the late seventeenth century. That civil order and political obedience to which all the monarchs had contributed from Edward IV onwards had been shaken by the civil war and its immediate aftermath, but was ultimately strengthened rather than destroyed by the shock. The political system which was to emerge in England between 1660 and 1689 bore little resemblance to the Tudor monarchy in any of its more obvious features, but it was nevertheless firmly rooted in the successes and limitations of the government which they had created.

APPENDIX

The following corrections and reappraisals should be read in connection with the pages and referred to:

p.14 ll. 1–7 At the same time the resources of government were overtaxed to sustain an aggressive and untenable position in Scotland, and the combination of these controversial policies with the Protector's autocratic political style further alienated his natural allies among the aristocracy.

p. 14. l. 24 Mary disappointed many of the expectations which had been aroused by her accession. Her political inexperience, and her deep distaste for the course of events in England during the preceding twenty years seriously impaired her relationship, not only with the political nation, but even with her own Council.

p.15 l. 5 The natural misfortunes of her reign exposed her to polemical attacks which seriously undermined her credibility. Her failures should not be over-emphasised, and the aristocratic experimentation with parliament does not now appear to have been as significant as I originally thought. In many ways her government was successful and well organised, but the main premises upon which it was based failed to convince either the political nation or her natural heir, both of whom had developed a sense of national priorities which Mary did not share.

p.15 ll. 26–8 It would be more accurate to say that it kept that institution in good working order, and maintained its political significance.

p.18 ll. 1–4 This constitutional revolution brought to power a group of men from the lower reaches of the 'political nation', and turned the traditional order, 'middle to top'. The alienation of these men from the 'political nation' has been exaggerated here.

p. 23 ll. 21–6 Specific pardons were pleaded in court by only about 10 per cent of defendants who appeared, but Henry VI issued some 12,000 'general' pardons between 1437 and 1460, which must have had the effect of deterring many potential plaintiffs from approaching the courts at all.

p. 28 It was perfectly possible for a substantial gentleman, even in a troubled area like Suffolk, to live out a long and peaceful life without ever becoming embroiled in legal or physical conflict. Colin Richmond, *John Hopton; a Fifteenth-century Suffolk Gentleman* (CUP, 1981).

p. 90 ll. 12–13 The original leaders appear to have been former household servants of Edward IV, prompted perhaps by personal loyalty, but the Duke of Norfolk appeared to have the situation well under control.

p. 93 ll. 17–25 He had for years been hailed by Welsh bardic poets as the 'son of prophecy' who was to restore the ancient British hegemony over England, but such expectations had been held (and disappointed) before, so that this support did not very readily translate into soldiers.

p. 118 ll. 6–10 Here the king followed a policy of binding the great Marcher Lords by indentures for the proper discharge of their offices, and started with his uncle Jasper Tudor, Duke of Bedford. This system did not amount to direct interference in the Lordships, but was fairly effective as a means of improving the standard of law enforcement.

p. 123 Henry is not remembered for the magnificence of his court, but he was much respected at the time as a generous and discriminating patron, who drew his inspiration from the Ducal court of Burgundy. He spent lavishly on jewels, which were a recognised form of investment, and on books, of which he was an avid collector. He transformed the small Royal Library of Edward IV into one of the most prestigious collections in Europe, and his image among renaissance scholars was far removed from the dowdy miser of subsequent folklore.

p. 130 ll. 7–11 This statement now appears to be too strong; the 'political nation' hankered rather for the unsatisfactory compromise which her father had left. The queen's authority was challenged only briefly, but its limitations were clearly revealed by her failure to create a party committed to the continuance of her policies.

p. 141 ll. 33–6 An attempt was made to remedy this situation by building up the power of Charles Brandon, Duke of Suffolk, in North Wales and the Lordship of Chirk, but Brandon, who was essentially a court peer, was unable to command sufficient local following.

p. 142 ll. 18–22 This statement has now been invalidated by the researches of Dr Guy. Wolsey's major instrument, although he did not invent it, was the Court of Star Chamber. Through this court he was able to exercise closer control over the Justices of the Peace, and occasionally to call to account major officials who had abused their trust, or used the intricacies of the common law to frustrate the ends of justice. His hankering after the Roman Law was an hypothesis of A. F. Pollard.

p. 142 ll. 32–5 St Germain did not, of course, add that certainty might be no substitute for justice, because the powerful traditions of the common lawyers made them notoriously blind to their own failings. His determination to expose those failings added greatly to the hatred which Wolsey incurred.

p. 164 ll. 27–9 It is now clear that he did not originate that policy, all the essentials of which were present in a memorandum of advice to the king drawn up in 1529 and known as the 'Collectanea satis copiosa'.

p. 173 ll. 27–8 Cromwell also showed considerable social idealism. His concept of the king's role in protecting the interests of the commonwealth laid the foundations for the social responsibility of central government.

p. 177 ll. 29–34 In spite of their statutory origin, these courts were not answerable to Westminster but to the chanceries which already existed in the Principality, and the judiciary in Wales consequently enjoyed an autonomy not accorded to any other part of the kingdom.

p. 183 l. 1 Several of these nobles and gentlemen had had close connections with Catherine, and were strongly sympathetic to Mary. They have been dubbed the 'Aragónese faction', and their role in the overall movement remains a controversial one. They had certainly suffered a humiliating reversal at Cromwell's hands after the fall of Anne Boleyn, and were willing to seize any opportunity to get rid of him. G. R. Elton, 'Politics and the Pilgrimage of Grace', *Studies in Tudor and Stuart Government and Politics*, III, 183–216.

p. 193 ll. 24–9 Conservative ecclesiastics had become seriously alarmed by the disruptive sermons of radical preachers claiming Cromwell's patronage, particularly in London, and their fears may also have communicated themselves to the king, helping to make the charge of sacramentarianism stick.

p. 201 ll.15–20 Many lay fraternities also disappeared under the terms of this Act, and the remainder disintegrated with the repudiation of Purgatory, leaving a gap in popular piety which was never really filled. J. J. Scarisbrick, *The Reformation and the English People*, 19–40.

p.205 l. 12 And above all by the debilitating campaign in Scotland.

p. 252 ll. 8–9 Elizabeth, not entirely convinced of his professions of goodwill, made her own preparations behind the scenes, but in this case the king was entirely sincere, and carefully stayed out of England during Mary's last illness to avoid complicating the situation.

p. 254 ll. 13–28 The existence of this 'pressure group' now appears highly unlikely in the sense suggested here, and Elizabeth probably needed no prompting in the direction of a protestant settlement. Whatever the queen may have intended in January, it seems clear that by March she was seeking a fully reformed establishment, along the lines that her brother had pioneered. The House of Lords had unwittingly encouraged her in that direction by passing the Supremacy bill and rejecting protestant uniformity. N. L. Jones, *Faith by Statute*.

p. 268 ll. 11–15 The rivalry of these two men was an important fact of life at court by the summer of 1560, but not as dominant as this statement would suggest. Cecil was not a courtier and not all Dudley's enemies were his friends.

p. 278 ll. 8–11 Far from consciously seeking increased control over policy, however, the members were predominantly concerned to keep their institution in being. Not only were they the sole constitutional curb upon royal absolutism, but also keenly aware that they were the last effective Estates in Europe.

p. 284 ll. 8–9 Throughout the country a substantial number of Marian priests continued to administer the sacraments, and to keep the traditional faith alive, but they had little contact with the mainstream of European catholicism, and their commitment to the papacy was not improving with time and isolation.

p. 284 ll. 24–32 It was also, increasingly, a faith of the aristocracy and their dependants; partly because it was a well-established Counter Reformation tactic to concentrate upon the upper ranks of society, and partly for reasons of convenience which were not always creditable to the missionaries.

pp. 300–5 In spite of her skill in managing them, Elizabeth was never overfond of parliaments. She was far more aware than were the members of the thinness of the ice beneath her feet. The House of Lords was still politically the more important, but the House of Commons represented the wealth of the country – not only because of the rapid rise in the size of the gentry class since 1540 but also because the obsolete forty shilling franchise and its urban equivalents by this time entitled over a quarter of the adult male population to vote. The queen was very willing to take her faithful Commons into partnership, but it had to be strictly on her terms, and the more often parliament met, the more difficult that became. It was for this reason that she was always careful to keep both Houses fully occupied about their proper business, which was legislation, and was never fully frank about her financial difficulties. The queen was more inclined to choose policies which she believed she could afford than seek means to pay for necessary action.

Inflation and evasion had, by 1585, reduced each parliamentary subsidy to about half its 1559 value, and although the Council threatened, no strenuous attempts were made either to improve collection or to update the assessments. The English taxation system was in many ways the most equitable in Europe, in that the poor paid little or nothing. However, the lightness of the burden, which played a major part in increasing the relative wealth of the English aristocracy, had by 1603 reduced the Crown to financial exhaustion. In the long run this was to expose its power to political erosion.

p. 305 l. 26 Unfortunately, the manner in which she did this enabled it to be claimed later that she had confessed to an improper use of the prerogative.

p. 332 James was, as he rightly pointed out, an 'old and experienced king', but his very success in Scotland proved to be in some ways a handicap. He approached his new subjects with a self-confidence which was not entirely justified.

p. 342 ll. 13–20 James was an orthodox Calvinist, but his view of the supremacy gave him some common ground with the supporters of *iure divino* episcopacy, and probably explains his promotion of the theologically uncongenial Bancroft after Whitgift's death.

p. 344 l. 28 They were also significantly better educated, as the lay aristocracy increasingly moved into the universities, and sent their sons to the schools which they and their immediate predecessors had endowed.

pp. 352–3 The account of James's relations with the puritans given here I now regard as quite unsatisfactory. Particularly, the Hampton Court Conference should be completely reassessed in the light of recent research. In some ways James was the ideal man to handle the religious situation of 1603. His Calvinism placed him in the mainstream of English protestant thinking, and his belief in an episcopal form of church government also prompted him to defend the *status quo*. In fact he found the Church of England much more congenial than the presbyterian Kirk, which had proved so independent and recalcitrant. Although he alarmed some of his bishops by his sympathetic reception of the Millenary petition, and by his decision to call the Hampton Court Conference, their fears were soon allayed. This was not because James quarrelled with the puritans, indeed he accepted a long list of moderate proposals for detailed reform, but because he entrusted the enforcement of these reforms to the bishops themselves, and took no particular pains to make sure that this was carried out. He was also slightly more sympathetic than Elizabeth had been to the autonomy of the church, encouraging his bishops to use their own jurisdiction, forbidding them by statute to alienate their lands, and returning impropriated tithes in royal hands. No puritan could object to these latter measures, but the king's willingness to allow Bancroft to conduct a small purge of non-conformists after 1603, and his failure to implement most of the Hampton Court reforms, produced a constant trickle of grumbles during the various sessions of the first parliament.

p. 354 ll. 17–27 There was puritan distrust of James's supposed catholic sympathies, but they were less emphatic and important than this passage would suggest.

pp. 354–5 Although the religious implications of his foreign policy produced suspicion and hostility, the later parliaments of the reign were singularly free from puritan agitations of a domestic nature. The king's obvious enthusiasm for the revised English Bible, which was to bear his name, and his support for the orthodox party at the Synod of Dort in 1619, reassured the majority of English protestants and held in check those doubts which his vacillating policy towards catholicism undoubtedly caused. The High Church or Arminian party made little progress after the Calvinist George Abbott replaced Bancroft in 1611, and the godly gentlemen of the House of Commons concluded that the king was theologically sound, and sufficiently willing to extend practical toleration to moderate puritans.

p. 359 ll. 32–5 Apart from this subsidy Act, there was again, as in 1614, no legislation, which not only indicates the extent to which normal procedures were disrupted, but also the fact that government could perfectly well be carried on without them.

p. 361 ll. 24–36 Although the Privy Councillors were better organised in this parliament than at any time since 1604, the king's three principal men of business, Bacon, Coke and Cranfield, were bitterly at odds. As we have already seen, Coke hated Bacon, and at the beginning of the session the Commons were treated to the spectacle of Coke and Cranfield urging them on to the establishment of a committee of inquiry into judicial abuses which was clearly aimed at the Lord Chancellor.

p. 362 It would be more accurate to say that the parliamentary session of 1621 gave an important warning of what could happen when factious divisions and poor management combined with a measure of determined opposition. Just as in 1614, the basic problem was the willingness of certain councillors to work out their private feuds at the expense of the king's service, and James's willingness to tolerate such behaviour. The consequences were actually worse than those of the Addled Parliament, because they included the fall of one of the king's ablest ministers at a time when he could be ill spared, and an unresolved deadlock over foreign policy, which raised again in an acute form the problem of the proper limitations of parliamentary action. There was still too little continuity of organisation or personnel to justify the use of a collective term.

p. 365 ll. 1–7 The 'conspiracy of rich men' now consisted of favourites and parasites who swarmed around the king and Buckingham, and the former's willingness, and ability, to provide a remedy was no longer trusted.

p. 367 ll. 11–35 If anything, his hold over Charles was more secure than over James, thanks partly to their shared experience in Spain. In spite of his close personal relationship with James, Buckingham was constantly on edge lest he be replaced in the royal favour by the same means which he himself had employed. No such fear seems to have touched his relationship with Charles, which appears to have had no physical aspect. James also retained an independent mind to the last, in spite of age and sickness. John Williams, Bishop of Lincoln, who became Lord Keeper in July 1621, was the king's own choice, although he took care not to offend the all-powerful favourite. Moreover, Williams was able to remain in office after he had fallen out with Buckingham in 1623, but he did not long survive the old king's death, being dismissed in October 1625.

p. 368 l. 31 The conversion of Buckingham's mother, Mary, in 1622 increased its strength and prestige.

p. 371 ll. 18–27 Cranfield was an obstacle to the war party, which by this time consisted of the unlikely coalition of Charles and Buckingham with Pembroke, Digges, Eliot and other 'country' spokesmen. In the circumstances the outcome of his impeachment was a foregone conclusion.

p. 384 ll. 34–8 Having abolished the monarchy and the House of Lords, they left the pattern of land ownership substantially unaltered. Abolishing the episcopate and the Anglican liturgy, they left the parochial structure and its supporting tithes. The opportunity for social revolution on Leveller lines was deliberately rejected.

p. 386 ll. 18–26 During the period which immediately followed the dissolution, the position of the Crown became somewhat stronger. In some quarters there was a revulsion against the tactics of Eliot and his associates, and a feeling that it was they rather than the king who were provoking conflict. A few years without a parliament might therefore have encouraged a return to normal co-operation. However, Charles remained aloof and inarticulate, making no move to take advantage of this hopeful spirit, and as the years passed apprehensions about the future of parliament returned with redoubled vigour.

p. 427 Many of the royalists were young men, and the age profile of the king's armies was consistently lower than that of parliament's throughout the war – an indication of the fundamental conservatism of most of those who supported the parliamentary cause.

p. 445 ll. 29–38 James had continued to wield the royal supremacy in the manner appropriate to a 'Godly Prince', but had not succeeded in pacifying the anti-catholic suspicions of his subjects, and had failed to capitalise upon his theological affinities with the Calvinists.

p. 458 ll. 16–19 The representatives of the congregations were invited, not nominated as suggested here. After some consultation with local officials, and with the gathered churches, a balanced list was drawn up by the Council of Officers, ranging from Fifth Monarchist tradesmen to pillars of county society.

SELECT BIBLIOGRAPHY

SECTION 1 GENERAL (Sources, contemporary works and studies covering two or more of the four periods into which this study is divided.)

A *Printed sources and contemporary works*

Acts of the Privy Council of England (1542–1604, 1613–1631) eds., J. R. Dasent, etc., London, 1890–1907, 1921–64.

Byrne, M. St C., ed., *The Lisle Letters*, 6 vols., Chicago/London, 1981.

Calendar of the Patent Rolls (1485–1509, 1547–1578) eds., R. H. Brodie, etc., London, 1914–1916, 1924–1929, 1936–1939, 1939–1982.

Calendar of State Papers, Domestic (1547–1704) eds., R. Lemon, etc., London, 1856–1947.

Calendar of State Papers, Foreign (1547–1592) eds., W. Turnbull, etc., London, 1861–1980.

Calendar of State Papers, Spanish (1485–1603) eds., G. A. Bergenroth, etc., London, 1862–1954.

Calendar of State Papers, Venetian (1202–1675) eds., Rawdon Brown, etc., London, 1864–1898, 1900–1940.

Elton, G. R., *The Tudor Constitution* (2nd edition), Cambridge, 1982.

Hall, Edward, *The Union of the Two Noble and Illustre Families of York and Lancaster*, London, 1542, ed., H. Ellis, London, 1809.

Hughes, P. L. and Larkin, J. F., eds., *Tudor Royal Proclamations*, New Haven, Conn., 1964–1969.

Hughes, P. L. and Larkin, J. F., eds., *Stuart Royal Proclamations*, vol. 1, 1603–1625, Oxford, 1973.

Journals of the House of Commons (1547–1714) London, 1742; repr., 1803.

Journals of the House of Lords (1509–1714) London, 1767; repr., 1846.

Kenyon, J. P., *The Stuart Constitution*, Cambridge, 1966.

Larkin, J. F., *Stuart Royal Proclamations*, vol. 2, 1625–1646, Oxford, 1983.

Smith, Sir Thomas, *De Republica Anglorum*, ed., Mary Dewar, Cambridge, 1982.
State Trials, A complete collection, eds., W. Cobbett, etc., London, 1816–1898.
Statutes of the Realm, eds., A. Luders, etc., London, 1810–1828.
Stow, John, *Annals*, London, 1605.
Vergil, Polydore, *The Anglica Historia, 1485–1537*, ed., Denys Hay, Camden Society, 3rd series, 74, 1950.
Williams, C. H., ed., *English Historical Documents, 1485–1558*, London, 1967.

B *Works of reference*
Bindoff, S. T., ed., *The House of Commons, 1509–1558*, 3 vols., London, 1982.
Clark, P. and Slack, P., *Crisis and Order in English Towns, 1500–1700*, London, 1972.
Dictionary of National Biography, eds., Leslie Stephen, etc., London, 1885–1903.
Elton, G. R., *Studies in Tudor and Stuart Government and Politics* [STS], 3 vols., Cambridge, 1974–1983.
Hasler, P. W., ed., *The House of Commons, 1558–1603*, 3 vols., London, 1981.
Heal, F. and O'Day, R., *Church and Society in England, Henry VIII–James I*, London, 1977.
Holdsworth, W. S., *A History of English Law*, London, 1922–1952.
Short Title Catalogue of books printed in England, Scotland and Ireland, and of English books printed abroad, 1475–1640, by A. W. Pollard and G. R. Redgrave, London, 1926; revised by W. A. Jackson and F. S. Ferguson, London, 1976. 1641–1700, by D. G. Wing, New York, 1945–1951.
Thirsk, Joan, ed., *The Agrarian History of England and Wales, 1500–1640*, Cambridge, 1967.

C *Studies and monographs*
Ashton, R., *The English Civil War; Conservatism and Revolution, 1603–1649*, London, 1978.
Bean, J. M. W., *The Decline of English Feudalism, 1215–1540*, Manchester, 1968.
Bellamy, J. G., *The Tudor Law of Treason*, London, 1979.

Challis, C. E., *The Tudor Coinage*, Manchester, 1978.
Cliffe, J. T., *The Yorkshire Gentry from the Reformation to the Civil War*, London, 1969.
The Puritan Gentry, London, 1984.
Coleman, D. C., *The Economy of England, 1450–1750*, London, 1977.
Coward, B., *The Stuart Age*, London, 1980.
Cross, M. C., *Church and People, 1450–1660*, London, 1976.
Davies, C. S. L., *Peace, Print and Protestantism, 1450–1558*, London, 1976.
Davis, J. C., *Utopia and the Ideal Society*, Cambridge, 1981.
Dietz, F. C., *English Government Finance, 1485–1558, Urbana*, Ill., 1920.
English Public Finance, 1558–1641, New York, 1932.
Elton, G. R., *England under the Tudors*, 2nd ed., London, 1974.
'Tudor Government; points of contact I, Parliament', STS.
'Tudor Government; points of contact II, the Council', STS.
'Tudor Government; points of contact III, the Court', STS.
'Parliament in the sixteenth century; functions and fortunes', STS.
Fletcher, A., *Tudor Rebellions*, London, 1968.
Foster, E. R., *The House of Lords, 1603–1642*, London, 1883–4.
Gleason, J. H., *The Justices of the Peace in England, 1558–1640*, Oxford, 1969.
Heinze, R. W., *The Proclamations of the Tudor Kings*, Cambridge, 1976.
Hill, C., *The Century of Revolution*, London, 1961.
Puritanism and Revolution, London, 1958.
'The many-headed monster in Tudor and Stuart England' in *From Renaissance to Counter Reformation*, ed., C. H. Carter, London, 1966.
Ives, E. W., 'The reputation of the Common Lawyers in English society, 1450–1550', *University of Birmingham Historical Journal*, 7, 1960.
Faction in Tudor England, Historical Association, 1979.
James, M. E., 'English politics and the concept of honour', *Past and Present*, Supp. 3, 1978.
Kerridge, E., *Agrarian Problems in the Sixteenth Century and After*, London, 1969.

Knowles, M. C., *The Religious Orders in England*, III, Cambridge, 1959.

Laslett, P., *The World We Have Lost*, London, 1965.

Loades, D. M., 'The press under the early Tudors', *Transactions of the Cambridge Bibliographical Society*, 4, 1964.

Lovejoy, A. O., *The Great Chain of Being*, Cambridge, Mass., 1936.

McGrath, P., *Papists and Puritans under Elizabeth I*, London, 1967.

Miller, H., 'Lords and Commons; relations between the two houses of parliament 1509–1558', *Parliamentary History*, I, 1983.

Morris, C., *Political Thought in England, Tyndale to Hooker*, London, 1953.

Neale, J. E., *Elizabeth I and Her Parliaments*, London, 1953–7.

O'Day, R., *The English Clergy; Emergence and Consolidation of a Profession, 1558–1642*, Leicester, 1979.

Ogilvie, C., *The King's Government and the Common Law, 1471–1641*, Oxford, 1958.

Outhwaite, R. B., *Inflation in Tudor and Early Stuart England*, 2nd ed., London, 1982.

Ramsey, P., *The Price Revolution in Sixteenth-century England*, London, 1971.

Reid, R., *The King's Council in the North*, London, 1921.

Rowse, A. L., *Tudor Cornwall*, London, 1951.

Russell, C., *The Crisis of Parliaments, 1509–1660*, Oxford, 1974.

Smith, A. G. R., *The Emergence of a Nation State, 1529–1660*, London, 1984.

Stone, L., *The Crisis of the Aristocracy, 1558–1641*, Oxford, 1965.

Thompson, J. A. F., *The Transformation of Medieval England, 1370–1529*, London, 1983.

Walzer, M., *The Revolution of the Saints*, London, 1966.

Williams, P., *The Tudor Regime*, Oxford, 1979.

Wernham, R. B., *Before the Armada*, London, 1966.

Youings, J., *Sixteenth-century England* (The Pelican Social History of Britain), London, 1984.

Youngs, F. A., *The Proclamations of the Tudor Queens*, Cambridge, 1976.

SECTION 2 PART I, 1450–1520

A *Printed sources and contemporary works*

Armstrong, C. A. J., *The Usurpation of Richard III by Dominico Mancini*, Oxford, 1936.
Bayne, C. G. and Dunham, W. H., eds., *Select Cases in the Council of Henry VII*, Selden Society, 1958.
Bruce, John, *History of the Arrival of Edward IV in England*, Camden Society, Old Series, I, 1838.
Dudley, Edmund, *The Tree of Commonwealth*, ed., D. M. Brodie, Cambridge, 1948.
Fortescue, Sir John, *The Governance of England*, ed., C. Plummer, London, 1885.
De laudibus legum Angliae, ed., S. B. Chrimes, Cambridge, 1949.
Gairdner, James, *Three Fifteenth Century Chronicles*, Camden Society, New Series, XXVIII, 1880.
Myers, A. R., ed., *English Historical Documents, 1327–1485*, London, 1969.
Paston Letters, ed., James Gairdner, London, 1910.
Pollard, A. F., ed., *The Reign of Henry VII from Contemporary Sources*, London, 1913–14.
Proceedings and Ordinances of the Privy Council of England (1386–1485), ed., N. H. Nicholas, London, 1834–7.
Rotuli Parliamentorum (1278–1504), London, 1832.
Warkworth, J., *A Chronicle of the First Thirteen Years of the Reign of King Edward IV*, ed., J. O. Halliwell, Camden Society, Old Series, X, 1839.

B *Studies and monographs*

Bellamy, J. G., *The Law of Treason in England in the Later Middle Ages*, Cambridge, 1970.
Crime and Public Order in England in the Later Middle Ages, London, 1973.
Bennett, H. S., *The Pastons and Their England*, Cambridge, 1922.
Blatcher, M., *The Court of King's Bench 1450–1550*, London, 1979.

Chrimes, S. B., *Henry VII*, London, 1973.

Dunham, W. H., Jr, *Lord Hastings' Indentured Retainers, 1461–1483*, New Haven, Conn., 1955.

Griffiths, R. A., *Henry VI*, London, 1981.

Jacob, E. F., *The Fifteenth Century*, Oxford, 1961.

Kingsford, C. L., *Prejudice and Promise in Fifteenth Century England*, Oxford, 1925.

Lander, J. R., *Conflict and Stability in Fifteenth Century England*, London, 1969.

Crown and Nobility, 1450–1509, London, 1976.

Government and Community, 1461–1509, London, 1980.

Lyle, H. M., *The Rebellion of Jack Cade*, Historical Association, 1950.

McFarlane, K. B., *The Nobility of Later Medieval England*, Oxford, 1973.

Ross, C., *Edward IV*, London, 1974.

Richard III, London, 1981.

Storey, R. L., *The End of the House of Lancaster*, London, 1966.

The Reign of Henry VII, London, 1968.

Thompson, J. A. F., *The Later Lollards, 1414–1520*, Oxford, 1965.

Wilkinson, B., *Constitutional History of England in the Fifteenth Century*, London, 1964.

Wolffe, B. P., *The Crown Lands 1461–1536*, London, 1970.

c *Articles*

Carpenter, C., 'Fifteenth-century English politics', *Historical Journal*, 26, 1983.

Chrimes, S. B., 'The reign of Henry VII; some recent contributions', *Welsh History Review*, 10, 1981.

Elton, G. R., 'Why the history of the early Tudor Council remains unwritten', STS.

'Henry VII; Rapacity and Remorse', STS.

Hurstfield, J., 'The revival of feudalism in early Tudor England', *History*, 37, 1952.

Keen, M. N., 'Treason trials under the law of Arms', *Transactions of the Royal Historical Society*, 5th series, 12, 1962.

Lander, J. R., 'Council, administration and councillors', *Bulletin of the Institute of Historical Research*, 32, 1959.

'Edward IV, the modern legend and a revision', *History*, 41, 1956.
'Attainder and forfeiture, 1453–1509', *Historical Journal*, 4, 1961.
McFarlane, K. B., 'Parliament and bastard feudalism', *TRHS*, 4th series, 26, 1944.
'The Wars of the Roses', *Proceedings of the British Academy*, 1965.
Scarisbrick, J., 'Cardinal Wolsey and the Common Weal' in Ives, E. W., Knecht, R. J. and Scarisbrick, J., *Wealth and Power in Tudor England*, London, 1978.
Virgoe, R., 'The composition of the King's council, 1437–1461', *BIHR*, 43, 1970.

SECTION 3 PART II, 1520–1570

A *Sources and contemporary works*

Cheke, Sir John, *The Hurt of Sedition*, London, 1549. Facsimile ed., Scolar Press, 1971.
Christopherson, J., *An Exhortation to All Men to Take Heed and Beware of Rebellion*, London, 1554. Facsimile ed., New York, 1973.
Dewar, M., ed., *A Discourse of the Common Weal of This Realm of England* (1549), Charlottesville, Va., 1969.
Donaldson, P. S., *A Machiavellian Treatise by Stephen Gardiner*, Cambridge, 1975.
Elyot, Sir Thomas, *The Book Named The Governor*, London, 1531, ed., S. E. Lehmberg, New York, 1962.
Foxe, J., *The Acts and Monuments of the English Martyrs*, London, 1563, 1570, ed., Josiah Pratt, London, 1870.
Gardiner, Stephen, *De vera obedientia oratio*, London, 1535, in P. Janelle, ed., *Obedience in Church and State*, Cambridge, 1930.
Goodman, Christopher, *How Superior Powers Ought to Be Obeyed*, Geneva, 1558, ed., C. H. McIlwain, New York, 1931.
Jewel, John, *An Apology or Answer in Defence of the Church of England*, London, 1564; in *Works*, ed., J. Ayre, Parker Society, 1850.

Jordan, W. K., ed., *The Chronicle and Political Papers of Edward VI*, London, 1966.

Letters and Papers of the Reign of Henry VIII, eds., James Gairdner, etc., London, 1862–1910.

Nichols, J. G., ed., *The Diary of Henry Machyn*, Camden Society, Old Series, XLII, 1848.

The Chronicle of Queen Jane, Camden Society, Old Series, XLVIII, 1850.

Ponet, John, *A Short Treatise of Politic Power*, Strasburg (?) 1556, in W. S. Hudson, *John Ponet: Advocate of Limited Monarchy*, London, 1942.

Proctor, J., *The History of Wyatt's Rebellion*, London, 1554, in E. Arber, *An English Garner*, London, 1903.

St German, C., *Dialogus de fundamentis legum Angliae*, London, 1532, translated and edited by W. Muchall, Cincinnati, 1874.

Sharp, Sir Cuthbert, ed., *Memorials of the Rebellion of 1569*, Newcastle, 1840.

Stanford, Sir William, *An Exposition of the King's Prerogative*, London, 1567.

B *Studies and monographs*

Baumer, F. le Van, *The Early Tudor Theory of Kingship*, New Haven, Conn., 1940.

Beer, B. L., *Northumberland*, Kent, Ohio, 1973.

Bush, M. L., *The Government Policy of Protector Somerset*, London, 1975.

Cornwall, J., *The Revolt of the Peasantry, 1549*, London, 1977.

Dickens, A. G., *Lollards and Protestants in the Diocese of York, 1509–1558*, Oxford, 1959.

The English Reformation, London, 1964.

Dodds, M. H. and R., *The Pilgrimage of Grace and the Exeter Conspiracy*, Cambridge, 1915.

Elton, G. R., *The Tudor Revolution in Government*, Cambridge, 1953.

Policy and Police, Cambridge, 1972.

Reform and Reformation, Cambridge, 1977.

Gould, J. D., *The Great Debasement*, Oxford, 1970.

Graves, M. A. R., *The House of Lords in the Parliaments of Edward VI and Mary I*, Cambridge, 1981.

Guy, J. A., *The Public Career of Thomas More*, Brighton, 1980.

Haigh, C., ed., *The Reign of Elizabeth I*, London, 1984.
Haugaard, W. P., *Elizabeth and the English Reformation*, Cambridge, 1968.
Hoak, D. E., *The King's Council in the Reign of Edward VI*, Cambridge, 1976.
Jones, N. L., *Faith by Statute*, London, 1982.
Jones, W. R. D., *The Tudor Commonwealth, 1529–1559*, London, 1970.
Jordan, W. K., *Edward VI: the Young King*, London, 1968.
Edward VI: the Threshold of Power, London, 1970.
Land, S. K., *Ketts Rebellion: the Norfolk Rising of 1549*, Ipswich, 1978.
Lehmberg, S. E., *The Reformation Parliament, 1529–1536*, Cambridge, 1970.
The Later Parliaments of Henry VIII, 1536–1547, Cambridge, 1977.
Levine, Mortimer, *The Early Elizabethan Succession Question, 1558–1568*, Stanford, Calif., 1966.
Loach, J. and Tittler, R., *The Mid-Tudor Polity*, London, 1980.
Loades, D. M., *Two Tudor Conspiracies*, Cambridge, 1965.
The Oxford Martyrs, London, 1970.
The Reign of Mary Tudor, London, 1979.
MacCaffrey, W., *The Shaping of the Elizabethan Regime*, Princeton, 1968.
Maconica, J. K., *English Humanists and Reformation Politics*, Oxford, 1965.
Pollard, A. F., *Wolsey*, London, 1929; new edition, London, 1965.
Prescott, H. F. M., *Mary Tudor*, London, 1952.
Scarisbrick, J. J., *Henry VIII*, London, 1968.
The Reformation and the English People, Oxford, 1984.
Smith, A. H., *County and Court*, Oxford, 1974.
Smith, L. B., *Henry VIII: the Mask of Royalty*, London, 1971.
Youings, J., *The Dissolution of the Monasteries*, London, 1972.

C *Articles*

Alsop, J. D., 'The theory and practice of Tudor taxation', *English Historical Review*, 97, 1982.
'The revenue commission of 1552', *Historical Journal*, 22, 1979.

Bateson, M., 'The Pilgrimage of Grace and Aske's examination', *English Historical Review*, 5, 1890.

Dickens, A. G., 'Sedition and conspiracy in Yorkshire during the latter years of Henry VIII', *Yorkshire Archaeological Journal*, 34, 1939.

Elton, G. R., 'Politics and the Pilgrimage of Grace', STS.

'Taxation for War and Peace in Early Tudor England', STS.

'Thomas More, Councillor', STS.

Gleason, J. H., 'Commissions of the Peace, 1554–1564', *Huntingdon Library Quarterly*, 18, 1955.

Haigh, C. A., 'Anticlericalism and the English Reformation', *History*, 68, 1983.

Harriss, G. L., 'Theory and practice in royal taxation; some observations', *EHR*, 97, 1982.

Hurstfield, J., 'Was there a Tudor despotism after all?', *TRHS*, 5th series, 17, 1967.

Ives, E. W., 'The genesis of the Statute of Uses', *EHR*, 82, 1967.

James, M. E., 'The first Earl of Cumberland and the decline of northern feudalism', *Northern History*, I, 1966.

'Obedience and dissent in Henrician England; the Lincolnshire Rebellion of 1536', *Past and Present*, 48, 1970.

Change and Continuity in the Tudor North, Borthwick Papers, 27, 1965.

A Tudor Magnate and the Tudor State, Borthwick Papers, 30, 1966.

Loach, J., 'Parliamentary opposition in the reign of Mary Tudor', unpublished Oxford D.Phil., 1973.

Pogson, R. H., 'Reginald Pole and the priorities of government in Mary Tudor's church', *Historical Journal*, 18, 1975.

Reid, R., 'The rebellion of the Earls, 1569', *TRHS*, New Series 20, 1906.

Smith, L. R., 'Treason trials in sixteenth century England', *Journal of the History of Ideas*, 15, 1954.

Youings, J., 'The Council in the West', *TRHS*, 5th series, 10, 1970.

SECTION 4 PART III, 1570–1630

A *Printed sources and contemporary works*

Allen, William, *A True, Sincere and Modest Defence of the English Catholics* (1584), ed., R. Kingdon, New York, 1965.

Camden, William, *Annales rerum anglicarum*, London, 1615, trs. H. Norton, London, 1688.

Cecil, William, *The Execution of Justice in England*, London, 1583, ed., R. Kingdon, New York, 1965.

Coke, Sir Edward, *Institutes of the Laws of England*, London, 1628–1644.

D'Ewes, Sir Simonds, *The Journal of all the Parliaments during the Reign of Queen Elizabeth*, ed., P. Bowes, London, 1682, 1693.

Doleman, R. (Robert Parsons), *A Conference about the Next Succession to the Crown of England*, Antwerp (?) 1594. Facsimile ed., Scolar Press, 1972.

Frere, W. H. and Douglas, C. E., eds., *Puritan Manifestos*, London, 1807. New edition, London, 1954.

Hooker, Richard, *Laws of Ecclesiastical Polity*, London, 1593, 1597, ed., W. Speed Hill, Cambridge, Mass., 1977–81.

James, I., *Works*, London, 1616, *Political Works*, ed., C. H. McIlwain, Cambridge, Mass., 1918.

Marprelate Tracts, 1588, 1589, ed., William Pierce, London, 1911.

Salisbury Manuscripts (Historical Manuscripts Commission): 3rd, 4th, 5th, 6th, 7th, 12th, 13th, 14th, 15th, 16th and 17th Reports, and appendices.

Tanner, J. R., ed., *Constitutional Documents of the Reign of James I*, Cambridge, 1930.

B *Studies and monographs*

Boynton, L., *The Elizabethan Militia*, London, 1967.

Cheyney, E. P., *A History of England from the Defeat of the Armada to the Death of Elizabeth*, New York, 1914–26.

Collinson, P., *The Elizabethan Puritan Movement*, London, 1967.

The Religion of Protestants, London, 1982.

English Puritanism, Historical Association, 1983.

Cross, M. C., *The Puritan Earl*, Cambridge, 1966.
Cruikshank, C. G., *Elizabeth's Army*, Oxford, 1946; 2nd edition, Oxford, 1966.
Handover, P. M., *The Second Cecil*, London, 1959.
Hill, C., *The Economic Problems of the Church*, Oxford, 1956.
Hurstfield, J., *The Queen's Wards*, London, 1958.
Lake, P. G., *Moderate Puritans and the Elizabethan Church*, Cambridge, 1982.
Lockyer, R., *Buckingham*, London, 1981.
MacCaffrey, W., *Queen Elizabeth and the Making of Policy, 1572–1588*, Princeton, 1981.
Palliser, D. M., *The Age of Elizabeth*, London, 1983.
Peck, L. L., *Northampton: Patronage and Politics at the Court of James I*, London, 1982.
Prestwich, M., *Politics and Profit under the Early Stuarts*, Oxford, 1966.
Ruigh, R. E., *The Parliament of 1624*, Cambridge, Mass., 1971.
Russell, C., ed., *The Origins of the English Civil War*, London, 1973.
Parliaments and English Politics, 1621–1629, Oxford, 1979.
Sharpe, K., *Faction and Parliament: Essays on Early Stuart History*, Oxford, 1978.
Smith, A. G. R., *Servant of the Cecils: the Life of Sir Michael Hickes*, London, 1977.
Supple, B., *Commercial Crisis and Change in England, 1600–1642*, Cambridge, 1959.
Thomson, G. S., *Lords Lieutenant in the Sixteenth Century*, London, 1923.
Usher, R. G., *The Rise and Fall of High Commission*, Oxford, 1913; new edition, Oxford, 1968.
Wernham, R. B., *After the Armada*, Oxford, 1984.
Williams, P., *The Council in the Marches of Wales under Elizabeth I*, Cardiff, 1958.
Zagorin, P., *The Court and the Country*, London, 1969.
Zaller, R., *The Parliament of 1621*, Berkeley, 1971.

c *Articles*

Elton, G. R., 'A high road to civil war?', STS.
Gay, E. F., 'The midland revolt and the inquisitions of depopulation', *TRHS*, New Series 18, 1904.

Haigh, C., 'From Monopoly to Minority: Catholicism in Early Modern England', *TRHS*, 5th series, 31, 1981.

Hoskins, W. G., 'The rebuilding of rural England, 1570–1640', *Past and Present*, 4, 1953.

Lambert, S., 'Procedure in the House of Commons in the Early Stuart period', *EHR*, 95, 1980.

Lee, Maurice, Jr, 'James I and the Historians', *Albion*, 16/2, 1984.

MacCaffrey, W. T., 'Place and patronage in Elizabethan politics', in *Elizabethan Government and Society*, eds., S.T. Bindoff, etc., London, 1961.

Peck, L. L., 'Corruption at the Court of James I; the Undermining of Legitimacy', in Malament, B., *After the Reformation*, Pennsylvania, 1980.

Read, C., 'William Cecil and Elizabethan public relations', in *Elizabethan Government and Society*.

Rich, E. E., 'The Elizabethan population', *Economic History Review* (2nd series), 2, 1949.

Russell, C., 'Parliamentary history in perspective, 1604–1629', *History*, 61, 1976.

Sainty, J. C., 'Lieutenants of Counties, 1585–1642', *BIHR Special Supplement* 8, 1970.

Shriver, F., 'Hampton Court revisited; James I and the puritans', *Journal of Ecclesiastical History*, 33, 1982.

Smith, A. G. R., 'The secretariats of the Cecils, c.1580–1612', *EHR*, 83, 1968.

Stone, L., 'The inflation of honours', *Past and Present*, 14, 1963.

Zaller, R., 'The concept of opposition in Early Stuart England', *Albion*, 12/2, 1980.

SECTION 5 PART IV, 1630–1660

A *Printed sources and contemporary works*

Abbott, W. C., ed., *The Writings and Speeches of Oliver Cromwell*, Cambridge, Mass., 1937–1947.

Clarendon, Edward, Earl of, *The History of the Rebellion*, Oxford, 1702–4.

D'Ewes, Sir Simonds, *Journal*, ed., W. Notestein, New Haven, Conn., 1923.

Filmer, Sir Robert, *Patriarcha and other Political Works*, ed., P. Laslett, Oxford, 1949.

Firth, C. H. and Rait, R. S., eds., *Acts and Ordinances of the Interregnum, 1642–1660*, London, 1911.

Gardiner, S. R., ed., *Documents of the Puritan Revolution, 1625–1660*, 3rd edition, Oxford, 1906.

Greaves, R. L. and Zaller, R., eds., *Biographical Dictionary of British Radicals in the Seventeenth Century*, vol. I, Brighton 1982; vol. 2, 1983.

Haller, W. and Davies, G., eds., *Leveller Tracts*, New York, 1944.

Hobbes, T., *Leviathan*, ed., M. Oakeshott, Oxford, 1955.

Petrie, C., ed., *The Letters, Speeches and Proclamations of King Charles I*, London, 1935.

Woodhouse, A. S. P., ed., *Puritanism and Liberty*, 2nd ed., London, 1974.

B *Studies and monographs*

Ashton, R., *The English Civil War*, London, 1978.

Aylmer, G. E., *The King's Servants*, 2nd ed., London, 1974.

The Interregnum, 1646–1660, London, 1972.

The State's Servants, London, 1973.

The Levellers in the English Revolution, London, 1975.

Carlton, C., *Charles I, the Personal Monarch*, London, 1983.

Firth, C. H., *Oliver Cromwell*, London, 1900.

Fletcher, A., *The Outbreak of the English Civil War*, London, 1981.

Frank, J., *The Levellers*, Cambridge, Mass., 1955.

Gardiner, S. R., *The History of the Great Civil War*, London, 1893.

The History of the Commonwealth and Protectorate, London, 1903.

Hexter, J. H., *The Reign of King Pym*, Cambridge, Mass., 1941.

James, M., *Social Problems and Policy during the English Revolution*, London, 1930; 2nd edition, London, 1964.

Kishlansky, M. A., *The Rise of the New Model Army*, Cambridge, 1980.

Lamont, W. M., *Godly Rule*, London, 1970.

Morrill, J. S., *The Revolt of the Provinces*, London, 1976.

ed., *Reactions to the English Civil War, 1642–1649*, London, 1982.

Nuttall, G., *Visible Saints*, Oxford, 1957.

Pearl, V., *London and the Outbreak of the Puritan Revolution*, Oxford, 1961.

Roots, I., *The Great Rebellion*, London, 1966.

Sharp, A., ed., *Political Ideas of the English Civil War, 1641–1649*, London, 1983.

Trevor-Roper, H., *Archbishop Laud*, 2nd edition, London, 1962.

Underdown, D., *Royalist Conspiracy in England, 1649–1660*, New Haven, Conn., 1960.

Pride's Purge, Oxford, 1971.

Wedgwood, C. V., *Strafford*, London, 1935; revised edition, London, 1962.

The King's Peace, London, 1955.

The King's War, London, 1958.

Weston, C. C. and Greenburg, J. R., *Subjects and Sovereigns*, Cambridge, 1981.

Woolrych, A., *Commonwealth to Protectorate*, Oxford, 1982.

Worden, B., *The Rump Parliament*, Cambridge, 1973.

Yule, G., *The Independents in the English Civil War*, Cambridge, 1958.

Zagorin, P., *A History of Political Thought in the English Revolution*, New York, 1954.

C *Articles*

Ashton, R., 'Charles I and the City', in *Essays on the Economic and Social History of Tudor and Stuart England*, ed., F. J. Fisher, Cambridge, 1961.

Aylmer, G. E., 'Crisis and regrouping in the political elites; England from the 1630s to the 1660s', in Pocock, J. G. A., ed., *Three British Revolutions: 1641, 1688, 1776*, Princeton, 1980.

Cotterell, M., 'Interregnum law reform; the Hale commission of 1652', *EHR*, 83, 1968.

Fisher, F. J., 'Puritanism, Politics and Society', in *The English Revolution*, ed., E. W. Ives, London, 1968.

Ives, E. W., 'Social change and the law', in *The English Revolution*.

Manning, B. S., 'The outbreak of the English Civil War', in *The English Civil War and After*, ed., R. H. Parry, London, 1970.

Nourse, G. B., 'Law reform under the Commonwealth and Protectorate', *Law Quarterly Review*, 75, 1959.

Pennington, D. H., 'The County Community at War', in *The English Revolution*.

'The rebels of 1642', in *The English Civil War and After*.

Roots, I., 'The central government and the local community', in *The English Revolution*.

Russell, C., 'The theory of treason in the trial of Strafford', *EHR*, 80, 1965.

Trevor-Roper, H., 'Oliver Cromwell, and his Parliaments', in *Essays Presented to Sir Lewis Namier*, eds., R. Pares and A. J. P. Taylor, London, 1956.

Woolrych, A., 'Oliver Cromwell and the rule of the Saints', in *The English Civil War and After*.

'The calling of Barebones' Parliament', *EHR*, 80, 1965.

INDEX